Natural Law and the Law of Nations in Eighteenth- and Nineteenth-Century Italy

Early Modern Natural Law

STUDIES AND SOURCES

VOLUME 6

The titles published in this series are listed at *brill.com/emnl*

Natural Law and the Law of Nations in Eighteenth- and Nineteenth-Century Italy

Edited by

Elisabetta Fiocchi Malaspina
Gabriella Silvestrini

BRILL

LEIDEN | BOSTON

The open access publication of this book has been realised with the support of the Swiss National Science Foundation.

Cover illustration: *A New Map of Italy* (1708), John Senex. Washington State University Libraries' Manuscripts, Archives, and Special Collections (MASC). Public Domain.

Names: Fiocchi Malaspina, Elisabetta, editor. | Silvestrini, Gabriella, 1961- editor.
Title: Natural law and the law of nations in Eighteenth- and Nineteenth-Century Italy / edited by Elisabetta Fiocchi Malaspina, Gabriella Silvestrini.
Description: Leiden ; Boston : Brill/Nijhoff, 2024. | Series: Early modern natural law : studies & sources, 2589-5982 ; volume 6 | Includes bibliographical references and index.
Identifiers: LCCN 2023039723 (print) | LCCN 2023039724 (ebook) | ISBN 9789004685123 (hardback) | ISBN 9789004685130 (ebook)
Subjects: LCSH: Natural law–History–18th century. | Natural law–History–19th century. | International law–Italy–History–18th century. | International law–Italy–History–19th century.
Classification: LCC K417.18 N38 2024 (print) | LCC K417.18 (ebook) | DDC 340/.112094509033–dc23/eng/20230929
LC record available at https://lccn.loc.gov/2023039723
LC ebook record available at https://lccn.loc.gov/2023039724

Typeface for the Latin, Greek, and Cyrillic scripts: "Brill". See and download: brill.com/brill-typeface.

ISSN 2589-5982
ISBN 978-90-04-68512-3 (hardback)
ISBN 978-90-04-68513-0 (e-book)
DOI 10.1163/9789004685130

This book is printed on acid-free paper and produced in a sustainable manner.

Contents

Acknowledgements

The following volume is the result of a series of seminars held at the University of Eastern Piedmont (Vercelli, Italy) between 2017 and 2019 in collaboration with the University of Zurich, which brought together a group of Italian scholars as part of the international research programme 'Natural Law 1625–1850: An International Project' (coordinated by Frank Grunert, Knud Haakonssen and Louis Pahlow). Merio Scattola joint the project, contributing Italian perspectives on its work, until his premature and unexpected death in 2015. With our seminars and the present volume, we are honoured to continue his legacy.

The multiplicity of modern variants of natural law has merged into the numerous research itineraries contained in the chapters of this book. These essays, in addition to providing various themes and perspectives for future scientific research, are the result of the collective effort made by all the colleagues who enthusiastically joined the project: we would like to thank them most warmly, not least for their attention and patience, especially during the period marked by the Covid-19 pandemic and its restrictions.

We would also like to thank Patrizia Delpiano, Germana Gandino, Andrea Pennini, Claudio Rosso, Riccarda Suitner and Edoardo Tortarolo, who attended the seminars we organized and contributed to the preliminary discussions in preparation for the book. We are also indebted to Simone Ghelli and Emanuele Salerno, who helped to revise bibliography and footnotes, and to Ralph Footring for copy-editing the chapters.

A special thanks goes to the editors of the book series 'Early Modern Natural Law: Studies & Sources', particularly to Knud Haakonssen for his insightful and valuable comments, as well as to the anonymous peer reviewers for their accurate and constructive suggestions.

The text of several chapters was translated from the Italian by the following: Matthew Armistead (Chapter 4, Gabriella Silvestrini; and Chapter 9, Frédéric Ieva); Filippo Valente (Chapter 6, Serena Luzzi; and Chapter 8, Vittor Ivo Comparato); and Chiara Rotondi (Chapter 11, Giuseppina De Giudici).

The seminars and the publication of this volume have been made possible by research funds of the Department of the Humanities, University of Eastern Piedmont, and of the University of Zurich, to which grateful acknowledgement is made, but to which no responsibility is attributed.

Notes on Contributors

Alberto Clerici
is Professor of History of Political Thought at the Faculty of Political Science of the University Niccolò Cusano in Rome. His main research fields include the history of early modern theories of sovereignty, resistance and the law of nations. He has published *Monarcomachi e giusnaturalisti nella Utrecht del Seicento. Willem van der Muelen e la legittimazione olandese della 'Glorious Revolution'* (Milano: Franco Angeli, 2007).

Vittor Ivo Comparato
is editor of the journal *Il Pensiero politico*. Professor emeritus, he has long taught History of Political Thought and Modern History at the Universities of Florence and Perugia. His research has mainly focused on the history of seventeenth-century French and Italian political thought, erudite libertinism and republicanism. His monographs include: *Giuseppe Valletta. Un intellettuale napoletano della fine del Seicento* (Napoli: Istituto Italiano di Studi Storici, 1970), *Uffici e società a Napoli (1600–1647): dell'ideologia del magistrato* (Firenze: Olschki, 1974); *Cyrano de Bergerac Politique* (Napoli: ESI, 1997) and *Utopia* (Bologna: il Mulino, 2005).

Giuseppina De Giudici
is Associate Professor of Medieval and Modern Legal History at the Department of Law, University of Cagliari. Her main research fields include the history of *jus gentium*, with a focus on the legal status of ambassadors in the modern age, and the history of the University of Cagliari and the teaching also of international law. Her books include Sanctitas legatorum: *Sul 'fondamento' dell'indipendenza giurisdizionale in età moderna* (Napoli: ESI, 2020). She is editor, together with Dante Fedele and Elisabetta Fiocchi Malaspina, of the collection of essays entitled *Soggettività contestate e diritto internazionale in età moderna* (Historia et ius, 2023, open access).

Elisabetta Fiocchi Malaspina
is Assistant Professor of Legal History at the Law Faculty of the University of Zurich. Her main research fields include the history of international law, circulation and diffusion of theories of natural law and law of nations in the eighteenth and nineteenth centuries, and the history of land ownership and land registration systems (in the nineteenth and twentieth centuries). She has published *L'eterno ritorno del* Droit des gens *di Emer de Vattel (secc. XVIII–XIX)* (Frankfurt: Max Planck Institute for European Legal History, 2017).

Frédéric Ieva
is Research Fellow in Modern History at the Department of Foreign Languages and Literature and Modern Cultures, University of Turin. His main research fields include the history of the Duchy of Savoy and the Kingdom of France in the seventeenth century, and the figure of Ercole Ricotti, the first professor of modern history at the University of Turin. His publications include: '"A poor imitation of Grotius and Pufendorf?" Biographical Uncertainties and the Laborious Genesis of Vattel's *Droit des gens*', in *The Legacy of Vattel's* Droit des gens, ed. Koen Stapelbroek and Antonio Trampus (London: Palgrave Macmillan, 2019), 53–76; (as editor) Ercole Ricotti, *Scritti sull'istruzione militare*, prefazione di Pierpaolo Merlin (Torino: Centro Studi di storia dell'Università di Torino, 2022); and *Illusioni di Potenza. La diplomazia sabauda e la Francia nel cuore del Seicento (1630–1648)* (Roma: Carocci, 2022).

Girolamo Imbruglia
now retired, has lectured in modern history at the University 'l'Orientale' of Naples. His main trends of research are the history of European Enlightenment, the history of historiography and the history of Christianity in early modern Europe, especially the history of the Society of Jesus and of heretical movements. His publications include: *Naples in the Eighteenth Century: The Birth and Death of a Nation State* (Cambridge: Cambridge University Press, 2000); *The Jesuit Missions of Paraguay and a Cultural History of Utopia (1568–1789)* (Brill: Leiden, 2017); *Utopia. Una storia politica da Savonarola a Babeuf* (Carocci: Roma, 2021); 'La religione sociniana. Culto e comunità', *Quellen und Forschungen aus italienischen Archiven und Bibliotheken* 102 (2022): 69–85; 'The Idea of Religion and Sacrifice from Grotius to Diderot's Encyclopedia', *History of European Ideas* 47(5) (2021): 1–18; 'Civilisation and Colonisation: Enlightenment Theories in the Debate between Diderot and Raynal', *History of European Ideas* 41(7) (2015): 2–25; 'Tribunal de la foi et tribunal de l'opinion publique au siècle des lumières. Giannone, Montesquieu, Beccaria', in *Censure et critique*, ed. Laurence Macé, Claudine Poulouin and Yvan Leclerc (Paris: Garnier, 2015), 333–352.

Francesca Iurlaro
holds a Ph.D. in law from the European University Institute (Florence, 2018). She was a Global Postdoctoral Fellow at New York University (2019–2020) and an Alexander von Humboldt Postdoctoral Fellow at the Max Planck Institute for Comparative Public Law and International Law (Heidelberg, 2020–2022). In her book *The Invention of Custom: Natural Law and The Law of Nations* (Oxford: Oxford University Press, 2021), she explores how topoi from classical antiquity shaped customary international law. In 2012 she received the

Alberico Gentili Prize for her translation of Alberico Gentili's *Lectionis Virgilianae Variae Liber* (1603), a legal commentary on Virgil's *Eclogues*.

Serena Luzzi
is Associate Professor of Modern History at the Department of Humanities, University of Trento. Her research fields include the Enlightenment, the circulation of natural law and Italian secularitazion. She is editor of Carlantonio Pilati's *Di una riforma d'Italia ossia dei mezzi di riformare i più cattivi costumi, e le più perniciose leggi d'Italia* (1767) (Roma: Storia e Letteratura, 2018).

Emanuele Salerno
is Senior Research Fellow and member of the Heisenberg project team on the Grotius Census Bibliography, generously funded by the Deutsche Forschungsgemeinschaft (SO 1807/2), at the Max Planck Institute for Comparative Public Law and International Law in Heidelberg. His research focuses on theoretical and practical tools for supporting international peace and security in a historical comparative framework. In addition to the early modern history and the history of political and legal international thought, his broader academic interests are the history of universities, book circulation, libraries and archives. He has published on the legal-political culture of the ruling class and cases of pragmatization of the law of nature and nations in eighteenth-century Tuscany.

Gabriella Silvestrini
is Associate Professor of History of Political Thought at the Department of Humanities, University of Eastern Piedmont. Her main research fields include the history of early modern natural law theories, republicanism, theories of punishment, the Enlightenment and Jean-Jacques Rousseau. She has published *Diritto naturale e volontà generale. Il contrattualismo repubblicano di Jean-Jacques Rousseau* (Torino: Claudiana, 2010).

Antonio Trampus
is Full Professor of Early Modern History at the Department of Linguistics and Comparative Cultural Studies, Ca' Foscari University, Venice. His research focuses on cultural history, history of political ideas and constitutionalism. His books include the critical edition of Benjamin Constant's commentary on Filangieri (Berlin: de Gruyter, 2012), the edited volume with K. Stapelbroek of *The Legacy of Vattel's* Droit des gens (Cham: Palgrave, 2019) and *Emer de Vattel and the Politics of Good Government: Constitutionalism, Small States and the International System* (Cham: Palgrave Macmillan, 2020).

Introduction

Elisabetta Fiocchi Malaspina and Gabriella Silvestrini

The project from which this volume derives set out to map the teachings of natural law and the law of nations by following how chairs were established in Italy from the mid-eighteenth to the mid-nineteenth century. The aim was to reconstruct the cultural and political contexts where such chairs were created, teachers' profiles, as well as their education, their sources and textbooks. If we consider the history of the Italian peninsula and its plurality of states, each with its particular traits, along with the influences that several political systems had on academic education and on the teaching of natural law and the law of nations, the subject is obviously extensive. The research needed to be multidisciplinary, drawing on a wide range of traditions, some highly specialized, for instance the history of universities (and especially of their faculties of law and philosophy), the history of public law, the history of the Italian Enlightenment and its main figures, elements of political and church history, and history of the circulation of ideas.

From the beginning, it was clear that the questions on when and how chairs were established could not leave out the philosophical, political, legal and religious meaning of conveyed theories, as well as the question of what types of conflicts and quarrels were involved: tradition versus modernity, Protestantism versus Catholicism, states against states, states against churches. In an attempt to avoid preconceived ideas about these major themes, we focused on how individual authors and professors employed and transformed doctrines of early modern natural law. In a nutshell, the problems were to understand what 'modern Protestant natural law'[1] could mean from the viewpoint of those authors and professors, and to determine whether it is possible to trace an 'Italian path' to natural law, or to identify an Italian specificity to political thought and perhaps the Enlightenment in the region.

1 On the multifaced aspects and traditions of Protestant natural law see Knud Haakonssen, 'Protestant Natural Law Theory: A General Interpretation', in *New Essays on the History of Autonomy: A Collection Honoring J. B. Schneewind*, ed. Natalie Brender and Larry Krasnoff (Cambridge: Cambridge University Press, 2004), 92–109; Knud Haakonssen and Michael Seidler, 'Natural Law: Law, Rights, and Duties', in *A Companion to Intellectual History*, ed. Richard Whatmore and Brian Young (Chichester: Wiley-Blackwell, 2015), 377–400. See also: Simone Zurbuchen, 'Protestant Natural Law', in *Encyclopedia of the Philosophy of Law and Social Philosophy*, ed. Mortimer Sellers and Stephan Kirste (Dordrecht: Springer, 2020), 1–6.

DOI:10.1163/9789004685130_002

The first step of the research was to expand the timeframe, traditionally established from 1726, when the first chair of public law was established in Italy, in Pisa, to the early nineteenth century, when the supposed downfall of natural law made way for historicism and positivism.[2] The analysis of the Italian case, in fact, persuaded us to extend both the *a quo* and *ad quem* dates. The 'chronology of chairs' could not clearly provide the organizing criterion for our research, for three closely related reasons. First, as in other parts of Europe, the creation of chairs represents the peak of a process rooted in the second half of the seventeenth century. This process was not a case of passive reception by Italian authors of a modern and Protestant natural law from the other side of the Alps as opposed to an outmoded Catholic tradition. Moreover, well before becoming independent, the discipline of natural law and the law of nations was introduced within Italian faculties of law and philosophy through courses on Pandects, Justinian *Institutes* and moral philosophy, as it was elsewhere. Finally, as in Germany and other parts of the world, the creation of these chairs continued during the nineteenth century, although perhaps later than anywhere else, and an inescapable arrival point is Italian unification, with the introduction of international law in the universities of the new Kingdom of Italy, formed in 1861. From the first chapter, devoted to Pisa (Emanuele Salerno), to the last, dealing with Cagliari (Giuseppina De Giudici), the itinerary might be defined as a shift from natural law and the law of nations to international law.

In this wider chronological perspective, a second outcome emerges: the 1750s no longer represent the moment of highest diffusion and circulation of 'Protestant' natural law. If anything, we might see that decade as a turning point within a more complex and wider framework which cannot be reduced to just the one issue, the struggle between Protestant and Catholic natural law.[3] Certainly, the transition from the figure of Benedict XIV (1740–1758),

2 For an account of the early end of natural law see Norberto Bobbio, *Thomas Hobbes and the Natural Law Tradition*, trans. Daniela Gobetti (Chicago, IL: Chicago University Press, 1993). For a different approach and analysis, see the recent contribution of Knud Haakonssen, 'Early Modern Natural Law Theories', in *The Cambridge Companion to Natural Jurisprudence*, ed. George Duke and Robert P. George (Cambridge: Cambridge University Press, 2017), 76–102, at 99: 'One of the ironies of the success of Kant's polemical efforts is that it is only in recent scholarship that it has become quite clear that his own work in the philosophy of law extended the life of natural law as a genre and an academic discipline well into the nineteenth century, and hence beyond the scope of this chapter'.

3 As Walter Rech has argued, 'International Law as a Political Language, 1600–1859', in *A History of International Law in Italy*, ed. Giulio Bartolini (Oxford: Oxford University Press, 2020), 48–78, at 55: 'Protestant natural law did not firmly set foot in Italy until the mid-

the 'enlightened pope', to that of Clement XIII (1758–1769) can be considered a moment of 'crisis' and 'growing alienation of Catholicism and Enlightenment'.[4] But, given the multiplicity of contexts and actors, the 'great fear'[5] of Catholic culture in the face of Protestant modernity is only one of many issues and not a fundamental interpretative criterion.

The research overarchingly led to a third outcome, which consists of the possibility of the definite rejection, in the field of modern natural law, of the image of an Italy lagging behind the more advanced northern European countries. If, from the chronological point of view of the creation of chairs in the faculties of law, such delay is undeniable, the idea of Italy as a place where doctrines coming from abroad were either passively disseminated or harshly contested is long outdated. That biased image was fed by some European travellers like Edward Gibbon,[6] as well as by some spokespeople both from the Italian Enlightenment, and later, from the Risorgimento (see Chapter 2, by Alberto Clerici). Concerning modern natural law, this image collapses as soon as we focus on the innovative nature of the practices of assimilation and translation; on the way traditions are reprocessed and reinvented; on cultural, linguistic and legal transfers. The various political and cultural contexts of the

---

eighteenth century, when it underpinned attempts at reform by enlightened despots across the peninsula'. On 'Catholic Enlightenment' see: Vincenzo Ferrone, 'Chiesa cattolica e modernità. La scoperta dei diritti dell'uomo dopo l'esperienza dei totalitarismi', in *Chiesa cattolica e modernità, Atti del convegno della Fondazione Michele Pellegrino*, ed. Franco Bolgiani, Vincenzo Ferrone and Francesco Margiotta Broglio (Bologna: Il mulino, 2004), 17–131; Patrizia Delpiano, *Church and Censorship in Eighteenth-Century Italy: Governing Reading in the Age of Enlightenment* (New York: Routledge, 2018). See the masterly studies of Franco Venturi, *Italy and the Enlightenment: Studies in a Cosmopolitan Century* (New York: New York University Press, 1972); idem, *Il Settecento riformatore*, vol. 5, *L'Italia dei lumi, 1764–1790* (Torino: Einaudi, 1987); Vincenzo Ferrone, *The Intellectual Roots of the Italian Enlightenment: Newtonian Science, Religion, and Politics in the Early Eighteenth Century* (Atlantic Highlands, NJ: Humanities Press International, 1995); idem, *The Enlightenment: History of an Idea* (Princeton: Princeton University Press, 2017). For a different perspective see *Law and the Christian Tradition in Italy: The Legacy of the Great Jurists*, ed. Orazio Condorelli and Rafael Domingo (London: Routledge, 2021).

4 See Mario Rosa, 'The Catholic *Aufklärung* in Italy', in *A Companion to the Catholic Enlightenment in Europe*, ed. Ulrich L. Lehner and Michael Printy (Leiden: Brill, 2010), 215–250, at 229–232.

5 Merio Scattola, 'Protestantesimo e diritto naturale cattolico nel XVIII secolo', in *Illuminismo e Protestantesimo* ed. Giulia Cantarutti and Stefano Ferrari (Milano: FrancoAngeli, 2010), 131–148, at 134.

6 As has been observed by Owen Chadwick, 'The Italian Enlightenment', in *The Enlightenment in National Context*, ed. Roy Porter and Mikulas Teich (Cambridge: Cambridge University Press, 1981), 90–105, at 91.

Italian states were part of a wider and dense network, wherein people and ideas circulated inside and outside Italy.

Due to the wider chronological perspective and the multiplicity of local contexts, this volume does not aim to give an all-encompassing picture, even in outline. More modestly, our intention is to suggest meaningful research itineraries, which can inspire future scientific developments. From a methodological viewpoint, two different, but closely intertwined, approaches were employed. First, we mapped several chairs throughout the Italian peninsula (Emanuele Salerno for Pisa, Alberto Clerici for La Sapienza in Rome, Elisabetta Fiocchi Malaspina for Pavia, Ivo Comparato for Perugia, Frédéric Ieva for Turin, Giuseppina De Giudici for Cagliari). The connection between law and politics, between curricula (often determined by governments) and teaching activities permitted us to highlight how this discipline was introduced and taught; what strategies professors adopted; the relationship between natural law and Roman law; how textbooks were selected and reinterpreted. The main sources were either manuscript lectures and notes in Italian university libraries or professors' published works.[7] Second, the analysis of how doctrines of natural law and the law of nations were interpreted and transformed has been fundamental to fully understand the different reasons for the introduction of this discipline in the colourful Italian political and cultural contexts.[8] Here, besides

7 Where no English version is cited, translations of these texts in the present volume are by the authors and/or by the translators of their contributions.

8 Much research has been done to trace the presence in Italy of the 'classics' of modern natural law and how they were received in Italy, mainly in the eighteenth century. Among the most important studies are: Diego Panizza, 'La traduzione italiana del "De iure naturae" di Pufendorf: giusnaturalismo moderno e cultura cattolica nel Settecento', *Studi Veneziani* 11 (1969): 483–528; Maurizio Bazzoli, 'Giambattista Almici e la diffusione di Pufendorf nel Settecento italiano', *Critica storica* 16 (1979): 3–100; Diego Quaglioni, 'Pufendorf in Italia. Appunti e notizie della prima diffusione della traduzione italiana del *De iure naturae et gentium*', *Il Pensiero Politico* 32 (1999): 23–250; Stefania Stoffella, 'Assolutismo e diritto naturale in Italia nel Settecento', *Annali dell'Istituto storico italo-germanico* 26 (2000): 137–175; ead., 'Il diritto di resistenza nel Settecento Italiano. Documenti per la storia della traduzione del De iure naturae et gentium di Pufendorf', *Magistrature et politique* 2 (2001): 173–199; Eugenio Garin, 'Appunti per una storia della fortuna di Hobbes nel Settecento italiano', *Rivista critica di storia della filosofia* 17(4) (2002): 514–527; *La recezione di Grozio a Napoli nel Settecento*, ed. Vittorio Conti (Firenze: Centro editoriale toscano, 2002); Philippe Audegean, 'Passions et liberté. Loi de nature et fondement du droit en Italie à l'époque de Beccaria', *Studi settecenteschi* 23 (2003): 197–278; Maria Rosa di Simone, 'L'influenza di Christian Wolff sul giusnaturalismo dell'area asburgica e italiana', in *Dal 'De Jure Naturae et gentium' di Samuel Pufendorf alla codificazione prussiana del 1794. Atti del convegno internazionale, Padova, 25–26 ottobre 2001*, ed. Marta Ferronato (Padova: Cedam, 2005), 221–268; Antonio Trampus, *Emer de Vattel and the Politics of Good Government: Constitutionalism, Small States and the International System* (Cham: Palgrave Macmillan, 2020).

textbooks, the objects of our research were critical comments and Italian translations of authors such as Pufendorf and Vattel (Serena Luzzi, Antonio Trampus), as well as the works of some internationally known Italian authors, such as the members of the Academy of Fists, Antonio Genovesi, Mario Pagano, Pasquale Stanislao Mancini and Luigi Taparelli d'Azeglio (Gabriella Silvestrini, Girolamo Imbruglia, Frédéric Ieva, Francesca Iurlaro). These two perspectives, namely the academic context and the wider cultural and political context, are tightly connected as the history of universities is inseparable from the theoretical contributions made to a shared European language, despite the heterogeneity of Italian contexts.

Part 1: Between Civil Law and the Law of Nature and Nations

The two opening chapters, devoted to Pisa and Rome, raise many questions for discussion. Salerno's essay inspects the Tuscan context, where the first Italian chair of public law was established in 1726. The renowned jurist and economist Pompeo Neri was appointed, though only for a short period. In 1738, a new chair of natural law and the law of nations was created. However, the discipline, in particular Grotius's works, had been present since the second half of the seventeenth century, becoming crucial in the early eighteenth century as a legal weapon to claim the ancient liberty of Florence against Imperial pretensions. Similarly, the conflict with the papacy, far from being a religious dispute, was a matter of territorial sovereignty in which natural law proved useful. A key figure within the academic environment is Giuseppe Averani (1662–1738), professor of civil law for more than forty years. The analysis of his works shows how the understanding of natural law and the law of nations is consistent with acknowledging the crucial role of Roman law. Yet, Averani carried out a methodological renewal emphasizing the primacy of principles and of theory over practice.

In his chapter, Alberto Clerici highlights the competition among Catholic educational institutions: the University, ruled by the pope, and the Jesuit College. The context is La Sapienza in Rome, where a formal chair of 'natural law, public law and the law of nations' was established in the Faculty of Law only in 1824. However, the actual teaching of natural law and the law of nations was introduced more than a century earlier, by Gian Vincenzo Gravina (1664–1718), in his courses on Roman law. Here the 'reception' led to a significant re-elaboration, and Gravina's work was well received by other European authors of the Enlightenment, such as Montesquieu and Gibbon. The link between Roman law and natural law was part of an attempt to explain the historical origin of laws, as well as to highlight the universal reason underlying them. While Gravina develops his view independently of Giambattista Vico, his successor to the chair of Pandects, Emmanuele Duni (1714–1781), explicitly resorted to the latter. Duni seems to have sought a 'third way' between Catholic natural law and Protestant natural law, combining natural law and history in an innovative way.[9]

The two following chapters are devoted to Lombardy and the chair of natural and public law established at the University of Pavia. Jean Baptiste Noël de Saint Clair was appointed in 1769 and served until 1796 and, as in previous cases, he initially included natural law and the law of nations in the teaching of Roman law, more precisely of Justinian *Institutes*. A natural law course would gradually emerge with the creation, at first, of a chair of public law and, eventually, of the previously mentioned chair of natural and public law. In the latter case, the competing actors were the Habsburg government and the local ruling class, represented by the Senate. The overall political context is also different from Rome; university reform was part of a wider plan aimed at reorganizing Lombardy's institutions. The first act was the centralization of educational institutions in the hands of the Habsburg government, which was determined to deprive the clergy of the education of the youth and, hence, of the ruling classes. As Elisabetta Fiocchi Malaspina points out, in the years before Saint Clair, Venanzio de Mays's presentation of and commentary on Justinian *Institutes* are imbued with references to natural law scholarship, both Catholic and Protestant (from Francisco Suárez to Hugo Grotius, from Samuel Pufendorf to Johann Gottlieb Heineccius). With the university reform and the official introduction of a chair in natural and public law at Pavia's Faculty of Law, the situation changed dramatically. The reform plan of legal studies from 1773, as well as Jean Baptiste Noël de Saint Clair's textbook manuscript, led to a redefinition of the hierarchical order of legal knowledge, of legal sources and of political power, which anticipates the broader institutional reforms in Lombardy.

In a complementary way, Gabriella Silvestrini focuses on the reorganization of studies in Lombardy in the light of the theories elaborated by the members of the Academy of Fists, who, together with their main collaborators, actively engaged in Habsburg reforms, against traditional local powers and

9 On the contrast between classical natural law and history, see Leo Strauss, *Natural Right and History* (Chicago, IL: University of Chicago Press, 1953); a first reconsideration of the historical dimension of modern natural law was in Alfred Dufour, *Droits de l'homme, droit naturel et histoire. Droit, individuel et pouvoir de l'Ecole du droit naturel à l'Ecole du droit historique* (Paris: Presses Universitaire de France, 1991).

knowledge. On the one hand, Beccaria's and the Verri brothers' theories appear to be a fully fledged philosophical foundation of the reform project. The core of their view, inspired by Francis Bacon and the *Encyclopédie*, was the unity of human knowledge deduced from first principles and human nature itself. On the other hand, the context of university reform allows us to understand better the intellectual intentions of the 'pugilists'. Far from being a rejection *in toto*, their criticism and appropriation of modern natural law theories were conceived as a rearticulation of the relationship between theory and practice, between philosophy, morality and law, to establish a new hierarchy of knowledge that could suit a new society aiming at the greatest happiness shared by the greatest number.

Part 2: Recoveries and Criticisms of Natural Law

The second part of the volume focuses on the circulation of ideas within two different areas of the Italian peninsula: the Kingdom of Naples and north-eastern Italy.

Girolamo Imbruglia's essay is devoted to Antonio Genovesi (1713–1769) and his school in Naples. Genovesi's teaching covers a wide spectrum, including natural law ethics and history, religion and government, economy and law. In his works, Genovesi dwelt upon education as an essential feature of citizens' growth and their participation in political reforms that would benefit society as a whole. Unlike French intellectuals of the Enlightenment, for him, natural law is not aimed at political transformation, but rather at citizens' education. Mario Pagano (1748–1799), one of Genovesi's most renowned disciples, carried out the shift from such educational function of natural law to its political use. As an active member of the 1799 Parthenopean Republic, Pagano shaped Genovesi's view, endowing, through a historical foundation of natural rights, political action with more relevance. Hence, within the Neapolitan context, natural law facilitated the transition not only from reform to revolution, but also from a rationalist to a historical foundation of natural rights.

In relation to the northern-eastern context, Serena Luzzi's essay focuses on the tension between law and religion, and on the various strategies employed to propagate and adjust Protestant natural law within a Catholic environment. Giambattista Almici (1717–1793) is the author of the first Italian translation of Samuel Pufendorf's *De iure naturae et gentium*, based on the French version by Jean Barbeyrac. Luzzi highlights how the encounter with theories from a Protestant tradition nourished a gradual and limited attempt by the political power to make itself more independent of the Catholic Church. The circulation of translations, essays and books aided finding an alternative to Scholastic natural law. In the second part of her chapter, Luzzi accounts some particularly significant reactions to Almici's translation, from the Dominican friar Giovanni Bonifacio Finetti to Carlantonio Pilati. The latter was the author of *Di una riforma d'Italia* (1767) and articulated a critique of natural law that was unprecedented in Italy.

In the north-eastern context, especially Venice, the theories of natural law and the law of nations were also characterized by a strong political stance. Through the reinterpretation and adaptation of treatises such as Emer de Vattel's *Droit des gens*, they provided an effective support to the governments of the small republics within the international system. Antonio Trampus devotes his chapter to the vicissitudes of the teaching of natural law at the University of Padua. On the one hand, Trampus presents the key figure of Giovanni Battista Bilesimo (1716–1799), who was appointed to the chair of natural law in 1764; on the other hand, he stresses the collective intellectual effort in introducing works coming from the Protestant world, such as Vattel's. The end of the Republic of Venice in the post-Restoration context entailed not only a transformation of the teaching of natural law in universities, but also its eclipse as a source because it was considered to be outmoded.

Part 3: From Natural Law and the Law of Nations to International Law

The third part of the volume spans chronologically from the end of the eighteenth century to the well into the nineteenth, especially the crucial moment in Italian history marked by the 'Risorgimento' and the process of unification, the main steps in which were the First Italian War of Independence in 1848 and the proclamation of the Kingdom of Italy in 1861.[10] With the 'Legge Casati' of 1859 reforming the whole education system, the teaching of natural law and the law of nations saw a transformation, while the new discipline of international law gradually emerged.

Ivo Comparato examines the official introduction of teaching of natural law and the law of nations at the University of Perugia after the reforms carried out between 1798 and 1799. The story of this chair is linked to the political events

10 A still useful and insightful introduction to the process of Italian unification is the classic book, with a selection of texts, edited by Denis Mack Smith, *The Making of Italy, 1796–1866* (London: Macmillan, 1988 [first published 1968]).

that took place up to Unification. Thanks to the analysis of texts adopted by professors such as Giuseppe Colizzi, Pietro Antonio Magalotti, Vincenzo Bini and Bonfiglio Mura, it is possible to highlight not only the different intellectual orientations, but also the most important disagreements between theories of natural law and the previous tradition. These debates were characterized by a recurring tension between the diffusion of liberal ideas and the papacy's measures, such as the 1824 Bull *Quod divina sapientia*, which suppressed the teaching of natural law and the law of nations, until it was restored in 1847.

An attempt to introduce a chair of *jus gentium* was made in Turin[11] as early as the 1730s. Yet, the strong opposition of the Curia prevented it. However, as Frédéric Ieva points out, during the eighteenth century, theories of natural law and the law of nations were taught in courses on moral philosophy. In the early nineteenth century, a chair of international law was established in the University of Turin, and the renowned jurist Pasquale Stanislao Mancini (1817–1888) was appointed to it in 1850. This chair acquired a strong symbolic political role during the national unification process. Indeed, during this period, Mancini had the opportunity to present his theory of nationality as the foundation of the law of nations, which influenced the public and private reception of international law significantly. For authors such as Pufendorf, Wolff and Vattel the *state* constitutes the main subject of the law of nations; instead, for Mancini, international law is the natural law of peoples, and consequently the primary factor is the *nation*, with its essential features of 'reason, race, language, customs, history, laws and religions'. From this perspective, the concept of nationality obtains an utterly new configuration as 'collective expression of liberty', as well as a 'holy and divine thing, like liberty itself'.

Another key figure from Piedmont is the Jesuit Luigi Taparelli d'Azeglio (1793–1862). Taparelli provided an original contribution to the reception of Protestant natural law theories, to the development of the so-called 'social doctrine of the Church', and to the reinterpretation of international law. As Francesca Iurlaro highlights, Taparelli's perspective combined Christian Wolff's doctrines with Catholic theology, especially Francisco Suárez's, dwelling upon the notions of *perfectio* and *concursus*, as well as the relationship between 'debt' and 'international love'. According to Taparelli, the

11 Since the sixteenth century, Turin had been the capital of the territories belonging to the Dukes and then Princes of Savoy, who acquired the Kingdom of Sardinia in 1720. Turin was then also the capital of that Kingdom, but Piedmont and Sardinia remained two distinct political entities until the beginning of the nineteenth century. See Anthony L. Cardoza and Geoffrey W. Symcox, *A History of Turin* (Torino: Einaudi, 2006).

definition of international order is a lengthy process of assimilation and mediation of theories, which, even though apparently distant, have many points in common, also concerning the elaboration of just war theories.

Giuseppina de Giudici examines the tension between the law of nations and international law, through a case study of the University of Cagliari from 1764, when a reform by Giovanni Battista Lorenzo Bogino (1701–1784) was implemented, until the official creation of a chair of international law with the Casati reform in the 1850s. De Giudici emphasizes the difference between the 1850s and the period between 1764 and 1849, when Cagliari, like many other Italian universities, had seen natural law and the law of nations taught indirectly, in courses on *jus civile* and *jus canonicum*. The University of Cagliari offers an example of the diverse and complex dynamics involved in the development of international law and the Italian school which had Mancini as its founder.

In conclusion, our book contributes to a rethinking of what has been conventionally understood as modern natural law. The essays collected here show that natural law has not only been the subject of a highly codified academic teaching, but also provided a broader conceptual and philosophical frame underlying the 'science of man'. Natural law is also a language wherein reform programmes of education and of politics have taken form, affecting a variety of discourses and literary genres. Even though a conceptual unity of natural law may exist, it should no longer be a problem to talk about modern natural laws, in the plural. The Italian debates we examine here show how authors were aware of a multiplicity of divisions: from the quarrel over whether the state of nature is a 'feral' state or not, to debates concerning the relationship between natural law and history, reason and passions, different theories on just war, and various political implications of social contract doctrine. Even with regard to the theme of secularization, a definition of modern natural law as a process of secularization contains the same questions and limits that generations of historians have encountered while dwelling upon the relationship between Enlightenment and religion.[12] Forms of materialism, irreligion or atheism do not necessarily entail a rejection of natural law. The specificity of the Italian case does not correspond to a particular conceptual or philosophical stance, like, for example, the primacy of history, of politics or of morals. Rather, it is the plurality of the *particular* ways in which these general features manifested

12 On the problematic concept of 'secularization' we share the insightful analysis by Ian Hunter, 'Secularization: The Birth of a Modern Combat Concept', *Modern Intellectual History* 12 (2015): 1–32.

themselves in Italy that allows us to grasp the richness of the Italian uses and interpretations of natural law: a plurality of theories that mirrors the plurality of contexts and actors, whose dramatic change with the process of unification shaped the birth and evolution of the Italian law of nations.

Bibliography

Audegean, Philippe, 'Passions et liberté. Loi de nature et fondement du droit en Italie à l'époque de Beccaria', *Studi settecenteschi* 23 (2003): 197–278.

Bazzoli, Maurizio, 'Giambattista Almici e la diffusione di Pufendorf nel Settecento italiano', *Critica storica* 16 (1979): 3–100.

Bobbio, Norberto, *Thomas Hobbes and the Natural Law Tradition*, trans. Daniela Gobetti (Chicago, IL: Chicago University Press, 1993).

Cardoza, Anthony L., and Geoffrey W. Symcox, *A History of Turin* (Torino: Einaudi, 2006).

Chadwick, Owen, 'The Italian Enlightenment', in *The Enlightenment in National Context*, ed. Roy Porter and Mikulas Teich (Cambridge: Cambridge University Press, 1981), 90–105.

Delpiano, Patrizia, *Church and Censorship in Eighteenth-Century Italy: Governing Reading in the Age of Enlightenment* (New York: Routledge, 2018).

di Simone, Maria Rosa, 'L'influenza di Christian Wolff sul giusnaturalismo dell'area asburgica e italiana', in *Dal 'De Jure Naturae et gentium' di Samuel Pufendorf alla codificazione prussiana del 1794. Atti del convegno internazionale, Padova, 25–26 ottobre 2001*, ed. Marta Ferronato (Padova: Cedam, 2005), 221–268.

Dufour, Alfred, *Droits de l'homme, droit naturel et histoire. Droit, individuel et pouvoir de l'Ecole du droit naturel à l'Ecole du droit historique* (Paris: Presses Universitaire de France, 1991).

Ferrone, Vincenzo, 'Chiesa cattolica e modernità. La scoperta dei diritti dell'uomo dopo l'esperienza dei totalitarismi', in *Chiesa cattolica e modernità, Atti del convegno della Fondazione Michele Pellegrino*, ed. Franco Bolgiani, Vincenzo Ferrone and Francesco Margiotta Broglio (Bologna: Il mulino, 2004), 17–131.

Ferrone, Vincenzo, *The Enlightenment: History of an Idea* (Princeton, MA: Princeton University Press, 2017).

Ferrone, Vincenzo, *The Intellectual Roots of the Italian Enlightenment: Newtonian Science, Religion, and Politics in the Early Eighteenth Century* (Atlantic Highlands, NJ: Humanities Press International, 1995).

Garin, Eugenio, 'Appunti per una storia della fortuna di Hobbes nel Settecento italiano', *Rivista critica di storia della filosofia* 17(4) (2002): 514–527.

Haakonssen, Knud, 'Protestant Natural Law Theory: A General Interpretation', in *New Essays on the History of Autonomy: A Collection Honoring J. B. Schneewind*, ed. Natalie Brender and Larry Krasnoff (Cambridge: Cambridge University Press, 2004), 92–109.

Haakonssen, Knud, and Michael Seidler, 'Natural Law: Law, Rights, and Duties', in *A Companion to Intellectual History*, ed. Richard Whatmore and Brian Young (Chichester: Wiley-Blackwell, 2015), 377–400.

Haakonssen, Knud, 'Early Modern Natural Law Theories', in *The Cambridge Companion to Natural Jurisprudence*, ed. George Duke and Robert P. George (Cambridge: Cambridge University Press, 2017), 76–102.

Hunter, Ian, 'Secularization: The Birth of a Modern Combat Concept', *Modern Intellectual History* 12 (2015): 1–32.

La recezione di Grozio a Napoli nel Settecento, ed. Vittorio Conti (Firenze: Centro editoriale toscano, 2002).

Law and the Christian Tradition in Italy: The Legacy of the Great Jurists, ed. Orazio Condorelli, and Domingo Rafael (London: Routledge, 2021).

Mack Smith, Denis, *The Making of Italy, 1796–1866* (1968) (London: Macmillan, 1988).

Panizza, Diego, 'La traduzione italiana del "De iure naturae" di Pufendorf: giusnaturalismo moderno e cultura cattolica nel Settecento', *Studi Veneziani* 11 (1969): 483–528.

Quaglioni, Diego, 'Pufendorf in Italia. Appunti e notizie della prima diffusione della traduzione italiana del *De iure naturae et gentium*', *Il Pensiero Politico* 32 (1999): 23–250.

Rech, Walter, 'International Law as a Political Language, 1600–1859', in *A History of International Law in Italy*, ed. Giulio Bartolini (Oxford: Oxford University Press, 2020), 48–78.

Rosa, Mario, 'The Catholic *Aufklärung* in Italy', in *A Companion to the Catholic Enlightenment in Europe*, ed. Ulrich L. Lehner and Michael Printy (Leiden: Brill, 2010), 215–250.

Scattola, Merio, 'Protestantesimo e diritto naturale cattolico nel XVIII secolo', in *Illuminismo e Protestantesimo*, ed. Giulia Cantarutti and Stefano Ferrari (Milano: FrancoAngeli, 2010), 131–148.

Stoffella, Stefania, 'Assolutismo e diritto naturale in Italia nel Settecento', *Annali dell'Istituto storico italo-germanico* 26 (2000): 137–175.

Stoffella, Stefania, 'Il diritto di resistenza nel Settecento Italiano. Documenti per la storia della traduzione del De iure naturae et gentium di Pufendorf', *Magistrature et politique* 2 (2001): 173–199, http://laboratoireitalien.revues.org/261.

Strauss, Leo, *Natural Right and History* (Chicago, IL: University of Chicago Press, 1953).

The Enlightenment in National Context, ed. Roy Porter and Mikulas Teich (Cambridge: Cambridge University Press 1981).

Trampus, Antonio, *Emer de Vattel and the Politics of Good Government: Constitutionalism, Small States and the International System* (Cham: Palgrave Macmillan, 2020).

Venturi, Franco, *Il Settecento riformatore*, vol. 5, *L'Italia dei lumi, 1764–1790* (Torino: Einaudi, 1987).

Venturi, Franco, *Italy and the Enlightenment: Studies in a Cosmopolitan Century* (New York: New York University Press, 1972).

Zurbuchen, Simone, 'Protestant Natural Law', in *Encyclopedia of the Philosophy of Law and Social Philosophy*, ed. Mortimer Sellers and Stephan Kirste (Dordrecht: Springer, 2020), 1–6.

PART 1

Between Civil Law and the Law of Nature and Nations

CHAPTER 1

Natural Law at the University of Pisa: From the *Ius civile* Teachings to the Establishment of the First Chair of *Ius publicum* in 1726

Emanuele Salerno

1 Introduction

The history of the teaching of modern natural law at the University of Pisa[1] formally started in 1738, during the rule of the new Grand Duke Francis Stephen Habsburg-Lorraine, with the reinstatement in the 'collegio dei giureconsulti' of the 'jus publicum' chair.[2] Only then, while reorganizing the teaching plan, was the chair equated with a chair of 'diritto della natura e delle genti' (law of nature and nations), and lessons on this subject began to appear in printed schedules.[3] However, on the basis of what happened at the universities in the Germanic area,[4] and the explicit reference in the acts establishing this second

1 On the Pisan *Studium*, see the collective work, based mainly on primary sources, *Storia dell'Università di Pisa* 2 vols (Pisa: Plus, 2000) (hereafter *StUniPi*). I would especially like to honour the memory of Professor Danilo Marrara for constantly encouraging me in pursuing archival research, during my research doctorate at the University of Pisa.

2 ASF, Consiglio di Reggenza, 1 (letter-book of correspondence between the Secretary of Tuscany in Vienna and the Regency in Florence), fol. 118r–v: 'Au Council de Régence, Vienne le 15 octobre 1738 […] Nous avons cru nécessaire d'y introduire, *au faire revivre une Chaire de Professeur du Droit naturel, des gens, et public de l'Empire,* laquelle nous avons conféré à l'Abbé Bandiera' (italics added). On this period, see Elisa Panicucci, 'Dall'avvento dei Lorena al Regno d'Etruria (1737–1807)', in *StUniPi*, vol. 2, I, 3–134.

3 ASP, Università 2, C I 2 (concise course contents are reported from the printed schedule '1739', i.e. academic year 1739/1740: Francesco Niccolò Bandiera 'aget de bello et summo imperio'), fols n.n.; more documentation is in ASF, Consiglio di Reggenza, 640 (from fasc. '1738'), fols n.n.

4 On the introduction of modern natural law since the second half of the seventeenth century, that is, while public law chairs were consolidated in Protestant universities, see Michael Stolleis, *Geschichte des öffentlichen Rechts in Deutschland* (München: Beck, 1988), vol. 1, 195–196, 276, 289. On the conceptual discontinuity within the lexical continuity of *ius publicum*, see Merio Scattola, *Dalla virtù alla scienza. La fondazione e la trasformazione della disciplina politica nell'età moderna* (Milano: FrancoAngeli, 2003), 330–390, already discussed in his *Das Naturrecht vor dem Naturrecht. Zur Geschichte des* ius naturae *im 16. Jahrhundert* (Tübingen: Niemeyer, 1999), 107–204.

 | DOI:10.1163/9789004685130_003

chair of public law,[5] the history of the teaching of modern natural law has been conventionally considered as starting with the institution of the first chair of 'jus publicum', in 1726.[6] The first chair of public law in Italy was indeed founded at the time of the government of the last Medici Grand Duke, Gian Gastone, during the dynastic crisis of the reigning family and the related international dispute between the Grand Duchy and the Holy Roman Empire: a *bellum diplomaticum* that, throughout the first decades of the eighteenth century, engaged the Tuscan ruling class and its jurists in defending the autonomy and independence of the Tuscan 'small state' against imperial expansion.[7]

However, the absence of the contents of the lectures given by the first teacher of the course (the abbot jurist Pompeo Neri, in the chair from 1727/1728 to 1728/1729) has compelled scholars to undertake an indirect institutional reconstruction, focusing at best on the *bellum litterarium* regarding the origin of the mythical *Littera Pisana/Florentina* of the *Digest* during the late 1720s.[8]

---

5 See the reports of the University administrator Cerati (1738), transcribed in appendices II and III to Niccola Carranza, *Monsignor Gaspare Cerati provveditore dell'Università di Pisa nel Settecento delle riforme* (Pisa: Pacini, 1974), 318–331 and 332–342.

6 See Danilo Marrara, 'Pompeo Neri e la cattedra pisana di "diritto pubblico" nel XVIII secolo', *Rivista di Storia del Diritto Italiano* 59 (1986): 173–202. On the Italian framework, see Italo Birocchi, 'L'insegnamento del diritto pubblico nelle Università italiane nel XVIII secolo', in *Science politique et droit public dans les facultés de droit européennes (XIIIe–XVIIIe siècle)*, ed. Jaques Krynen and Michael Stolleis (Frankfurt am Main: Klostermann, 2008), 549–581.

7 On the Medici succession, see Marcello Verga, *Da 'cittadini' a 'nobili'. Lotta politica e riforma delle istituzioni nella Toscana di Francesco Stefano* (Milano: Giuffrè, 1990), 13–64, and idem, *Alla morte del re. Sovranità e leggi di successione nell'Europa dei secoli XVII–XVIII* (Roma: Salerno, 2020), 82–100; Matthias Schnettger, 'Dynastische Interessen, Lehnsrecht und Machtpolitik. Der Wiener Hof und die Anwartschaft der Kurfürstin Anna Maria Luisa von der Pfalz auf die toskanische Erbfolge (1711–1714)', *Mitteilungen des Instituts für Österreichische Geschichtsforschung* 108 (2000): 351–371; Emanuele Salerno, 'Giusnaturalismo e cultura giuspolitica nella Toscana del primo Settecento. Il *Discorso sopra la successione della Toscana* di Niccolò Antinori (1711)', *Archivio Storico Italiano* 173 (2015): 31–64. Most of the literature on the treatment of legal arguments in international politics of the period can be found – with extensive references to primary sources – in Frederik Dhondt, *Balance of Power and Norm Hierarchy: Franco-British Diplomacy After the Peace of Utrecht* (Leiden: Brill, 2015). For the scholarly debate on the need to investigate the history of international law from comparative and local perspectives, see Giulio Bartolini, 'What Is a History of International Law in Italy For? International Law Through the Prism of National Perspectives', in *A History of International Law in Italy*, ed. Giulio Bartolini (Oxford: Oxford University Press, 2020), 3–15 (esp. 3–10).

8 See Enrico Spagnesi, 'Il diritto', in *StUniPi*, vol. 1, I, 191–257 (esp. 248–257), and vol. 2, II, 461–570 (461–468); Giuliano Marini, 'Dal Diritto naturale alla Filosofia del diritto', in *StUniPi*, vol. 2, II, 635–661.

Nevertheless, the presence of numerous primary sources makes it possible to reinterpret the establishment of the first public law chair as a *terminus ad quem* of an earlier process. Indeed, a process of gradual introduction and use of modern natural law by Pisan academics, from the end of the seventeenth century, is demonstrated not only by funeral orations dedicated to the main law professors (often the only sources used by historians for their accounts), but also by many neglected sources, such as library catalogues, judicial decisions and legal consultations, as well as government booklets. Furthermore, the early process of circulation and reception of modern natural law is confirmed by the publication, in 1703, of an academic dissertation, titled *De jure belli, et pacis disputatio*, in which Grotius is explicitly mentioned. This first text, together with those that arose during the *bellum diplomaticum*, are actually fundamental for understanding the two perspectives (only at times convergent) of legal education and international politics, through which the process of institutionalization of natural law at the University of Pisa was developing. Actually, it should be remembered that the author of one of the first texts on the troubled Tuscan succession (with sophisticated quotations from Grotius's and Pufendorf's natural law doctrines), Senator and State Councillor Niccolò Francesco Antinori, served also as 'Auditore' – that is, the main central official – of the Pisan *Studium*.[9]

This chapter therefore describes this early stage, essential to interpreting the conditions in which the first public law chair of Italy was founded. The study of legal education in the late seventeenth and early eighteenth century will allow a more in-depth understanding of both the development of natural law in teaching practice throughout the long eighteenth century, and the features of the two processes of reception, respectively for educational and political purposes. In fact, although both processes were founded on appreciation of the centrality of Roman law and philosophy in the construction of doctrines by the so-called 'modern natural law school', and developed through mediation of traditional Roman legal culture of the Pisan 'historical-critical school', there were some differences. In this initial phase, the didactic reception was indirect, although not entirely implicit, whereas the political reception was direct and explicit.

---

9 See Emanuele Salerno, '*Stare pactis* and Neutrality. Grotius and Pufendorf in the Political Thought of the Early Eighteenth-Century Grand Duchy of Tuscany', in *War, Trade and Neutrality: Europe and the Mediterranean in Seventeenth and Eighteenth Centuries*, ed. Antonella Alimento (Milano: FrancoAngeli, 2011), 188–202, and idem, 'Giusnaturalismo e cultura giuspolitica nella Toscana del primo Settecento' (on Antinori's career, n. 14).

2 Continuity of Programmes: The Primacy of Roman Law, but First Traces of Modern Natural Law

In the period of the last two Medici Grand Dukes, Cosimo III (1670–1723) and Gian Gastone (1723–1737), the *Studium* of Pisa preserved the profile of state school, consolidated since its reopening in 1543 by Duke Cosimo I. The College of Jurists continued to be consulted by the prince in an advisory capacity and legal education was primarily addressed to the civil class and directed towards practice, both in the justice courts and in the various state magistracies.

Despite the renewal of the teaching method through the reception of legal humanism, since the beginning of the seventeenth century, the programme of legal studies remained focused, as in other Italian *Studia*, on teaching the two *Corpora iuris*, without fundamental changes from the statutory regulation for the reopening in 1543. The teachings of civil and canon law were divided into three levels, respectively entrusted to the 'istitutisti', extraordinary and ordinary professors, preserving the institution of 'concorrenza'.[10] The first two classes covered preparatory courses, in elementary exegetical terms; ordinary professors were in charge of interpreting sections of the *Digest* and the *Codex*, or the *Decretales* of Pope Gregory IX.[11]

The reasons for the continuity of this tradition trace back to the hierarchy of sources for the legal system in force in the Tuscan Grand Duchy and in neighbouring states. At that time – as Pompeo Neri would explain later to the new Habsburg-Lorraine dynasty – Roman and canon law were applied in all Tuscan courts of justice. Roman law (with the annexed parts on feudal matters) was considered *ius commune*, that is, with residual and supplementary function over statutory and municipal laws (canon law had a different status). Consequently, of the four bodies of written laws in force, the content of Roman and canon law was an essential element of the university curriculum. Meanwhile, education on statutory and municipal laws, including customary law derived from the interpretation of Tuscan justice courts (whose judgments also had regulatory functions of 'nomofilachia' and of verification of the laws in force), remained delegated to practical apprenticeship.[12]

---

10 That is, the simultaneous activation of multiple courses on the same subject, allowing students to choose different teachers and enabling the organization of circular disputes as supplementary educational activities.

11 See Danilo Marrara, 'L'età medicea (1543–1737)', in *StUniPi*, vol. 1, I, 79–187 (legal course contents, 129–130), and vol. 1, II, 571–656; Danilo Barsanti, 'I docenti e le cattedre', in *StUniPi*, vol. 1, II, 475–480, 505–566, and vol. 2, I, 269–416.

12 See Pompeo Neri [Badia], *Discorso primo* (report on the compilation of a new code of municipal laws of Tuscany, 31 May 1747), ed. Marcello Verga, in Verga, *Da 'cittadini' a*

University legal education continued to unfold through 'public lectures' and 'repetitions to the column',[13] 'domestic lectures' and, for competing lectures on civil and canon law, 'circular disputes'.[14] It should be noted that since 1566 the hereditary prince Francesco de' Medici established an obligatory oath of Catholic allegiance for candidates to final exams, beyond oaths of loyalty to the prince (including by clergymen), obedience to the rector, and observance of university laws (already required by the Statutes). The degree examination, the only mandatory exam in the five-year curriculum, was oral and divided into two phases: first, oral presentation of assigned contents, that is, a fragment from each of the two *Corpora iuris*; and second, a response to the objections from the commissioners.[15]

The years between the late seventeenth century and the 1730s have been considered by historians as a period in which the Medici dynastic crisis negatively influenced the functioning of the University. Moreover, in the 1690s, the Catholic orthodoxy of Grand Duke Cosimo III led to interventions against the freedom of teaching. This was because, in addition to the texts of Aristotle, prescribed by the Statutes, a group of professors also dealt with the doctrines of Anaxagoras, Plato, Democritus and Epicurus, among the ancient authors, and of Galileo and Gassendi, among the modern ones, in their courses of natural philosophy.[16]

'nobili', 317–346. On the legal professions in Tuscany, see Daniele Edigati, *Avvocati e procuratori nella Toscana d'Antico Regime. Le professioni forensi dalla tutela alla disciplina di polizia* (Bologna: Il Mulino, 2021).

13 That is, in the courtyard of the University building.

14 Here and below, English translations from Italian and Latin sources are by the present author.

15 On the degree examination, see Marrara, 'L'età medicea (1543–1737)', 171–187. Since 1611, law students had been required to present certificates of attendance for all three levels to be admitted to final exam; ibid., 174.

16 On the university context, see Carranza, *Monsignor Gaspare Cerati*, 5–9, 18–21, 38–48, and Marrara, 'L'età medicea (1543–1737)', 150–163. On the period, see Eric Cochrane, *Florence in the Forgotten Centuries, 1527–1800* (Chicago, IL: University of Chicago Press, 1973), 231–396. The framework of the political and cultural decadence that accompanied Cosimo III's government has been partly blurred in *La Toscana di Cosimo III*, ed. Franco Angiolini, Vieri Becagli and Marcello Verga (Firenze: Edifir, 1993), but the 1690s are in any case still considered as marking a break in the reform projects of the first two decades of his princehood. For the long-term cultural benefits of the European tours made by the last Medici princes, Cosimo III and Giovan Gastone, especially in the Netherlands, see Elena Fasano Guarini, 'Cosimo III de' Medici', and Maria Pia Paoli, 'Gian Gastone de' Medici', both in *Dizionario Biografico degli Italiani* (Roma: Istituto dell'Enciclopedia Italiana), vol. 30 (1984), 54–61 and vol. 54 (2000), 397–407, respectively (and further references there); see also Henk Th. van Veen and Andrew P. McCormick, *Tuscany and the Low Countries: An Introduction to the Sources and an Inventory of Four Florentine Libraries* (Firenze: Centro Di, 1984).

Nevertheless, alongside these suspect classical and modern philosophers, the works of major modern natural law theorists were also present in the libraries[17] available to professors of the University of Pisa, as systematic investigation into the principal libraries of Florence and Pisa confirms.[18] The head of neo-humanistic jurisprudence, Giuseppe Averani,[19] who taught civil law for forty years, had a seventeenth edition of Grotius's *De iure belli ac pacis* (*IBP*), probably that published in Jena in 1673.[20] His lesser-known colleague Giacomo Tiburzio Tommaso Monti had the edition of 1680, that is, the first edition with the commentary of Johannes Fredericus Gronovius,[21] whose intellectual relationship with the Medici court (later continued by his sons) dated back to the early 1640s.[22] But interest in these works exceeded the circle of jurists and, although banned by the Roman *Index*, they were also owned by clergymen. In the library of Camaldolese Guido Grandi,[23] professor of philosophy and math-

17 On the Italian framework of book production, circulation and censorship, see Renato Pasta, 'Mediazioni e trasformazioni: operatori del libro in Italia nel Settecento', *Archivio Storico Italiano* 172 (2014): 311–354.

18 Here follow – for the first time – the results of a systematic examination into book ownership marks conducted in the libraries of Florence and Pisa. The editions are numbered in reference to the scholarly bibliography of Grotius and Pufendorf, hereafter *BG* and *BP*; *BG*: Jacob ter Meulen and Pieter Johan Jurrian Diermanse, *Bibliographie des écrits imprimés de Hugo Grotius* (La Haye: M. Nijhoff, 1950); *BP*: Horst Denzer, *Moralphilosophie und Naturrecht bei Samuel Pufendorf* (München: Beck, 1972), 359–373.

19 On his intellectual profile, see Niccola Carranza, 'Averani, Giuseppe', in *Dizionario Biografico degli Italiani* (Roma: Istituto dell'Enciclopedia Italiana, 1962), vol. 4, 658–659, and see below in this chapter. Averani taught civil law from 1685/1686 to 1725/1726.

20 I thank librarian Mauro Bernardini of the University Library of Pisa for having guided me in the examination of book ownership marks and various inventories of Averani's collection, reported recently in Maria Augusta Morelli Timpanaro, 'Il testamento segreto di Giuseppe Averani (1728). Il suo costante attaccamento allo studio pisano e ad alcuni colleghi', *Bollettino Storico Pisano* 75 (2006): 287–309.

21 The Hague: A. Leers, 1680 (BUP, B.o.5.8; *BG*: 583); Monti taught civil law from 1720/1721 to 1734/1735.

22 On the meaning of the *iter italicum* for J. F. Gronovius, who stayed in Florence for two months between 1640 and 1641, see Fabrizio Lomonaco, Lex regia. *Diritto, filologia e fides historica nella cultura politico-filosofica dell'Olanda di fine Seicento* (Napoli: Guida, 1990), 41–80, now also in English, although with some typographical errors, under the title *New Studies on Lex Regia* (Bern-New York: Peter Lang, 2011), 71–98. His son Jacob taught Greek and rhetoric at the University of Pisa (1673/1674); later, Gronovius's other son, Laurens Theodor, came to Florence to study the *Littera* of the *Digest* (1679–1682). On this, see Tammo Wallinga, 'Laurentius Theodorus Gronovius (1648–1724)', *Tijdschrift voor Rechtsgeschiedenis* 65 (1997): 459–495.

23 See Ugo Baldini, 'Grandi, Guido', in *Dizionario Biografico degli Italiani* (Roma: Istituto dell'Enciclopedia Italiana, 2002), vol. 58, 494–507; Grandi taught from 1700/1701 to 1733/1734.

ematics, there was the first edition with notes by Jean Barbeyrac, in Latin, of the *De iure* by Grotius (1720), as well as a seventeenth-century edition of the *De Cive* by Hobbes (1696).[24] The Servite Gerardo Capassi,[25] court theologian and professor of scholastic theology, owned two editions of the *De iure*, one in Latin (1696–1703),[26] with the comments by Willem Van der Muelen as well as by Gronovius, and the first edition translated into French and annotated by Barbeyrac (1724).[27] His 'brother' and pupil, Francesco Raimondo Adami,[28] then professor of dogmatic theology, possessed – like Capassi – two editions of the major natural law work of Grotius, a seventeenth-century edition (1651)[29] and the first edition with notes by Barbeyrac, in Latin (1720).[30] An interesting picture, corroborating the hypothesis that the study of the circulation of modern natural law at the University of Pisa in the first half of the eighteenth century should be expanded beyond the boundaries of the legal teachings.[31]

Evidence of the introduction and use of natural law by the professors of law and its circulation among them is also found in some eighteenth-century

---

24 Amsterdam: Janssonius van Waesberge, 1720 (*BG*: 602); Amsterdam: H. & Viduam Th. Boom, 1696; for these entries see BUP, *Catalogo alfabetico della Libreria Grandiana* [ca. 1780], MS 387.

25 See Franco A. Dal Pino, 'Capassi, Gerardo', in *Dizionario Biografico degli Italiani* (Roma: Istituto dell'Enciclopedia Italiana, 1975), vol. 18, 387–391; Capassi taught from 1683/1684 to 1726/1727.

26 Utrecht: W. van de Water, 1696–1703 (BMRF, 6.C.III.62; *BG*: 590).

27 Amsterdam: P. de Coup, 1724 (BNCF, B.17.3.13; *BG*: 654); he also owned the *Commentariorum de rebus suecicis libri XXVI* of Pufendorf (Utrecht: J. Ribbius, 1686; BNCF, Palat. 29.2.8.3; *BP*: 8.1).

28 See Giovanni Miccoli, 'Adami, Francesco Raimondo', in *Dizionario Biografico degli Italiani* (Roma: Istituto dell'Enciclopedia Italiana, 1960), vol. 1, 233–234; Adami taught from 1744/1745 to 1767/1768 and again from 1774/1775 to 1788/1789.

29 Amsterdam: J. Jansson, 1651 (BMRF, 6.D.VIII.10; *BG*: 576).

30 Amsterdam: J. Janssonius van Waesberge, 1720 (BMRF, 6.J.VI.44; *BG*: 602); he also owned Grotius's *De veritate religionis christianae* (Amsterdam: L. & D. Elzevier, 1662; BMRF, 6.B.XII.7; *BG*: 959).

31 Moreover, the contacts between Grotius and Galileo in the 1630s, and the report on the censorship of Grotius's *IBP* by Paganino Gaudenzi, professor of humanities at the Pisan *Studium* from 1628/1629 to 1648/1649 (also teaching feudal law from 1630/1631), would deserve further study. On Grotius's relations with Italy and the *IBP*'s reception by Roman Catholic circles, see Harm-Jan van Dam, 'Italian Friends: Grotius, De Dominis, Sarpi and the Church', *Nederlands Archief Voor Kerkgeschiedenis/Dutch Review of Church History* 75 (1995): 198–215; Henk Nellen, *Hugo Grotius: A Lifelong Struggle for Peace in Church and State, 1583–1645* (Leiden: Brill, 2015), 378–379 and *passim*; Nicholas Hardy, *Criticism and Confession: The Bible in the Seventeenth Century Republic of Letters* (Oxford: Oxford University Press, 2017), 219–240 (esp. 221, n. 91, and 224, n. 102).

sources. Already in the mid-eighteenth century, the Florentine literary periodical *Novelle letterarie*, on the occasion of the death of Giovanni Bonaventura Neri Badia (1657–1742),[32] former professor of civil law for five years and then high magistrate, remembered his commitment to 'derive principles of justice and equality from the sources of nature and of public law',[33] hitherto neglected, in order to better interpret the spirit of the laws, statutes and customs of different peoples. Similarly, for the funeral honours of the above-mentioned professor Giuseppe Averani (1662–1738),[34] his pupil Antonio Niccolini celebrated his teacher as the one who 'raised us from the study of Roman laws to the contemplation of the reason of nature and nations, thus man can become not only expert in law, but creator of new and good laws'.[35] Niccolini continued, 'he ahead of everyone pointed out to us how easily we could acquire possession of the reason of nature and nations' through the study of philosophy (namely, the principles of the just, honest and decorous that are found in Roman law), and through learning about history.[36] Also the pupil of both these professors, Bernardo Tanucci (1698–1783),[37] who taught civil law for over ten years in Pisa, was described as the teacher who commented on Justinian's *Institutiones*, including reference to the law of nature and nations.[38] Indeed, Tanucci recommended the study of the classics of the 'modern natural law school' for learning public law by those preparing to enter public life, years after his own teaching experience.[39]

These professors, with their texts, offer the elements necessary to understand the reception of modern natural law at the University of Pisa up until the founding of the first public law chair in 1726, entrusted to Pompeo Neri

32 See Daniele Edigati, 'Neri Badia, Giovanni Bonaventura', in *Dizionario Biografico dei Giuristi Italiani. XII–XX secolo*, ed. Italo Birocchi et al. (Bologna: Il Mulino, 2013), 1423–1424. G. B. Neri Badia taught civil law from 1683/1684 to 1688/1689, then became judge, and from 1719 'Auditore della Consulta', that is, the official of the supreme judicial court responsible for the control of justice administration and dispensation by the prince's grace.

33 *Novelle letterarie* (Firenze: n.p., con licenza de' superiori, 1742), no. 12, Firenze, 23 March 1742, cols 177–178.

34 See Mario Montorzi, 'Averani, Giuseppe', in *Dizionario Biografico dei Giuristi Italiani. XII–XX secolo*, ed. Italo Birocchi et al. (Bologna: Il Mulino, 2013), 128–130.

35 Antonio Niccolini, 'Delle lodi di Giuseppe Averani [...] 1745', in Giuseppe Averani, *Lezioni Toscane* (Firenze: Gaetano Albizzini, 1744–1761), vol. 2, iii–xxxix, at xxiii.

36 Ibid., xxiv.

37 See Anna Vittoria Migliorini, 'Tanucci, Bernardo', in *Dizionario Biografico dei Giuristi Italiani. XII–XX secolo*, ed. Italo Birocchi et al. (Bologna: Il Mulino, 2013), 1931–1934.

38 Angelo Fabroni, *Historia Academiae Pisanae* (Pisis: Gaetanus Mugnainus, 1791–1795), vol. 3, 332.

39 On this, see Salerno, '*Stare pactis* and Neutrality', 190–191, and further references there.

(1707–1776)[40] by the Grand Duke Gian Gastone under an extraordinary procedure, in view of the 'long, faithful and attentive service' of his father, Giovanni Bonaventura Neri Badia.[41]

From these traces it is clear that in the late seventeenth and early eighteenth century, as already noted by historians, despite no innovation of the traditional *ratio studiorum* of legal studies emerging from the teaching programmes, the process of renewal of legal teaching and of opening to European law schools – which began with the introduction of the humanistic jurisprudence method – was also developed in the direction of the 'modern natural law school'.

At any rate, so far no attention has been paid to the first explicit confirmation of the introduction of Grotius to the official academic context, that is, the academic exercise *De jure belli, et pacis disputatio* of 1703,[42] associated with the head of Pisan neo-humanistic jurisprudence, Giuseppe Averani. Formally attributed to the German Philipp Wilhelm von Sutter, under the direction of Averani (who appears on the title page as *praeses*), this text was published at the grand ducal printing house, richly gilded, and dedicated to the Grand Duke Cosimo III. The dedication celebrated the Grand Duke's neutral policy and exalted the political virtues of that Medici as a ruler capable of keeping the Tuscan small state at peace. As shown in the following pages, the central thesis of the text responded to the political debate on interstate relations of Tuscany during the War of Spanish Succession (1701–1713/1714).

The *De jure belli, et pacis disputatio* of 1703 casts light on both perspectives of the process of introduction, circulation and use of modern natural law in the Pisan academic context, that is, legal education and international politics, revealing at the same time the primacy of the political function in the early stage of this reception process. Then, in order to reconstruct, first of all, the conditions of legal teaching practice of this period, we must refer to the professorship and work of Giuseppe Averani.

3 Renewal of the Method: Averani, Natural Law and Grotius

The renewal of the study of law at the University of Pisa has been traced back to the reception of legal humanism, which occurred at the beginning of

40 See Marcello Verga, 'Neri, Pompeo', in *Dizionario Biografico dei Giuristi Italiani. XII–XX secolo*, ed. Italo Birocchi et al. (Bologna: Il Mulino, 2013), 1520–1523.

41 Doc. IV, in Appendix to Marrara, 'Pompeo Neri', 200.

42 Philipp Wilhelm von Sutter [*praeses* Giuseppe Averani], *De jure belli, et pacis disputatio* (Florentiae: typis Regiae Celsitudinis, apud Petrum Antonium Brigonci, superiorum licentia, 1703); the copy used here is in BNCF, Magl.20.2.140.

the seventeenth century. The credit for penetration of the work and method of Cujas, Duaren, Doneau and Favre has been given to Niccolò Buonaparte from San Miniato, who taught civil law at the Pisan *Studium* for over thirty years, starting in 1609. During the seventeenth century, the Pisan law school was developed (preferring the erudite approach of humanistic jurisprudence, rather than the systematic one) by a pupil of Buonaparte, Bartolomeo Chesi, as well as by Pietro Paolo Borromei and Anton Maria Rilli, until it gained particular European relevance with Giuseppe Averani, who was a pupil of Borromei, Rilli and Francesco Maria Ceffini.[43]

Averani's legal training occurred within the 'historical-critical school' of Pisa, but in addition to law, the Florentine jurist cultivated interests in the natural sciences, following an experimental anti-scholastic orientation (whose rationalist approach would also be manifested in his method of teaching law). This was an eclecticism that he shared and developed with his older brothers Benedetto,[44] classicist and professor also at the University of Pisa, and Niccolò,[45] lawyer and astronomer, editor of the Florentine edition of the *Opera omnia* by Gassendi (1727). This edition was produced during the cultural renewal centred on the revival of Galileo's thought, in which Giuseppe intervened directly, participating in the Florentine edition of the *Opere di Galileo Galilei* (1718).[46] It is therefore appropriate to quote an eighteenth-century source stating that the Averani brothers formed 'a Triumvirate very rarely found in the same house, and perhaps unique in the same generation'.[47]

Averani's long career as professor of *ius civile* began in the academic year 1685/1686, as soon as he obtained his degree *in utroque iure*, and continued for-

43 On these members of the Pisan law school, see *ad vocem* in *Dizionario Biografico dei Giuristi Italiani. XII–XX secolo*, ed. Italo Birocchi et al. (Bologna: Il Mulino, 2013). On the Italian neo-humanistic law school, see Italo Birocchi, *Alla ricerca dell'ordine. Fonti e cultura giuridica nell'età moderna* (Torino: Giappichelli, 2002), 317–334; idem, 'Introduzione', in Francesco Rapolla, *De jurisconsulto*, ed. Italo Birocchi (Bologna: Il Mulino, 2006), 9–70 (esp. 14–34).

44 On Benedetto Averani (1645–1707), see Niccola Carranza, 'Averani, Benedetto', in *Dizionario Biografico degli Italiani* (Roma: Istituto dell'Enciclopedia Italiana, 1962), vol. 4, 657–658.

45 On Niccolò Averani (*ca.* 1650–1727), see Niccola Carranza, 'Averani, Niccolò', in *Dizionario Biografico degli Italiani* (Roma: Istituto dell'Enciclopedia Italiana, 1962), vol. 4, 659–660.

46 On this cultural renewal process and the associated publications, see Vincenzo Ferrone, *The Intellectual Roots of the Italian Enlightenment: Newtonian Science, Religion, and Politics in the Early Eighteenth Century*, trans. Sue Brotherton (Amherst: Humanities Press, 1995; originally published in Italian, 1982), 41–62.

47 Marco Lastri, *ad vocem*, in *Raccolta d'elogi d'uomini illustri toscani* (Lucca: Benedini, 1774), vol. 4, 682.

mally until the year of his death, 1738, although his teaching activities ceased from the academic year 1726/1727 for health reasons.[48]

The core elements of his didactics clearly emerge from his inaugural address of the academic year at the end of his career, which may well represent the educational commitment of a lifetime.[49] The eclectic jurist's text is an exhortation to students and princes (from 1688 he was tutor for Gian Gastone's legal studies) to oppose the spread of a conception of legal science strictly practice-oriented and detached from theory. For him, this attitude was the main cause of the decrease in enrolment and, above all, of the decline of jurisprudence, as well as all other scientific disciplines for the conservation and development of the state, happiness and protection of humanity. The polemical target of Averani was the pragmatic jurists ('haec vorago, quae absorbet profectus omnium, qui seditiosis Pragmaticorum vocibus auscultant'), that is, those who, neglecting the laws of the *Corpus iuris civilis*, attribute legal authority to the 'opiniones' of the 'doctores', often for mere financial interests. The consequence of this cultural decline also affected the administration of justice and hence the state.[50]

The controversy between legal theorists and practitioners was restated by Averani, who favoured the historical-philological approach of legal humanism, as did the law school to which he belonged. It is precisely the humanistic jurisprudence that has to be considered the common ground between the Pisan 'historical-critical school' and the Dutch 'elegant school'. The attention to direct study of the sources of Roman law through history and philology, deep knowledge of classical history, literature and philosophy, and aversion to Aristotelian scholasticism, are all useful elements to understand Averani's interest in Grotius's work[51] and his role as director of the above-mentioned *De jure belli, et pacis disputatio* of 1703. Therefore, before examining in depth the

48 ASF, Consiglio di Reggenza, 640 (fasc. 'Ruolo dello Studio dell'Anno 1727'), fols n.n.

49 Giuseppe Averani, *Oratio de jurisprudentia, medicina, theologia per sua principia addiscendis Pisis habita anno 1723* (Veronae: n.p., n.d.); the publication of this inaugural lecture is due to Averani's pupil, Bernardo Tanucci, who dedicated the print to Giovanni Bonaventura Neri Badia, who was the mentor for his legal apprenticeship.

50 Ibid., 7–8.

51 For the scholarly debate on the Grotian tradition, see the journal *Grotiana*. On the legacy of Roman law and philosophy in Grotius's *IBP*, see (with special regard to his use of the historical method) Massimo Panebianco, *Ugo Grozio e la tradizione storica del diritto internazionale* (Napoli: Editoriale Scientifica, 1974), 21–36, 38–66; (with particular emphasis on his use of the rhetorical method) Benjamin Straumann, *Roman Law in the State of Nature: The Classical Foundations of Hugo Grotius' Natural Law* (Cambridge: Cambridge University Press, 2015), esp. 14–16, 41–50, 70–82. On Dutch jurisprudence of the period, see Reinhard Zimmermann, 'Roman-Dutch Jurisprudence and Its Contribution

product of his teaching career, the *Interpretationes juris*, whose first edition was published in Leiden in 1716,[52] thanks to members of the Dutch law school, Brenkman, Noodt and Bynkershoek,[53] it seems appropriate to discuss the text of this academic dissertation.

The *disputatio* on the law of war and peace of 1703 begins with the dedication to Grand Duke Cosimo III signed by the German Philipp Wilhelm von Sutter,[54] who belonged to the Palatinate court and was married to a lady-in-waiting of the Electress Palatine Maria Luisa Medici, daughter of Cosimo III.[55] The dedication praises the Grand Duke's policy of neutrality. It highlights the political virtue of the prince, able to preserve the Tuscan small state at peace during a period of wars in Europe and Italy, by contrast: war, indeed, is considered the necessary means to ensure peace in an international order dominated by expansionist policies. This idea is then further developed in thesis number I, which opens the dissertation.[56]

The first thesis[57] also presents all the fundamental terms: natural law, law of nations, state of nature, the relationship between law of nations and natural law, as well as the relationship between war, state of nature and peace. Each concept is anchored to a fragment of the *Corpus iuris civilis* (hereafter *CI*) and illustrated with reference to classical authors only.[58] Through this text it is therefore possible to identify the fragments of the *CI* considered by the author to be the basis of the discourse on natural law.

---

to European Private Law', *Tulane Law Review* 66 (1992): 1685–1721; and Wallinga, 'Laurentius Theodorus Gronovius (1648–1724)', 490–495. On Dutch political culture, see Alberto Clerici, *Monarcomachi e giusnaturalisti nella Utrecht del Seicento. Willem Van der Muelen e la legittimazione olandese della* Glorious Revolution (Milano: FrancoAngeli, 2007). On the natural law teachers (and their textbooks) at Dutch universities in the eighteenth century, see Corjo J. H. Jansen, 'Over de 18e eeuwse docenten natuurrecht aan Nederlandse universiteiten en de door hen gebruikte leerboeken', *Tijdschrift voor Rechtsgeschiedenis* 55 (1987): 103–115 (esp. table, 114–115).

52 Giuseppe Averani, *Interpretationes juris* (books 1–2, Lugduni Batavorum: apud Petrum Vander Aa, Bibliopolam et typographum ordinarium Academiae et Urbis, 1716).

53 Ibid., 'Typographus lectori'; Gaetano Albizzini, 'Memorie e notizie spettanti alla vita di Giuseppe Averani avvocato fiorentino', in Averani, *Lezioni Toscane*, vol. 1, ix–xli, at xxviii.

54 Sutter [Averani *praeses*], *De jure belli, et pacis disputatio*, 3–6.

55 On Sutter's biography, see Salerno, '*Stare pactis* and Neutrality', 193, n. 21.

56 The exercise has a total of fifteen theses.

57 Sutter [Averani *praeses*], *De jure belli, et pacis disputatio*, 7–9: 'Thesis I. There is peace, there is war: that is proper to natural law, this is introduced by the law of nations' (here and below the thesis's title is translated from Latin).

58 Namely, Cicero, Livy, Sallust, Virgil, Ovid, Seneca, Tibullus, Velleius Paterculus, Demosthenes, Aristotle, Thucydides, Saint Augustine.

The state of nature is a peaceful ideal (D.1.1.3), but war has been introduced by the law of nations (D.1.1.5 as a form of legal protection; I.1.2.2), a law which is common to all peoples as it is based on natural reason (I.1.2.1–2). Here an interesting distinction is made between state of nature and natural law: the communion of goods, the liberty of men, and peace are not considered natural law precepts but, rather, the original condition of the state of nature. Consequently, the law of nations, by introducing war, has not eliminated but only supplemented natural law, since this is immutable (I.1.2.11). In the last part, the main thesis is reiterated: because of human ambition, peace is achieved through war, and thus war serves to preserve the state of nature, not to subvert it. Interestingly, the author illustrates the connotation of immutability of natural law, not only by citing its divine origin (I.1.2.11), but also by referring to its application in civil law.[59]

The first explicit quotation of Grotius's *De iure belli ac pacis* appears in thesis III,[60] when the author makes a survey of the definitions of war, 'status per vim certantium, qua tales sunt' (*IBP*, book 1, ch. 1 [par. 2]). It is inserted immediately after that of Lipsius and before a long series of references to modern German public lawyers such as Althusius, Schönborner, Bocer, Liebenthal and Obrecht. The distinctive characteristics of war are, therefore, identified in the public form (vs private) and in the exercise of force (vs discussion) between two peoples (vs conflicts within the same people). In fact, in the last part, the author extensively quotes a passage from Cicero, according to which the use of force is the way to resolve disputes suitable to beasts, which man can use only if unable to use discussion;[61] the same quotation was used by Grotius in discussing just war (i.e. 1.2.1).

Just war is the subject of the theses IV and V.[62] This theme, of course, recurred in Florentine public and political discourse from the Middle Ages, combining elements taken from legal and moral sources.[63] Among such sources, Grotius's natural law was now included. Here the reference to Grotius

59 Sutter [Averani *praeses*], *De jure belli, et pacis disputatio*, 8–9: I.1.15.3; D.4.5.8; D.7.5.2.1; D.50.17.188.1.

60 Ibid., 12–14: 'Thesis III. War can be defined as a conflict between two peoples fighting using force'.

61 Cicero, *De officiis*, book 1 [11.34].

62 Sutter [Averani *praeses*], *De jure belli, et pacis disputatio*, 15: 'Thesis IV. There are two kinds of war: one is undertaken to defend and the other to offend'; 16–18: 'Thesis V. Both kinds of war can be just, if undertaken by legitimate authority and just cause'.

63 For the international literature on this subject, see Ryan Greenwood, 'The Just War in Florentine Political Discourse c. 1200–1400', *Jus Gentium: Journal of International Legal History* 4 (2019): 351–382.

(2.1) is placed between those of the major theologians (Augustine, Bellarmine, Ambrose, Diana, Molina and others) to illustrate the two types of war, defensive and offensive. The distinction is introduced by the assertion that injury is just cause for war, 'belli justa causa est injuria', followed by an extensive quotation from Augustine,[64] used by Grotius in illustrating the justifiable causes of war (i.e. 2.1.2). When the imminent offence is rejected, war is defensive, and when an offence already given is avenged, war is offensive.[65] Both types of war, therefore, are to be considered just if those wars are undertaken by legitimate authority and for just cause; the author, however, does not specify further the typology, and only refers the reader to the theologians, including Grotius, without any theoretical development of the discourse.[66]

Thesis VII[67] also deals with just war, arguing that war is also legitimate between Christian princes, by proving that it is not incompatible with natural law, law of nations, divine law, canon and civil law. Here there are two references to Grotius's work, but the scheme of the whole thesis recalls that of the second chapter of the first book of *IBP*. The first reference to Grotius (1.2) is introduced when natural law is discussed, and the sources used here are the same as those presented by Grotius, both the Old Testament and Cicero,[68] and the fragments of the *CI*.[69] The other reference to Grotius (1.2.8), inserted among the theologians Bellarmine, Lupus and González, is in the section where it is claimed that there is no conflict with canon law, and where the interpretation of the twelfth canon of the Council of Nicaea is cited, as in the *De iure*.[70] Ultimately, the sources of the different branches of law are borrowed from the text of Grotius, except those in the section dedicated to civil law, which are not directly discussed in the second chapter of the *IBP*'s first book.

Finally, worthy of mention is thesis IX, titled 'The faith given to the enemy, whether by war commander or private individual, has to be kept'.[71] The thesis opens with the assertions of Augustine, Quintilian and Ambrose[72] on the obli-

---

64 Sutter [Averani *praeses*], *De jure belli, et pacis disputatio*, 15: Augustine, *Quaestiones in Heptateuchum*, book VI, q. 10.

65 Sutter [Averani *praeses*], *De jure belli, et pacis disputatio*, 15.

66 Ibid., 16–18.

67 Ibid., 20–22: 'Thesis VII. Just war is also legitimate among Christian princes'.

68 Ibid., 21: Genesis 14 [20]; Cicero, *De finibus*, 3 [16] (to which the passage from *De officiis*, 1.4.11, is added).

69 Sutter [Averani *praeses*], *De jure belli, et pacis disputatio*: D.43.16.27; D.1.1.3; D.9.2.4pr.

70 Although originally this reference was placed in par. 9, no. 11 of Grotius's *De iure*.

71 Sutter [Averani *praeses*], *De jure belli, et pacis disputatio*, 26–27.

72 Ibid., 26: Augustine, *Epistola* 189 [6; ad Bonifacium]; Quintilian, *Declamationes*, 343 [12]; Ambrose, *De officiis ministrorum*, 1.29 [140].

gation to keep faith ('fides') with enemies, followed by the author's comment that the law of nations is common to the warring parties. This conception is then reinforced by quotations from Livy, Cicero and other classics,[73] on the law of nations as common to all men, including enemies. For the author, it is from the communion of the law of nations with enemies that the communion of conventions and commitments descends.[74] Indeed, in this section, the law of nations seems to lose its conventional nature, in order to demonstrate that respecting agreements is in accordance with natural equality, as some fragments of the *CI* also taught.[75] And it is precisely at this point that the author refers to Grotius, jurist among jurists (Hotman, Hunnius, Vinnen and Du Faur de Saint-Jorry [P. Faber]), quoting the well-known chapter concerning faith between enemies (3.19), from which all the aforementioned quotations are indeed taken (i.e. 3.19.1.2), with the exception of those from *CI*. The question of the inviolability of agreements signed with the enemy is a very controversial point among natural law theorists, and it is on this subject that the doctrines of Grotius and Pufendorf differ, mainly on the basis of the former's *stare pactis* principle and the latter's dynamic conception of state interests.[76] It seems significant that in the dissertation of the German von Sutter, conducted under the direction of Averani, Pufendorf is never mentioned.

---

73 Sutter [Averani *praeses*], *De jure belli, et pacis disputatio*, 26: Livy, *Ab urbe condita*, 5 [27.6]; Cicero, *De officiis*, 3 [29.108]. Other authors mentioned are: Seneca, Quintilian, Demosthenes, Apuleius, Cornelius Nepos and Lactantius.

74 Sutter [Averani *praeses*], *De jure belli, et pacis disputatio*, 26: 'sed si cum hostibus est communion juris gentium, est etiam communion conventium et obligationum', which is followed by references: D.2.14.5; D.1.1.5; I.1.2.

75 See the note above.

76 See Pufendorf, *ING*, 8.7.2, where the above-mentioned chapter of Grotius is judged to be moralistic. On this subject the bibliography is vast, because it calls into question the dualist conception of the law of nations; most of the references can be found in: Kari Saastamoinen, 'Pufendorf on the Law of Sociability and the Law of Nations', in *The Law of Nations and Natural Law 1625–1800*, ed. Simone Zurbuchen (Leiden: Brill, 2019; open access https://brill.com/view/title/39292), 107–131; Simone Zurbuchen, 'Defining the Law of Nations: The *École romande du droit naturel* and the Lausanne Edition of Grotius' *De jure belli ac pacis* (1751–1752)', in *The Law of Nations and Natural Law*, 253–277; and in Randall Lesaffer, 'The Nature of Europe's Classical Law of Nations', in *The Oxford Handbook of the Sources of International Law*, ed. Samantha Besson and Jean d'Aspremont (Oxford: Oxford University Press, 2017), 99–117. On the Grotian conception of trust, see Hans Blom, 'Hugo Grotius on Trust, Its Causes and Effects', in *Trust and Happiness in the History of European Political Thought*, ed. Laszlo Kontler and Mark Somos (Leiden: Brill, 2017), 76–98, and further references there. For a fine-grained analysis of the Pufendorfian realist conception of international order and politics, see Maurizio Bazzoli, *Stagioni e teorie della società internazionale* (Milano: LED, 2005), 139–171.

The deliberated quotation of Grotius's work in this supplementary teaching activity, though exceptional, is important. In fact, on the one hand, the explicit discussion of Grotius's doctrines (albeit in elementary terms) in a text on an academic occasion and dedicated to the Grand Duke gives evidence of the now legitimate reception of the Dutch jurist in the context of official culture. On the other hand, the theme of international politics addressed in this dissertation identifies the original privileged field of application of modern natural law *auctoritates* by Tuscan state jurists throughout the process of institutionalization of natural law. Below, this will be seen to have developed in the context of the *bellum diplomaticum* between the Grand Duchy and the Empire, up until establishment of the first chair of public law in 1726. But although Averani's forty-year teaching career has been recognized as the foundation of the training of important members of the Tuscan ruling class, including several professors of the University of Pisa,[77] it is still necessary to examine the work, *Interpretationes juris*, produced by his long teaching activity and published for the first time in Leiden in 1716 through the members of the Dutch elegant school.[78] Moreover, although in this text modern natural law theorists are never mentioned, some passages correspond to the arguments in Grotius's *De iure*. After all, knowledge of the Dutch jurist is widely testified by the dissertation of 1703.

4 Renewal of the Method: Averani, Roman Law and Grotius

In the aforementioned inaugural lecture, Averani describes the task of public education as assisting students to assimilate the fundamental principles of the various scientific disciplines for the benefit of public utility, that is, for society and the state.[79] The idea of the learning process originates from a rational-

77 Niccola Carranza, 'L'Università di Pisa e la formazione culturale del ceto dirigente toscano del Settecento', *Bollettino Storico Pisano* 33–35 (1964–1966): 469–537.

78 Averani, *Interpretationes juris* (1st edition, books 1–2, Lugduni Batavorum: apud Petrum Vander Aa, Bibliopolam et typographum ordinarium Academiae et Urbis, 1716); (2nd edition, books 1–2, 'priore multo emendatior', Lugduni Batavorum: apud Joh. et Herm. Verbeek bibliop[olas], 1736); (1st edition, books 3–5, 'opus postumum, continens interpretationum juris libros tres posteriores', Lugduni Batavorum: apud Petrum/Balduinum Vander Aa, 1746); (1st edition, books 1–5, 'editio novissima', Lugduni: typis Petri Bruyset, sumptibus Fratrum de Tournes, 1751); (2nd edition, books 1–5, 'editio novissima', Neapoli: ex typis Josephi Campi, sumptibus Vincentii de Aloysio, 1777–1785); (3rd edition, books 1–5, 'editio novissima', Maceratae: ex typographia Josephi Mancini-Cortesi, 1832–1833).

79 Averani, *Oratio de jurisprudentia*, 8, 21.

ist conception of human being, nature and science.[80] Considering science as consisting of principles and rules that become structured over time, Averani states that training must be long, gradual and directed primarily to the theoretical aspects of disciplines,[81] so that students can learn them thoroughly, acquiring the ability to exercise critical intelligence.[82]

Legal education must be based on in-depth study of the *leges* of the *Corpus iuris civilis*, since only in this way can students acquire the legal science and the experience necessary to practise their profession in the law courts. Only with detailed knowledge of the laws will they be able to deal with actual cases and resolve contradictions between the divergent opinions of the jurists,[83] thus offering their positive contribution to the administration of justice and therefore to citizens.[84] In front of the jurists in training, Averani's attention was aimed at promoting the legacy of the true masters ('antistites') of legal science, that is, those who in past centuries had undertaken the work of interpretation, conciliation and commentary of the laws, as against the still current dissemination of the work of pragmatic lawyers,[85] considered to be destroyers of jurisprudence.[86]

In his *Interpretationes juris*, therefore, Averani placed at the centre of his exposition only the fragments of the Justinian compilation. The interpretation examines, first, the grammar and lexicon of the text, and then verifies its correspondence with the 'intention of the legislator', through comparison with other legal provisions of the *CI* and with classical history and literature. Averani's goal is to show the intrinsic rationality of Roman law by his own original interpretations, to which he comes after discussing traditional and modern ones, such as those of Cujas, Duaren, Doneau and Favre,[87] which, however, are mentioned only briefly, because the exposition is based on the laws.

Legal historians have rightly noted the introduction of the logic of 'explicatio' and 'demonstratio' in the discussion of fragments,[88] a method that dis-

80 Ibid., 9.

81 Ibid., 10–12, 21.

82 Ibid., 14.

83 Ibid., 15–16, 18.

84 Ibid., 16.

85 On the criticisms and merits of the pragmatic jurists, see Giuseppe Ermini, 'I "prammatici" nella storia del diritto dell'età moderna', *Archivio Storico Italiano* 135 (1977): 425–446.

86 Averani, *Oratio de jurisprudentia*, 16–17.

87 Among these, Cujas is certainly the most quoted author; in the five books he is mentioned at least forty times.

88 Montorzi, 'Averani, Giuseppe', 129.

tinguishes the 'modern natural law school' from traditional jurisprudence.[89] But although Averani criticized the degeneration of Bartolism and promoted the return to the study of legal principles, the teaching practice in the course on civil law was to provide students with the tools to operate in courts of justice, where mainly private law issues were argued by applying the *ius commune* based on Roman law. It is therefore not surprising that, in the five books of Averani's *Interpretationes juris*, the reference to natural law appears almost exclusively in the illustration of questions and institutions of private law dedicated to the legal category of the *obligatio naturalis*.[90] Similarly, the lack of quotations from authors of the 'modern natural law school' does not surprise. Only Grotius is mentioned, but even then not with reference to his greatest natural law work, but to his commentary on the Old Testament ('Numer. cap. 27.6 et seqq. ibi et Grotius').[91]

With reference to Grotius, it should be noted that, although in a residual part of the examination of the *deprecatio* to the *Lex Rhodia de iactu* (D.14.2.9), the author makes incisive criticism of the hegemonic claims of the Holy Roman Empire, which expresses arguments corresponding to those in the *IBP* on the refusal to conceive German imperial jurisdiction as equivalent to that of the ancient Roman Empire and on the foundation of the state sovereignty:

> The ancient interpreters, too sweet, estimated that world domination had remained at the disposal of the Emperor *until the present time* [in Latin: 'ad hoc aevi']. Totally absurd. The Roman Emperor was once master of the world he possessed and held under his dominion ['quem possidebat et ditione tenebat']. The Roman people were master of all nations, obviously of those they had subdued with weapons and war, or

---

89 Norberto Bobbio, 'Il giusnaturalismo', in *Storia delle idee politiche economiche e sociali*, ed. Luigi Firpo (Torino: Utet, 1980), vol. 4, I, 491–558, at 502.

90 Averani, *Interpretationes juris*: on the legacy of pupil (D.29.2.89), book 2, ch. 8; on the obligations of the pupil without tutor (D.12.6.41 and D.44.7.59), 2.14; see other examples in 2.10, 2.15, 2.24, 3.27–28, 5.10, 5.32. On the controversial category of the *obligatio naturalis* in Roman law, whose bibliography is extremely vast because it refers to the more general problem of the concept of *ius naturale* in classical jurisprudence, see Alberto Burdese, 'La "naturalis obligatio" nella più recente dottrina', *Studi Parmensi* 32 (1983): 45–79, together with Guglielmo Nocera, *Ius naturale nella esperienza giuridica romana* (Milano: Giuffrè, 1962), and Lorena Atzeri, 'Natura e ius naturale fra tradizione interna ed esterna al Corpus Iuris giustinianeo', in *Testi e problemi del giusnaturalismo romano*, ed. Dario Mantovani and Aldo Schiavone (Pavia: IUSS Press, 2007), 715–758. On the ways of interpreting the *Digest*, see *Interpretare il Digesto: storia e metodi*, ed. Dario Mantovani and Antonio Padoa Schioppa (Pavia: IUSS Press, 2014), and further references there.

91 Ibid., book 3, ch. 28, sect. 11.

> conquered by the fear of Roman power, or induced by the public utility ['vel publica ductas utilitate'], or lured by friendship, and had subjugated under their authority and dominion ['sub imperium ditionemque subjunxerat']. So the Emperor *at the present time* ['hoc tempore'] is the master of those peoples who are subject to his power and authority ['quae sunt ejus potestati, imperioque subjectae'], of those provinces that he possesses and which he commands. But how little part of the Roman Empire does he possess? No differently, other kings, princes and peoples are the masters of those nations and provinces that are subjected to their dominion and power ['quae sunt eorum ditioni, potestatique subjectae']. In fact, they acquired them with the same art, and the same ways, with which the Roman people obtained the empire of the world. There is, therefore, no reason why they [the Romans] should be masters of the world they obtained but not those others who obtained their provinces by similar means.[92]

Although Grotius is not mentioned, the thesis proposed by Averani in the text from his teaching is entirely in conformity with that of the Dutch jurist (i.e. in 2.9.11 and 2.22.13). In particular, the above passage expresses a conception of internal and external sovereignty of states, used during the international controversy with the Empire to defend the autonomy and independence of the Tuscan small state – on that occasion with explicit reference to the *auctoritas* of Grotius. We find this argument both in Averani and Neri Badia, in their pupil Tanucci as well as the Archbishop of Pisa, Francesco Frosini.

5 Political Use of Natural Law: Defending the Tuscan Small State against Imperial Expansion

As seen, in the academic dissertation of 1703, the instrumental connection between modern natural law and international politics was already identified and strategically implemented. It is therefore not surprising that a more advanced political use of the texts of Grotius and Pufendorf can be observed during the *bellum diplomaticum* between the Grand Duchy and the Empire during the early decades of the eighteenth century. On several occasions,

92 Ibid., 3.5.11 (italics added). The original Latin of the last sentences is very effective: 'Nulla igitur ratio potest excogitari, cur ille [the Roman people] fuerit dominus mundi, quem fuit adeptus, hi [other kings, princes and peoples] non sint domini provinciarum, quas similiter adepti feurunt'.

indeed, Tuscan jurists used the great natural law theorists to promote specific principles of public law in international public opinion to defend the internal and external sovereignty of their state. First of all, it was a matter of defending the autonomy and independence of the city of Florence (and its dominion) against imperial pretensions to consider the entire Grand Duchy as a fief to invest in, once the male line of the Medici family had died out. These claims, as is known, were then also enshrined in Article 5 of the so-called Quadruple Alliance Treaty of London on 2 August 1718.[93]

Historically identified as Giuseppe Averani and Giovanni Bonaventura Neri Badia, the authors of the government's booklet *De libertate civitatis Florentiae* (1722) used the authority of Grotius and Pufendorf to demonstrate to the international political community and the Emperor Charles VI the legal effects of the continued exercise of sovereignty by the people of Florence[94] in both the republican and the princely regime.

Among the diplomatic sources, historical narratives and legal doctrines, the authors cite extensive passages from Grotius and Pufendorf, first to support the applicability of extinctive prescription also to imperial sovereignty (*IBP*, 2.4.4–5; 2.22.13; *ING*, 8.5.9).[95] Then, Grotius's authority is used to trace the various agreements between the Florentine Republic and the European princes, including emperors, back to the category of unequal alliances. With this type of alliance, according to Grotian doctrine, subjects retain their full sovereignty: even when a payment of money is made, even if the agreement implies that one is under the protection ('in fide') of the other. As a result, the imperial decree of Charles V (28 October 1530) is interpreted as an act (i.e. a 'laudum') of an arbitrator, who had been elected by the Republic itself in the full exercise of sovereignty in the Capitulations (12 August 1530), whose initial normative formula 'intendendosi sempre, che sia conservata la libertà' (always acknowledging that liberty must be preserved) is obviously highlighted. Therefore, the

93 That is, 30 CTS 415; on this, see Paolo Alatri, *L'Europa dopo Luigi XIV* (Palermo: Sellerio, 1986), 165–167; and Randall Lesaffer, 'The 18th-Century Antecedents of the Concert of Europe II. The Quadruple Alliance of 1718', in *Oxford Historical Treaties* (Oxford: Oxford University Press, online edition 2017, https://opil.ouplaw.com/page/592).

94 Giuseppe Averani and Giovanni Bonaventura Neri Badia, *De libertate civitatis Florentiae ejusque dominii* (1st edition: Pisis: n.p., 1721 [but 1722]; 2nd edition n.p., 1722); here, the continued exercise of sovereignty is claimed as: 'vetustissima jura omnimodae Libertatis Florentiae Ditionis', 3; 'jus omnimodae et absolutae libertatis, quo semper ab antiquissimis temporis usi sunt Florentini in toto suo territorio', 4; 'absoluta libertas, ab omni jurisdictione prorsus immunis', 6 (here and below the quotations are taken from the 2nd edition).

95 Ibid., 14, 41–42.

words 'fides' and 'devotio' used in the imperial award must be interpreted only as referring to a title of protection ('titulus protectionis') and not as founding and assigning a new jurisdiction ('jurisdictio') to the Empire over the Florentine state (*IBP*, 1.3.21–22).[96] Furthermore, Grotius is widely quoted to affirm the principle of public law relating to the legal continuity of the sovereignty of the people's body in political regime changes, such as during the transition from a republic to an elective kingdom, which the Tuscan authors equate to what had happened in the history of the city of Florence in the transition from the republic to the principality (*IBP*, 2.9.8 and 2.16.16).[97]

Even the Archbishop of Pisa, Francesco Frosini,[98] who had graduated in law from the University of Pisa (and who played an important formal role in the university system),[99] in his contemporary manuscript 'Discorso legale sopra la libertà dello Stato fiorentino' quoted Grotius extensively along with his commentators, Gronovius, Van der Muelen and Ziegler. The aim was to demonstrate that Charles V's *laudum* (28 October 1530) was not meant to acquire sovereignty, and therefore could not be used in the imperial texts as proof of 'suppression of the ancient liberty of Florence'.[100]

To support this thesis, Frosini resorts to Grotius's doctrines – mostly by means of Van der Muelen's commentaries – first, to show that the will of the Emperor had not been to subject the Florentine state. This would have violated the provisions established by him in previous public agreements (the League of Barcelona with the Medici Pope, Clement VII, and the Capitulations made by the Republic), producing serious violations of public law (unworthy of his role). He would have offended the public faith, which is the foundation of justice and peaceful human coexistence, and he would have infringed the principle of fairness, which is the basis of the virtue of the ruler (*IBP*, 3.20.51; 2.25.1).[101] He would have contravened the law of nations, according to which the auxiliary troops are entitled only to movable goods (*IBP*, 3.6.23–24).[102]

96 Ibid., 17, 27, 50–53.

97 Ibid., 57.

98 On Frosini's intellectual profile, see Carlo Fantappiè, 'Frosini, Francesco', in *Dizionario Biografico degli Italiani* (Roma: Istituto dell'Enciclopedia Italiana, 1998), vol. 50, 609–611.

99 On this, see Marrara, 'L'età medicea (1543–1737)', 180–187.

100 Francesco Frosini, 'Discorso legale sopra la libertà dello Stato fiorentino e la niuna sua dependenza dall'Imperio [di Mons. Frosini Arcivescovo di Pisa]. Per quem reges regnant ipse dirigat consilium meum', [1715–1722?], MS, in ASF, Miscellanea Medicea, 147, fasc. 3, fols 129r–174r; the author's name appears in the title of the MS copy preserved in BANL, Corsiniana, 1199 [35.D.4], fols 5r–43v. References hereafter follow this order: 131r (ASF); 7v (BANL).

101 Ibid., 134r–135r; 9v–10v.

102 Ibid., 135r–v; 11r.

Furthermore, he would have eliminated the just cause of war, namely the reintegration into government of the Medici family, who had been violently stripped of their power, making the war unlawful (*IBP*, 2.1.2.2).[103] Ultimately, Frosini shows that the imperial decree ('lodo') had been an unequal alliance, and thus could not have founded any jurisdiction or subjection of the Florentine state to the Empire, resulting from an act of the Emperor as arbitrator (*IBP*, 1.3.21; 3.20.51).[104] In the last part of the text, the author reinforces his thesis by noting that the interpretation of the imperial decree – as an act not directed at acquisition of sovereignty – had been observed by the parties for almost two centuries. Here, the Archbishop recalls Grotius, again using Van der Muelen's commentary (*IBP*, 2.4.1), to whom Pufendorf is added (*ING*, 4.12),[105] because both natural lawyers founded the restriction of the subjects' claims precisely on the natural law that originates from the need to ensure public peace. Thus, the text closes by arguing, with another reference to Grotius and reinforced by further citations from German public law jurists, that even imperial sovereignty falls into extinctive prescription (*IBP*, 2.22.13).[106]

Bernardo Tanucci, too, made extensive use of Grotius and his 'greatest commentator Pufendorfio' (in addition to Heinrich Cocceji, Gronovius and Barbeyrac) and Wolff, Huber and Thomasius, in the third chapter of his *Dritto della Corona di Napoli sopra Piombino*.[107] That is the chapter which the author considered the summary of his *Vindiciae Italicae*, that is, the dissertations produced by invitation of the Florentine Secretary of State for War, Carlo Rinuccini, after the Treaty of London of 1718 and during the international controversy of the early decades of the eighteenth century between the Grand Duchy and the Empire.[108]

---

103 Ibid., 137r; 12v.

104 Ibid., 143v–145v; 18r–20r, and 153r–154v; 26v–28r.

105 Ibid., 164r–165r; 35v–36r.

106 Ibid., 170r–171v; 40r–41r.

107 Bernardo Tanucci, *Dritto della Corona di Napoli sopra Piombino* (n.p., n.d; written in 1736 and published post 1759), ch. 3, 67–94. The main part of ch. 3 was written around 1726–1728, as reported in the letters from Bernardo Tanucci to Lorenzo Mehus, from Naples, 1781–1783, MSS, in BRF, Riccardiano, 3497, fols 1r–8v.

108 On Tanucci's political culture, see Marcello Verga, 'Dai Medici ai Lorena. Aspetti del dibattito politico in Toscana nell'Epistolario del Tanucci', in *Bernardo Tanucci e la Toscana* (Firenze: Olschki, 1986), 171–215; and Mario D'Addio, 'Impero, feudalesimo e storia d'Italia nel pensiero civile di Tanucci', in *Bernardo Tanucci statista letterato giurista*, ed. Raffaele Ajello and Mario D'Addio (Napoli: Jovene, 1988), vol. 1, 25–56. On Rinuccini, see Emanuele Salerno, 'Rinuccini, Carlo', in *Dizionario Biografico degli Italiani* (Roma: Istituto dell'Enciclopedia Italiana, 2016), vol. 87, 610–614.

Here, the modern natural law theorists are cited as *auctoritates* to support the principles of public law against the pretension of reviving imperial sovereignty over the Italian territories, supported through the alleged legal continuity of the title of Emperor from the days of the ancient Roman Empire. In summary, Tanucci argues through extensive quotations from Grotius and Pufendorf, and also recalling in footnotes the texts of Gronovius and of Noodt on the *lex regia*, that sovereignty originally resides in the people. Consequently, since Italians no longer wanted to elect any Emperor after Frederick I Barbarossa, they had regained their liberty, as Pufendorf had also written. Tanucci cites the passage in which the German jurist had refuted those who denied that, in periods of interregnum, sovereignty returned to the people: 'potestatem imperandi ad populum reverti' the German lawyer had written, to which Tanucci also adds a reference to Grotius (*ING*, 7.7.7 and *IBP*, 1.3.7; 2.9.8).[109] According to Tanucci, after Charlemagne, all Emperors had always been elected by Italians. Even Otto I had been called by Italians to free them from Berengario's tyranny. Thus, after Otto's intervention (as an auxiliary and consultant), Italians had returned to 'nativa libertà' (native liberty), as natural law theorists had taught (*IBP*, 3.9.9 and *ING*, 8.6.21 and 26).[110] Ultimately, for the Tuscan jurist, the medieval 'Kingdom of Italy' had been an elective kingdom that could not have been alienated or united with Germany. This was because 'an elective King' was not able 'to alienate Italy to Germany':

> No Italian state was transferred by German Emperors who first had possessed it [i.e. the Emperors could not cede any Italian state if they did not own it first]. All the investitures of the pompous Italic Code are fiefdoms offered by tyrants who through violence had acquired unjust power, and had no right, other than tacit consent or violence, or some incipient consent of the people, and therefore could neither alienate, nor offer up.[111]

This political use of modern natural law theorists' texts demonstrates the extensive expertise acquired by the Tuscan ruling class of the early eighteenth century and confirms interstate relations as the privileged field of application.

---

109 Tanucci, *Dritto della Corona di Napoli sopra Piombino*, 72–73.

110 Ibid., 76–77.

111 Ibid., 80–81. On the invalidity of such acts, both Grotius and Pufendorf (*IBP*, 1.3.11 and *ING*, 8.5.10) are mentioned at the beginning of the third chapter, 70, as well as in the conclusion, to reiterate that there could be no legal continuity of the title of Emperor since the times of the ancient Roman Empire (*IBP*, 2.22.13 and *ING*, 8.5.9, and *De statu Imperii Germanici*, 1.14), 85–86.

A similar approach can also be observed in judicial use, where the citation of natural law *auctoritates* is deemed necessary in the same field of *inter gentes* law.

6 Judicial Use of Natural Law: The Natural Law of Nations Addressing External Public Law Cases

In reference to the Pisan academics, the collection of judicial decisions and legal consultations *Decisiones et responsa juris*, by Giovanni Bonaventura Neri Badia and his son Pompeo Neri,[112] is a particularly valuable source for examining the judicial use of natural law. In fact, although the natural law theorists, Grotius, Hobbes, Pufendorf, Huber and Suárez, are often cited *ad abundantiam*,[113] their *auctoritas* is deemed indispensable in cases where public law matters between sovereign states were discussed. In addition, the decisions of G. B. Neri Badia, some of which date back to the late 1690s, confirm the Tuscan jurist's extensive knowledge of the authors of the 'modern natural law school', even before the beginning of the eighteenth century.[114]

Of particular interest is the 'Responsum I' of Pompeo Neri.[115] This text, dating back to the early 1730s, is in fact almost contemporary with his teaching in the new Pisan chair of public law. As is known, the first chair of *ius publicum*, although established in 1726, was activated only later, for the two academic years of 1727/1728 and 1728/1729. During this period, Pompeo Neri appears to have taught only seventeen lessons,[116] the contents of which are still unknown.

112 Giovanni Bonaventura Neri Badia [and Pompeo Neri], *Decisiones et responsa juris* (Florentiae: ex typographia Josephi Allegrini, [Pisoni] & soc., 1769–1776).

113 See, ibid.: by Giovanni Bonaventura Neri Badia, 'Decisio V Senensis' (1696; ref. Suárez), vol. 1, 33–43; 'Dec. VIII Senensis' (n.d., post 1695; Suárez), vol. 1, 52–72; 'Dec. L' (n.d.; Grotius), vol. 1, 449–451; 'Dec. LXIV' (n.d., post 1703; Suárez), vol. 1, 515–528; and by Pompeo Neri, 'Decisio I' (1736; Hobbes, Pufendorf, Grotius, F. Vásquez), vol. 2, 229–273.

114 See the note above for his decisions from the end of the seventeenth century. The expert use of Pufendorf's and Grotius's works by G. B. Neri Badia is then particularly attested in his 'Responsa XIX–XXI' (n.d., post. 1716), vol. 2, 151–188, on the testament of Elector Palatine Johann Wilhelm, husband of Anna Maria Luisa Medici, daughter of Grand Duke Cosimo III (esp. 158–159, 161–169, 176–177).

115 Pompeo Neri, 'Responsum I' (n.d., post. 1730), in Neri Badia, *Decisiones et responsa juris*, vol. 2, 383–392.

116 ASF, Consiglio di Reggenza, 640 (fasc. '1728' and '1729', and the 'Ristretto delle lezzioni' [*sic*]), fols n.n.: in the first academic year he only gave eight lessons, being nominated at the end of the last 'Terzeria'; in the second only nine (out of seventy). In the fascicle '1737', a draft note on the professors at the Florentine *Studium* states that Pompeo Neri

However, analysing this, Neri's consultation on the question of border regulation between the Grand Duchy and the Papal State, it is possible to grasp the sophisticated expertise acquired by the young jurist on the doctrines of the greatest natural law authors, and to understand why resorting to them was necessary.

Indeed, from the first pages, Neri points out that, since the question involves two states/sovereigns, the interpretation must be based not only on *ius commune*, but also on the 'naturale diritto delle genti' (natural law of nations).[117] Grotius is used at the beginning of this legal opinion to affirm that the Pope is obliged to accept the exchange of land requested by the Grand Duke on the basis of the 'first principles of natural justice according to the famous axiom *Quod tibi non nocet etc.* [D.39.3.1.11; D.39.3.2.5]', an axiom explained by reference to the Dutch jurist (*IBP*, 2.2.6).[118] The instance brought by the Grand Duke, in fact, satisfies two conditions, the necessity and usefulness for neighbouring peoples, and the absence of damage to the defendant (Principality of the Holy See). It thus matches the exception of the exclusive exercise of the right of ownership over goods; by means of this exception, the original right to make use of goods as if they were still in common is revived, as Grotius had written.

Pufendorf and Hobbes, too, are cited to illustrate the Pope's obligation to accept the exchanges, but with reference to 'the only law, which obliges the sovereigns', that is, the security and the welfare of the people.[119] Through these references, Neri argues that no papal bull, including *De non infeudando*, can limit the Pope's actual sovereignty. In fact, in any state the existence of a supreme and full power ('summam et plenam potestatem') is necessary, and this can be divided and limited in order to moderate the will of the sovereign prince's arbitrariness through promises and agreements. But these have no binding force on the sovereign unless they attribute specifically to certain institutional subjects a part of the sovereignty over particular matters; much less are they binding in the case of 'necessità legale' (legal necessity), that is, a necessary act for the correct execution of the convention already established and approved by the parties (*ING*, 7.6; 7.2; 7.4–5; *De Cive*, 7.17).[120]

In the final part, the quotations from Grotius, together with his greatest commentators, Boecler, Van der Muelen and Barbeyrac, give further evidence

was appointed in 1728 as professor at the Pisan *Studium* but after being asked to assist the prince directly he moved to Florence and thus was enabled to read there.

117 Neri, 'Responsum I', 386, no. 2, and 388, no. 4.

118 Ibid., 386, no. 3.

119 Ibid.

120 Ibid., 389, nos 12–18.

of Neri's in-depth knowledge of the doctrines of the Dutch natural law jurist. These last references serve to emphasize the exceptional nature of the case under discussion, since the exchanges concern only limited, depopulated areas and proved advantageous and necessary to the peoples. Consequently, Grotius's doctrine on the indispensable consent of the people, in the total or partial alienation of states by sovereigns, could not be applied. In the case examined, using the two exceptions of public utility and necessity, silence of the people had to lead to the presumption of consent, as Grotius had specified (*IBP*, 2.6.3–4 and 2.6.7–8).[121]

7 Conclusion

At the University of Pisa, traces of the introduction, circulation and use of, and indeed reliance on, modern natural law are already recorded alongside the classes of *ius civile* during the last decades of the seventeenth century and in the early eighteenth century. The first explicit evidence of Grotius in the official academic context was in 1703, associated with the activity of one of the most important professors, Giuseppe Averani, not in the field of civil law but, rather, in external public law, that is, in the field of law of war and peace. The same field, that is, interstate relations and *inter gentes* law, appeared as the preferred field in the judicial and political use of natural law. Ultimately, the process of institutionalization of modern natural law in the Pisan academic context has emerged as developing in the context of the *bellum diplomaticum* between the Grand Duchy and the Empire, ending two decades later with the establishment of the first chair of *ius publicum* in 1726.

Unquestionably, the Roman legal culture of the Pisan historical-critical school directed and mediated the reception of modern natural law doctrines. However, depending on the purposes for which the texts of the great authors of the 'modern natural law school' were used, it is possible to observe some differences. The reception of natural law for educational purposes was indirect with respect to that aimed at international politics (binding for the Tuscan small state). This is because legal education was traditionally directed to practice in the internal fora, that is, Tuscan courts of justice, in which mainly private law issues were dealt with, by means of *ius commune*, based on Roman law. Its political use, instead, was addressed to the European system of courts and diplomats, that is, the external fora of interstate relations among sovereign

121 Ibid., 391–392, nos 34–37.

states, in which Roman law had become ineffective and therefore recourse to the *auctoritates* of the natural law of nations was direct and explicit.

At the University of Pisa, therefore, partly due to external factors such as the *bellum diplomaticum*, modern natural law theories spread gradually among law professors until the establishment of the first public law chair in 1726, under the government of the last Medici Grand Duke, Gian Gastone. Employing an extraordinary procedure, the chair was entrusted to the jurist abbot Pompeo Neri, but the teaching was conducted for just two academic years, 1727/1728 and 1728/1729. Fresh archival research has revealed that he taught only a very few lessons. Although the content of the lessons has not been found, deeper examination of other contemporary sources has revealed the advanced expertise acquired by the young jurist with regard to the modern natural law doctrines of the major authors, necessary in dealing with cases of external public law.

The public law professorship was reconstituted only ten years later, in the academic year 1738/1739, under the government of the new Grand Duke, Francis Stephen Habsburg-Lorraine. The teaching was then entrusted to a doctor of theology, abbot Francesco Niccolò Bandiera, who taught for nearly thirty years, until 1765/1766, in a very different political scenario.[122]

These research results suggest that the study of legal education in the last Medici period is still essential, not only to clarify the relationship between Roman law, natural law and public law, both internal and external (therefore, to comprehend the development of modern natural law in academic culture), but also to understand the legal-political culture of the Tuscan ruling class, and how this culture led the institutionalization of natural law at the University of Pisa, until the foundation of the first public law chair in Italy, in 1726.

Archival Sources

ASF: Archivio di Stato, Firenze, Italy, Consiglio di Reggenza, 1 (Copialettere del carteggio della Segreteria di Toscana a Vienna con la Reggenza; Dispacci e lettere, 28 July 1737–18 December 1739), and 640 and 641 (Ruoli dell'Università di Pisa); Miscellanea Medicea, 147 (Notizie di Firenze; Questione della libertà dello Stato fiorentino e della sua autonomia dall'Impero).

122 Bandiera's teaching dealt with universal public law, and in the official reports he specified that he followed mainly the doctrines of Grotius and Pufendorf, and that on the question of the resistance of subjects he supported the opinion of passive obedience. See ASF, Consiglio di Reggenza, 641 (fasc. '1748'), fols n.n.

ASP: Archivio di Stato, Pisa, Italy, Università 2, C I 2 (Ruoli dell'Università).

BANL: Biblioteca dell'Accademia Nazionale dei Lincei e Corsiniana, Roma, Italy, Corsiniana, 1199 [35.D.4] (Raccolta di scritture, e memorie appartenenti alle cose occorse nella Corte di Firenze e negoziati avuti colla corte di Roma dall'anno 1730 al 1740).

BRF: Biblioteca Riccardiana, Firenze, Italy, Riccardiano, 3497 (Lettere diverse all'Ab. Mehus e al Marchese Cosimo Riccardi).

BUP: Biblioteca Universitaria, Pisa, Italy, Manoscritti, 387 (Catalogo alfabetico della Libreria Grandiana).

Bibliography

Abbreviations

BG: Jacob ter Meulen and Pieter Johan Jurrian Diermanse, *Bibliographie des écrits imprimés de Hugo Grotius* (La Haye: M. Nijhoff, 1950).

BMRF: Biblioteca Marucelliana, Firenze.

BNCF: Biblioteca Nazionale Centrale, Firenze.

BP: Horst Denzer, *Moralphilosophie und Naturrecht bei Samuel Pufendorf* (München: Beck, 1972), 359–373.

CI: *Corpus iuris civilis.*

IBP: Grotius, *De iure belli ac pacis.*

ING: Pufendorf, *De iure naturae et gentium.*

fasc.: fascicle

fol.: folio

n.d.: no date

n.n.: not numbered

n.p.: no place/no publisher

StUniPi: *Storia dell'Università di Pisa*, 2 vols (Pisa: Plus, 2000).

Alatri, Paolo, *L'Europa dopo Luigi XIV* (Palermo: Sellerio, 1986).

Albizzini, Gaetano, 'Memorie e notizie spettanti alla vita di Giuseppe Averani avvocato fiorentino', in Giuseppe Averani, *Lezioni Toscane* (Firenze: Gaetano Albizzini, 1744–1761), vol. 1, ix–xli.

Atzeri, Lorena, 'Natura e ius naturale fra tradizione interna ed esterna al Corpus Iuris giustinianeo', in *Testi e problemi del giusnaturalismo romano*, ed. Dario Mantovani and Aldo Schiavone (Pavia: IUSS Press, 2007), 715–758.

Averani, Giuseppe, *Interpretationes juris* [...] (books 1–2, Lugduni Batavorum: apud Petrum Vander Aa, Bibliopolam et typographum ordinarium Academiae et Urbis,

1716); (books 1–5, 'editio novissima', Lugduni: typis Petri Bruyset, sumptibus Fratrum de Tournes, 1751).

Averani, Giuseppe, *Oratio de jurisprudentia, medicina, theologia per sua principia addiscendis Pisis habita anno 1723* (Veronae: n.p., n.d.).

Averani, Giuseppe, and Giovanni Bonaventura Neri Badia, *De libertate civitatis Florentiae ejusque dominii* (1st edition Pisis: n.p., 1721 [but 1722]; 2nd edition n.p., 1722).

Baldini, Ugo, 'Grandi, Guido', in *Dizionario Biografico degli Italiani* (Roma: Istituto dell'Enciclopedia Italiana, 2002), vol. 58, 494–507.

Barsanti, Danilo, 'I docenti e le cattedre', *Storia dell'Università di Pisa* (Pisa: Plus, 2000), vol. 1, II, 475–480, 505–566; vol. 2, I, 269–416.

Bartolini, Giulio, 'What Is a History of International Law in Italy For? International Law Through the Prism of National Perspectives', in *A History of International Law in Italy*, ed. Giulio Bartolini (Oxford: Oxford University Press, 2020), 3–15.

Bazzoli, Maurizio, *Stagioni e teorie della società internazionale* (Milano: LED, 2005).

Birocchi, Italo, *Alla ricerca dell'ordine. Fonti e cultura giuridica nell'età moderna* (Torino: Giappichelli, 2002).

Birocchi, Italo, 'Introduzione', in Francesco Rapolla, *De jurisconsulto*, ed. Italo Birocchi (Bologna: Il Mulino, 2006), 9–70.

Birocchi, Italo, 'L'insegnamento del diritto pubblico nelle Università italiane nel XVIII secolo', in *Science politique et droit public dans les facultés de droit européennes (XIIIe–XVIIIe siècle)*, ed. Jaques Krynen and Michael Stolleis (Frankfurt am Main: Klostermann, 2008), 549–581.

Blom, Hans, 'Hugo Grotius on Trust, Its Causes and Effects', in *Trust and Happiness in the History of European Political Thought*, ed. Laszlo Kontler and Mark Somos (Leiden: Brill, 2017), 76–98.

Bobbio, Norberto, 'Il giusnaturalismo', in *Storia delle idee politiche economiche e sociali*, ed. Luigi Firpo (Torino: Utet, 1980), vol. 4, I, 491–558.

Burdese, Alberto, 'La "naturalis obligatio" nella più recente dottrina', *Studi Parmensi* 32 (1983): 45–79.

Carranza, Niccola, 'Averani, Benedetto', in *Dizionario Biografico degli Italiani* (Roma: Istituto dell'Enciclopedia Italiana, 1962), vol. 4, 657–658.

Carranza, Niccola, 'Averani, Giuseppe', in *Dizionario Biografico degli Italiani* (Roma: Istituto dell'Enciclopedia Italiana, 1962), vol. 4, 658–659.

Carranza, Niccola, 'Averani, Niccolò', in *Dizionario Biografico degli Italiani* (Roma: Istituto dell'Enciclopedia Italiana, 1962), vol. 4, 659–660.

Carranza, Niccola, 'L'Università di Pisa e la formazione culturale del ceto dirigente toscano del Settecento', *Bollettino Storico Pisano* 33–35 (1964–1966): 469–537.

Carranza, Niccola, *Monsignor Gaspare Cerati provveditore dell'Università di Pisa nel Settecento delle riforme* (Pisa: Pacini, 1974).

Clerici, Alberto, *Monarcomachi e giusnaturalisti nella Utrecht del Seicento. Willem Van der Muelen e la legittimazione olandese della* Glorious Revolution (Milano: FrancoAngeli, 2007).

Cochrane, Eric, *Florence in the Forgotten Centuries, 1527–1800* (Chicago, IL: University of Chicago Press, 1973).

D'Addio, Mario, 'Impero, feudalesimo e storia d'Italia nel pensiero civile di Tanucci', in *Bernardo Tanucci statista letterato giurista*, ed. Raffaele Ajello and Mario D'Addio (Napoli: Jovene, 1988), vol. 1, 25–56.

Dal Pino, Franco A., 'Capassi, Gerardo', in *Dizionario Biografico degli Italiani* (Roma: Istituto dell'Enciclopedia Italiana, 1975), vol. 18, 387–391.

Denzer, Horst, *Moralphilosophie und Naturrecht bei Samuel Pufendorf* (München: Beck, 1972).

Dhondt, Frederik, *Balance of Power and Norm Hierarchy: Franco-British Diplomacy After the Peace of Utrecht* (Leiden: Brill, 2015).

Edigati, Daniele, *Avvocati e procuratori nella Toscana d'Antico Regime. Le professioni forensi dalla tutela alla disciplina di polizia* (Bologna: Il Mulino, 2021).

Edigati, Daniele, 'Neri Badia, Giovanni Bonaventura', in *Dizionario Biografico dei Giuristi Italiani. XII–XX secolo*, ed. Italo Birocchi et al. (Bologna: Il Mulino, 2013), 1423–1424.

Ermini, Giuseppe, 'I "prammatici" nella storia del diritto dell'età moderna', *Archivio Storico Italiano* 135 (1977): 425–446.

Fabroni, Angelo, *Historia Academiae Pisanae*, 3 vols (Pisis: Gaetanus Mugnainus, 1791–1795).

Fantappiè, Carlo, 'Frosini, Francesco', in *Dizionario Biografico degli Italiani* (Roma: Istituto dell'Enciclopedia Italiana, 1998), vol. 50, 609–611.

Fasano Guarini, Elena, 'Cosimo III de' Medici, granduca di Toscana', in *Dizionario Biografico degli Italiani* (Roma: Istituto dell'Enciclopedia Italiana, 1984), vol. 30, 54–61.

Ferrone, Vincenzo, *The Intellectual Roots of the Italian Enlightenment: Newtonian Science, Religion, and Politics in the Early Eighteenth Century*, trans. Sue Brotherton (Amherst: Humanities Press, 1995; originally published in Italian, 1982).

Frosini, Francesco, 'Discorso legale sopra la libertà dello Stato fiorentino e la niuna sua dependenza dall'Imperio [di Mons. Frosini Arcivescovo di Pisa]. Per quem reges regnant ipse dirigat consilium meum', [1715–1722?], MS, in ASF, Miscellanea Medicea, 147, fasc. 3, fols 129r–174r; and in BANL, Corsiniana, 1199 [35.D.4], fols 5r–43v.

Greenwood, Ryan, 'The Just War in Florentine Political Discourse c. 1200–1400', *Jus Gentium: Journal of International Legal History* 4 (2019): 351–382.

Hardy, Nicholas, *Criticism and Confession: The Bible in the Seventeenth Century Republic of Letters* (Oxford: Oxford University Press, 2017).

Interpretare il Digesto: storia e metodi, ed. Dario Mantovani and Antonio Padoa Schioppa (Pavia: IUSS Press, 2014).

Jansen, Corjo J. H., 'Over de 18e eeuwse docenten natuurrecht aan Nederlandse universiteiten en de door hen gebruikte leerboeken', *Tijdschrift voor Rechtsgeschiedenis* 55 (1987): 103–115.

La Toscana di Cosimo III, ed. Franco Angiolini, Vieri Becagli and Marcello Verga (Firenze: Edifir, 1993).

Lesaffer, Randall, 'The 18th-Century Antecedents of the Concert of Europe II. The Quadruple Alliance of 1718', in *Oxford Historical Treaties* (Oxford: Oxford University Press, online edition 2017), https://opil.ouplaw.com/page/592 (accessed 21 January 2023).

Lesaffer, Randall, 'The Nature of Europe's Classical Law of Nations', in *The Oxford Handbook of the Sources of International Law*, ed. Samantha Besson and Jean d'Aspremont (Oxford: Oxford University Press, 2017), 99–117.

Lomonaco, Fabrizio, Lex regia. *Diritto, filologia e fides historica nella cultura politico-filosofica dell'Olanda di fine Seicento* (Napoli: Guida, 1990).

Lomonaco, Fabrizio, *New Studies on Lex Regia* (Bern: Peter Lang, 2011).

Marini, Giuliano, 'Dal Diritto naturale alla Filosofia del diritto', in *Storia dell'Università di Pisa* (Pisa: Plus, 2000), vol. 2, II, 635–661.

Marrara, Danilo, 'L'età medicea (1543–1737)', in *Storia dell'Università di Pisa* (Pisa: Plus, 2000), vol. 1, I, 79–187; vol. 1, II, 571–656.

Marrara, Danilo, 'Pompeo Neri e la cattedra pisana di "diritto pubblico" nel XVIII secolo', *Rivista di Storia del Diritto Italiano* 59 (1986): 173–202.

Meulen, Jacob ter, and Pieter Johan Jurrian Diermanse, *Bibliographie des écrits imprimés de Hugo Grotius* (La Haye: M. Nijhoff, 1950).

Miccoli, Giovanni, 'Adami, Francesco Raimondo', in *Dizionario Biografico degli Italiani* (Roma: Istituto dell'Enciclopedia Italiana, 1960), vol. 1, 233–234.

Migliorini, Anna Vittoria, 'Tanucci, Bernardo', in *Dizionario Biografico dei Giuristi Italiani. XII–XX secolo*, ed. Italo Birocchi et al. (Bologna: Il Mulino, 2013), 1931–1934.

Montorzi, Mario, 'Averani, Giuseppe', in *Dizionario Biografico dei Giuristi Italiani. XII–XX secolo*, ed. Italo Birocchi et al. (Bologna: Il Mulino, 2013), 128–130.

Morelli Timpanaro, Maria Augusta, 'Il testamento segreto di Giuseppe Averani (1728). Il suo costante attaccamento allo studio pisano e ad alcuni colleghi', *Bollettino Storico Pisano* 75 (2006): 287–309.

Nellen, Henk, *Hugo Grotius: A Lifelong Struggle for Peace in Church and State, 1583–1645* (Leiden: Brill, 2015).

Neri Badia, Giovanni Bonaventura [and Pompeo Neri], *Decisiones et responsa juris* (Florentiae: ex typographia Josephi Allegrini, [Pisoni] & soc., 1769–1776).

Neri [Badia], Pompeo, *Discorso primo* (report on the compilation of a new code of municipal laws of Tuscany, 31 May 1747), ed. Marcello Verga, in Marcello Verga, *Da 'cittadini' a 'nobili'. Lotta politica e riforma delle istituzioni nella Toscana di Francesco Stefano* (Milano: Giuffrè, 1990), 317–346.

Niccolini, Antonio, 'Delle lodi di Giuseppe Averani […] 1745', in Giuseppe Averani, *Lezioni Toscane* (Firenze: Gaetano Albizzini, 1744–1761), vol. 2, iii–xxxix.

Nocera, Guglielmo, *Ius naturale nella esperienza giuridica romana* (Milano: Giuffrè, 1962).

Novelle letterarie (Firenze: n.p., con licenza de' superiori, 1742).

Panebianco, Massimo, *Ugo Grozio e la tradizione storica del diritto internazionale* (Napoli: Editoriale Scientifica, 1974).

Panicucci, Elisa, 'Dall'avvento dei Lorena al Regno d'Etruria (1737–1807)', in *Storia dell'Università di Pisa* (Pisa: Plus, 2000), vol. 2, I, 3–134.

Paoli, Maria Pia, 'Gian Gastone de' Medici, granduca di Toscana', in *Dizionario Biografico degli Italiani* (Roma: Istituto dell'Enciclopedia Italiana, 2000), vol. 54, 397–407.

Pasta, Renato, 'Mediazioni e trasformazioni: operatori del libro in Italia nel Settecento', *Archivio Storico Italiano* 172 (2014): 311–354.

Raccolta d'elogi d'uomini illustri toscani. Compilati da vari letterati fiorentini (Lucca: Benedini, 1770–1774).

Saastamoinen, Kari, 'Pufendorf on the Law of Sociability and the Law of Nations', in *The law of Nations and Natural Law 1625–1800*, ed. Simone Zurbuchen (Leiden: Brill, 2019), 107–131, https://doi.org/10.1163/9789004384200_007 (accessed 21 January 2023).

Salerno, Emanuele, 'Giusnaturalismo e cultura giuspolitica nella Toscana del primo Settecento. Il *Discorso sopra la successione della Toscana* di Niccolò Antinori (1711)', *Archivio Storico Italiano* 173 (2015): 31–64.

Salerno, Emanuele, 'Rinuccini, Carlo', in *Dizionario Biografico degli Italiani* (Roma: Istituto dell'Enciclopedia Italiana, 2016), vol. 87, 610–614.

Salerno, Emanuele, '*Stare pactis* and Neutrality. Grotius and Pufendorf in the Political Thought of the Early Eighteenth-Century Grand Duchy of Tuscany', in *War, Trade and Neutrality: Europe and the Mediterranean in Seventeenth and Eighteenth Centuries*, ed. Antonella Alimento (Milano: FrancoAngeli, 2011), 188–202.

Scattola, Merio, *Dalla virtù alla scienza. La fondazione e la trasformazione della disciplina politica nell'età moderna* (Milano: FrancoAngeli, 2003).

Scattola, Merio, *Das Naturrecht vor dem Naturrecht. Zur Geschichte des* ius naturae *im 16. Jahrhundert* (Tübingen: Niemeyer, 1999).

Schnettger, Matthias, 'Dynastische Interessen, Lehnsrecht und Machtpolitik. Der Wiener Hof und die Anwartschaft der Kurfürstin Anna Maria Luisa von der Pfalz auf die toskanische Erbfolge (1711–1714)', *Mitteilungen des Instituts für Österreichische Geschichtsforschung* 108 (2000): 351–371.

Spagnesi, Enrico, 'Il diritto', in *Storia dell'Università di Pisa* (Pisa: Plus, 2000), vol. 1, I, 191–257; vol. 2, II, 461–570.

Stolleis, Michael, *Geschichte des öffentlichen Rechts in Deutschland*, 4 vols (München: Beck, 1988–2012).

Storia dell'Università di Pisa, vol. 1, *1343–1737* (I–II) (Pisa: Pacini, 1993; reprint Pisa: Plus, 2000); vol. 2, *1737–1861* (I–III) (Pisa: Plus, 2000).

Straumann, Benjamin, *Roman Law in the State of Nature: The Classical Foundations of Hugo Grotius' Natural Law* (Cambridge: Cambridge University Press, 2015).

Sutter, Philipp Wilhelm von [*praeses* Giuseppe Averani], *De jure belli, et pacis disputatio* (Florentiae: typis Regiae Celsitudinis, apud Petrum Antonium Brigonci, superiorum licentia, 1703).

Tanucci, Bernardo, *Dritto della Corona di Napoli sopra Piombino* (n.p., n.d; published post 1759).

Van Dam, Harm-Jan, 'Italian Friends: Grotius, De Dominis, Sarpi and the Church', *Nederlands Archief Voor Kerkgeschiedenis/Dutch Review of Church History* 75 (1995): 198–215.

Veen, Henk Th. Van, and Andrew P. McCormick, *Tuscany and the Low Countries: An Introduction to the Sources and an Inventory of Four Florentine Libraries* (Firenze: Centro Di, 1984).

Verga, Marcello, *Alla morte del re. Sovranità e leggi di successione nell'Europa dei secoli XVII–XVIII* (Roma: Salerno, 2020).

Verga, Marcello, *Da 'cittadini' a 'nobili'. Lotta politica e riforma delle istituzioni nella Toscana di Francesco Stefano* (Milano: Giuffrè, 1990).

Verga, Marcello, 'Dai Medici ai Lorena. Aspetti del dibattito politico in Toscana nell'Epistolario del Tanucci', in *Bernardo Tanucci e la Toscana* (Firenze: Olschki, 1986), 171–215.

Verga, Marcello, 'Neri, Pompeo', in *Dizionario Biografico dei Giuristi Italiani. XII–XX secolo*, ed. Italo Birocchi et al. (Bologna: Il Mulino, 2013), 1520–1523.

Wallinga, Tammo, 'Laurentius Theodorus Gronovius (1648–1724)', *Tijdschrift voor Rechtsgeschiedenis* 65 (1997): 459–495.

Zimmermann, Reinhard, 'Roman-Dutch Jurisprudence and Its Contribution to European Private Law', *Tulane Law Review* 66 (1992): 1685–1721.

Zurbuchen, Simone, 'Defining the Law of Nations: The *École romande du droit naturel* and the Lausanne Edition of Grotius' *De jure belli ac pacis* (1751–1752)', in *The Law of Nations and Natural Law 1625–1800*, ed. Simone Zurbuchen (Leiden: Brill, 2019), 253–277, https://doi.org/10.1163/9789004384200_012 (accessed 21 January 2023).

CHAPTER 2

Reception and Reinterpretation: Natural Law and the Law of Nations at the Roman 'Sapienza' in the Eighteenth Century

Alberto Clerici

1 An Unexciting Path?

Undoubtedly, the history of the *ius naturae et gentium* in early modern Rome – conceived both as an intellectual tradition and as a new academic discipline coming from Protestant lands – has not attracted much attention from historiography. Scholars have been more interested in the birth of 'public law' and modern 'public international law' on the nineteenth-century Italian Peninsula[1] or, concerning the eighteenth century, the creation and development of official university chairs of 'Law of Nature and of Nations' have aroused greater interest.[2] Moreover, the *ius naturae et gentium* has often been seen, in Italian legal history, only in the light of the traditional conflict between the *mos gallicus* and *mos italicus*, and not as an integral part of the intellectual trajectory of a specific academic subject – albeit multifaceted – already widespread in many parts of Europe.[3] Moreover, of all the so-called 'ancient States' of

1 Luigi Nuzzo, *Origini di una Scienza. Diritto internazionale e colonialismo nel XIX secolo* (Frankfurt am Main: Klostermann, 2012).

2 Italo Birocchi, 'L'insegnamento del diritto pubblico nelle Università italiane nel XVIII secolo', in *Science politique et droit public dans les facultés de droit européennes (XIIIe–XVIIIe siècle)*, ed. Jacques Krynen and Michael Stolleis (Frankfurt am Main: Klostermann, 2008), 549–558; Paolo Alvazzi del Frate, 'La "découverte" du droit constitutionnel. La culture juridique française et les débuts de la science du droit public en Italie à l'époque révolutionnaire', in *Modernisme, tradition et acculturation juridique*, ed. Bart Coppein, Fred Stevens and Laurent Waelkens (Bruxelles: Koninklijke Vlaamse Academie van België voor Wetenschappen en Kunsten, 2011), 175–180; and the essays by Vittor Ivo Comparato, 'Il diritto di natura a Perugia tra la Repubblica romana e l'Unità', and by Maria Rosa Di Simone, 'L'Unità d'Italia e l'insegnamento del diritto pubblico all'Università di Roma', *Annali di storia delle università italiane* 18 (2014): 221–242, 301–312.

3 On the birth of the new discipline see *The Law of Nations and Natural Law 1625–1800*, ed. Simone Zurbuchen (Leiden: Brill, 2019). Arguably, most of this scholarship has had a limited impact on international work in the field, for linguistic reasons.

DOI:10.1163/9789004685130_004

pre-unified Italy, the Papal States could have been considered the least interesting context to look for the reception of Protestant natural law. They were of course the bulwark of Catholic orthodoxy and Roman law, part of the 'most archaic Italy' (*l'Italia più arcaica*), as Franco Venturi famously put it,[4] and for that reason 'less efficient, less rational and less rationalizable' than other regions, for example Naples, Milan and Venice. Indeed, a long-established opinion sees the eighteenth and nineteenth-century papacy as an irremediably old-fashioned and close-minded cultural world, backward and averse to changes, therefore unsuitable for acknowledging the novelties of the Enlightenment. This unfavourable image was partly caused by the anti-clerical stance of many figures of the Italian *Risorgimento*,[5] had a very long life and gave birth to many controversies among historians, who, for the most part, may well have considered the study of modern natural law in Enlightenment Rome as an unexciting path. However, the most insightful scholarship has rightly criticized this straightforward unenthusiastic picture of the Papal States,[6] by emphasizing the need to identify different phases in their history, and by highlighting the cultural contribution of a greater variety of actors in Roman intellectual life, starting from the Popes themselves, up to writers, artists, scholars (both lay and ecclesiastic), publishers, booksellers and government officials, as well as putting in better light the role played by cafés, academies, universities and the like. Certainly, the manifold difficulties of the slow, tortuous reception of the ideas of the Enlightenment in the Papal States cannot be denied. But my intention here is not to look for hard (if not impossible) to find cases of plain and unhesitating acceptance of the most innovative and provocative ideas of the Enlightenment in eighteenth-century Rome, where 'tradition' was still a cultural value of paramount importance, and where the universities were undoubtedly anchored to old-fashioned methods and weakened by internal

4 *Illuministi italiani*, vol. 7, *Riformatori delle antiche repubbliche, dei ducati, dello Stato pontificio e delle isole*, ed. Giuseppe Giarrizzo, Gianfranco Torcellan and Franco Venturi (Milano: Ricciardi, 1965), ix–x.

5 Take for instance Giuseppe Garibaldi, one of the most celebrated heroes of Italian unification, who defined the Catholic Church as 'a contagious and perverse sect'. See Giuseppe Garibaldi, *Edizione nazionale degli scritti di Giuseppe Garibaldi: Epistolario*, vol. 6, *1861–1862* (Bologna: Cappelli, 1932), 93.

6 Marina Caffiero, 'Roma nel Settecento tra politica e religione. Dibattito storiografico e nuovi approcci', *Dimensioni e problemi della ricerca storica* 1 (2000): 81–100; Margaret C. Jacob, *The Secular Enlightenment* (Princeton: Princeton University Press, 2019), 204–206, and especially the several contributions in *Filippo Maria Renazzi. Università e cultura a Roma tra Settecento e Ottocento*, ed. Maria Rosa Di Simone, Carla Frova and Paolo Alvazzi Del Frate (Bologna: Il Mulino, 2019).

power struggles.[7] Instead, more modestly, I would like to add a few to the 'small and limited germs of renewal' that even Venturi saw in the papacy of the time,[8] by focusing on the interesting ways in which a few distinguished professors at La Sapienza received but at the same time adapted and adjusted some famous – or infamous – authors of early modern natural law and the law of nations, conceived as a plural endeavour and not as a clearly homogenous philosophical school. Also, I hope to show that it is unfair to maintain that, in Rome, 'for the actual encounter with the scientific and rationalist outlook we cannot look to the universities'.[9] Notwithstanding the many difficulties in finding the available sources, due to the vicissitudes of the archives concerning La Sapienza,[10] and the lack of accurate manuscript copies of university lectures relevant to our topic,[11] luckily the major figures in the reception of *ius naturae et gentium* at the *Studium Urbis* wrote and published several works, from which we can get a fairly precise picture of the ideas and methods they adopted in university teaching.

I will concentrate on Gian Vincenzo Gravina (1664–1718) and Emmanuele Duni (1714–1781), whose lives and teachings will be linked to the intellectual life of papal Rome and to the intricate history of the academic choices that led eventually to the formal establishment in the Law Faculty at La Sapienza of a chair of 'natural law, public law and the law of nations'. This happened only in 1824, but the subject had already been at least partially formalized as a course on 'natural law and the law of nations' at the Faculty of Philosophy and Arts since 1788.

---

7 There were two major conflicts in Rome: one between the *avvocati concistoriali*, the governing body of La Sapienza, and the professors; and the other between Sapienza itself and the still prestigious Jesuit Roman College. See Maria Rosa Di Simone, *La 'Sapienza' romana nel Settecento. Organizzazione Universitaria e Insegnamento del Diritto* (Roma: Edizioni dell'Ateneo, 1980).

8 *Illuministi*, xii.

9 This is the opinion of Hanns Gross, *Rome in the Age of Enlightenment: The Post-Tridentine Syndrome and the Ancien Regime* (Cambridge: Cambridge University Press, 1990), 243.

10 Giuliana Adorni, 'L'archivio dello *Studium Urbis* fra Archivio di Stato di Roma e Archivio Segreto Vaticano', *Annali di storia delle università italiane* 22 (2018): 243–259.

11 In the Historical Archives of the Pontifical Gregorian University I have located a very well preserved manuscript copy of the lectures on *jus naturae et gentium* at the Sapienza by Father Giovanni Battista Piccadori (1766–1829) in 1808, when this subject was taught from the chair of ethics: Curia, FC 273 2, fols 1–323, *Juris Naturae, ac Gentium Praelectiones, quas in Sapientiae Gymnasio habuit I.B. Piccadori*. Anno 1808. For later years, we also have the revised lectures of Francesco Norcia (1797–ca. 1870), the first professor of natural law and law of nations since 1824 (this time at the Faculty of Law), published as *Iuris naturae et gentium institutiones in usum auditorum adornatae*, 2 vols (Roma: Contedini, 1830).

2 'Tricks of Acrobats' and 'Child's Fables'

It is true that the Roman cultural environment, on the eve of the eighteenth century, was rather refractory to new ideas in the liberal arts, as in science. The Celestine Father Celestino Galiani (1681–1753), one of the leading exponents of Italian Newtonianism in Naples and Rome, and professor of church history at La Sapienza from 1718, wrote to a friend in 1705 about scientific experiments: 'what is to be feared is not so much the Inquisitor as the belief of men who hold [experiments] to be little more than tricks of acrobats'.[12] The situation was difficult also regarding the introduction of the new vision of the relationship between morality and politics coming from natural jurisprudence. Scepticism about this new vogue was famously expressed by Cardinal Giovanni Battista De Luca (1614–1683), a very influential figure in legal studies in Rome at the end of the seventeenth-century (though very critical of the corruption of academic teaching at La Sapienza).[13] In a series of writings, De Luca repeatedly scorned 'modern' natural law tenets, such as the primeval community of goods and lands, and the theories of the origins of law and society, as 'child's fables' and 'chimeras', urging law students and magistrates to stick strictly to legal practice. Indeed, the brilliant but short-lived teaching of Marc-Antoine Muret (1526–1585), a star of legal humanism and professor at the Sapienza from 1563 to 1585, had by De Luca's time been long forgotten.[14] In De Luca's eyes, the main problem of natural law was that, apart from precepts directly derived from divine law, it was of little practical use, since 'we do not know in which volumes such laws are recorded, what their tenor is, what were the authors and legislators, and what authority obliged also the sovereign

12 Vincenzo Ferrone, *The Intellectual Roots of the Italian Enlightenment: Newtonian Science, Religion, and Politics in the Early Eighteenth Century*, trans. Sue Brotherton (Amherst: Humanities Press, 1995, orig. publ. in Italian 1982), 11. On Galiani, besides Ferrone's many studies, see Koen Stapelbroek, *Love, Self-Deceit, and Money: Commerce and Morality in the Early Neapolitan Enlightenment* (Toronto: University of Toronto Press, 2008), ch. 2, and idem, *Commercio, passioni e mercato. Napoli nell'Europa del Settecento* (Milano: FrancoAngeli, 2020), 60–90.

13 De Luca was very close to popes Alexander VII and Innocent XI, and frequented the Roman academy of Queen Christina of Sweden. He was appointed cardinal in 1681, after more than thirty years of legal practice in all fields of jurisprudence. See Aldo Mazzacane, 'Giovan Battista De Luca', in *Dizionario Biografico degli Italiani* (Roma: Istituto dell'Enciclopedia Italiana, 1990), vol. 38, 340–347.

14 Francesca Loverci, 'Gli studi umanistici dal Rinascimento alla Controriforma', in *Storia della Facoltà di Lettere e Filosofia de La Sapienza*, ed. Lidia Capo and Maria Rosa Di Simone (Roma: Viella, 2000), 199–243.

princes'.[15] Moreover, a commitment to natural law could lead to 'errors and fables from which many misunderstandings about the power of princes may arise'.[16] It is clear that the tradition of natural law De Luca was referring to was not the 'orthodox Catholic' one, but the dangerous one coming from modern Protestant writers. This is apparent in a passage of *Il cavaliere e la dama* (The knight and the lady, 1675), an interesting picture of Roman culture at the time, where De Luca makes a scornful catalogue of these 'new' ideas:

> The invention and introduction of many things, even modern ones, are accredited by some people as if those things were not there before. Such as the introduction of civil life, and the society of men in civic society, as well as in inhabited places, almost as if they lived on their own as wild beasts in caves, or in the woods, grazing on acorns and other wild fruits. Such laughable childishness! Or even the introduction of 'mine' and 'yours' and property, almost as if before it did not exist, and everything was common. Or the introduction of coins, and consequently that of the purchase and sale, almost as if before because there was no money (a necessary instrument of such a contract), only barter was in use. Or even that there were some original authors, and introducers of laws, and letters, and sciences, and arts.[17]

A similar scepticism permeates also De Luca's notion of *ius gentium*, and especially the idea of *ius gentium primarium*, the law of nations stemming from 'a kind of rational instinct among men, and from perennial custom among nations'.[18] De Luca rejected the proper legal character of such law, especially as far as the law of war was concerned, since it lacked the formal structure of civil litigation with a dedicated judge. Consequently, he considered the law of war – and other aspects of the *ius gentium* – as a matter of state, regulated

15 Giovanni Battista De Luca, *Il Principe cristiano pratico* (Roma: Stamperia della Camera Apostolica, 1680), 207.

16 Giovanni Battista De Luca, *Il dottor volgare, ovvero il compendio di tutta la legge civile, canonica, feudale, e municipale*, vol. 6, *Dello stile legale* (Colonia: Modesto Fenzio, 1740 [1673]), 499; idem, *Principe cristiano*, 194. On De Luca's sceptical conception of natural law and its relationship to other branches of law, see Alessandro Dani, *Un' immagine secentesca del diritto comune. La teoria delle fonti del diritto nel pensiero di Giovanni Battista De Luca* (Bologna: Monduzzi, 2008), ch. 1; see also Maria Rosa Di Simone, 'Doveri e diritti delle "dame" nel pensiero di Giovanni Battista De Luca', *Historia et ius* 15 (2019): 1–22.

17 Giovanni Battista De Luca, *Il cavaliere e la dama* (Roma: Dragondelli, 1675), 33.

18 Dani, *Immagine secentesca*, 55–56.

by *lex politica* more than jurisprudence,[19] and his *Dottor volgare* has a rather cynical remark about the vagueness of this body of notions:

> And from this it follows that each one figures this law of nations in his own way, and he considers himself very wise at it, hence for the most part it is used as an excuse, or in order to mantle force and oppression by the powerful upon the weak.[20]

But a commitment to the new 'modern' vision of natural law could have had far more serious consequences in those days than the simple jokes of De Luca. In 1690 the Inquisition started a trial on a presumptive heretical sect known as 'The Whites' (*I Bianchi*), involving a number of persons in Rome and Milan from different social classes, education and backgrounds, including a few professors of La Sapienza.[21] The first informer and accuser, one Francesco Picchitelli, told the Holy Inquisitors that, among other dangerous and blasphemous things, the members of this coterie held that 'we must not believe in anything, except in the law that nature teaches us: do not do to others what you do not like, eat, drink and live happily'.[22] This charge was accepted in the course of the proceedings – which included torture in some cases – by a few of the defendants. Filippo Alfonsi, poet and librarian, in a clumsy attempt to soften his position, blamed his companions for having 'entangled his mind' with ideas such as 'that we must not believe in any law, not even the Catholic one, all made for political reasons, except the Law of Nature'.[23] And he added that 'when discussing such matters, they called it philosophizing, and they said they were becoming Philosophers', a very interesting remark for the question of how natural law was perceived at that time, namely, not only as a strictly legal subject, but also (and especially) a philosophical one.

---

19 Giovanni Battista De Luca, *Theatrum veritatis et justitiae* (Venetiis: Paulum Balleonium, 1716), vol. 15.1, 115b, at n. 1: 'de hoc iure agere non pertinet ad professores fori externi pro iudicio contentioso, cum potius id pertineat ad illam legem, quae politica dicitur, atque huiusmodi violationis judex vel ultor sit potius eventus belli, sive ea maior vis bellica, quae dicitur ultima ratio rerum'.

20 De Luca, *Dottor volgare*, 'proemio', 61–62.

21 The proceedings of the trial, now in the Archives of the Holy Office in Rome, have been studied by Vittorio Frajese, *Dal libertinismo ai Lumi. Roma 1690–Torino 1727* (Roma: Viella, 2016), 9–41.

22 Frajese, *Dal libertinismo*, 13 (quoting from the original manuscript of the trial proceedings): 'che non si ha da credere a niente ma alla legge che ci insegna la natura: non fare ad altri quello che non piace a te, mangiare, bevere, e stare allegramente'.

23 Ibid.: 'che non si deve credere ad alcuna legge, nemmeno alla Cattolica, fatte tutte per Politica, ma solo alla Legge della Natura'.

Finally, it must also be considered that, apart from the patent general suspicion of cultural innovation, the delay in the reception and discussion of *ius naturae et gentium* at the Sapienza (compared with other universities such as Pisa)[24] was further hindered by its academic competition with the prestigious Jesuit Roman College, where the teaching of more orthodox Scholastic natural law had a strong tradition thanks to the work of its famous former professors Robert Bellarmine, Juan de Mariana and Francisco Suarez.[25]

Thus, only slowly, at the end of the seventeenth century, the gloomy opinion on and position of natural law and the law of nations at the Sapienza began to change, thanks to a combination of cultural and political causes. On the one hand, it was a question of fighting formalism, dogmatism and the exclusively practical attitude to legal studies, and, on the other hand, of proposing a methodological alternative to the predominant Aristotelian, Scholastic and Jesuit natural law. Given this agenda, it is not surprising that the main innovations at La Sapienza were introduced with a focus on the close ties between philology, philosophy and history in the study of law, and a keen interest in the style and ideas of legal humanism and *scuola culta*, as well as in the intellectual suggestions coming from the Neapolitan cultural environment of the *Investiganti* and the works of Giambattista Vico (1668–1744).[26] Furthermore, this quest was certainly helped by the reforming action of some popes, and by their attempts – not always completely successful – to rationalize and modernize the general plan of studies within the 'official' Roman university. In 1701 Clement XI, an admirer of Gravina, established a special congregation for papal academies, to which Gravina contributed.[27] Between 1744 and 1748 Benedict XIV, himself a scholar and an acquaintance of many illustrious men of the Enlightenment, also proposed a reform project for La Sapienza. If the real value of his plan is controversial, it is nevertheless possible to admit that Prospero Lorenzo Lambertini, also as a pope, remained an intellectually

24 See Chapter 1 of the present volume, by Emanuele Salerno.

25 Marina Formica, 'Il secolo dei Lumi', in *Storia della Facoltà di Lettere e Filosofia de La Sapienza*, ed. Lidia Capo and Maria Rosa Di Simone (Roma: Viella, 2000), pp. 305–339, at p. 314.

26 The multiple intellectual exchanges and networks between Rome and Naples in the early eighteenth century have been well analysed by Raffaele Ajello, 'Cartesianesimo e cultura oltremontana al tempo dell'*Istoria civile*', in *Pietro Giannone e il suo tempo*, ed. Raffaele Ajello (Napoli: Jovene, 1980), vol. 1, 3–81. For our purpose, see especially Felix Waldmann, 'Natural Law and the Chair of Ethics in the University of Naples, 1703–1769', *Modern Intellectual History* 19 (2022): 54–80.

27 Di Simone, *La 'Sapienza' romana nel Settecento*, 84–91.

curious man and moderately open to novelty.[28] It was he, for example, who supported Emmanuele Duni for the chair of the Pandects at the Sapienza. Then, in 1788 Pope Pius VI issued a series of regulations for the University, which partially formalized, as we will see, the teaching of natural law and the law of nations in the Faculty of Philosophy. Finally, in 1824 Leo XII published the decree *Quod divina sapientia*, addressed to the reform of the Roman university, and providing for the first official chair of 'Natural law, public law, and the law of nations', now moved to the Faculty of Law.[29]

3 *Ius naturae et gentium* at the Sapienza: The Teaching and the Chair

As said, there was no chair devoted to 'natural law' or 'law of nations' at the Sapienza before 1824. In 1812 Giovanni Ferri de Saint-Constant (1755–1830), Rector of the University newly appointed by the Napoleonic government, lamented the absence of a course 'du droit naturel et du droit des gens', but remarked that 'the old regulations [of the University] had in a way filled this void by instructing the professor of moral philosophy to teach the elements of natural law'.[30] Ferri de Saint-Constant provides us with the interesting information that notions of the subject were given not as a part of the curriculum of studies offered by the Faculty of Law (*Classe dei leggisti*), but within the Faculty, or *Classe*, of 'Philosophy and Arts'. In fact, he was referring to the already mentioned regulations of the Sapienza issued by Pope Pius VI in an effort to improve the life and reputation of the institution. The regulations for the Faculty of Philosophy and Arts stated:

> The Reader of Ethics, at the first hour of the morning, every year, lectures on the subject and, deriving it from the principles of natural law and the law of nations, truly gives the elements of public law.[31]

This line shows how *ius naturae et gentium* and *ius publicum* were, at that time, clearly intertwined, if not identified one with the other, as already happened

28 Gaetano Greco, *Benedetto XIV: Un canone per la Chiesa* (Roma: Salerno, 2011); *Benedict XIV and the Enlightenment: Art, Science, and Spirituality*, ed. Rebecca Messbarger, Christopher M. S. Johns and Philip Gavitt (Toronto: University of Toronto Press, 2017).

29 Enrico Flaiani, *L'Università di Roma dal 1824 al 1852. Docenti, programmi ed esami tra le riforme di Leone XII e quelle di Pio IX* (Città del Vaticano: Archivio Segreto Vaticano, 2012).

30 Paolo Alvazzi del Frate, *Università napoleoniche negli "Stati romani". Il rapport di Giovanni Ferri de Saint-Constant sull'istruzione pubblica, 1812* (Rome: Viella, 1995), 151.

31 *Regolamento dell'Archiginnasio romano* (Roma: Camera Apostolica, 1788), 42.

in other parts of Europe.[32] As a matter of fact, when in 1824 the first official chair for this subject was created in Rome, it was named *Diritto di natura, diritto pubblico e delle genti*,[33] but at that time it was integrated into legal studies, mainly thanks to the earlier action of canon law professor Giovanni Devoti (1744–1820), who had been a pupil of Emmanuele Duni.[34] This reflects another important aspect of the history of *ius naturae et gentium* at the Sapienza, namely the internal fighting between faculties and professors, which was linked to the thorny question of the uncertain nature of this discipline, divided between theory and practice.

Indeed, even if the first official chair of natural law and the law of nations was created in 1824, the sources reveal that in 1788 this area of studies seemed to possess, at least informally, its own autonomy within the moral and legal disciplines. For example, the widely available gazette *Notizie per l'Anno 1788* stated that Aurelio Gama of the Order of the Clerics Regular Minor (also known as Adorno Fathers) was appointed the first professor of *gius naturale, et delle genti*. In 1794 the chair passed to Gama's religious brother Giovanni Battista Piccadori (1766–1829), who became General of his Order and counsellor of the Holy Office and Index congregations in Rome.[35] His manuscript lectures from 1808, even though formally given as part of the Ethics classes, were titled 'lectures on natural law and the law of nations, given at the Sapienza University'. This is confirmed by Filippo Maria Renazzi's celebrated *History* of the Sapienza, published in four volumes between 1803 and 1806, where Piccadori was mentioned as having succeeded Gama 'in teaching the principles of nat-

32 Merio Scattola, *Dalla virtù alla scienza. La fondazione e la trasformazione della disciplina politica nell'età moderna* (Milano: FrancoAngeli, 2002).

33 Cf. 'Metodo generale di pubblica istruzione ed educazione per lo Stato Pontificio', Archivio Segreto Vaticano, Rome, Italy, Segreteria di Stato, Interni, 1824, b.532, 45, fasc.1, published in Flaiani, *L'Università di Roma*, 101.

34 Devoti was a member of the special commission appointed by Pope Pius VII in 1816 for the reformation of academic studies in Rome, eventually culminating in the *Quod divina sapientia*, issued in 1824, by when Devoti had died. For his plea on moving the teaching of natural law and the law of nations to the Faculty of Law, see Nicola Spano, *L'Università di Roma* (Roma: Mediterranea, 1935), 69. Members of this commission included cardinals Ercole Consalvi and Bartolomeo Pacca, both very interested in modern natural law. For their use of Vattel even in legal practice, see Elisabetta Fiocchi Malaspina, *L'eterno ritorno del* Droit des gens *di Emer de Vattel (secc. XVIII–XIX). L'impatto sulla cultura giuridica in prospettiva globale* (Frankfurt am Main: Max Planck Institute for European Legal History, 2017), 152–157.

35 Philippe Boutry, *Souverain et pontife: Recherches prosopographiques sur la Curie Romaine à l'âge de la Restauration 1814–1846* (Roma: Publications de l'École française de Rome, 2002), 467. Open access: http://books.openedition.org/efr/1860 (accessed 11 May 2021).

ural law and the law of nations'.[36] Piccadori held the assignment until 1824, when, as we have seen, the chair was officially named and moved to the Law Faculty under Francesco Norcia (1797–after 1870), who kept it until 1836.[37]

So, it cannot be denied that the formalization of *ius naturae et gentium* within academic teachings in Rome happened at a very late stage. However, to have a full picture of the matter it is essential to look also at the less formal and less explicit reception of Protestant natural law from the very beginning of the eighteenth century up to the regulations of 1788. It is in this period, in fact, that we find the first and most significant signs and sources of this complex process of reaction and readjustment of the natural law tradition, with its now inseparable appendix of the law of nations. And here it is necessary to look, above all, at legal studies, where obviously the concepts of 'natural law' and 'law of nations' were discussed within the usual framework of Roman jurisprudence, even if without any great novelty, as we have seen, apart from the exceptional figure of Muret. But new methodologies, new themes and new authors started to show up in Rome after Gian Vincenzo Gravina was called to the chair of the Pandects in 1699.

4 Gian Vincenzo Gravina (1664–1718)

Gravina was born in Calabria, southern Italy.[38] He studied under the eminent Italian cartesian Gregorio Caloprese and, in Naples, under the jurist

36 Filippo Maria Renazzi, *Storia dell'Università degli Studi di Roma detta comunemente la Sapienza* (Roma: Pagliarini, 1803–1806), vol. 4, 422. Renazzi (1745–1808) taught criminal law at the Sapienza for many years. His *Elementa juris criminalis* (1773) shows a wide use of authors from the tradition of *ius naturae et gentium*. See Gigliola di Renzo Villata, 'Alle origini degli "Elementa": quali i "semina castae, veraeque criminalis scientiae"?', in *Filippo Maria Renazzi*, 136–138.

37 Flaiani, *L'Università di Roma*, 44, n. 76.

38 On Gravina, see especially Carlo Ghisalberti, *Gian Vincenzo Gravina giurista e storico* (Milano: Giuffrè, 1962); Amedeo Quondam, *Cultura e ideologia di Gianvincenzo Gravina* (Milano: Mursia, 1968); Di Simone, *La 'Sapienza' romana nel Settecento*, 84–91; Carla San Mauro, 'Gian Vincenzo Gravina', in *Dizionario Biografico degli Italiani* (Roma: Istituto dell'enciclopedia italiana, 2002), vol. 58, 756–764; Fabrizio Lomonaco, *Filosofia, diritto e storia in Gianvincenzo Gravina* (Roma: Edizioni di Storia e Letteratura, 2006); Carla San Mauro, *Gianvincenzo Gravina giurista e politico* (Milano: FrancoAngeli, 2006); Enrico Zucchi, 'Tirannide e stato di natura. Sul rifiuto dell'assolutismo giusnaturalista nelle *Tragedie Cinque* di Gian Vincenzo Gravina', in *Prima e dopo il Leviatano*, ed. Merio Scattola and Paolo Scotton (Padova: Cleup, 2014), 193–226; Gaetano Antonio Gualtieri, *Gian Vincenzo Gravina tra estetica, etica e diritto. Dialoghi, discorsi, trattati* (Venezia: Marsilio, 2021).

Serafino Biscardi and the professor of Greek, Gregorio Messere. They introduced Gravina to the importance of the study of history and erudition, the cult of the Classics and the predilection for legal humanism and its most important exponents: Alciato, Cujas, Donellus, Hotman. In 1689 Gravina followed Cardinal Francesco Pignatelli to Rome and began to earn a solid reputation for his manners and scholarship. He corresponded with learned men such as Antonio Magliabechi, Friedrich Benedikt Carpzov and Johann Georg Graevius, and quickly found his place in the intellectual world of papal Rome. On good terms with both Innocent XII and his successor, Clement XI, Gravina became professor of civil law at La Sapienza in 1699, and in 1703 he also held the chair of canon law. He died in 1718, just after having accepted a position at the University of Turin by invitation of Vittorio Amedeo II of Savoy.

A man of vast interests and erudition, Gravina is the author of a substantial number of works in different fields. His main achievement in legal studies, the *Originum iuris civilis libri tres*, appeared in Leipzig in 1708, under the auspices of Johann Burckhard Mencke (1674–1732), director of the well-known periodical *Acta eruditorum*.[39] The book was well received and later praised by Montesquieu and Gibbon, among others.[40] In fact, Gravina had been called to Rome by Cardinal Albani (later to become Pope Clement XI) precisely in order to vivify the spectrum of the teaching of law. According to Giovan Battista Passeri (1694–1780), a pupil of Gravina at the Sapienza, it was Albani who proposed Gravina's name to the pope, by stressing that 'Roman jurisprudence had to be repolished as it had already been done in other nations'.[41] Another early recognition of the originality of Gravina's method comes once again from Renazzi, for whom Gravina

> was the first who after the era of Alciatus and Muretus, undertook to treat and illustrate among the Italians – and especially in Rome – Jurisprudence with the lights of Philosophy, with the principles of public law,

39 Fabrizio Lomonaco, *Il commercio delle idee. Contributi allo studio dei periodici europei del Sei-Settecento* (Milano: FrancoAngeli, 2021), 33–82. I quote from the 1713 Naples edition in three volumes, edited by Fabrizio Lomonaco in 2004 as Gianvincenzo Gravina, *Originum juris civilis libri tres*, ed. Fabrizio Lomonaco, foreword by Fulvio Tessitore, 3 vols (Napoli: Liguori, 2004).

40 On the immediate fortune of the *Originum*, see Lomonaco, *Filosofia, diritto e storia*, 199–229. On Gravina and Montesquieu (with reference to *Esprit des lois*, vol. 1, 3), see Ghisalberti, *Gian Vincenzo Gravina*, 4–5; on Gibbon and Gravina, see Giuseppe Giarrizzo, *Edward Gibbon e la cultura europea del Settecento* (Napoli: Istituto Italiano di Studi Storici, 1954), 195–196.

41 Giovan Battista Passeri, *Vita di Gianvincenzo Gravina*, in Gravina, *Opere scelte* (Firenze: Batelli, 1926).

> and with all the necessary Greek and Latin erudition. It is true that he benefited much from the works of many very learned French and German interpreters of Roman Law, unknown in Italy at the time, not only to the crowd of forensic *Giureconsulti*, but also to public professors in universities. But it is to his great credit to know precisely these authors and to be able to take advantage of them.[42]

Gravina participated in the reorganization of studies at the Roman university and, animated by a profound anti-Jesuitism, took action to revive the importance of Sapienza *vis-à-vis* the Roman College. A staunch opponent of probabilism, in his oration *De instauratione studiorum* Gravina invited his colleagues to refrain from the use of casuistry, 'in order not to add further torments to the normal difficulty of legal interpretation'.[43] Gravina's approach to the study of law was essentially rational, historical and philological.[44] His involvement in the Neapolitan cultural environment, the same one Vico frequented,[45] had pushed him to study the juridical dimension of human life from two fundamental points of view: time and space.[46] On the one hand, a crucial aspect of his method consisted in the investigation of the actual historical links between natural law and civil law (essentially Roman law), understood as a search for the profound *origins* of the rules of man's behaviour.[47] On the other hand, Gravina devoted himself early to the definition of the *universal* character of law and knowledge in general. Indeed, one of his public lectures as professor of the Pandects at the Sapienza addressed precisely – and appropriately

---

42 Renazzi, *Storia dell'Università degli Studi di Roma*, vol. 4, 81.

43 Gian Vincenzo Gravina, *Oratio de instauratione studiorum*, in *Scritti critici e teorici*, ed. Amedeo Quondam (Bari: Laterza, 1973), 356.

44 Vincenzo Ferrone, *The Politics of Enlightenment: Constitutionalism, Republicanism, and the Rights of Man in Gaetano Filangieri*, trans. Sophus A. Reinert (London: Anthem Press, 2012), 72–73. According to Ferrone, Gravina 'deserves credit for having launched a new tradition of political studies based on the historical and more generally philosophical analysis of the existing nexuses of politics and law', 72.

45 But Fabrizio Lomonaco has rightly stressed the need to study Gravina in his own right, without the recurring temptation to see him only as a possible forerunner of Vico. See Lomonaco, *Filosofia, diritto e storia*, 3–5.

46 Fabrizio Lomonaco, *Le* Orationes *di G. Gravina: scienza, sapienza e diritto* (Napoli: La città del Sole, 1997), 10–11.

47 Ghisalberti, *Gian Vincenzo Gravina*, 18–19. Gravina's interest in the historical analysis of law is already visible in his *Specimen prisci iuris* (in *Opuscula*: 1696) and *De ortu et progressu iuris civilis liber, qui est Originum primus* (Napoli, 1701). But of course the search for the 'origins' of justice and jurisprudence constitutes the key aspect (reflected in the title itself) of Gravina's masterwork *Originum juris civilis libri tres* (Leipzig, 1708, translated into French in 1766).

enough – the topic of 'sapientia universa'.[48] Within this lecture Gravina proposed a view of human history in seven steps, according to the development of *sapientia*. His desire for innovation in human knowledge is made clear when Gravina rejoiced that philosophy had now become finally free from 'Aristotelian servitude', finding truth 'from nature itself' (*ex ipsa natura*) and thanks to the contribution of figures such as Telesius, Patrizi, Bacon, Gassendi, Galilei and Descartes.[49]

Unfortunately, we do not have the texts of the Gravina's lectures at the Sapienza, but we can obtain an adequate picture of his ideas on *ius naturae et gentium* from his numerous other works, above all from the second book *De iure naturali, gentium et XII Tabularum* of his masterpiece *Originum iuris civilis libri tres* (1708), a reconstruction of the genesis of civil law, natural law and the law of nations in ancient times, dedicated to Pope Clement XI. A convinced advocate of the legal humanism of *mos gallicus*, in the list of his favourite authors, in addition to Donellus, Alciato, Duarenus and the beloved Cuiacius, Gravina also recruited Hugo Grotius.[50] It is true that he mentioned the Dutch scholar only twice in his *Originum juris civilis*,[51] but Gravina seems to have been influenced by him precisely on topics of *ius gentium*, such as the belief in the original common ownership of lands and the freedom of the seas.[52] Interestingly, his discussion of the right of war and peace in the *Originum* proceeds with an inversion, beginning with the right of peace, followed by the right of

48 Gian Vincenzo Gravina, *In auspicatione studiorum de sapientia universa*, published in the *Orationes* (Napoli: 1712). As we will see, the concept of 'universal jurisprudence' or *giurisprudenza universale* also features at the centre of Emmanuele Duni's works.

49 Gravina, *Oratio de instauratione studiorum*, 381: 'At philosophia ex aristotelica servitute manumissa, scientiam initio per Telesium potissimum et Patricium et Ficinum in Platone, aliisque graecis philosophis venabatur; iampridem vero a Bacone, Gassendo, Galilaeo, Cartesio, ex humanae mentis angustiis ad rerum universitatem traducta, causarum veritatem haurit ex ipsa natura'. However, the rejection of Aristotelianism and the focus on natural philosophy does not imply, for Gravina, the complete adherence to radical forms of metaphysics or atheism. See Lomonaco, *Le* Orationes, 19–20.

50 Gian Vincenzo Gravina, *De conversione doctrinarum* (1694), in *Scritti critici e teorici*, 148. Adriana Luna-Fabritius, 'Providence and Uses of Grotian Strategies in Neapolitan Political Thought, 1650–1750', in *Sacred Polities, Natural Law and the Law of Nations in the 16th–17th Centuries*, ed. Hans W. Blom (Leiden: Brill, 2022), 314–342, at 331, states that Gravina 'was one of the most important readers of Grotius in this period'.

51 Guido Fassò, *Vico e Grozio* (Napoli: Guida, 1971), 19–20. See Gravina, *Originum*, vol. 2, 15, p. 223, with reference to Grotius, *De iure belli ac pacis*, III.15.1–2, on the *ius post bellum* and the law of victory.

52 Gravina, *Originum*, vol. 2, 10, pp. 165–166.

war.[53] He also shared with Grotius a keen interest in ancient Stoicism, usually seen in his system as a fundamental partner to Platonism. But just as modern natural law thinkers used Stoicism in a new way, Gravina's Platonism was miles away from 'the pious Platonism of Ficino and the Italian Renaissance', and it did not mean hostility to modernity.[54]

Gravina's attitude to Hobbes is a complex one.[55] From the anthropological point of view, on the one hand, Gravina condemned the idea of natural selfishness in humanity, which he attributed to Machiavelli and, well before him, to the Sophists (Hobbes being a mere 'emulator').[56] On the other hand, he recognized an important but not a decisive role for passions and the 'law of the body' in the determination of human behaviour. In fact, speaking of a 'double natural law' in human beings, there is also the 'law of reason' to be taken into account. In that sense, reason and passions are both inherent in humanity (as opposed to animals, which possess only instincts), with the former superior to the latter, unfolding progressively from the original state thanks to God's Providence.[57] Thus, in a sort of blending of Christian Platonism and Christian Stoicism, according to Gravina the goal of the wise man is to find harmony and equilibrium between reason and passions, in a quest for the balance between the particular nature of individuals and the universal nature of Creation.[58] From a legal point of view, understanding the relationship between reason and passions appears crucial to Gravina also in order to find the correct interpretation of the different definitions of natural law and

53 Ibid., II, 13–14, pp. 220–221. According to Gravina, the rules of peace logically come before those of war, because his Platonic and Christian anthropology envisages war only as a violation of the provisions of reasonable sociability and peaceful commerce.

54 Jonathan Israel, *Enlightenment Contested: Philosophy, Modernity, and the Emancipation of Man. 1670–1752* (Oxford: Oxford University Press, 2006), 525.

55 See the remarks by Lomonaco in the introduction to Gravina, *Originum*, xxxi–xxxiv. For Gravina's constitutionalism as opposed to Hobbesian absolutism, see Zucchi, 'Tirannide e stato di natura'.

56 Gravina, *Oratio de instauratione studiorum*, 355. He also attacked Hobbes's defence of matriarchal society (*De Cive*, IX, 3) in *Originum*, II, 10, 165.

57 Gravina, *Originum*, II, 2–4, 157–159. It must be said that Gravina, apart from a single reference to Providence, aptly eschews all thorny theological problems in his work, keeping it as much as possible at the legal, historical and philosophical level. A reason for that might have been his at least partially unorthodox views on sacred history, ancient wisdom and natural philosophy. See Frajese, *Dal libertinismo ai Lumi*, 91–132.

58 See Gravina, *Originum*, II, 4, 160: 'Hence the Stoics said that to live according to nature is a virtue transmitted to us by the law of reason, by which the particular nature of men is reconciled with the universal nature of all things' (*Hinc vivere secundum naturam, ipsam Stoici dixerunt, esse virtutem traditam nobis ab lege rationis, qua peculiaris hominum, et rerum universa natura conciliantur*).

ius gentium given by Ulpian and by Gaius in the *Corpus iuris civilis*.[59] Indeed, the idea of 'moderation' coming from knowledge, reason and wisdom appears to be central to Gravina's outlook. Moderation is also the paramount virtue of the *sapientes*, granting them a natural right to rule over the ignorant (*ius sapientioris*)[60] and providing the main weapon to fight the unavoidable 'diseases of rational nature', or vices, described by Gravina in a clear Machiavellian tone.[61] From the more political point of view, this *ius sapientioris*, or aristocracy of virtue, whose outcome should be seen in the laws of a community, means for Gravina that political power cannot and should not be held by all members of the society, thus departing from ideas of popular sovereignty or the natural equality of men as upheld by other figures in the tradition of *ius naturae et gentium*.[62] However, in many of his legal and literary works Gravina also attacked absolutism and tyranny, whose ideas he identified (perhaps too hastily) with Bodin and Grotius.[63] Particularly relevant here is Gravina's critical remark against the Dutch jurist in his posthumously published *De imperio et iurisdictione*, since it involves one of Grotius's most controversial statements, concerning the possibility of 'voluntary enslavement' or intentional deprivation of liberty by individuals.[64] Generally speaking, Gravina preferred a kind of enlightened monarchy, subject to the rule of law and reason and assisted by wise magistrates and counsellors from the middle class.[65]

The origin of political community, for Gravina, is still tied to the fundamental concept of family, and its traditional structure. But it is interesting to note that Gravina also puts the family at the beginning of the law of nations, since it is precisely in order to please their needs and acquire what they miss that

59 *Digest* 1.1.1.3–4 (Ulpian) and *Digest* 1.1.9 (Gaius), discussed – without explicit acknowledgement – in Gravina, *Originum*, II, 1, 155–156.

60 Gravina, *Originum*, II, 17, 224–225.

61 See ibid., II, 7, 162–163, for the description of the chasm between the infinite generation of desires and the impossibility of man's contentment without recourse to reason and wisdom, echoing Machiavelli's 'mala contentezza' in *Discorsi sopra la prima deca di Tito Livio*, vol. 1, 37.

62 See San Mauro, *Gianvincenzo Gravina*, 90–94; Zucchi, 'Tirannide e stato di natura', 214.

63 Gian Vincenzo Gravina, *De imperio et iurisdictione* (Catania: Giannotta, 1907), 23–33. Whether Bodin and Grotius can be called 'absolutists', and whether they were considered as such by their contemporaries, are still debated questions. Useful remarks are made in Daniel Lee, *Popular Sovereignty in Early Modern Constitutional Thought* (Oxford: Oxford University Press, 2016), chs 6 and 8.

64 Gravina, *De imperio et iurisdictione*, 23: 'Homines enim liberi, quorum non est commercium, transire nequunt in proprietatem imperantis, unde non possunt venire nisi sub potestate, atque ex voluntate propria'. See Grotius, *De iure belli ac pacis*, 1.3.8.1. Gravina's work was written in 1743, but published only in 1907.

65 San Mauro, *Gianvincenzo Gravina*, 81–104.

families, under the guidance of natural reason, search for relationships and exchanges with other families. Hence, the law of nations, defined as 'ratio illa, quae non uni familiae, sed pluribus regendis est instituta, cumque pluribus gentium communicata', derives from basic economic needs, and Gravina can title the relevant chapter of *Originum* 'De iure Gentium, et Origine Commerciorum'. Once again, he stresses the importance of 'the law of reason', conceived as the 'mother' of the law of nations[66] and as the guiding light for fostering peace and avoiding wars. The crucial role attributed by Gravina to reason, also in the law of nations, reveals his participation in a major discourse of early modern *ius naturae et gentium*, that on the legitimacy of wars against the so-called 'enemies of mankind'. Indeed, it is the capability of recognising and following reason that draws a line between men and beasts. Appealing to the Ciceronian notions of 'societas hominum' and 'communis hostis omnium',[67] usually attributed to pirates and brigands and already used for example by Alberico Gentili and Hugo Grotius,[68] Gravina makes clear that 'whoever goes astray from virtue, and unleashes passions from its commands, changing from reason to instincts, is a criminal, and an enemy of human nature' (*hostis humanae naturae*).[69] The same image is repeated in the chapter on the law of war ('De jure belli'), where Gravina states that if a nation violates 'the bond of human society' (*foedus humanae societatis*), then other nations can legitimately wage a just war against those 'enemies of mankind' (*hostis humanitatis*).[70] And so crucial to him is the power of reason over *feritas* that Gravina does not hesitate to resolutely defend the rule of *sapientes* over the 'barbarians'.[71]

5 Emmanuele Duni (1714–1781)

If Gravina's innovative teaching at La Sapienza lasted for about twenty years, his later colleague Emmanuele or Emanuele Duni did even better, holding the

66 Gravina, *Originum*, II, 14, 221: 'rationis lex, quae mater est juris gentium'.

67 Cicero, *De Officiis*, I.50 and III.107.

68 See Walter Rech, *Enemies of Mankind: Vattel's Theory of Collective Security* (Leiden: Brill, 2013), 54–70.

69 Gravina, *Originum*, II, 9, 165.

70 Ibid., II, 14, 221.

71 Ibid., II, 15, 223, in a discussion on the justness of Roman conquests, squeezed between two quotations from Grotius (*De iure belli ac pacis*, III.15.1 and III.15.11.12). Gravina strongly defends the justice of Roman wars, only directed – in his opinion – against 'barbarians', and always following 'humanity'. The issue had been debated at least since Alberico Gentili's *De armis romanis* (1599).

chair of the Pandects for almost thirty years, from 1753 until his death in 1781.[72] Like Gravina, Duni was born in southern Italy (Matera), and like him he was trained at the great Neapolitan school of law, perhaps attending the last 'private' lessons of Giambattista Vico,[73] who always remained a crucial figure for Duni, to the point that he was accused of being a mere plagiarist, with little or no originality.[74]

In recent years, however, attempts have been made to do justice to Duni's ability as a teacher and to his openness to new ideas and to new readings. He was, indeed, a 'popularizer' of Vico, but not devoid of a certain dignity of his own.[75] According to Achille Gennarelli, Duni's brother Egidio Romualdo, a musician of some reputation, introduced him to the Parisian erudite circles during a sabbatical Emmanuele spent in France, where he allegedly met even Voltaire. Indeed, Duni's *Origine, e progressi del cittadino e del governo civile di Roma* (1763–1764), a careful reconstruction of the social, legal and political development of the Roman Republic,[76] was favourably reviewed by the Parisian *Gazette littéraire de l'Europe* and translated into German in 1829 (without acknowledgement of its real author) by Wilhelm von Eisendecher (1803–1880). Other evidence of Duni's European network is his letter of April 1763 to the English consul in Venice, John Strange, where he praised the British

72 Mauro Di Lisa, 'Duni Emmanule', in *Dizionario Biografico degli Italiani* (Roma: Istituto dell'Enciclopedia Italiana, 1993), vol. 42, 19–26; Max Ascoli, *Saggi vichiani*, vol. 1, *La filosofia giuridica di Emmanuele Duni* (Roma: Garroni, 1928); Maria Guercio, 'E. Duni storico del diritto', *Archivio della società romana di Storia Patria* 98 (1974): 147–173. See also the introduction to the eighteenth-century edition of Duni's complete works by Achille Gennarelli, 'Notizie di Emmanuele Duni', in *Opere complete di Emmanuele Duni* (Roma: Tipografia Camerale, 1845), vol. 1, i–xxiii; Renazzi, *Storia dell'Università di Roma*, 253. To my knowledge, the most up-to-date study of Duni is in Giovanni Scarpato, *Giambattista Vico dall'età delle riforme alla Restaurazione. La Scienza nuova tra Lumi e cultura cattolica, 1744–1827* (Roma: Aracne, 2018), 69–126.

73 The question is debated: Di Lisa rejects that possibility, while Scarpato seems to think it plausible, considering that Antonio Genovesi also attended Vico's private academy from 1736.

74 Benedetto Croce, *Bibliografia Vichiana, accresciuta e rielaborata a cura di Fausto Nicolini* (Napoli: Ricciardi, 1947), 268–269.

75 As already avowed by Di Simone, *La 'Sapienza' romana*, 197–202. See also Fabrizio Lomonaco, *Tracce di Vico nella polemica sulle origini delle pandette e delle XII tavole nel Settecento italiano* (Napoli: Liguori, 2005), 37–40.

76 Benedetto Staij, the ecclesiastical censor who gave the *imprimatur* to Duni's work, judged the book as 'very useful', and admired the 'new lights' (*nuovi lumi*) used by the author to clarify the sometimes complex vicissitudes of Roman society. See Alberto Tinto, 'Giovanni Komarek tipografo a Roma nei secoli XVII–XVIII e i suoi campionari di caratteri', *La Bibliofilia* 75 (1973): 189–225.

cultural world and lamented the fact that in Rome 'the purity of [legal] doctrine lies buried'.[77] But perhaps the main contribution to Duni's notoriety came from two important literary polemics. The first one was linked to his first major work, *Saggio sulla giurisprudenza universale* (An essay on universal jurisprudence), which appeared in 1759 in the Roman cultural periodical *Giornale de' letterati*,[78] sponsored by Benedict himself, and it was then published in Rome as a monograph in 1760. The essay was heavily influenced by Vico's system. One specific idea, that of the original 'ferality' of the first men, stimulated Vico's enemy Bonifacio Finetti (1707–1782), a Dominican and author of the *De principiis iuris naturae et gentium adversus hobbesium, pufendorfium, thomasium, wolfium et alios* (1764).[79] There, Finetti criticized both Duni and his master, Vico, an attack to which Duni replied, generating in turn a long rejoinder from Finetti, the *Apologia del genere umano accusato d'essere stato una volta bestia* (An apology for humankind, accused of having been once upon a time a beast, 1768). The second debate was tied to Duni's denunciation of the abbot Louis-Clair Du Bignon (1738–?), whom he had met in Italy in 1765, for plagiarism.[80] In the same year Du Bignon published *Histoire critique du gouvernement romain* in Paris, raising Duni's (overall unfair)[81] accusation of plagiarism – with reference to his *Origine e progressi* – in an article in the *Gazette Littéraire*, and Du Bignon's reply. Melchior von Grimm (1723–1807) soon joined the debate in the *Correspondance littéraire*, which he co-edited with Diderot.[82] Later in his life Duni refined and updated his *Saggio* of 1760, giving it a new structure and analysing new authors (such as Thomasius and Wolff), and published it as *La Scienza del Costume o sia sistema sul dritto universale* (Napoli: stamperia Simoniana, 1775), a systematic work summarizing his reflections on natural jurisprudence.

---

77 See Franco Venturi, 'Elementi e tentativi di riforma nello stato pontificio del Settecento', *Rivista Storica Italiana* 4 (1963): 778–817.

78 *Giornale de' letterati per gli anni* MDCCLVIII, *e* MDCCLIX, art. XXI, 305–359.

79 The volume was published under the name of Finetti's brother, Giovanni Francesco, and dedicated to Maria Theresa of Austria. On Finetti, see Merio Scattola, 'Protestantesimo e diritto naturale cattolico nel XVIII secolo', in *Illuminismo e protestantesimo*, ed. Giulia Cantarutti and Stefano Ferrari (Milano: FrancoAngeli, 2010), 131–148; and see also Chapter 6, by Serena Luzzi, in the present volume.

80 Mouza Raskolnikoff, 'Vico, l'histoire romaine et les érudits français des Lumières', *Mélanges de l'école française de Rome* 96 (1984): 1051–1077.

81 See Scarpato, *Giambattista Vico*, 105–118.

82 Franco Venturi, *L'antichità svelata e l'idea del progresso in N. A. Boulanger, 1722–1759* (Bari: Laterza, 1947), 153.

Since 1753 Duni had won a position at the Sapienza thanks to the support of the pope himself,[83] the 'enlightened' Benedict XIV. As said, Duni kept the crucial chair of *Pandette* for almost thirty years, so his impact on at least two generations of students should not be underestimated. Duni's interest in the literature on *ius naturae et gentium* is already clearly visible in his *Saggio sulla giurisprudenza universale*, a fair example of what he is likely to have taught his pupils at the Sapienza. As a matter of fact, the final pages of the essay offer one of the first (if not the first) critical review in Italy of another classic of eighteenth-century natural law, Emer de Vattel's newly published *Du droit des gens* (1758). But the discussion of Vattel is only the conclusion of a long journey 'in the midst of a stormy sea of writings [...] for the most part coming from beyond the Alps', as Duni confesses in the dedicatory letter of the volume to the great statesman and man of letters Bernardo Tanucci (1698–1783).[84] This journey finally took him into the 'harbour of wisdom of the incomparable and (let us say frankly) of the great philosopher, philologist and jurist Giambattista Vico'. So, as in Gravina, also in Duni we find an attempt to find a 'third way' for approaching the issue of 'universal jurisprudence' (explicitly identified by Duni with 'natural law and the law of nations'),[85] between the old-fashioned Thomism and the Protestant 'innovators'. The route to follow was clearly the historicist method of Gravina and Vico, based on a philological analysis of the temporal and spatial origins of law.[86] Thus, the influence of Vico and Gravina appeared unequivocal in the idea that civil law, as well as the law of nations, cannot be fully understood without recourse to philosophy and philology, as Duni himself confessed to John Strange in the above-mentioned letter of 1763.[87] From our perspective, the most interesting part of the essay is the last one, where Duni investigates the relationship between natural law

---

83 Or, better, by the 'precise command' of His Holiness (*ordine espresso*): see Archivio di Stato di Roma, Rome, Italy, Università di Roma, 88, fol. 245v.

84 Emmanuele Duni, *Saggio sulla giurisprudenza universale*, in *Opere complete di Emmanuele Duni*, vol. 3, 4.

85 Ibid., 10.

86 For an attempt to look at Vico in the light of the recent historiography on *ius naturae et gentium*, see Walter Rech, 'History and Normativity: Vico's "Natural Law of Nations"', *Journal of the History of International Law* 17 (2015): 147–169.

87 Quoted in Venturi, 'Elementi e tentativi di riforma', 791: 'The laws and customs of men, and consequently of all nations, cannot be dealt without having recourse to the light of philosophy, nor will we ever know how to point out their origin and nature without the help of philosophy, which is the mother of every human understanding' (*Le leggi, ed i costumi degli uomini, ed in conseguenza delle nazioni tutte, non si possono trattare senza ricorrere ai lumi filosofici, né mai sapremo additarne la loro origine, indole e natura senza l'aiuto della filosofia ch'è la madre d'ogni umano intendimento*).

and the law of nations by analysing the works of Grotius, Hobbes, Pufendorf, Selden and Vattel.[88] A first important implication is that civil law, while falling within the sphere of utility and 'certainty' (*il certo*), maintains a relationship with the authentic 'truth' (*il vero*) of natural law that is based on the common rationality of man, who, even before living in a juridical society, participates in the universal society of reason. Following Vico, Duni argued that the different nations at the time of their foundation autonomously gave themselves a 'natural law of nations' (*diritto naturale delle genti*) which constituted the outcome of the 'additions or deductions' of natural law proper. In contrast, according to Duni, Hobbes and the 'most erudite' Grotius had denied any connection between natural and civil law, and had instead explained the basic uniformity between the legal systems of the various nations through an *a posteriori* procedure based on 'consent'. It was, in Duni's eyes, an abstract solution, where the authentic foundation of *ius gentium* should have arisen from a philological investigation. And, as in Vico, the whole formation process of this 'natural law of nations' is guaranteed by Divine Providence:

> Therefore, where they [the modern interpreters of natural law] place the birth of the law of nations in that small area of civil law that is found to be uniform among them [the nations], I on the contrary claim that the civil law is the son of the law of nations, and not the other way around, as they claimed to establish against all reasonableness, encouraged [lit. flattered] by the ease with which Hobbes was able to get away with it. But they did not realize that Hobbes had in mind to establish an entire system of jurisprudence far from any principle of Divine Providence.[89]

However, the reference to Providence cannot mask the novelty of a vision that makes the 'natural law of nations' both historical *and* natural at the same time. Duni (as Vico before him) entirely rejects the Hobbesian reduction of the law of nations to natural law. Singularly enough, by the 'natural law of nations' he intended a law of nations that was 'natural' precisely because it was customary and conventional, evolving from nations' concrete and ever-changing

88 Duni is not explicit about the editions he used to quote these authors. He cites a long passage in Latin from Hobbes's *De Cive* and refers to Pufendorf's *De iure naturae et gentium* in French (undoubtedly from the translation of Jean Barbeyrac). He quotes Grotius frequently, but only once with a precise reference to his *De iure belli ac pacis* in Latin. As to Vattel, Duni puts the title *Du droit des gens* only in a footnote, while discussing a few arguments from the book.

89 Duni, *Saggio sulla giurisprudenza universale*, 35–36.

needs. Also, in another crucial passage simplified from Vico, Duni claims that, in order to fully understand the development of the 'natural law of nations', one has to study 'with the metaphysical lights' the pre-historical period, those times 'obscure' and 'fabled' when men lacked the use of reason and lived like beasts. It follows that natural reason was not originally created in humanity by God, and consequently the principles of natural law were discovered and discernible by individuals and nations only through history, and in different 'stages', starting from a 'feral state' of man (*stato ferino*).[90]

It was this claim by Vico and reaffirmed by Duni that attracted Finetti's criticism. The unorthodox position of Vico and Duni[91] is highlighted by the fact that in his *Apologia* Finetti lists together Jean-Jacques Rousseau, Vico and Duni. Actually, he considers the two Italians even more pernicious than the Genevan, as 'Rousseau describes his lawless savages in the form of fiction or hypothesis, while Vico and Duni assert that these lawless beasts really and truly existed'.[92] It should be noted that Duni's *Risposta* to Finetti, on the theme of the animal behaviour of primordial humans, actually contained an element that was foreign to Vico's works, and that could instead be seen in relation to Rousseau's famous *Discours sur l'origine et les fondements de l'inégalité parmi les hommes* (1755). I refer to the comparison between the primordial men and the modern savages of the Indies, which Duni established on the basis of *De l'origine des Lois, des Arts et des Sciences* (1758)[93] by Antoine Goguet, a 'modern and most erudite' writer.[94] Anyway, the dispute apparently had a certain echo, as another passage in Finetti's *Apologia* points to a very interesting remark about how Duni's teachings had been received as unusual at the Sapienza in Rome, causing a bitter clash between two parties, the 'ferals' and the 'anti-ferals' (*ferini e antiferini*):

---

90 Ibid., 42–43.

91 See Pierre Girard, 'Les conditions de l'anthropologie politique chez Vico et Genovesi', in *Polis e Polemos. Giambattista Vico e il pensiero politico*, ed. Gennaro Maria Barbuto and Giovanni Scarpato (Milano: Mimesis, 2022), 247–249.

92 [Bonifacio Finetti], *Apologia del genere umano accusato d'essere stato una volta bestia, in cui si dimostra la falsità dello stato Ferino degli antichi uomini colla Sacra Scrittura* (Venezia: Radici, 1768), 86: 'E si noti che Rousseau dipinge i suoi selvaggi senza legge in foggia di finzione o sia d'ipotesi; mentre Vico e Duni ammettono come stati veramente e realmente al mondo i bestioni esleggi'.

93 An Italian translation appeared in Naples in 1762. See Scarpato, *Giambattista Vico*, 76–77.

94 Emmanuele Duni, *Risposta ai dubbi proposti dal signor Gianfrancesco Finetti sopra il Saggio sulla giurisprudenza universale di Emmanuele Duni* (Roma: Amidei, 1766), in *Opere complete di Emmanuele Duni*, vol. 3, 48.

> Duni was joined by a number of his colleagues; but the greater and wiser part of those professors (as far as we have been told from Rome) were truly sickened by the indecent manners he had in such a literary question and consequently were not at all persuaded by his reasons, or rather his cabal and sophisms. So, a kind of war broke out between those scholars, some strongly condemning him, and others defending him with equal commitment: hence they formed like two parties of *ferini* and *antiferini*.[95]

Overall, Duni's conception of the *ius naturae et gentium* is the same as that found in other important figures of the Italian Catholic *Aufklärung* of the time, such as Appiano Buonafede (1716–1793) and Antonio Genovesi (1713–1769).[96] The idea was to separate, in the Protestant tradition and in 'modern authors' in general, the figures who were too radical and far from orthodoxy (such as Hobbes, Spinoza and Helvétius) and those who could be partly 'saved' for their erudition or for their reasonable intuitions (such as Grotius, Pufendorf, Locke, Montesquieu and Vattel). Indeed, in the preface to *La Scienza del Costume* Duni shows a positive attitude towards the 'illustrious writers' on *ius naturae et gentium*, 'massime Oltramontani', who 'have deserved, and will always deserve perpetual praise'.[97] Duni seems to be particularly sympathetic with Grotius, 'a man of supreme qualities'. While the Dutch jurist mistakenly searched for the foundation of the law of nations in universal consent, nevertheless, 'being the most learned and the most versed of all in erudition, he clearly saw that the foundation of the law of nations could not be the same principle as that of the law of nature'. Even more, in *La Scienza del Costume* Duni dared to defend one of Grotius's most controversial ideas, namely, that natural law keeps its validity

95 Finetti, *Apologia*, 4: 'A Duni si sono uniti alquanti dei suoi colleghi; ma la maggiore e più saggia parte di quei professori (per quanto ci è stato riferito da Roma), siccome sono restati sommamente nauseati dall'indecente maniera da lui tenuta in una quistione letteraria, così non sono restati punto persuasi dalle sue ragioni, o piuttosto cabale e sofismi. Quindi s'è accesa una spezie di guerra tra quegli eruditi, alcuni condannandolo fortemente, ed altri difendendolo con eguale impegno: onde si son formati come due partiti di *ferini* e *antiferini*'.

96 Elisabetta Fiocchi Malaspina, *L'eterno ritorno del* Droit des gens; Alberto Clerici, 'Vattel in the Papal States. The Law of Nations and Anti-Prussian Propaganda in Italy at the Time of the Seven Years' War', in *The Legacy of Vattel's* Droit Des Gens, ed. Koen Stapelbroek and Antonio Trampus (Basingstoke: Palgrave, 2019), 207–234; Adriana Luna-Fabritius, 'Pufendorf's Sociability in (Italian) Translation', in *Passions, Politics and the Limits of Society*, ed. Heikki Haara, Koen Stapelbroek and Mikko Immanen (Berlin: De Gruyter, 2020), 235–258.

97 Duni, *La Scienza del Costume*, 10–12.

etiamsi daremus non esse Deum, and that, consequently, an atheist could well have access to it. It is true – says Duni – that in the heart of the atheist the observance of the precepts of nature, understood as laws prescribed by God, does not reign, but it is equally true that the atheist, as gifted with intelligence like others, will not be able to escape the knowledge that these regulations 'have a degree of validity' (*aliquem locum haberent*) even for the person of the atheist. So Grotius does not contradict himself when he claims that God is the author of natural law, and that the latter can also be known by atheists. Although the atheist does not recognize the force of obligation in the laws of nature, he, too, could not deny with his own reason (*coi propri lumi*) that such and no other should be the conduct of our actions, namely, that which is dictated to us by our Nature.[98]

All in all, it seems that the students of the Sapienza found themselves faced with a teacher well prepared and endowed with a certain originality, considering the context of Papal Rome. From a strictly political point of view, too, Duni seems to have had unconventional ideas. Undoubtedly, his *Origine e progressi* is primarily a work of social and legal history (again in the footsteps of Vico), where we do not find any particular references to or quotations from the canon of modern natural law.[99] However, the concepts of 'nature' and 'human nature' find ample space within the volume, where they are used in an eminently political sense. Duni showed with historical expertise the advent of the popular government of ancient Rome through the political struggle for the affirmation of the 'natural ideas of freedom born with man himself', and the 'desire, inspired us by Nature, to free ourselves from the tyranny of others'. Political turmoil was the tool through which the Roman populace (*plebe*) reached full awareness of the ineluctable tension inherent in human nature and started to reflect on 'the pure law of humanity, which does not recognize the reason for inequality between man and man'.[100] It is more than plausible that Duni, in addition to Vico, read Rousseau (as implied by Finetti). Another crucial piece of evidence comes from a passage in *La Scienza del Costume* where Duni blends Christianity and Enlightenment to attack war, slavery and above all private property as contrary to natural law. The ownership of goods combined with the right to transfer them to others are the causes

98 Ibid., 20.

99 The sources used by Duni are mainly taken from Roman history. The literary model, starting from the title itself, appears to be Gravina's *Originum*.

100 Emmanuele Duni, *Origine e progressi del cittadino e del governo civile di Roma* (Roma: Bizzarrini Komarek, 1763–1764). I quote from *Opere complete di Emmanuele Duni*, vols 1 and 2, 24, 102, 106.

of the inequality that we see in civil societies. Nature admits only the use of things common to all, not a privative and absolute right of ownership.[101]

6 Concluding Remarks

Undoubtedly, the process of introducing and receiving Protestant (and generally 'updated') literature on natural law in papal Rome was slow, yet it happened. Focusing on the world of universities,[102] we have seen how for about half a century, thanks to personalities such as Gravina and Duni, attempts were made to revive legal studies and critically select the sources and themes of the new modern natural law, between reception and reinterpretation. The primary goal was to find an alternative to the traditional visions – perceived by now as inadequate – both of pedantic medieval law and of Jesuit scholasticism, without of course fully endorsing the Protestants. To do so, Gravina and Duni turned to history and philosophy, taking the quest for the 'origins' of human conduct as their main objective. In a way, they brought to Rome the best part of that vital and innovative cultural world that was Naples in the seventeenth and eighteenth centuries. The question we have tried to address is not so much to know when and to what extent the 'modern' *ius naturae et gentium* was finally taught in Rome, but rather to demonstrate the efforts of a few, maybe 'exceptional' figures, to renew a part of jurisprudence in a hostile cultural environment.

Archival Sources

Archivio di Stato di Roma, Rome, Italy, Università di Roma, 88.
Archivio Segreto Vaticano, Rome, Italy, Segreteria di Stato, Interni, 1824.
Archivio Storico della Pontificia Università Gregoriana, Rome, Italy, Curia, FC 273 2.

101 Duni, *La Scienza del Costume*, 202: 'Non si può negare, che fin dalla più remota antichità gli uomini abbiano introdotto molti costumi, che per niun conto possono riferirsi al dritto mero Naturale, come le guerre, la schiavitù, le manumisioni, e sopra tutto il dominio privativo, o sia la proprietà dei beni unita al dritto di trasferirgli ad altri, che poi ha cagionato quell'ineguaglianza, che scorgiamo nelle Società Civili. La Natura non ammette che il puro uso delle cose comune a tutti, e non un dritto privativo, ed assoluto di proprietà'.

102 There is a need for more comprehensive research on *ius naturae et gentium* in Rome, based also on the study of academies, cafes, periodicals, correspondence, as well as arts and sciences.

Bibliography

Adorni, Giuliana, 'L'archivio dello *Studium Urbis* fra Archivio di Stato di Roma e Archivio Segreto Vaticano', *Annali di storia delle università italiane* 22 (2018): 243–259.

Ajello, Raffaele, 'Cartesianesimo e cultura oltremontana al tempo dell'*Istoria civile*', in *Pietro Giannone e il suo tempo*, ed. Raffaele Ajello (Napoli: Jovene, 1980), vol. 1, 3–81.

Alvazzi del Frate, Paolo, *Università napoleoniche negli "Stati romani". Il rapport di Giovanni Ferri de Saint-Constant sull'istruzione pubblica*, 1812 (Rome: Viella, 1995).

Alvazzi del Frate, Paolo, 'La "découverte" du droit constitutionnel. La culture juridique française et les débuts de la science du droit public en Italie à l'époque révolutionnaire', in *Modernisme, tradition et acculturation juridique*, ed. Bart Coppein, Fred Stevens and Laurent Waelkens (Bruxelles: Koninklijke Vlaamse Academie van België voor Wetenschappen en Kunsten, 2011), 175–180.

Ascoli, Max, *Saggi vichiani*, vol. 1, *La filosofia giuridica di Emmanuele Duni* (Roma: Garroni, 1928).

Benedict XIV and the Enlightenment: Art, Science, and Spirituality, ed. Rebecca Messbarger, Christopher M. S. Johns and Philip Gavitt (Toronto: University of Toronto Press, 2017).

Birocchi, Italo, 'L'insegnamento del diritto pubblico nelle Università italiane nel XVIII secolo', in *Science politique et droit public dans les facultés de droit européennes (XIIIe–XVIIIe siècle)*, ed. Jacques Krynen and Michael Stolleis (Frankfurt am Main: Klostermann, 2008), 549–558.

Boutry, Philippe, *Souverain et pontife: Recherches prosopographiques sur la Curie Romaine à l'âge de la Restauration 1814–1846* (Roma: Publications de l'École française de Rome, 2002).

Caffiero, Marina, 'Roma nel Settecento tra politica e religione. Dibattito storiografico e nuovi approcci', *Dimensioni e problemi della ricerca storica* 1 (2000): 81–100.

Clerici, Alberto, 'Vattel in the Papal States. The Law of Nations and Anti-Prussian Propaganda in Italy at the Time of the Seven Years' War', in *The Legacy of Vattel's* Droit Des Gens, ed. Koen Stapelbroek and Antonio Trampus (Basingstoke: Palgrave, 2019), 207–234.

Comparato, Vittor Ivo, 'Il diritto di natura a Perugia tra la Repubblica romana e l'Unità', *Annali di storia delle università italiane* 18 (2014): 221–242.

Croce, Benedetto, *Bibliografia Vichiana, accresciuta e rielaborata a cura di Fausto Nicolini* (Napoli: Ricciardi, 1947).

Dani, Alessandro, *Un'immagine secentesca del diritto comune. La teoria delle fonti del diritto nel pensiero di Giovanni Battista De Luca* (Bologna: Monduzzi, 2008).

De Luca, Giovanni Battista, *Il cavaliere e la dama* (Roma: Dragondelli, 1675).

De Luca, Giovanni Battista, *Il dottor volgare, ovvero il compendio di tutta la legge civile, canonica, feudale, e municipale* (Colonia: Modesto Fenzio, 1740 [1673]).

De Luca, Giovanni Battista, *Il Principe cristiano pratico* (Roma: Stamperia della Camera Apostolica, 1680).

De Luca, Giovanni Battista, *Theatrum veritatis et justitiae* (Venetiis: Paulum Balleonium, 1716).

Di Lisa, Mauro, 'Emmanuele Duni', in *Dizionario Biografico degli Italiani* (Roma: Istituto dell'Enciclopedia Italiana, 1993), vol. 42, 19–26.

Di Renzo Villata, Gigliola, 'Alle origini degli "Elementa": quali i "semina castae, veraeque criminalis scientiae"?', in *Filippo Maria Renazzi. Università e cultura a Roma tra Settecento e Ottocento*, ed. Maria Rosa Di Simone, Carla Frova and Paolo Alvazzi Del Frate (Bologna: Il Mulino, 2019), 136–138.

Di Simone, Maria Rosa, 'Doveri e diritti delle "dame" nel pensiero di Giovanni Battista De Luca', *Historia et ius* 15 (2019): 1–22.

Di Simone, Maria Rosa, 'L'Unità d'Italia e l'insegnamento del diritto pubblico all'Università di Roma', *Annali di storia delle università italiane* 18 (2014): 301–312.

Di Simone, Maria Rosa, *La 'Sapienza' romana nel Settecento. Organizzazione Universitaria e Insegnamento del Diritto* (Roma: Edizioni dell'Ateneo, 1980).

Duni, Emmanuele, *La Scienza del Costume o sia sistema sul dritto universale* (Napoli: stamperia Simoniana, 1775).

Duni, Emmanuele, *Origine e progressi del cittadino e del governo civile di Roma* (Roma: Bizzarrini Komarek, 1763–1764).

Duni, Emmanuele, *Risposta ai dubbi proposti dal signor Gianfrancesco Finetti sopra il Saggio sulla giurisprudenza universale di Emmanuele Duni* (Roma: Amidei, 1766), in *Opere complete di Emmanuele Duni* (Roma: Tipografia Camerale, 1845).

Duni, Emmanuele, *Saggio sulla giurisprudenza universale* (1760), in *Opere complete di Emmanuele Duni* (Roma: Tipografia Camerale, 1845), 1–63.

Fassò, Guido, *Vico e Grozio* (Napoli: Guida, 1971).

Ferrone, Vincenzo, *The Politics of Enlightenment: Constitutionalism, Republicanism, and the Rights of Man in Gaetano Filangieri*, trans. Sophus A. Reinert (London: Anthem Press, 2012, orig. publ. in Italian 2008).

Ferrone, Vincenzo, *The Intellectual Roots of the Italian Enlightenment: Newtonian Science, Religion, and Politics in the Early Eighteenth Century*, trans. Sue Brotherton (Amherst: Humanities Press, 1995, orig. publ. in Italian 1982).

Filippo Maria Renazzi. Università e cultura a Roma tra Settecento e Ottocento, ed. Maria Rosa Di Simone, Carla Frova and Paolo Alvazzi Del Frate (Bologna: Il Mulino, 2019).

Finetti, Bonifacio, *Apologia del genere umano accusato d'essere stato una volta bestia, in cui si dimostra la falsità dello stato Ferino degli antichi uomini colla Sacra Scrittura* (Venezia: Radici, 1768).

Fiocchi Malaspina, Elisabetta, *L'eterno ritorno del* Droit des gens *di Emer de Vattel (secc. XVIII–XIX). L'impatto sulla cultura giuridica in prospettiva globale* (Frankfurt am Main: Max Planck Institute for European Legal History, 2017).

Flaiani, Enrico, *L'Università di Roma dal 1824 al 1852. Docenti, programmi ed esami tra le riforme di Leone XII e quelle di Pio IX* (Città del Vaticano: Archivio Segreto Vaticano, 2012).

Formica, Marina, 'Il secolo dei Lumi', in *Storia della Facoltà di Lettere e Filosofia de La Sapienza*, ed. Lidia Capo and Maria Rosa Di Simone (Roma: Viella, 2000), 305–339.

Frajese, Vittorio, *Dal libertinismo ai Lumi. Roma 1690–Torino 1727* (Roma: Viella, 2016).

Garibaldi, Giuseppe, *Edizione nazionale degli scritti di Giuseppe Garibaldi: Epistolario*, vol. 6, *1861–1862* (Bologna: Cappelli, 1932).

Gennarelli, Achille, 'Notizie di Emmanuele Duni', in *Opere complete di Emmanuele Duni* (Roma: Tipografia Camerale, 1845), vol. 1, i–xxiii.

Ghisalberti, Carlo, *Gian Vincenzo Gravina giurista e storico* (Milano: Giuffrè, 1962).

Giarrizzo, Giuseppe, *Edward Gibbon e la cultura europea del Settecento* (Napoli: Istituto Italiano di Studi Storici, 1954).

Girard, Pierre, 'Les conditions de l'anthropologie politique chez Vico et Genovesi', in *Polis e Polemos. Giambattista Vico e il pensiero politico*, ed. Gennaro Maria Barbuto and Giovanni Scarpato (Milano: Mimesis, 2022), 247–249.

Gravina, Gian Vincenzo, *De conversione doctrinarum* (1694), in *Scritti critici e teorici*, ed. Amedeo Quondam (Roma: Laterza, 1973).

Gravina, Gian Vincenzo, *De imperio et iurisdictione* (Catania: Giannotta, 1907).

Gravina, Gian Vincenzo, *In auspicatione studiorum de sapientia universa*, in *Orationes* (Napoli: 1712).

Gravina, Gian Vincenzo, *Oratio de instauratione studiorum*, in *Scritti critici e teorici*, ed. Amedeo Quondam (Bari: Laterza, 1973).

Gravina, Gian Vincenzo, *Originum juris civilis libri tres* (Leipzig, 1708), ed. with an introduction by Fabrizio Lomonaco (Napoli: Liguori, 2004).

Greco, Gaetano, *Benedetto XIV: Un canone per la Chiesa* (Roma: Salerno, 2011).

Gross, Hanns, *Rome in the Age of Enlightenment: The Post-Tridentine Syndrome and the Ancien Regime* (Cambridge: Cambridge University Press, 1990).

Gualtieri, Gaetano Antonio, *Gian Vincenzo Gravina tra estetica, etica e diritto. Dialoghi, discorsi, trattati* (Venezia: Marsilio, 2021).

Guercio, Maria, 'E. Duni storico del diritto', *Archivio della società romana di Storia Patria* 98 (1974): 147–173.

Illuministi italiani, vol. 7, *Riformatori delle antiche repubbliche, dei ducati, dello Stato pontificio e delle isole*, ed. Giuseppe Giarrizzo, Gianfranco Torcellan and Franco Venturi (Milano: Ricciardi, 1965).

Israel, Jonathan, *Enlightenment Contested: Philosophy, Modernity, and the Emancipation of Man. 1670–1752* (Oxford: Oxford University Press, 2006).

Jacob, Margaret C., *The Secular Enlightenment* (Princeton, NJ: Princeton University Press, 2019).

Lee, Daniel, *Popular Sovereignty in Early Modern Constitutional Thought* (Oxford: Oxford University Press, 2016).

Lomonaco, Fabrizio, *Filosofia, diritto e storia in Gianvincenzo Gravina* (Roma: Edizioni di Storia e Letteratura, 2006).

Lomonaco, Fabrizio, *Il commercio delle idee. Contributi allo studio dei periodici europei del Sei-Settecento* (Milano: FrancoAngeli, 2021).

Lomonaco, Fabrizio, *Le* Orationes *di G. Gravina: scienza, sapienza e diritto* (Napoli: La città del Sole, 1997).

Lomonaco, Fabrizio, *Tracce di Vico nella polemica sulle origini delle pandette e delle XII tavole nel Settecento italiano* (Napoli: Liguori, 2005).

Loverci, Francesca, 'Gli studi umanistici dal Rinascimento alla Controriforma', in *Storia della Facoltà di Lettere e Filosofia de La Sapienza*, ed. Lidia Capo and Maria Rosa Di Simone (Roma: Viella, 2000), 199–243.

Luna-Fabritius, Adriana, 'Providence and Uses of Grotian Strategies in Neapolitan Political Thought, 1650–1750', in *Sacred Polities, Natural Law and the Law of Nations in the 16th–17th Centuries*, ed. Hans W. Blom (Leiden: Brill, 2022), 314–342.

Luna-Fabritius, Adriana, 'Pufendorf's Sociability in (Italian) Translation', in *Passions, Politics and the Limits of Society*, ed. Heikki Haara, Koen Stapelbroek and Mikko Immanen (Berlin: De Gruyter, 2020), 235–258.

Mazzacane, Aldo, 'Giovan Battista De Luca', in *Dizionario Biografico degli Italiani* (Roma: Istituto dell'Enciclopedia Italiana, 1990), vol. 38, 340–347.

Norcia, Francesco, *Iuris naturae et gentium institutiones in usum auditorum adornatae*, 2 vols (Roma: Contedini, 1830).

Nuzzo, Luigi, *Origini di una Scienza. Diritto internazionale e colonialismo nel XIX secolo* (Frankfurt am Main: Klostermann, 2012).

Passeri, Giovan Battista, *Vita di Gianvincenzo Gravina*, in Gravina, *Opere scelte* (Firenze: Batelli, 1926).

Piccadori, Giovanni Battista, *Iuris naturae et gentium institutiones in usum auditorum adornatae* (Roma: Contedini, 1830).

Quondam, Amedeo, *Cultura e ideologia di Gianvincenzo Gravina* (Milano: Mursia, 1968).

Raskolnikoff, Mouza, 'Vico, l'histoire romaine et les érudits français des Lumières', *Mélanges de l'école française de Rome* 96 (1984): 1051–1077.

Rech, Walter, 'History and Normativity: Vico's "Natural Law of Nations"', *Journal of the History of International Law* 17 (2015): 147–169.

Rech, Walter, *Enemies of Mankind: Vattel's Theory of Collective Security* (Leiden: Brill, 2013).

Regolamento dell'Archiginnasio romano (Roma: Camera Apostolica, 1788).

Renazzi, Filippo Maria, *Storia dell'Università degli Studi di Roma detta comunemente la Sapienza* (Roma: Pagliarini, 1803–1806).

San Mauro, Carla, 'Gian Vincenzo Gravina', in *Dizionario Biografico degli Italiani* (Roma: Istituto dell'Enciclopedia Italiana, 2002), vol. 58, 756–764.

San Mauro, Carla, *Gianvincenzo Gravina giurista e politico* (Milano: FrancoAngeli, 2006).

Scarpato, Giovanni, *Giambattista Vico dall'età delle riforme alla Restaurazione. La Scienza nuova tra Lumi e cultura cattolica, 1744–1827* (Roma: Aracne, 2018).

Scattola, Merio, 'Protestantesimo e diritto naturale cattolico nel XVIII secolo', in *Illuminismo e protestantesimo*, ed. Giulia Cantarutti and Stefano Ferrari (Milano: FrancoAngeli, 2010), 131–148.

Scattola, Merio, *Dalla virtù alla scienza. La fondazione e la trasformazione della disciplina politica nell'età moderna* (Milano: FrancoAngeli, 2002).

Spano, Nicola, *L'Università di Roma* (Roma: Mediterranea, 1935).

Stapelbroek, Koen, *Commercio, passioni e mercato. Napoli nell'Europa del Settecento* (Milano: FrancoAngeli, 2020).

Stapelbroek, Koen, *Love, Self-Deceit, and Money: Commerce and Morality in the Early Neapolitan Enlightenment* (Toronto: University of Toronto Press, 2008).

The Law of Nations and Natural Law 1625–1800, ed. Simone Zurbuchen (Leiden: Brill, 2019).

Tinto, Alberto, 'Giovanni Komarek tipografo a Roma nei secoli XVII–XVIII e i suoi campionari di caratteri', *La Bibliofilia* 75 (1973): 189–225.

Venturi, Franco, 'Elementi e tentativi di riforma nello stato pontificio del Settecento', *Rivista Storica Italiana* 4 (1963): 778–817.

Venturi, Franco, *L'antichità svelata e l'idea del progresso in N. A. Boulanger, 1722–1759* (Bari: Laterza, 1947).

Waldmann, Felix, 'Natural Law and the Chair of Ethics in the University of Naples, 1703–1769', *Modern Intellectual History* 19 (2022): 54–80.

Zucchi, Enrico, 'Tirannide e stato di natura. Sul rifiuto dell'assolutismo giusnaturalista nelle *Tragedie Cinque* di Gian Vincenzo Gravina', in *Prima e dopo il Leviatano*, ed. Merio Scattola and Paolo Scotton (Padova: Cleup, 2014), 193–226.

CHAPTER 3

The Teaching of Natural Law and Universal Public Law at the University of Pavia in the Late Eighteenth Century

Elisabetta Fiocchi Malaspina

1 Introduction

For the teaching of natural law and universal public law at the University of Pavia, the second half of the eighteenth century was a crucial period. Between 1771 and 1773, the Habsburg university reforms gave a decisive impetus to radical change in the university's organization and curricula of the faculty of law.[1]

Important studies have dealt not only with the University of Pavia but especially with its faculty of law in this period. Maria Carla Zorzoli dedicated several of her writings to the study and transcription of primary sources, such as the legal theses in *utroque iure* discussed between 1772 and 1796, which are preserved at the State Archives of Pavia.[2] Maria Gigliola di Renzo Villata described in numerous essays the organization of the law faculty, taking into consideration the projects for academic reform, the jurists and their training in Lombardy during the eighteenth century.[3]

---

1 For a complete overview of the history of the University of Pavia, particularly between the eighteenth and nineteenth centuries, see the important volumes edited by Dario Mantovani, *Almum Studium Papiense. Storia dell'Università di Pavia* (Milano: Cisalpino Istituto Editoriale Universitario, 2012–2020).

2 Maria Carla Zorzoli, *Le tesi legali all'Università di Pavia nell'età delle riforme: 1772–1796* (Milano: Istituto Editoriale Cisalpino-La Goliardica, 1980); ead., 'La formazione dei giuristi lombardi nell'età di Maria Teresa: il ruolo dell'Università', in *Economia, istituzioni, cultura in Lombardia nell'età di Maria Teresa*, vol. 3, *Istituzioni e società*, ed. Aldo de Maddalena, Ettore Rotelli and Gennaro Barbarisi (Bologna: Il Mulino, 1982), 743–769; ead., 'L'Università di Pavia (1535–1796). L'organizzazione dello studio', in *Storia di Pavia, IV: L'età spagnola e austriaca* (Milano: Banca del Monte di Lombardia, 1995), vol. 1, 427–481; ead., 'La Facoltà di Giurisprudenza nell'Università di Pavia (1535–1796)', in *Studi di Storia del Diritto* (Milano: Giuffrè, 1996), vol. 1, 483–516.

3 Maria Gigliola di Renzo Villata, 'Diritto, didattica e riforme nella Pavia settecentesca tra tradizione manoscritta e testi a stampa', in *Dalla pecia all'e-book. Libri per l'Università: stampa, editoria, circolazione e lettura. Atti del Convegno internazionale di studi. Bologna, 21–25 ottobre 2008*, ed. Gian Paolo Brizzi and Maria Gioia Tavoni (Bologna: Clueb, 2009),

Following these important research projects, this contribution aims to analyse the establishment of the chair of natural law and universal public law immediately after the Habsburg reform became effective. This chair will be examined in its wider context by reconstructing the phases prior to its official establishment, and also considered in detail with regard to the reform plans adopted between 1771 and 1773. Attention will also be given to the influence of the teaching of natural law theories on sovereign rulers, on those who carried out the reform, on the professors in charge and on the students of the faculty of law.

Jean Baptiste Noël de Saint Clair was professor of natural and public law at the University of Pavia from 1769 to 1796. His long teaching career enables us to analyse and critically reconstruct his choices of legal sources, topics and textbooks for his lectures on natural law and the law of nations. The manuscript notes of his lectures, titled *Institutiones iuris naturalis et iuris publici universalis*[4] and *Institutiones iuris naturalis*,[5] still unpublished and preserved at the University Library of Pavia, will form part of this investigation.

Saint Clair's lectures on natural law and universal public law were the starting point for the reflections of the former Jesuit, professor of metaphysics at the University of Pavia, Andrea Draghetti, and we will return to Draghetti and his treatise titled *Ethica societatis jesu elucubrata duo in volumina divisa, quorum unum generalem, alterum specialem amplectitur* (1818).

The circulation of the theories of natural law and public law in the northern part of the Italian peninsula was marked by the continuous and incessant

---

297–329. See also ead., '1740–1765: un declino inarrestabile? Il Senato milanese "recalcitrante" tra misure riformistiche di ripiego e modesti segni di rinnovamento dell'Ateneo pavese' and '1765–1771: Gli anni decisivi per la riforma. Dall'incubazione ai risultati', in *Almum Studium Papiense*, vol. 2.1, 63–82, 83–114. And also ead., 'Tra Vienna, Milano e Pavia: un piano per un'università "dall'antico lustro assai decaduta" (1753–1773)', in *Gli statuti universitari: tradizione dei testi e valenze politiche. Atti del Convegno internazionale di studi, Messina-Milazzo, 13–18 aprile 2004*, ed. Andrea Romano (Bologna: Clueb, 2007), 507–546; ead., 'Le droit public en Lombardie au XVIIIe siècle et l'Europe', in *Science politique et droit public dans les facultés de droit européennes (XIIIe–XVIIIe siècle)*, ed. Jacques Krynen and Michael Stolleis (Frankfurt am Main: Klostermann, 2008), 583–612; ead., 'Introduzione. La formazione del giurista in Italia e l'influenza culturale europea tra Sette e Ottocento: il caso della Lombardia', in *Formare il giurista. Esperienze nell'area lombarda tra Sette e Ottocento*, ed. Maria Gigliola di Renzo Villata (Milano: Giuffrè, 2004), 1–106.

4 Jean Baptiste Noël de Saint Clair, *Institutiones iuris naturalis et iuris publici universalis*, 1784–1785, MS, Biblioteca Universitaria di Pavia, Manoscritti Aldini, 265.

5 Jean Baptiste Noël de Saint Clair, *Institutiones iuris naturalis*, MS, Biblioteca Universitaria di Pavia, Manoscritti Aldini, 208.

work of professors who, in accordance with royal directives, adopted textbooks and preferred authors such as Pufendorf, Wolff and Heineccius, either translated into Italian or re-edited in the same language. This chapter will demonstrate how natural law and universal public law theories at various levels assumed an important role in the training of jurists in eighteenth-century Lombardy.

2 The First Half of the Eighteenth Century in Pavia: Venanzio de Mays and the Teaching of *Iuris publici et civilis*

In the first half of the eighteenth century, the University of Pavia experienced a difficult period, with low student enrolment, insufficient financial resources and strong competition from neighbouring universities. One such was the University of Turin, to which the Constitution of 1729 had given a new order, enabling it to attract more students.[6]

In an endeavour to put an end to this difficult situation, the Senate of Milan was appointed to direct the University. In 1730, the Senate invited the *Podestà* (the chief civic magistrate) of Pavia to prepare a report concerning a series of interventions that would improve the 'good government' of the University. The *Podestà* suggested a change in the faculty of law and particularly in the organization of legal studies.[7] In 1741, there were no chairs of natural and public law, and these subjects did not even appear in the curricula.[8]

In 1742, the number of professorships for civil law was drastically reduced and the professorship of public law was established,[9] while in 1747, the chair of legal history was created.[10] Venanzio de Mays was appointed professor of public law in 1742, a chair titled 'ad lecturam iuris publici et civilis'.[11] He taught this subject until 1772.[12] His lectures were deemed 'worthy of the common

6 Baldo Peroni, 'La riforma dell'Università di Pavia nel Settecento', in *Contributi alla storia dell'Università di Pavia: pubblicati nell'XI centenario dell'Ateneo* (Pavia: Tipografia cooperativa, 1925), 115–174, at 120.

7 Ibid., 125.

8 Ibid., 121.

9 Ibid., 125.

10 Zorzoli, *Le tesi legali all'Università di Pavia*, 15.

11 Maria Gigliola di Renzo Villata, 'De Mays Venanzio', in *Dizionario Biografico dei Giuristi Italiani* (*XII–XX secolo*), ed. Italo Birocchi et al. (Bologna: Il Mulino, 2013), vol. 1, 304–305; Zorzoli, *Le tesi legali all'Università di Pavia*, 18.

12 *Memorie e documenti per la storia dell'Università di Pavia e degli uomini più illustri che v'insegnarono* (Pavia: Stabilimento Tipografico-Librario Successori Bizzoni, 1878), 97.

applause',[13] although, as Maria Rosa di Simone points out, they were 'traditionalist' and based essentially on natural and Roman law.[14]

In 1738, de Mays published a treatise titled *Institutiones juris naturae et gentium ad usum cupidae legum juventutis singulis titulis institutionum juris civilis accomodatae excellentissimo Mediolanensi senatui nuncupatae*.[15] The sources used in this text ranged from Latin and religious texts to the authors of legal humanism, such as Jacques Cujas (described as 'the most erudite') and Budé, to works on natural law, such as *De iure belli ac pacis* and *Mare liberum* of Grotius and *De iure naturae et gentium* of Samuel Pufendorf.[16] There are also references to the *Elementa iuris naturae et gentium* of Heineccius, to *De legibus* of Suarez, as well as several references to Vincenzo Gravina, especially to his *De ortu et progressu iuris civilis*.[17] De Mays clarified that the theories of Pufendorf,

13 Pietro Ballerini, *Il metodo di S. Agostino negli studj* (Milano: Giuseppe Galeazzi, 1772), 48.

14 Maria Rosa di Simone, 'L'Unità d'Italia e l'insegnamento del diritto pubblico all'Università di Roma', *Annali di storia delle università italiane* 18 (2014): 301–312, at 302; di Renzo Villata, '1740–1765: un declino inarrestabile?', 64. See also Maria Rosa di Simone, 'I curricula giuridici', in *Le università napoleoniche. Uno spartiacque nella storia italiana ed europea dell'istruzione superiore. Atti del Convegno internazionale di studi, Padova-Bologna 13–15 settembre 2006*, ed. Piero Del Negro and Luigi Pepe (Bologna: Clueb, 2008), 145–167.

15 Venanzio de Mays, *Institutiones juris naturae et gentium ad usum cupidae legum juventutis singulis titulis institutionum juris civilis accomodatae excellentissimo Mediolanensi senatui nuncupatae* (Mediolani: Ex typographia Josephi Pandulphi Malatesta, 1738).

16 Di Renzo Villata, 'De Mays Venanzio', 304–305. This happened eighteen years before the first Italian translation, by Giovambattista Almici, of Samuel von Pufendorf, *Il diritto della natura e delle genti o sia sistema generale de' principii li più importanti di morale, giurisprudenza, e politica, rettificato, accresciuto, e illustrato da Giovambattista Almici* (Venezia: Pietro Valvasense, 1757–1759). For the reception of Pufendorf in Italy, see Chapter 6 of the present volume, by Serena Luzzi. See also Diego Panizza, 'La traduzione italiana del "De iure naturae" di Pufendorf: giusnaturalismo moderno e cultura cattolica nel Settecento', *Studi Veneziani* 11 (1969): 483–528; Maurizio Bazzoli, 'Almici e la diffusione di Pufendorf nel Settecento Italiano', *Critica Storica* 16 (1979): 3–100; idem, 'Aspetti della recezione di Pufendorf nel Settecento italiano', in *Dal "De Jure Naturae et gentium" di Samuel Pufendorf alla codificazione prussiana del 1794. Atti del convegno internazionale, Padova, 25–26 ottobre 2001*, ed. Marta Ferronato (Padova: Cedam, 2005), 41–60; Diego Quaglioni, 'Pufendorf in Italia. Appunti e notizie della prima diffusione della traduzione italiana del *De iure naturae et gentium*', *Il Pensiero Politico* 32 (1999): 235–250; Stefania Stoffella, 'Assolutismo e diritto naturale in Italia nel Settecento', *Annali dell'Istituto storico italo-germanico* 26 (2000): 137–175; ead., 'Il diritto di resistenza nel Settecento Italiano. Documenti per la storia della traduzione del *De iure naturae et gentium* di Pufendorf', *Laboratoire italien: Politique et société* 2 (2001): 173–199, http://laboratoireitalien.revues.org/261 (accessed 28 September 2019). Concerning the reception of Grotius in Italy, see *La recezione di Grozio a Napoli nel Settecento*, ed. Vittorio Conti (Florence: Centro Editoriale Toscano, 2002), and Chapter 5 of the present volume, by Girolamo Imbruglia.

17 Di Renzo Villata, 'De Mays Venanzio', 304.

Selden and Grotius were considered only when they were functional and useful in the context and did not conflict with the doctrine of the Church.[18]

De Mays was of fundamental importance for his introduction of a way of teaching inspired by the *mos gallicus*, in contrast to the *mos italicus*, predominant in the Italian peninsula at the time.[19] These humanistic currents, as Italo Birocchi rightly pointed out, entered into the academic legal discourse, creating an opening for discussion of legal issues, the relationship between citizens and the state and, above all, how civil society should be governed.[20] De Mays, in fact, is a key figure in understanding to what extent the *mos gallicus* current of thought influenced the creation of a new programme of studies in the faculty of law and the introduction of a specific chair of natural and universal public law.[21]

In 1757 a first plan of reform was drawn up, with the aim of modifying the order of studies, for example by reducing the number of chairs considered 'superfluous', regulating the admission of students and giving teaching assignments to illustrious professors.[22] On 24 November 1765, Maria Theresa established a Council of Studies composed of five members whom the director appointed: these included Gian Rinaldo Carli, who was responsible for drafting a reform plan for the studies of mathematics, systematic and experimental physics; Michele Daverio for ecclesiastical studies; and Giuseppe Pecis for logic, metaphysics, rhetoric and oriental languages.[23]

For the faculty of law, senator Nicola Pecci was commissioned to draft the 'Piano degli Studi legali' (legal studies plan) together with the 'Piano generale degli Studi' (general studies plan). Pecci elaborated a highly practical plan with the collaboration of Venanzio de Mays: for the chair of natural law he proposed as textbook Samuel Cocceii's *Dissertationes proemiales XII in quibus principia Grotiana circa ius naturae* […] *ad iustam methodum revocantur*; and for the chair of public law he suggested the themes that should be addressed by the

18 De Mays, *Institutiones juris naturae et gentium*, 5.

19 Italo Birocchi, *Alla ricerca dell'ordine. Fonti e cultura giuridica nell'età moderna* (Torino: Giappichelli, 2002), 319. See also Elio Tavilla, 'Beccaria, l'anti-juriste. Critiques de la culture juridique et résistances aux réformes dans l'Italie du XVIIIe siècle', in *Le bonheur du plus grand nombre. Beccaria et les Lumières*, ed. Philippe Audegean et al. (Lyon: ENS Éditions, 2017), 97–110.

20 Italo Birocchi, *Alla ricerca dell'ordine*, 319.

21 At the time when de Mays taught, Cesare Beccaria was studying law in Pavia. See Chapter 4 of the present volume, by Gabriella Silvestrini.

22 Peroni, 'La riforma dell'Università di Pavia nel Settecento', 126.

23 Ibid.

teacher.[24] Pecci, in fact, distinguished between 'primary' public law – international treaties and their interpretation; diplomacy; status, rights and duties of the ambassador – and 'secondary' public law, which regulated the internal affairs of the nation, illustrating, for example, the different forms of government.[25]

In 1768, Pietro Paolo Giusti stressed in his *Memoria sulla riforma generale degli Studi nella Lombardia austriaca* (report on the general reform of studies in Austrian Lombardy) the need to pay more attention to public and universal public law in order to assert a highly formative means of understanding social rights, forms of government and international relations.[26]

3 Natural Law and Universal Public Law in the 'Piano disciplinare' and the 'Piano scientifico' (1771–1773)

In 1771 Maria Theresa approved the university reform, which was further modified in 1773.[27] This reform plan, described in detail by Zorzoli, consisted of two parts: the first, the 'Piano disciplinare' (disciplinary plan), reorganized the administrative structures of the University of Pavia, while the second, known as the 'Piano scientifico' (scientific plan), regulated the curricula within the individual faculties. The 'Piano scientifico' stipulated that there be annual lectures in natural and universal public law, civil law, legal history and feudal law, criminal law and canon law, while Pandects and treatises of canon law were offered only as biennial lectures.[28]

The Habsburg reform laid the foundation for an enlightened curriculum for the law faculties. As the new statutes put it: 'Security, property, peace and harmony are the most essential and precious goods within societies. They are procured and preserved by the Law, with that most noble Philosophy, based on the intimate knowledge of human heart'.[29]

24 di Renzo Villata, 'Diritto, didattica e riforme nella Pavia settecentesca', 303.

25 Ibid.

26 Ibid., 305.

27 Ibid., 306.

28 Zorzoli, *Le tesi legali all'Università di Pavia*, 25.

29 'La sicurezza, la proprietà, la pace, l'armonia nelle Società sono beni i più essenziali, ed i più preziosi. A procurarli, e conservarli tende la Giurisprudenza colla più nobile Filosofia, fondata sulla intima cognizione del cuore umano': 'Piano scientifico per l'Università di Pavia', in *Statuti e ordinamenti della Università di Pavia dall'anno 1361 all'anno 1859. Raccolti e pubblicati nell'XI centenario dell'Ateneo* (Pavia: Tipografia cooperativa, 1925), 228–255, at 235.

The academic plan was the fruit of contemporary Enlightenment jurisprudence. The reformists regarded the reform as the end of the *mos italicus* from a methodological point of view and as the beginning of legal education oriented towards the 'gradual and universal system of legal principles'.[30] Discussions evolved around which printed books should be used in lessons:[31] at first, in fact, the Habsburg government thought it would suggest the textbooks that professors should use: Chancellor Wenzel Anton von Kaunitz-Rietberg in 1769 wrote to the Minister Plenipotentiary Carlo Gottardo Firmian to suggest that for natural and universal public law, it would be appropriate to choose between *De officio hominis et civis* by Pufendorf and *Elementa iuris naturae et gentium* by Heineccius.[32] However, with the reform, freedom of choice was established: teachers were free to choose a textbook at the beginning of the academic year, and then the teacher's choice was submitted to the governing body and the magistrate of studies.[33]

The scientific plan for the chair of natural and public law expressly stated that the subject was the 'sublime science from which all the foundations of jurisprudence are developed'.[34] Natural law acquired a central role within the Habsburg reform as a subject of practical and preparatory study. In fact, future jurists were expected not only to know the mechanisms of the organization of civil society but also to be prepared to justify the exercise of political authority in society.[35]

In the introduction to natural and public law, moral philosophy was used to outline the existence of human freedom, and the duties of individuals and the relations that are established between people: 'the principles of such relations of men with other men depend on the desire for happiness, the aversion to pain, equality, freedom, equal independence of men among themselves in the original state of Nature'.[36]

This was followed by a discourse on the state of nature, the creation of civil society, contracts, the formation of family and its legal consequences. The

30 di Renzo Villata, 'Diritto, didattica e riforme nella Pavia settecentesca', 302.

31 Ibid.

32 Peroni, 'La riforma dell'Università di Pavia nel Settecento', 151–152.

33 Ibid. See also Zorzoli, *Le tesi legali all'Università di Pavia*, 13.

34 'scienza sublime colla scorta della quale si sviluppano tutti i fondamenti della giurisprudenza': 'Piano scientifico per l'Università di Pavia', 235–236.

35 Ibid., 236.

36 'i principii di tali rapporti dell'uomo cogli altri Uomini dipendono dal desiderio della felicità, dall'avversione al dolore, dalla uguaglianza, libertà, indipendenza uguale degli Uomini fra loro nello stato originario di Natura'. Ibid., 236.

aim was to analyse natural law by putting aside all 'speculative discussions'[37] that were based on common ideas and sentiments rather than on scientific foundations. In this way, natural law 'becomes a clear compendium of science, easy for anyone to understand'.[38]

Natural law was often introduced through a historical overview in which the different theories of philosophers or jurists over the centuries were presented. This first part, focused on humanity in the state of nature, was followed by the introduction of public law and the formation of civil society, the objectives and rights and duties of individuals as well as the rights and duties of those who govern:

> The duties and rights of the supreme power demand vigilance for the tranquillity and the peace and security of the entire State. They, therefore, require appropriate laws for the direction of the actions of citizens, and for the prevention of crimes, or for punishing them in order to dissuade them through fear of punishment from committing them. They also require the establishment of magistrates, officers, and ministers who administer justice, and the dispositions upon which the good order of judgments, the police, and all that is necessary for the benefit of society depend.[39]

The curriculum also included lessons on the separation of powers and the foundation of legislative, executive and judicial power within the state. This was followed by the analysis of relations between states, introducing the concept of sovereignty, equality and independence, by elaborating on: 'the conventions, treaties and mediations that govern relations between nations, the modalities of wars, peace treaties and trade, privileges, immunities and qualities of the Ministers of the Nations'.[40]

---

37 Ibid.

38 'diviene una scienza chiara e compendiosa, facile a chicchessia'. Ibid., 235.

39 'I doveri e diritti della suprema potestà esigono vigilanza per la tranquillità e la quiete e sicurezza dello Stato in tutta la sua estensione. Richiedono dunque leggi opportune per la direzione delle azioni de' cittadini, e per prevenire i delitti, o per punirli affine d'allontanar col timore della pena dal commetterli. Richiedono ancora la destinazione di magistrati, uffiziali e ministri che amministrino la giustizia, e le disposizioni, dalle quali dipende il buon ordine dei giudizi, la polizia, e tutto ciò che è necessario al vantaggio della società'. Ibid., 235–236.

40 'Si daranno notizie sulle convenzioni, trattati e mediazioni che regolano i rapporti tra le nazioni; le modalità delle guerre, i trattati di pace e di commercio; i privilegi, le immunità e qualità dei Ministri delle Nazioni'. Ibid.

It is interesting to note that professors commonly adopted a very practical approach by including examples to clarify and illustrate the 'abstract theories'.[41]

From a general point of view, the Habsburg reform proposed significant changes in the curricula. The strong focus on natural and universal public law also affected the status of other courses. The course in Roman law, for example, lost its importance and was offered only as an introductory course;[42] criminal law, on the other hand, acquired the status of a separate subject and was directly linked to the principles of public law. As far as canon law was concerned, the course focused on analysing of the relationship between State and Church.[43]

In this period, the texts of Heineccius became central to the teaching of Roman law, the Pandects and civil law. For the course on the Pandects, given by Antonio Filippo Bassiano Bigoni in the academic year 1774–1775, there is an explicit reference in its official programme to 'duce Heineccio',[44] and the textbook for Giuseppe Gaspare Belcredi's lectures was Heineccius' *Antiquitates romanae*.[45] Elia Giardini and Pietro Biffignandi, also lecturers in civil law the late eighteenth and early nineteenth centuries, used Heineccius's *Elementa iuris secundum ordinem Institutionum* and *Elementa iuris secundum ordinem Pandectarum*, 'holding them to be convenient due to order, clarity and brevity'.[46]

4 Jean Baptiste Noël de Saint Clair and *Institutiones iuris naturalis et iuris publici universalis*

Jean Baptiste Noël de Saint Clair was a professor of natural and universal public law at the law faculty of the University of Pavia from 1769 to 1796, a

41 Ibid.

42 'l'uso dei principi di diritto romano fosse inadeguato o addirittura dannoso'. Ibid.

43 Zorzoli, *Le tesi legali all'Università di Pavia*, 33–34.

44 Claudia Bussolino, '1771–1780: La riforma attuata', in *Almum Studium Papiense*, vol. 2.1, 115–128, at 124, n. 71.

45 di Renzo Villata, 'Diritto, didattica e riforme nella Pavia settecentesca', 311.

46 Elisabetta D'Amico, 'La riforma luosiana degli studi giuridici pavesi', in *Giuseppe Luosi, giurista italiano ed europeo. Traduzioni, tradizioni e tradimenti della codificazione. A duecento anni dalla traduzione in italiano del Code Napoléon (1806–2006). Atti del Convegno Internazionale di Studi (Mirandola-Modena, 19–20 ottobre 2006)*, ed. Elio Tavilla (Modena: Archivio Storico Edizioni APM, 2009), 115–139, here particularly 121: 'giudicate assai convenienti per ordine, chiarezza e brevità'.

period coinciding with the introduction of the Habsburg reforms. Through Saint Clair's teaching, it is possible to examine how the Habsburg directives were applied and how they influenced the syllabus of natural and universal public law.[47]

He taught for about thirty years, changing his teaching programme and consequently his textbooks as required. For the academic year 1786–1787, he announced that he would lecture on *Heineccii elementa iuris naturae et gentium secundum editionem veneta*.[48] We have no manuscript for those lectures, but for the academic year 1784–1785, we have a manuscript titled *Institutiones iuris naturalis et iuris publici universalis* and another, *Institutiones iuris naturalis*, which was substantially based on the previous work but without the section on public universal law.

In the prolegomenon of *Institutiones iuris naturalis et iuris publici universalis*, he analyses the meaning of natural law, the diversity of human actions in 'internae', 'externae' and 'mixtae', followed by the division between law and obligation, with references to Grotius. Subsequently, the discussion stretches from the meaning of consciousness to the state of nature. Following the prolegomenon, the first part of the manuscript is dedicated to natural law, particularly to man's duties towards God and himself for preservation and perfection.[49]

There follow the duties towards society and the family and duties relating to material things, where Saint Clair dwells on the various ways of acquiring property, focusing on the distinction between *inter vivos* and *mortis causa*. The last section of the first part (on natural law) is dedicated to 'De officiis erga alios quod attinet ad modo, quibus jus suum cuique persequi licet in statu naturali'. He concentrates on duelling and war, where he deals with the

47 For Jean Baptiste Noël de Saint Clair, see di Renzo Villata, 'Diritto, didattica e riforme nella Pavia settecentesca', 317–318. And also ead., 'Introduzione. La formazione del giurista in Italia', 61; ead., 'Un avvocato lombardo tra *ancien régime* e "modernità": Giovanni Margarita', in *Avvocati e avvocatura nell'Italia dell'Ottocento*, ed. Antonio Padoa Schioppa (Bologna: Il Mulino, 2009), 425–520, at 438; ead., 'Le droit public en Lombardie au XVIIIe siècle et l'Europe', 593 ff.

48 di Renzo Villata, 'Diritto, didattica e riforme nella Pavia settecentesca', 317–318.

49 Saint Clair, *Institutiones iuris naturalis et iuris publici universalis*, 66–67: 'Quare cum homo ad bona non animi solum, sed etiam corporis, per quae scilicet corpus conservatur, atque perficitur, sibi naturali lege comparanda obligetur, consequens est, ut ad vitam, sine qua conservari corpus non potest, servandam; proindeque ad vitae periculum, nisi majoris boni obtinendi ratio aliud suadeat, declinandum teneatur'.

causes of a lawful war, the definition of the enemy, and offensive and defensive war.[50]

The second part is dedicated to universal public law and starts with a long reflection on civil society in general, its origin and how to obtain governmental power in the form of a republic or monarchy. It then continues by outlining the duties of rulers towards citizens and the duties of citizens.[51]

In the last part of the manuscript, Saint Clair elaborates on the meaning of the law of nations, following Wolff's definition – later taken up by Vattel – that understood the law of nations as natural law applied to relations between states. Following Wolff's distinction between the concepts of the necessary, voluntary and customary law of nations, he illustrates in detail his theory of the 'civitas maxima'.[52] With regard to the concepts of equality, sovereignty and independence of states, he refers directly to Vattel, whom he cites as 'Watelius', and describes his positions as 'acute'.[53] The lessons continue with the absolute duties of states, which derive from natural law, the hypothetical duties 'quae ex dominorum, ac territorium distinctione oriuntur' and the voluntary duties that arise from the signing of an international treaty. A specific section is devoted to the amicable settlement of disputes between states, with implicit references to Vattel's *Droit des gens*.[54]

---

50 di Renzo Villata, 'Diritto, didattica e riforme nella Pavia settecentesca', 317–318; Saint Clair, *Institutiones iuris naturalis et iuris publici universalis*, 148: 'Et quia ex dictis patet iustam belli causam in sola inesse mali repulsione, aut reparatione, sequitur perinde esse sive per errorem, sive per dementiam, ac furorem, sive per malitiam hujusmodi malum, aut periculum nobis obveniat. Bellum autem ad solam vindictam susceptam consistere non posse cum interno illo amore, quo etiam inimicos a nobis prosequendos esse, jam alibi demostravimus'.

51 Ibid., 157 ff.

52 Ibid., 157 ff.

53 Saint Clair wrote: 'Ex quo fit, ut duo etiam populi inter se naturali libertate gaudere intelligantur, quamvis uni, eidemque summo imperanti obnoxii sint, si suas quisque separatas rationes habeat, suisque peculiaribus utatur legibus fundamentalis, quemadmodum acute animadvertit Watelius'. Ibid., 237.

54 In chapter 18 of the second book, Vattel specifies that 'the disputes that arise between nations or their rulers originate either from contested rights or from injuries received. A nation ought to preserve the rights which belong to her; and the care of her own safety and glory forbids her to submit to injuries'. He specifically underlines the maxims of the law of nations respecting the mode of terminating disputes between different states, focusing on amicable accommodation, compromise, mediation, arbitration and conference and congresses: Emer de Vattel, *The Law of Nations, or Principles of the Law of Nature, Applied to the Conduct and Affairs of Nations and Sovereigns, with Three Early Essays on the Origin and Nature of Natural Law and on Luxury*, ed. Béla Kapossy and Richard Whatmore (Indianapolis, IN: Liberty Fund, 2008), book II, ch. 18, § 323 ff., 448 ff.

Saint Clair ended his *Institutiones iuris naturalis et iuris publici universalis* with a section on international peace treaties, 'de pace et pacis pactione', and a paragraph on ambassadors, 'de legationibus', where he embraced Vattel's theories concerning the 'representative character' of ambassadors and the ensuing ranking of different kinds of ministers, as well as the right to send ambassadors and the honours due to ambassadors.[55]

It is relevant that the former Jesuit Andrea Draghetti (1736–1825) was strongly influenced by Saint Clair's *Institutiones*. Draghetti had joined the Society of Jesus in 1752 and had been a professor of metaphysics at the imperial college of Brera in Milan, where he was considered 'one of the brightest and sharpest minds of that academic environment'.[56] In 1773, with the suppression of the Society of Jesus, he had lost his chair at Brera; thereafter he taught for a short time in Novara and in 1778 was appointed to teach logic and metaphysics at the University of Pavia.[57]

Inspired by Saint Clair, Draghetti published in 1818 a work titled *Ethica societatis jesu elucubrata duo in volumina divisa, quorum unum generalem, alterum specialem amplectitur*. The first volume is dedicated to the *Ethica generalis*, where he divides his examination into natural law, public law and the law of nations; in the second volume, titled *Ethica specialis*, the object of analysis is the passions, virtues and vices, and happiness, and here Draghetti takes

55 Saint Clair, *Institutiones iuris naturalis et iuris publici universalis*, 279–280. In chapter 6 of book IV of his *Law of Nations*, 'Of the several Orders of public Ministers, – of the representative Character, – and of the Honours due to Ministers', Vattel declares 'what is, by way of pre-eminence, called the *representative character*, is the faculty possessed by the minister, of representing his master even in his very person and dignity' (Vattel, *The Law of Nations*, book IV, ch. 6, § 70, 691), going on to say, 'the representative character, so termed by way of pre-eminence, or in contradistinction to other kinds of representation, constitutes the minister of the first rank, the ambassador' (§ 71). Vattel distinguished between ordinary and extraordinary ambassadors, a dichotomy dictated by reasons inherent in their missions (ibid.). Under them were the *envoys*, without any power of representation as such, and so ministers on a second level (§ 73, 692). The third level, the *residents*, represented the person of the sovereign not in his dignity but only in his affairs (ibid.). According to Vattel, owing to ceremonial complexity, another figure had been created, with no particular determination of character: the *minister*, charged with representing the sovereign in an unspecified manner (§ 74, 692). The plenipotentiary minister, lastly, although 'without any particular determination of character', had in practice acquired a role immediately inferior to that of ambassador (ibid.).

56 'una delle menti più profonde e acute dell'ambiente scolastico milanese': Mauro Bucarelli, 'Draghetti, Andrea', in *Dizionario Biografico degli Italiani* (Roma: Istituto dell'Enciclopedia Italiana, 1992), vol. 41, 629–630.

57 Ibid.

a strong position against Kant's metaphysics and ideas of the relationship between philosophy and religion.[58]

If we carefully compare the two texts, it is possible to see that Draghetti's first volume, *Ethica generalis*, is mostly a transcription of the *Institutiones iuris naturalis et iuris publici universalis* of Saint Clair, with additions and modifications. In the introduction to the volume, Draghetti says that he followed the 'Manuscriptis Ticinensi Athenæo'.[59] Compared with Saint Clair, Draghetti in most cases eliminates the titles of the various paragraphs; in others, he changes titles or subtitles; he also often refers to Grotius, Hobbes and Barbeyrac, while Saint Clair only makes implicit references to them.[60]

There are no sources to substantiate that Saint Clair corresponded with Draghetti, despite the similarity of their manuscripts. Draghetti eventually acquired a greater reputation than Saint Clair. In 1783 he entered the royal courts as a tutor to the sons of Archduke Ferdinand Charles Anthony, governor of Lombardy, and later he taught philosophy to the future Duke of Modena, Francis IV, to whom he would always remain attached.[61]

5 Juridical Theses on Natural and Universal Public Law

An interesting aspect of the Habsburg reform plan and its practical application, as far as concerns the law faculty and the teaching of natural and public law, is the public discussion of theses.[62] Zorzoli has perceptively observed that analysis of these arguments allows us to reconstruct how the reform was applied in practice. While scholarly demands had specified the syllabus in

58 Andrea Draghetti, *Ethica societatis jesu elucubrataduo in volumina divisa, quorum unum generalem, alterum specialem amplectitur* (Regii: Davolium, 1818), vol. 2, '*Ethica specialis*, sect. III, cap. III, 474 ff.

59 'Triplex inde habetur Ethicæ generalis pars, eodem ordine pertractanda. Præ ceteris, qui tripartitam materiam hanc pro Tyronibus nuperrime pertractarunt, Sanclerium sequemur in *Manuscriptis Ticinensi Athenæo* publice ab eo traditis; quibus tamen addere, demere, refragari, subrogare liberum nobis esse volumus, quotiescumque ratio ulla probabilis id suadeat, ut constabit infra'. Draghetti, *Ethica*, vol. 1, *Ethica generalis*. See also *Memorie e documenti per la storia dell'Università di Pavia*, 309, 468.

60 Draghetti, *Ethica*, 128, 156, 200–201, 230.

61 Bucarelli, 'Draghetti Andrea', 630.

62 Zorzoli, *Le tesi legali all'Università di Pavia*, 37. According to the reform plan, students had to take three exams in order to complete a course: an oral exam on all subjects of teaching in front of all members of the faculty, a written exam and finally the public exam.

great detail, the choice of topics for graduating students appeared decidedly freer.[63]

In line with the programme of Saint Clair's course, his students seemed to prefer for their theses a great variety of authors, such as Grotius, Pufendorf, Heineccius and Voet, as well as Thomasius and Wolff.[64] The topics of theses in natural and public law largely included the social contract, the state of nature, the origin of civil society, and the justification of the rights and duties of the sovereign to intervene in civil society.[65]

On 22 June 1775, candidate Rocco Marliani rejected the state of nature theorized by Hobbes as a state of war, arguing instead that peace naturally prevailed.[66] On 14 June 1776, Antonio Maria Sesti also discussed whether the 'status belli non est status hominis naturalis' together with civil law topics such as the legal status of minors and the *restitutio in integrum*.[67] On 11 June 1777, Luigi Rusca made an analysis of the law of love as the only principle of natural law, as proposed by Heineccius.[68] This topic was also taken up on 18 May1790, by Francesco Predabissi, who focused on the connection between human actions and benevolence.[69] On 14 June 1790, Camillo Renati discussed the positions of Pufendorf and Grotius with regard to the conclusion of contracts; two days later, Gaspare Visconti compared the theories of Hobbes with those of Rousseau on the state of nature.[70]

As far as public law was concerned, most of the graduating students dealt with issues relating to the legitimacy of war: Siro Quarti discussed on 13 June 1777 'ut bellum sit legitimum, belli indictio non est necessaria'[71] and on the same day Francesco Zutti discussed the lawfulness of reprisals.[72] Numerous theses examined the lawfulness of war in general and of religious wars in particular. For example, on 20 June 1785, Francesco Carloni considered 'Iniustum est bellum quod populus popolo indicit ut avitam religionem deieret et propriam amplectatur',[73] while on 30 May 1789, Andrea Castelli contested the doctrines that legitimized war for religious reasons.[74]

63 Ibid., 62.
64 Ibid.
65 Ibid.
66 'Theses in utroque iure', in Zorzoli, *Le tesi legali all'Università di Pavia*, 95, n. 13.
67 Ibid., 103, n. 12.
68 Ibid., 112–113, n. 7.
69 Ibid., 316, n. 14.
70 Ibid., 324, n. 41.
71 Ibid., 114, n. 11.
72 Ibid., 114, n. 13.
73 Ibid., 237–238, n. 35.
74 Ibid., 303, n. 36.

In line with natural law thinking and recent theories on the law of nations, students were called upon to take a stand also on issues such as the form of declarations of war,[75] the killing of prisoners,[76] immunities of ambassadors,[77] as well as the treatment of enemies,[78] the spoils of war,[79] the use of poison[80] and of gunpowder,[81] and compensation for the damage caused by war.[82] Many of the discussions also concerned trade issues: the freedom to trade,[83] interventions aimed at its limitation by the Prince,[84] and monopoly,[85] with particular attention to trade with foreigners[86] and with enemies.[87]

6 Conclusions: Natural Law, Universal Public Law, and the Law of Nations in Pavia in the First Half of the Nineteenth Century

The teaching of natural law and universal public law had a significant impact on the training of Lombard jurists. Lombard lawyers referred to the theories of natural law and the law of nations learned at university, quoting them, for example, in their *Allegationes*.[88] The questions of natural law and universal public law had already been discussed thirty years before the constitution of the chair in those subjects. As we have seen, Venanzio de Mays, participating in the plan drawn up by Pecci, helped to identify significant elements that characterized the academic reform. Mays's inclination towards *mos gallicus* inevitably led him to conceive academic teaching differently from how it had been in the past: the choice of textbooks by the professors indicated their preference for the theories of natural law and the law of nations and for clear

75 Ibid., 342, n. 51.

76 Ibid., 207, n. 46.

77 Ibid., 268, n. 22.

78 Ibid., 266, n. 13.

79 Ibid., 234, n. 22; 281–281, n. 9.

80 Ibid., 401, n. 43.

81 Ibid., 329, n. 7: 'Pulveris pirii usum satis non congrum jure naturae et gentium, et bono exercituum esse propugnamus'.

82 Ibid., 354, n. 51.

83 Ibid., 106, n. 22.

84 Ibid., 213, n. 7.

85 Ibid., 415, n. 15.

86 Ibid., 262–263, n. 3.

87 Ibid., 344, n. 54.

88 The interest in Vattel's theories in the Milanese legal context is also found in references in the *Allegationes*; see di Renzo Villata, 'Introduzione. La formazione del giurista in Italia', 64 ff.

treatises suitable for an audience of students, works successfully used also in other European and other Italian contexts.

In his lectures, Jean Baptiste Noël de Saint Clair did not hesitate to offer students a broader overview of the different theories on natural law, universal public law and the law of nations. In addition, he explained to his students how the discipline was currently characterized by continuous cultural and social interconnections from several European contexts, stressing how it was taught, circulated and adapted.

The teaching of natural law and universal public law took shape in an academic context characterized by the rigid rules established by the Habsburg reform. However, a unique space was created for professors as well as students, in which Saint Clair could teach natural law and generally enlightened jurisprudence, which was taken up by his students in their legal theses.

Subsequent reforms and governmental changes eventually separated natural law from universal public law and the law of nations. In the Napoleonic period, in fact, the 'Piano di Studj e di disciplina per le Università nazionali' (the plan of studies and discipline for national universities) of 31 October 1803 divided studies into three categories: mathematics and physics (in fact, all natural sciences), moral and political science (all social sciences, including law) and literature.[89]

For the course in moral philosophy and natural law, a programme was envisaged that focused on the traditional scheme of duties towards God, towards fellow men and towards oneself. Moral philosophy 'has its foundations in the natural faculties of man himself, from the exercise of which the intellectual and moral virtues are born, which are the means for preserving happiness'.[90] An essential part was devoted to the inalienable rights of man with regard to

---

89 *Foglio Officiale della Repubblica Italiana*, n. 1–15 (Milano: Dalla Reale Stamperia, 1803), 155–179. For the law faculty of the University of Pavia at the beginning of the nineteenth century, see Elisabetta D'Amico, 'La facoltà giuridica pavese dalla riforma francese all'Unità', *Annali di Storia delle università italiane* 7 (2003): 111–126. See also Luciano Muselli, 'La Facoltà di Giurisprudenza nell'Ottocento', in *Storia di Pavia, v: L'età moderna e contemporanea* (Milano: Banca Regionale Europea, 2000), 445–475; idem, 'I docenti della Facoltà giuridica pavese tra Cattolicesimo e Liberalismo', *Annali di Storia Pavese* 22–23 (1995): 459–464; idem, 'Da Tamburini a Foscolo: la facoltà legale pavese tra didattica giuridica e suggestioni di cultura globale', *Annali di storia pavese* 20 (1991): 91–101.

90 'doveri che ha l'uomo verso Dio, verso i suoi simili, e verso sé stesso, [la filosofia morale] ha i suoi fondamenti nelle facoltà naturali dell'uomo stesso, dall'esercizio delle quali nascono le virtu' intellettuali e morali, che sono i mezzi per conservare la felicità': 'Piano di Studj e di disciplina per le Università nazionali', in *Statuti e ordinamenti della Università di Pavia dall'anno 1361*, 284–285.

himself, to family and society. The course on public law and the law of nations was focused on international customs, pacts, alliance treaties, trade treaties and the illustration of theories on just war and peace negotiations.[91]

The 'Classe delle Scienze morali e politiche' included a chair of history and diplomacy. History was defined as 'the repository of the success that legislation, customs and institutions had among the various nations',[92] while the course on diplomacy analysed the various international treaties concluded throughout history, with particular attention paid to the principles contained in them, as well as to the 'spirit of them'.[93]

The course on public law and the law of nations was considered to cover a 'broad and important subject',[94] encompassing the study of international treaties and the theories concerning just and unjust wars. Public law, in fact, 'is what comes from the governing power of a great society of men, that is, a population. This power, conferred upon one or more men, constitutes the various forms of Governments, from which they issue laws limiting the Authorities, duties, and reciprocal rights of Magistrates and Citizens, and restricting or restraining social upheavals with the force entrusted to the governing power'.[95]

The special chair of public law and the law of nations, introduced by the Napoleonic reform, was given to Gabba in 1803–1804 and the following years to Abbot Giuseppe Prina,[96] who became director of the prestigious College of

91 Ibid., 285.

92 'Essa è il deposito del successo, ch'ebbero tra le varie Nazioni le legislazioni, i costumi, gl'istituti'. Ibid.

93 Ibid.

94 Ibid.

95 'è quello che deriva dalla potestà reggente una grande società di uomini, cioè una popolazione. Questa potestà, riposta in uno o più uomini, costituisce le varie forme de' Governi, dai quali emanano le leggi che limitano le Autorità, i doveri, i diritti reciproci de' Magistrati e de' Cittadini, e comprimono o frenano con la forza affidata al potestà reggente i turbamenti della società'. Ibid.

96 His cousin and namesake, appointed by Napoleon as finance minister of the Kingdom of Italy (1805–1814), was killed during the popular uprisings of 20 April 1814. Abbot Prina had arrived that day from Pavia to bring him to safety, disguising him as a priest. Minister Prina underestimated the gravity of the situation and remained in Milan. Alessandro Manzoni witnessed the tragic event, which also inspired his *Betrothed*. The 'attack on the bakers' ovens' illustrated in chapter 12 of the novel is undoubtedly inspired by the massacre of Prina. For the Abbot Prina and his cousin, see Luigi Ratti, *Il ministro Prina cento anni dopo la sua morte, su documenti e particolari inediti* (Milano: Vallardi, 1914), 37. Minister Prina graduated from Pavia on 12 May 1787, and was considered a brilliant student. The choice of themes for his public discussions ranged over criminal and civil law to natural law and universal public law (*Socialia officia tum privata tum publica ex commiseratione deduci omnia possunt*): 'Theses in utroque iure', in Zorzoli, *Le tesi legali all'Università di Pavia*, 265, n. 11.

Caccia in Pavia and used Lampredi's *Theoremata juris publici universalis* for his lectures during his career as professor.[97]

The chair of natural law had a different fate: it was assigned to the Jansenist abbot Pietro Tamburini (1737–1827) from 1797 to 1818. Tamburini had previously had other posts and was a professor at the University of Pavia for a total of more than forty years. Tamburini published his lectures on moral philosophy, natural and public law, and these seven volumes represent an important source for tracing the development of the discipline of natural law at the beginning of the nineteenth century, as well as the interconnections between natural law and Enlightenment theories.[98]

Archival Sources

Biblioteca Universitaria di Pavia, Manoscritti Aldini, 208 and 265.

Bibliography

Almum Studium Papiense. Storia dell'Università di Pavia, ed. Dario Mantovani (Milano: Cisalpino Istituto Editoriale Universitario, 2012–2020).

---

97 D'Amico, 'La facoltà giuridica pavese dalla riforma francese', 112 ff.

98 These volumes were published between 1803 and 1812: Pietro Tamburini, *Introduzione allo studio della Filosofia morale col Prospetto di un corso della medesima dei diritti dell'Uomo, e delle Società del cittadino abb. Pietro Tamburini professore sulla università di Pavia, membro del Collegio elettorale dei dotti, e Direttore del Collegio Nazionale. Tomo I contenente la Introduzione, e la I parte del Prospetto* (Pavia: Eredi di Pietro Galeazzi, 1803) and the last volume *Continuazione delle lezioni di Filosofia morale e di naturale e sociale diritto. Tomo VII e ultimo* (Pavia: Eredi di Pietro Galeazzi, 1812). Alberto Carrera has recently reconstructed his impact on the legal culture of Lombardy, *Pietro Tamburini 'Giurista'. Per una storia della cultura giuridica giansenista italiana* (PhD diss., University of Milan, 2015), https://irlh.unimi.it/?page_id=984&lang=it (accessed 28 September 2019). See also Pietro Stella, 'Pietro Tamburini nel quadro del giansenismo italiano', in *Pietro Tamburini e il giansenismo lombardo. Atti del Convegno internazionale in occasione del 250° della nascita (Brescia, 25–26 maggio 1989)*, ed. Paolo Corsini and Daniele Montanari (Brescia: Morcelliana, 1993), 193; Paola Vismara, 'Pietro Tamburini e il "dispotismo pontificio"', in *Il giansenismo e l'Università di Pavia. Studi in ricordo di Pietro Stella*, ed. Simona Negruzzo (Milano: Giuffrè, 2012), 95–114; Dale K. Van Kley, 'From the Catholic Enlightenment to the Risorgimento: The Exchange Between Nicola Spedalieri and Pietro Tamburini, 1791–1797', *Past & Present* 224(1) (2014): 109–162; Alberto Carrera, 'Dalla tolleranza religiosa alla "libertà del pensare". La riflessione dell'abate giansenista Pietro Tamburini (1737–1827), docente alla università di Pavia', *Italian Review of Legal History* 2 (2017): 1–16.

Ballerini, Pietro, *Il metodo di S. Agostino negli studj* (Milano: Giuseppe Galeazzi, 1772).

Bazzoli, Maurizio, 'Almici e la diffusione di Pufendorf nel Settecento Italiano', *Critica Storica* 16 (1979): 3–100.

Bazzoli, Maurizio, 'Aspetti della recezione di Pufendorf nel Settecento italiano', in *Dal 'De Jure Naturae et gentium' di Samuel Pufendorf alla codificazione prussiana del 1794. Atti del convegno internazionale, Padova, 25–26 ottobre 2001*, ed. Marta Ferronato (Padova: Cedam, 2005), 41–60.

Birocchi, Italo, *Alla ricerca dell'ordine. Fonti e cultura giuridica nell'età moderna* (Torino: Giappichelli, 2002).

Bucarelli, Mauro, 'Draghetti Andrea', in *Dizionario Biografico degli Italiani* (Roma: Istituto dell'Enciclopedia Italiana, 1992), vol. 41, 629–630.

Bussolino, Claudia, '1771–1780: La riforma attuata', in *Almum Studium Papiense. Storia dell'Università di Pavia*, vol. 2.1, *Dall'età austriaca alla nuova Italia*, ed. Dario Mantovani (Milano: Cisalpino Istituto Editoriale Universitario, 2015), 115–128.

Carrera, Alberto, 'Dalla tolleranza religiosa alla "libertà del pensare". La riflessione dell'abate giansenista Pietro Tamburini (1737–1827), docente alla università di Pavia', *Italian Review of Legal History* 2 (2017): 1–16, https://irlh.unimi.it/?page_id=984&lang=it (accessed 28 September 2019).

Carrera, Alberto, *Pietro Tamburini 'Giurista'. Per una storia della cultura giuridica giansenista italiana* (PhD diss., University of Milan, 2015).

D'Amico, Elisabetta, 'La facoltà giuridica pavese dalla riforma francese all'Unità', *Annali di Storia delle università italiane* 7 (2003): 111–126.

D'Amico, Elisabetta, 'La riforma luosiana degli studi giuridici pavesi', in *Giuseppe Luosi, giurista italiano ed europeo. Traduzioni, tradizioni e tradimenti della codificazione. A duecento anni dalla traduzione in italiano del Code Napoléon (1806–2006). Atti del Convegno Internazionale di Studi (Mirandola-Modena, 19–20 ottobre 2006)*, ed. Elio Tavilla (Modena: Archivio Storico Edizioni APM, 2009), 115–139.

de Mays, Venanzio, *Institutiones juris naturae et gentium ad usum cupidae legum juventutis singulis titulis institutionum juris civilis accomodatae excellentissimo Mediolanensi senatui nuncupatae* (Mediolani: Ex typographia Josephi Pandulphi Malatesta, 1738).

di Renzo Villata, Maria Gigliola, '1740–1765: un declino inarrestabile? Il Senato milanese "recalcitrante" tra misure riformistiche di ripiego e modesti segni di rinnovamento dell'Ateneo pavese', in *Almum Studium Papiense. Storia dell'Università di Pavia*, vol. 2.1, *Dall'età austriaca alla nuova Italia*, ed. Dario Mantovani (Milano: Cisalpino Istituto Editoriale Universitario, 2015), 63–82.

di Renzo Villata, Maria Gigliola, '1765–1771: Gli anni decisivi per la riforma. Dall'incubazione ai risultati', in *Almum Studium Papiense. Storia dell'Università di Pavia*, vol. 2.1, *Dall'età austriaca alla nuova Italia*, ed. Dario Mantovani (Milano: Cisalpino Istituto Editoriale Universitario, 2015), 83–114.

di Renzo Villata, Maria Gigliola, 'De Mays Venanzio', in *Dizionario Biografico dei Giuristi Italiani (XII–XX secolo)*, ed. Italo Birocchi et al. (Bologna: Il Mulino, 2013), vol. 1, 304–305.

di Renzo Villata, Maria Gigliola, 'Diritto, didattica e riforme nella Pavia settecentesca tra tradizione manoscritta e testi a stampa', in *Dalla pecia all'e-book. Libri per l'Università: stampa, editoria, circolazione e lettura. Atti del Convegno internazionale di studi. Bologna, 21–25 ottobre 2008*, ed. Gian Paolo Brizzi and Maria Gioia Tavoni (Bologna: Clueb, 2009), 297–329.

di Renzo Villata, Maria Gigliola, 'Introduzione. La formazione del giurista in Italia e l'influenza culturale europea tra Sette e Ottocento: il caso della Lombardia', in *Formare il giurista. Esperienze nell'area lombarda tra Sette e Ottocento*, ed. Maria Gigliola di Renzo Villata (Milano: Giuffrè, 2004), 1–106.

di Renzo Villata, Maria Gigliola, 'Le droit public en Lombardie au XVIIIe siècle et l'Europe', in *Science politique et droit public dans les facultés de droit européennes (XIIIe–XVIIIe siècle)*, ed. Jacques Krynen and Michael Stolleis (Frankfurt am Main: Klostermann, 2008), 583–612.

di Renzo Villata, Maria Gigliola, 'Tra Vienna, Milano e Pavia: un piano per un'università "dall'antico lustro assai decaduta" (1753–1773)', in *Gli statuti universitari: tradizione dei testi e valenze politiche. Atti del Convegno internazionale di studi, Messina-Milazzo, 13–18 aprile 2004*, ed. Andrea Romano (Bologna: Clueb, 2007), 507–546.

di Renzo Villata, Maria Gigliola, 'Un avvocato lombardo tra *ancien régime* e "modernità": Giovanni Margarita', in *Avvocati e avvocatura nell'Italia dell'Ottocento*, ed. Antonio Padoa Schioppa (Bologna: Il Mulino, 2009), 425–520.

di Simone, Maria Rosa, 'I curricula giuridici', in *Le università napoleoniche. Uno spartiacque nella storia italiana ed europea dell'istruzione superiore. Atti del Convegno internazionale di studi, Padova-Bologna 13–15 settembre 2006*, ed. Piero Del Negro and Luigi Pepe (Bologna: Clueb, 2008), 145–167.

di Simone, Maria Rosa, 'L'Unità d'Italia e l'insegnamento del diritto pubblico all'Università di Roma', *Annali di storia delle università italiane* 18 (2014): 301–312.

Draghetti, Andrea, *Ethica societatis jesu elucubrata duo in volumina divisa, quorum unum generalem, alterum specialem amplectitur* (Regii: Davolium, 1818).

Foglio Officiale della Repubblica Italiana, n. 1–15 (Milano: Dalla Reale Stamperia, 1803), 155–179.

La recezione di Grozio a Napoli nel Settecento, ed. Vittorio Conti (Firenze: Centro Editoriale Toscano, 2002).

Memorie e documenti per la storia dell'Università di Pavia e degli uomini più illustri che v'insegnarono (Pavia: Stabilimento Tipografico-Librario Successori Bizzoni, 1878).

Musselli, Luciano, 'Da Tamburini a Foscolo: la facoltà legale pavese tra didattica giuridica e suggestioni di cultura globale', *Annali di storia pavese* 20 (1991): 91–101.

Musselli, Luciano, 'I docenti della Facoltà giuridica pavese tra Cattolicesimo e Liberalismo', *Annali di Storia Pavese* 22–23 (1995): 459–464.

Musselli, Luciano, 'La Facoltà di Giurisprudenza nell'Ottocento', in *Storia di Pavia, V: L'età moderna e contemporanea* (Milano: Banca Regionale Europea, 2000), 445–475.

Panizza, Diego, 'La traduzione italiana del "De iure naturae" di Pufendorf: giusnaturalismo moderno e cultura cattolica nel Settecento', *Studi Veneziani* 11 (1969): 483–528.

Peroni, Baldo, 'La riforma dell'Università di Pavia nel Settecento', in *Contributi alla storia dell'Università di Pavia: pubblicati nell'XI centenario dell'Ateneo* (Pavia: Tipografia cooperativa, 1925), 115–174.

'Piano di Studj e di disciplina per le Università nazionali', in *Statuti e ordinamenti della Università di Pavia dall'anno 1361 all'anno 1859. Raccolti e pubblicati nell'XI centenario dell'Ateneo* (Pavia: Tipografia cooperativa, 1925), 276–309.

'Piano scientifico per l'Università di Pavia', in *Statuti e ordinamenti della Università di Pavia dall'anno 1361 all'anno 1859. Raccolti e pubblicati nell'XI centenario dell'Ateneo* (Pavia: Tipografia cooperativa, 1925), 228–255.

Pufendorf, Samuel von, *Il diritto della natura e delle genti o sia sistema generale de' principii li più importanti di morale, giurisprudenza, e politica, rettificato, accresciuto, e illustrato da Giovambattista Almici* (Venezia: Pietro Valvasense, 1757–1759).

Quaglioni, Diego, 'Pufendorf in Italia. Appunti e notizie della prima diffusione della traduzione italiana del *De iure naturae et gentium*', *Il Pensiero Politico* 32 (1999): 235–250.

Ratti, Luigi, *Il ministro Prina cento anni dopo la sua morte, su documenti e particolari inediti* (Milano: Vallardi, 1914).

Stella, Pietro, 'Pietro Tamburini nel quadro del giansenismo italiano', in *Pietro Tamburini e il giansenismo lombardo. Atti del Convegno internazionale in occasione del 250° della nascita (Brescia, 25–26 maggio 1989)*, ed. Paolo Corsini and Daniele Montanari (Brescia: Morcelliana, 1993), 151–204.

Stoffella, Stefania, 'Assolutismo e diritto naturale in Italia nel Settecento', *Annali dell'Istituto storico italo-germanico* 26 (2000): 137–175.

Stoffella, Stefania, 'Il diritto di resistenza nel Settecento Italiano. Documenti per la storia della traduzione del *De iure naturae et gentium* di Pufendorf', *Laboratoire italien: Politique et société* 2 (2001): 173–199, http://laboratoireitalien.revues.org/261 (accessed 28 September 2019).

Tamburini, Pietro, *Continuazione delle lezioni di Filosofia morale e di naturale e sociale diritto. Tomo VII e ultimo* (Pavia: Eredi di Pietro Galeazzi, 1812).

Tamburini, Pietro, *Introduzione allo studio della Filosofia morale col Prospetto di un corso della medesima dei diritti dell'Uomo, e delle Società del cittadino abb. Pietro Tamburini professore sulla università di Pavia, membro del Collegio elettorale dei dotti, e Direttore del Collegio Nazionale. Tomo I contenente la Introduzione, e la I parte del Prospetto* (Pavia: Eredi di Pietro Galeazzi, 1803).

Tavilla, Elio, 'Beccaria, l'anti-juriste. Critiques de la culture juridique et résistances aux réformes dans l'Italie du XVIIIe siècle', in *Le bonheur du plus grand nombre. Beccaria et les Lumières*, ed. Philippe Audegean et al. (Lyon: ENS Éditions, 2017), 97–110.

Van Kley, Dale, 'From the Catholic Enlightenment to the Risorgimento: The Exchange Between Nicola Spedalieri and Pietro Tamburini, 1791–1797', *Past & Present* 224(1) (2014): 109–162.

Vattel, Emer de, *The Law of Nations, or Principles of the Law of Nature, Applied to the Conduct and Affairs of Nations and Sovereigns, with Three Early Essays on the Origin and Nature of Natural Law and on Luxury*, ed. Béla Kapossy and Richard Whatmore (Indianapolis, IN: Liberty Fund, 2008).

Vismara, Paola, 'Pietro Tamburini e il "dispotismo pontificio"', in *Il giansenismo e l'Università di Pavia. Studi in ricordo di Pietro Stella*, ed. Simona Negruzzo (Milano: Giuffrè, 2012), 95–114.

Zorzoli, Maria Carla, 'La Facoltà di Giurisprudenza nell'Università di Pavia (1535–1796)', in *Studi di Storia del Diritto* (Milano: Giuffrè, 1996), vol. 1, 483–516.

Zorzoli, Maria Carla, 'La formazione dei giuristi lombardi nell'età di Maria Teresa: il ruolo dell'Università', in *Economia, istituzioni, cultura in Lombardia nell'età di Maria Teresa*, vol. 3, *Istituzioni e società*, ed. Aldo de Maddalena, Ettore Rotelli and Gennaro Barbarisi (Bologna: Il Mulino, 1982), 743–769.

Zorzoli, Maria Carla, *Le tesi legali all'Università di Pavia nell'età delle riforme: 1772–1796* (Milano: Istituto Editoriale Cisalpino-La Goliardica, 1980).

Zorzoli, Maria Carla, 'L'Università di Pavia (1535–1796). L'organizzazione dello studio', in *Storia di Pavia, IV: L'età spagnola e austriaca* (Milano: Banca del Monte di Lombardia, 1995), vol. 1, 427–481.

CHAPTER 4

The Law of Nature and Nations in the Mirror of the Academy of Fists: Reforms, Philosophy, Law and Economy

Gabriella Silvestrini

1 Introduction

The institutional reorganization of Lombardy during the reign of Maria Theresa reached its highest point and its paradigmatic moment in the reform of the university. That work took around two decades to complete, from 1753 to 1773,[1] and represents an exemplary case inasmuch as it prefigured the new centralized model of state administration that revoked the power of intermediary bodies: the Milanese Senate was deprived of its authority over educational matters in 1765, all elements of which, from the appointment of teachers, to the administration of schools and colleges, to the design of curricula up to the awarding of academic qualifications, became a prerogative of the Habsburg sovereign. It was in these decisive years of reform that the most significant theoretical works of the 'Milanese school' were produced: Pietro Verri's *Meditazioni sulla felicità* (1763), Cesare Beccaria's *Dei delitti e delle pene* (1764) and the periodical *Il Caffè* (1764–1766). The link between the Lombard Enlightenment and the reform process in Lombardy is well known, even though there were the ups and downs brought about by changes in the personal relations between the main protagonists, in particular (but not only) the rift between Beccaria and the Verri brothers at the end of 1766, and also by the expectations, successes and disappointments of the Lombard Enlightenment thinkers with regard to Viennese politics.[2]

---

1 See the previous chapter, by Elisabetta Fiocchi Malaspina. I would like to thank Gianni Francioni for his helpful comments to a first draft of this chapter.

2 The term 'école de Milan' was coined by Voltaire. For a guide on the sources and a bibliography of the Lombard Enlightenment updated to 2014, see the website http://illuminismolombardo.it/. See also Philippe Audegean, *La philosophie de Beccaria: savoir punir, savoir écrire, savoir produire* (Paris: Vrin, 2010); *Cesare Beccaria. La controverse pénale XVIIIe–XXIe siècle*, ed. Michel Porret and Élisabeth Salvi (Rennes: Presses Universitaires de Rennes, 2015); Pierre Musitelli, *Le flambeau et les ombres: Alessandro Verri, des Lumières à*

I will not revisit events that are already familiar nor seek to corroborate whether or to what extent the alliance between the exponents of the Austrian government and the members of the Academy of Fists[3] was undermined by the different objectives and political cultures of the various protagonists.[4] My aim is instead to reconsider the relationship between natural law and utilitarianism in the key works of the 'Milanese school', as well as to rethink the relationship between contractualism and legal positivism, using the debates and the public education reform plans as the interpretative context.

As has been authoritatively and repeatedly confirmed, the educational reform had a conceptual framework grounded in natural law, and natural law also gave the new Habsburg power theoretical legitimacy. Equally significant, and no less charged with ideological meaning, was the 'utilitarian' concern with public happiness, with the common good being a substantive goal of government policy.[5] The motto of the 'Milanese school', 'the greatest happiness shared among the greatest number', echoed in several variations and is also present in the *Memoria sopra la riforma generale degli studi nella Lombardia austriaca*, which was probably written by Pietro Paolo Giusti at the end of

---

la Restauration (1741–1816) (Paris: École française de Rome, 2016); *Il caso Beccaria. A 250 anni dalla pubblicazione del 'Dei delitti e delle pene'*, ed. Vincenzo Ferrone and Giuseppe Ricuperati (Bologna: Il Mulino, 2016); *Le bonheur du plus grand nombre. Beccaria et les Lumières*, ed. Philippe Audegean et al. (Lyon: ENS, 2017); Sophus A. Reinert, *The Academy of Fisticuffs: Political Economy and Commercial Society in Enlightenment Italy* (Cambridge, MA: Harvard University Press, 2018); John Bessler, *The Celebrated Marquis: An Italian Noble and the Making of the Modern World* (Durham, NC: Carolina Academic Press, 2018); Peter Garnsey, *Against the Death Penalty: Writings from the First Abolitionists – Giuseppe Pelli and Cesare Beccaria*, texts translated and with historical commentary by Peter Garnsey (Princeton, NJ: Princeton University Press, 2020); and the journal *Beccaria. Revue d'histoire du droit de punir* (Geneva: Georg, 2015–). See also Richard Bellamy, 'Introduction', in Cesare Beccaria, *On Crimes and Punishments and Other Writings*, ed. Richard Bellamy (Cambridge: Cambridge University Press, 1995), ix–xxx. Henceforth this English translation will be used, abbreviated as *CPO*.

3 The Academy was a well-known informal society or circle, founded by Pietro Verri, that met regularly from 1761 to 1766 in Verri's house in Milan and was the centre of the Lombard Enlightenment. The name comes from the fact that someone had told the group that met at Verri's house had argued and punched each other. Criticizing formal academies, they decided to call themselves the Academy of Fists (or Fisticuffs, according to Reinert). It was a satirical and ironic gesture of appropriating criticism.

4 The Habsburg view implied the primacy of the State, whereas the Lombard thinkers embraced liberalism and the defence of civil rights, according to Adriano Cavanna, 'La codificazione del diritto nella Lombardia austriaca', in *Economia, istituzioni, cultura in Lombardia nell'età di Maria Teresa*, 3 vols, ed. Aldo De Maddalena, Ettore Rotelli and Gennaro Barbarisi (Bologna: Il Mulino, 1982), vol. 3, 611–657, at 632.

5 Giulio Guderzo, 'La riforma dell'università di Pavia', in *Economia, istituzioni, cultura in Lombardia*, vol. 3, 852.

1768, in which it is stated that: 'nothing should be of greater interest than how to spread the greatest amount of knowledge to the greatest proportion of the nation'.[6]

In the copious documentation that accompanied the reform of the university, the coexistence of natural law and 'utilitarianism' does not seem to have caused problems. Was this a foregone conclusion for those involved, or did it immediately appear to be a mismarriage, at least in the eyes of the radical intellectuals writing for *Il Caffè*? The latter hypothesis would imply the existence of an unbridgeable gap between radical demands for reform made by the members of the Academy of Fists and the actual implementation of those same reforms from the late 1760s to the early 1770s. What is more, even from the point of view of criminal law and its teaching, which was equally subject to the winds of change, the question is far from irrelevant: was the principle of the 'mildness of punishment', at the heart of the call for the abolition of torture and the death penalty, inspired by a completely secularized, utilitarian and positivist view of criminal justice, or was it instead part of a view that ultimately referred to the idea of natural justice?

I share the view of other contributors to this volume that there was a reception leading to a critical reappraisal and reformulation of the main themes of the modern tradition of natural law and the law of nations. In the context of the university reform it is possible to demonstrate that the critique of the tradition of natural law in *Il Caffè* does not constitute a complete rejection of natural law and of the study of law.

In the next two sections I respectively consider critiques of the natural law tradition made by the 'pugilists' and give thought to the reinterpretation of this tradition by some of them: the *gius di natura* (natural law), together with public law and contractualist theories, will appear as the true language of the reforms. In section 4 I will highlight how the critique of jurisprudence and the adherence to the emerging science of economics were not meant to replace legal science with the science of 'public economy', but were aimed at a reformulation of the hierarchy of knowledge that saw the 'citizen philosopher' at the top of the scale. In complete harmony with the plan of university reform, members of the Academy of Fists looked to a new type of expert who could

6 Maria Gigliola di Renzo Villata, '1765–1771: Gli anni decisivi per la riforma. Dall'incubazione ai risultati', in *Almum Studium Papiense. Storia dell'Università di Pavia*, vol. 2.1, *Dall'età austriaca alla nuova Italia*, ed. Dario Mantovani (Milano: Cisalpino Istituto Editoriale Universitario, 2015), 83–114, at 99. On Pietro Paolo Giusti, see Carla Federica Gallotti, 'Diffusione dei lumi e crisi delle riforme in Spagna nella testimonianza di Pietro Paolo Giusti (1772–1781)', *Studi Settecenteschi* 11–12 (1988–1989): 237–303.

recover the original principles of the sciences, in particular the new 'philosophical jurist'. As section 5 highlights, it was in fact Beccaria who in this role proved himself capable of 'discovering' the principles of criminal justice.[7] Finally, in section 6, I will focus on the very close connections, even from a biographical point of view, between the Lombard Enlightenment and university reform.

2 The Academy of Fists and Natural Law: Which Natural Law?

The harshest and most radical critique of natural law by the authors of *Il Caffè* can be found in an unpublished article by Alfonso Longo,[8] which contains a satirical depiction of humans, described through the fiction of an assembly of dogs. In the name of brute force and of a materialist vision of reality, the entire text condemns without qualification all pretence to truth and universal justice, and it culminates in a corrosive conclusion: 'This canine assembly reserves the full, inalienable, natural right to publish these laws even in countries yet to be discovered, and even on the moon, since our power extends that far, as is clearly demonstrated by the way we howl at it'.[9] Having survived among Pietro Verri's unpublished papers, Longo's essay could be construed as

---

7 Beccaria was awarded the title of Doctor of Law by the University of Pavia in 1758. He was probably a student of Venanzio De Mays, who was teaching public law at that institution. See Elisabetta Fiocchi, 'De Mays, Venanzio', https://naturallawdatabase.thulb.uni-jena.de/item/natlaw_196. Beccaria later wrote, in his celebrated letter to Morellet of 26 January 1766, of his 'conversion to philosophy', in Cesare Beccaria, *Edizione Nazionale delle Opere di Cesare Beccaria*, ed. Luigi Firpo and Gianni Francioni, 16 vols (Milano: Mediobanca, 1984–2014, henceforth abbreviated as *EN*), vol. 4, *Carteggio* (*parte I: 1758–1768*), ed. Carlo Capra, Renato Pasta and Francesca Pino Pongolini (Milano: Mediobanca, 1994), 222; *CPO*, 122. On Beccaria as a competent jurist, see Loredana Garlati, 'Tradition et réformisme. Les inspirateurs culturels du Beccaria processualiste', in *Le bonheur du plus grand nombre. Beccaria et les Lumières*, 63–77; ead., 'Beccaria: Filosofo acclamato del passato e giurista misconosciuto del futuro', in *Dialogando con Beccaria. Le stagioni del processo penale italiano*, ed. Giovanni Chiodi and Loredana Garlati (Torino: Giappichelli, 2015), 1–30.

8 On Alfonso Longo, see Carlo Capra, 'Longo, Alfonso', *Dizionario Biografico degli Italiani* (Roma: Istituto dell'Enciclopedia Italiana, 2005), vol. 65, 687–692; Maria Francesca Turchetti, 'Alfonso Longo e l'Accademia dei Pugni (con quattro lettere inedite)', *Archivio storico lombardo* 140 (2014): 152–185.

9 'Del diritto naturale de' cani', in *'Il Caffè' 1764–1766*, 2nd edition revised, ed. Gianni Francioni and Sergio Romagnoli (Torino: Bollati Boringhieri, 1998, hereafter cited as *Caffè*), vol. 2, 836. *Il Caffè* was a periodical published from June 1764 until November 1766, and then unified in two volumes, the first volume 'from June 1764 to May 1765', the second 'from June 1765 until the next year'. See Gianni Francioni, 'Storia editoriale del "Caffè"', in *Caffè*, vol. 1, lxxxi–cxlvi.

the truth hidden behind the pages destined for publication, a sort of esoteric lesson beneath words exposed to the rigour of criticism and censorship.

Given this interpretation, the articles by Alessandro Verri published in volume 2 of *Il Caffé* (in particular, the praise of Carneades over Grotius) at first glance appear to be an indisputable attack on the 'law of nature', which is contrasted with the principle of utility as a foundation of human societies and their institutions. On this reading, the juridical perspective of natural law would be contrasted with a new form of 'economic' knowledge: the calculation of interests and the predictability of human passions. The principle of utility that replaces natural law, a new economic reason that marginalizes the old jurisprudence, the philosopher who takes the place of the jurist: these would be the ideas shared by the group of intellectuals linked to the Academy of Fists on the anthropological, epistemological and institutional level.[10] These ideas appear to have been sketched already in Pietro Verri's *Meditazioni sulla felicità* and in the first draft of Beccaria's *Dei delitti e delle pene*. In the *Meditazioni* Verri adopted for the first time in Italian the maxim of the 'greatest possible happiness shared with the greatest possible equality'[11] and made it part of a unified anthropology that explains all human actions as effects of pleasure and pain, that is, of interest in a broad sense, physical and moral. Rejecting what he took to be Shaftesbury and Hutcheson's dualism, which envisaged the possibility of a 'disinterested' love of one's neighbour compatible with self-love, Pietro Verri, like Helvétius, believed that even compassion originated in a desire to escape pain.[12] Despite the reference to the social contract as the foundation

10 See Luigi Ferrajoli, 'Beccaria e Bentham', *Diciottesimo secolo* 4 (2019): 75–84, at 77; and Philippe Audegean, 'Droit naturel et droit à la vie. Beccaria lecteur de Hobbes', *Diciottesimo secolo* 4 (2019): 33–45. For a different position, see Gianni Francioni, 'Beccaria, philosophe utilitariste' (first Italian edition 1990), in *Le bonheur du plus grand nombre. Beccaria et les Lumières*, 23–44; and Dario Ippolito, 'Contrat social et peine capitale. Beccaria contre Rousseau', in *Rousseau et l'Italie. Littérature, morale et politique*, ed. Philippe Audegean, Magda Campanini and Barbara Carnevali (Paris: Harmattan, 2017), 147–176.

11 For the history and the different interpretations of this 'utilitarian' maxim, from Francis Hutcheson to Jeremy Bentham, see Robert Shackleton, 'The Greatest Happiness of the Greatest Number: The History of Bentham's Phrase', *Studies on Voltaire and the Eighteenth Century* 90 (1972): 1641–1682. As Gianni Francioni highlights, Pietro Verri read Hutcheson's *Inquiry* in the French translation by Marc-Antoine Eidous, *Recherches sur l'origine des idées que nous avons de la beauté et de la vertu*, 2 vols (Amsterdam [i.e. Paris], 1749); cf. Gianni Francioni, 'Nota introduttiva', in Pietro Verri, *Meditazioni sulla felicità* (1763), in *Edizione Nazionale delle Opere di Pietro Verri*, vol. 1, *Scritti letterari, filosofici e satirici*, ed. Gianni Francioni (henceforth *ENPV*, vol. 1) (Roma: Edizioni di Storia e Letteratura, 2014), 685–687.

12 On Francis Hutcheson in Italy, see Chapter 6 of the present volume, by Serena Luzzi.

of societies and of the law, mention of natural law appears to be absent in this 1763 text: the phrase 'law of nature' refers exclusively to the mechanism of the passions and to the love of pleasure, and the term 'law' designates the law in force in political societies. The natural liberty partly forfeited through the social contract is not defined as a right. This, therefore, should be interpreted as a form of contractualism without natural law.[13]

The language of natural law is almost entirely absent also in the first manuscript version of Beccaria's *Dei delitti e delle pene*, in which terms like 'interest', 'natural sentiments of mankind' and 'self-love' recur frequently. The 'right to security' explicitly alludes to a political right, inasmuch as it is one 'which each citizen has earned'.[14] There is only one instance in which we encounter a concept above the positivist legal horizon, namely the 'rights of humanity'.[15] This one occurrence does not seem to weaken the framework of legal positivism that appears to structure the whole text with great consistency, beginning with the definitions both of law, seen as 'the restraint necessary to hold particular interests together, without which they would collapse into the old state of unsociability', as well as of justice.[16] Thus also in this case we are faced with a contractualism that is anti-natural law and clearly positivist, being closely connected with a materialism that denies human freedom and, in analogy with the physical world, sees humanity as motivated solely by the 'force which attracts us, like gravity, to our own good'.[17]

From the first autograph manuscript onward, Beccaria's work included references to the union of the soul with the body, to the connection between morality and politics, and to the rights of humanity. All these references should, however, be dismissed as being a form of self-censorship or purely rhetorical concessions within a new horizon of thought that, in the mid-eighteenth century, was completely secularized, partly through a materialism

13 *ENPV*, vol. 1, 734–762.

14 *Dei delitti e delle pene. Prima redazione*, ed. Gianni Francioni, in *EN*, vol. 1, 152. This formulation remains until the 'fifth' edition, ibid., 48; *CPO*, 9; on the complicated publication history of *Dei Delitti*, see Richard Bellamy's *Introduction*, *CPO*, xli–xliv.

15 *EN*, vol. 1, 157: 'the rights of humanity and the invincible truth'. From the first edition onwards, this expression becomes 'the rights of men'. *EN*, vol. 1, 54; *CPO*, 30.

16 *EN*, vol. 1, 140. The same formulation is repeated in the published editions, ibid., 32; *CPO*, 11.

17 *EN*, vol. 1, 146 and 41; *CPO*, 19. Cf. Jérôme Ferrand, 'La nécessité, passager clandestin de l'abolitionnisme beccarien', in *Le bonheur du plus grand nombre. Beccaria et les Lumières*, 127–138. For a 'Christian' interpretation of Beccaria's works, see Maria Gigliola di Renzo Villata, 'Cesare Beccaria (1738–1794)', in *Law and the Christian Tradition in Italy: The Legacy of the Great Jurists*, ed. Orazio Condorelli and Rafael Domingo (London: Routledge, 2021), 331–347.

inspired by Lucretius. The different stages in the drafting of the *Delitti*, which ended with the 'fifth' edition of 1766, reflected the attempt to make these theses in the first edition ever less heterodox, above all under the pressure of vehement charges of irreligiousness that rained down on the head of the anxious Beccaria, whom Ferdinando Facchinei accused of wanting to repudiate natural law.[18]

But, we might ask, does the denial of the existence of a law of nature established by God imply the rejection of natural law? In other words, who was right: the abbot Ferdinando Facchinei, who included Beccaria in the ranks of the 'modern publicists' who, according to him, denied natural law, or Jeremy Bentham, who detected incoherent residues of natural law in *Dei delitti*?[19]

As has been authoritatively argued, natural law has been defined in many ways;[20] it does not necessarily imply a theological foundation but can easily fit within a materialist or at least secular horizon of thought. On the one hand, Grotius's rationalist perspective was used, for example by Pierre Bayle, to advance the theory of the virtuous atheist. On the other, from Hobbes to Pufendorf to Locke, the possibility of knowing natural law through natural reason could coexist with the idea that the obligation to follow this law originates in divine will.[21] Conversely, as the line running from Grotius to Wolff,

---

18 See Paolo Preto, 'Facchinei, Ferdinando', in *Dizionario Biografico degli Italiani* (Roma: Istituto dell'Enciclopedia Italiana, 1994), vol. 44, 29–31; Alberto Bondolfi, 'Beccaria et la religion: la réaction de Facchinei et du Saint-Office', in *Le moment Beccaria: naissance du droit pénal moderne (1764–1810)*, ed. Philippe Audegean and Luigi Delia (Liverpool: Liverpool University Press/Voltaire Foundation, 2018), 33–42. On the self-censorship by members of the Academy of Fists, see Gianni Francioni, 'Censura e autocensura nella rivista "Il Caffè"', in *Varianti politiche d'autore. Da Verri a Manzoni*, ed. Beatrice Nava (Bologna: Pàtron, 2019), 15–57.

19 On the question of natural rights, see Herbert L. A. Hart, 'Bentham and Beccaria', in idem, *Essays on Bentham: Studies in Jurisprudence and Political Theory* (Oxford: Clarendon Press, 1982), 40–52; Jean-Pierre Cléro, 'Un tournant dans la conception du droit pénal: Beccaria and Bentham', in *Entre droit et morale: la finalité de la peine*, ed. Annette Sousa Costa (Bern: Peter Lang, 2010), 63–98; Emmanuelle de Champs, 'Bentham et l'héritage de Beccaria: du *Projet d'un corps complet de législation* aux *Traités de législation civile et pénale*', in *Cesare Beccaria. La controverse pénale*, 99–110.

20 See *The Cambridge Companion to Natural Jurisprudence*, ed. George Duke and Robert P. George (Cambridge: Cambridge University Press, 2017), especially the 'Introduction' by the editors, 1–13, and the chapter by Knud Haakonssen, 'Early Modern Natural Law Theories', 76–102.

21 On Bayle and natural law, see Elena Muceni, *Apologia della virtù sociale. L'ascesa dell'amor proprio nella crisi della coscienza europea* (Milano: Mimesis, 2018), 95–132. On the different theories of obligation in the tradition of natural law, see Tim Hochstrasser, *Natural Law Theories in the Early Enlightenment* (Cambridge: Cambridge University Press, 2000), and Chapter 10 of the present volume, by Francesca Iurlaro.

Burlamaqui and Vattel demonstrates, an authentically religious position did not necessarily imply adherence to a voluntarist theory of natural obligation.

Among the most representative authors in the materialist wing of the *philosophes* in the middle of the eighteenth century, both Diderot and Helvétius were far from making a radical rejection of natural law. The most significant case is that of Diderot, who in the entry 'Droit naturel' of the *Encyclopédie* suggested that the criterion for just and unjust was to be found in the general will of the human species. The idea of a hypothetical 'general assembly' of rational beings mentioned by Diderot appears to echo Wolff's ideal of the *civitas maxima*, although for Diderot this would be the foundation not only of the law of nations, but also of the 'truly inalienable natural rights' of humanity.[22]

As for Helvétius, although he clearly did not set out to discuss natural law theories, it would be wrong to consider him a critic of natural law because of his atheism or his materialism. On the contrary, natural law raises its head in *De l'esprit* – albeit incidentally, as if it were something that went without saying – in the context of a critique of tyrannical and arbitrary power. Such power is accused of deterring men from educating themselves in natural law, public law and the law of nations.[23] There is an undeniable link between ignorance of these sciences and the violation of human rights, which can occur where the principle of the happiness of the minority holds sway: 'In policed countries, the art of legislation has often consisted in making an infinite number of men

22 Denis Diderot, 'Droit naturel', in *Encyclopédie, ou dictionnaire raisonné des sciences, des arts et des métiers, etc.*, ed. Denis Diderot and Jean le Rond d'Alembert, University of Chicago, ARTFL Encyclopédie Project (autumn 2022 edition), ed. Robert Morrissey and Glenn Roe, https://encyclopedie.uchicago.edu (accessed on 14 January 2023). English translation of select passages are given in Denis Diderot, *Political Writings*, ed. and trans. John Hope Mason and Robert Wokler (Cambridge: Cambridge University Press, 1992), 17–21. Cf. Peter Schröder, 'Natural Law and Enlightenment in France and Scotland – A Comparative Perspective', in *Early Modern Natural Law Theories: Contexts and Strategies in the Early Enlightenment*, ed. Tim J. Hochstrasser and Peter Schröder (Dordrecht: Springer, 2003), 297–317; Ann Thomson, 'French Eighteenth-Century Materialists and Natural Law', *History of European Ideas* 42 (2016): 243–255.

23 C[laude]-A[drien] Helvétius, *De l'esprit, or, Essays on the mind, and its several faculties* (London: Albion Press, 1810), Essay II, ch. 12, 98: 'Now, in most arbitrary governments, the citizens cannot, without displeasing a despotic prince, employ themselves in the study of the law of nature, or in that of the public, moral, and political. They dare not ascend to the first principles of those sciences, nor form grand ideas'. See also Essay IV, ch. 15, 473. On Helvétius' republicanism, see David Wootton, 'Helvétius: From Radical Enlightenment to Revolution', *Political Theory* 28 (2000): 307–336.

subservient to the happiness of a few; in keeping, for this purpose, the multitude under oppression, and in violation all the privileges of humanity they have a right to demand'.[24]

As has often been stressed, Beccaria appears to have taken inspiration from this passage when writing the introduction to his main work. His knowledge of the *Encyclopédie* and of Diderot's 'Droit naturel' entry is certainly beyond doubt, not only because of its prosopopoeia of the thief who chooses a life of crime, 'gambling' on a happy life in exchange for moments of suffering: Diderot's 'violent reasoner' is without question an example of an 'apologia of injustice'.[25] The mention of the 'rights of humanity' is, from the first version of *Dei delitti*, full of references to inalienable natural rights.

Hence the embrace of materialist theories does not in itself indicate a rejection of natural law. For a historical understanding of Beccaria and the members of the Academy of Fists when criticizing traditional knowledge and proposing a reform of the law, one must therefore disregard whatever religious ideas one may harbour and instead consider more deeply the close connections with a broader cultural and social reform.

3 The Modern Innovators and the New Language of Natural Law, the Law of Nations, and the Social Contract

Before verifying whether some form of natural law continued to constitute the more or less implicit theoretical framework of *Dei delitti e delle pene*, we must consider the way in which the authors of the natural law tradition are mentioned in the works of Beccaria and the *Il Caffè* authors. From this perspective not only must one bear in mind the plurality of natural law traditions, which were quite familiar to these internationally minded Italian authors, but one must also avoid undervaluing the way these traditions were constantly reinterpreted. As such, beyond the specificity of individual intellectual and

---

24 Helvétius, *De l'esprit*, Essay I, ch. 3 ('Of ignorance'), 18 (footnote). See also Essay II, ch. 17, 175–176 (footnote *): 'In most of the empires of the East, they have not even the least idea of the laws of nature and nations [...] Whoever should endeavour to enlighten the people in this respect, would almost constantly expose himself to the fury of the Tyrant [...] In order to violate with the greater impunity the laws of humanity, they will have their subjects ignorant of what, as men, they have a right to expect from the prince, and of the tacit contract by which he binds himself with the people'.

25 Echoing, while paraphrasing, the title of the essay by Céline Spector, *Éloges de l'injustice. La philosophie face à la déraison* (Paris: Seuil, 2016); on Diderot and the violent reasoner, see 95–122.

professional paths, it is possible to discern a polemical intent shared by the members of the Academy of Fists that also corresponds to the peculiarity of the Lombardy context during the age of Maria Theresa and Leopold II.[26]

The group gathered around the academy, although largely coming from families of the patriciate, battled against the two pillars that supported the power of the local aristocracy, who opposed the reform policies desired by Vienna: the Church and the Senate, of which Count Gabriele Verri, father of the Verri brothers, was a member. The intellectual activities of the members of the group were thus motivated by a twofold (but indivisible) philosophical-cultural and political-professional aspiration: on the one hand, that of gaining entry into the enlightened republic of letters, pursuing fame and influencing public opinion; and on the other, that of supporting the Habsburg government and constructing a curriculum that would prepare them for participation in the new ruling group, searching for a suitable role, including in economic terms.

To this end, the politics of book dedications and submissions did not diverge from the normal practice of the era and certainly did not reduce the philosophical and scientific significance of the works. Unlike the French *philosophes*, who were excluded from government and universities, the intellectuals linked to *Il Caffè* acted in a context similar to a wide variety of European local realities in which the clash of powers and institutions offered the possibility of imagining reform paths and of obtaining occupations in the institutions, posts which might include, albeit not necessarily, academic careers. In this respect the Milanese environment seems to have been not dissimilar to that of Switzerland, if we consider, for example, Emer de Vattel, whose literary and philosophical activity was clearly oriented to finding a position at home or abroad.[27]

If the Senate and the ecclesiastical institutions were the main enemies, even from the personal point of view – especially for Pietro and Alessandro Verri, who, more than the others, had to endure the rigid views of their family – the polemical targets on the theoretical level were the pillars on which these authorities rested, which can be summarized in two words: tradition and whim. All the philosophical and political battles waged by the *Il Caffè* authors can be linked to these two.

---

26 The bibliography on the Lombardy context is vast, but see at least Carlo Capra, *La Lombardia austriaca nell'età delle riforme, 1706–1796* (Torino: Utet, 1987).

27 See *Concepts and Contexts of Vattel's Political and Legal Thought*, ed. P. Schröder (Cambridge: Cambridge University Press, 2021).

In the *Orazione panegirica sulla giurisprudenza milanese*, composed by Pietro Verri and discussed by the members of the Academy of Fists in 1763, a representative of tradition, supposedly personifying Senator Gabriele Verri, takes the floor. He denounces the corruption of the century and the 'ultramontane' poisons that were spreading throughout Italy thanks to 'modern inept innovators', all the while looking, however, with relief at the Milanese area where the power of local courts remained intact.[28] The object of this ironic polemic was the existing local legislation, the Nuove Costituzioni of 1541, criticized for clashing with nature and for its lack of proportion between crimes and punishments, in particular in cases which carried the death penalty. That work presented the same arguments later taken up by Beccaria for the impunity of crimes of conscience, abortions, sexual indiscretions, as well as on the right to emigrate.

Apart from the Nuove Costituzioni, the institution that was directly attacked was the Milanese Senate, then made up of only jurists.[29] This was a body that united 'the person of the legislator and the judge' and kept for itself the power both to interpret laws and to judge according to equity. In this attack on the Milanese political scene specifically, as well as local laws and the Senate, Pietro Verri also criticized the doctrinal tradition on which they were predicated, in particular the ideas of the jurists Bossi, Claro, Sacchi, Tiraqueau, Mantica, Menocchio, De Luca and Fulgosio, against whom he set the authors who had introduced 'a new language of *Gius naturale, Gius delle genti, Patto Sociale*'. The text unhesitatingly named the 'modern innovators' who were opposed to that tradition: Voltaire, and then Bacon and Montesquieu with regard to the separation of legislative and judicial power, and the Rousseau of *Emile*, who had been condemned by the Paris parliament. Pietro Verri considered Rousseau to be a supporter of natural law. The practice of torture was also denounced, for being contrary 'to the inalienable natural right to self-defence'.[30]

---

28 ENPV, vol. 1, 426 and 425.

29 On the Milanese Senate and its eighteenth-century decline, see Ugo Petronio, *Il Senato di Milano: istituzioni giuridiche ed esercizio del potere nel ducato di Milano da Carlo V a Giuseppe II* (Milano: Giuffrè, 1969).

30 ENPV, vol. 1, 430. On natural law as a common language, see Maurizio Bazzoli, 'Aspetti della recezione di Pufendorf nel Settecento italiano', in *Dal* De Jure naturae et gentium *di Samuel Pufendorf alla codificazione prussiana del 1794*, ed. Marta Ferronato (Padova: Cedam, 2005), 41–60, at 52. For a more nuanced reading of the legal culture criticized by Beccaria and the Verri brothers, see Maria Gigliola di Renzo Villata, 'Avant Beccaria. La culture juridique à l'épreuve du temps', in *Le bonheur du plus grand nombre. Beccaria et les Lumières*, 47–61.

If we compare this text with what was published in *Il Caffè* and the works of Beccaria, we can see that the polemic was not directed at the science of law in general, but at the 'reigning Jurisprudence' in the Milanese area, from a point of view that ran parallel to the Austrian government's reform programme, in which members of the Academy of Fists and their collaborators actively participated.

In the first volume of *Il Caffè* Alessandro Verri criticized the Justinian Code for being cumbersome and contradictory, and for making no reference to the 'constant and general principles of justice' that were at the root of all useful laws.[31] Nevertheless, the mass of Justinian laws contained not only opinion, but sometimes also reason, and the *Institutes* were defined as 'the only ordered code of Roman laws'.[32] According to him, the greatest degeneration lay in the rediscovery of Roman law by the glossators and commentators, Irnerius, Accursius, Bartolus and Baldus. Alessandro took up this analysis of Roman law again in his essay *Ragionamento sulle istituzioni civili* (1765), where he explained in greater detail why he approved of the *Institutes*: 'they are the only real code that we have', since, by setting out 'the elements of the law taken as general rules and without reference to particular cases', they expose 'the principles for deciding questions', in order to educate young people.[33] Outlining the main stages of the establishment of the common law in Europe, Verri emphasized the gulf between theory and practice, between erudite jurisconsults and forensic jurisprudence, which became a legal language unknown to those coming from the university and the study of the *Institutes*. And while the jurists of local courts and all the legal practitioners were educated on local practices and statutes, producing a sort of Pyrrhonism insofar as 'jurisprudence changes with the post-horses',[34] the development of legal science, starting with Cujas, had led to a similar disorder, by increasing the number of books and interpretations. In this way, the proliferation of laws and

31 Alessandro Verri, *Di Giustiniano e delle sue leggi* (1764), in *Caffè*, vol. 1, 185. More than simply setting out a radical criticism of Roman law, Verri aimed at a renewal of it, as did other authors such as Giovanni Maria Lampredi, based on the idea of its 'tendential "correspondence" to natural law', as Maria Gigliola di Renzo Villata writes regarding Lampredi, in 'Introduzione. La formazione del giurista in Italia e l'influenza culturale europea tra Sette e Ottocento: il caso della Lombardia', in *Formare il giurista. Esperienze nell'area lombarda fra Sette e Ottocento*, ed. Maria Gigliola di Renzo Villata (Milano: Giuffrè, 2004), 1–106, at 36.

32 *Caffè*, vol. 1, 183.

33 *Caffè*, vol. 2, 573; a little later (574) Alessandro specifies: 'their brevity makes them merely an idea of a code'.

34 Ibid., 580.

doctrines led to a sort of anarchy in which the sheer number of laws paradoxically meant an absence of law. Arbitrariness of interpretation inevitably followed the disorder of jurisprudence and affected in particular the right of ownership.[35]

The reform of civil law and its procedures proposed by Alessandro Verri, in agreement with other *Il Caffè* authors, was aimed at ending this disorder by introducing a new code that was both universal and suitable for the growth of trade and relations between citizens that marked the modern era. Consequently, criticism of the excessive number of laws and professionals in the public sphere went hand in hand with the awareness of a new and different function for jurisprudence. There was also the consciousness of the difficulty of enacting a reform whose end was that of removing legislative power from the legal experts and the judges through the introduction of laws that were clear, simple and necessary rules for guaranteeing not only the institution of property but also, and primarily, the 'universal good'.

The main protagonist of this reform that aimed more at destroying than building was to be the 'jurisconsult philosopher',[36] who had the collective profile of *Il Caffè*'s contributors and embodied the figure of the expert ideally suited to the task of renewing the educational institutions. Developing a new code in fact required a jurisconsult with expertise in Roman law, in particular the *Digest*, and who had an understanding of the treatises that offered clear expositions of all aspects of jurisprudence, such as Heineccius's and Domat's.[37] However, at the same time he had also to be a 'philosopher' in the sense of understanding the infinite multiplicity of social relations ('commerce, the new arts, new customs, the contracts of various types') and intellectually able to 'tie the many threads into a knot'.[38]

It is interesting to observe that both volumes of *Il Caffè* included an index of topics; in the first volume we find under 'Public economy' not only essays on commerce, luxury and contraband but also the articles 'On the Fideicommissum' by Alfonso Longo and 'On the Legislation of Justinian' by Alessandro Verri, alongside 'Political Thoughts' by Sebastiano Franci.[39] Thus, from the point of view of the *Il Caffè* editors, there was a close link between ethics, politics, law and public economy – a connection that we see again a few years

35 Ibid., 585.
36 Ibid., 599.
37 Ibid., 598.
38 Ibid., 598–599.
39 *Caffè*, vol. 1, 7; in the second volume the topic is enlarged: 'On Legislation and Public Economy' (vol. 2, 409).

later in the inaugural lecture for the chair of cameral sciences delivered by Beccaria on 9 January 1769. In this, while denouncing the times and places in which 'private jurisprudence became the public legislator', he presented 'public economy' as a science that was also important for the study of civil law since it was aimed at 'the invariable law of utility and the eternal norms of universal equity'.[40] For him, therefore, it was not a question of replacing law with economy, but of re-establishing the right relationships between disciplines and professions, overcoming the general subordination of jurisprudence to 'private justice', a subordination that had had the effect of enabling the rise of the 'anti-political canon' that rewarded inertia at the expense of work: 'These and others are the effects of restricting jurisprudence within the boundaries of private justice when it ought to embrace all the greatest principles of morals and politics'.[41]

The reference to the 'greatest principles of morals and politics', in the plural, cannot be interpreted only as a reference to the formula of maximum happiness for the greatest possible number. Morals and politics relate to the language of the 'law of nature', of the 'law of nations' and of the 'social contract' mentioned by Pietro Verri in the *Orazione panegirica*.

In essence, if we return to Alessandro Verri's essay on Carneades and Grotius, the conclusion was certainly not that of rejecting *in toto* the science of the law of nature and nations. As in the case of Roman law, the critique did not involve a total rejection, but a qualified reconsideration that marked a radical break not only with the representatives of tradition, like Senator Gabriele Verri, but also with those who, like Venanzio de Mays, had introduced the teaching of this discipline into the chair of public law.[42] While in Italy the success of Grotius and Pufendorf in the mid-eighteenth century was reflected in the translation of their works, the members of the Academy of Fists, and in particular the Verri brothers and Beccaria, had already distanced themselves from those authors in favour of Montesquieu, Vattel and Rousseau.

Alessandro's critique of Grotius was radical and took to the utmost the accusation of tyranny and despotism made by Rousseau. The contraposition of Carneades and Grotius served to shed light on what Alessandro saw as the contradictory arguments of the latter to justify slavery on the basis of a presumed 'law of nature' as well as his arguments on the possibility of making pacts of unconditional subordination, which Verri saw as a form of voluntary

40 *EN*, vol. 3, 85; *CPO*, 132.
41 *EN*, vol. 3, 86; *CPO*, 132.
42 See Chapter 3 of the present volume, by Elisabetta Fiocchi Malaspina.

servitude so extreme that it involved the obligation to renounce one's right of defence and advantage:

> He who, out of delirium and fatuity hands his limbs over to someone who might beat him and kill him with impunity, or make him drag a cart and bury him in a prison because of such a contract, according to the dictates of the law of nature would be guilty of a crime against nature and of breaking a contract if he were to attempt to escape from such servitude, all because in a moment of madness he transferred to someone else his right of existence and there is no longer any action that his own limbs can perform that is his. Such a person has become a thing.[43]

These are ideas that recall the essential statements of *Dei delitti e delle pene*, making explicit the basic premises of contract theory: there are reasons why contracts can be null and void, and these mainly coincide with the principle of voluntariness and rationality, and whose justice or injustice depend on the advantage of the contracting parties.

This made it possible to pour criticism on the theories of Grotius, who, it was considered, by confusing law with fact, justified both tyranny and tyrannicide and sedition, and allowed a right of war that granted permission to commit any atrocity against the enemy: 'The voice of nature screams against these blood writings'. The conclusion was a rehabilitation of Carneades in the very name of the rights of nature:

> Who therefore, Carneades or Grotius, has violated justice? Who has praised the rights of nature only to prove himself ignorant of them and to violate them, or who was less hypocritical, more human, when he professed them and put the chimeras to flight, appearing to destroy them only in the eyes of those who did not understand him?[44]

The condemnation of Grotius continued in Alessandro's article 'Di alcuni sistemi del pubblico diritto' (1766), which went on to criticize also the theories of Pufendorf and Gravina on the origins of society. Albeit in different ways, all three of these authors were thought to justify war against nations that violated 'the first laws of humanity'. Grotius, in particular, was deemed to hold that it was permissible to punish primitive peoples as if they were 'enemies of the

43 *Caffè*, vol. 2, 717.

44 Ibid., 720.

human race'. At this point Verri made a criticism of the 'humanitarian' war that justified conquest in the name of compassion:

> They conquer and then pay a jurisconsult. This doctrine may be dictated by compassion but not by law. It makes one nation the judge of another without any convention and without any need. I do not see what this law can be based on when the ferocious customs of the barbarians do not offer any disadvantage, either by fact or by example.[45]

Verri was undoubtedly aware of the debates on the various currents of natural law, the different positions on the power to punish and on just war, and his preference for the doctrines of Rousseau, although not explicitly cited in these two contributions to *Il Caffè*, and for Vattel is undeniable:

> Among the large ranks of publicists it seems to me that Mr Vattel has grasped the truth and is the one who has stripped this science of chimeras and misunderstandings by reducing it to a system of ideas, not words. He establishes the principle that nations must seek their happiness and perfectibility since this leads them to happiness itself. He imposes some worthwhile duties. Nobody can argue with them. His principle is based on the human heart as it is, not as we might wish it to be.[46]

In this way Vattel was considered the author who was able to develop the science of public law (or the law of nations) by basing it on the true interests of the nations.

If we pause to consider the meaning of this praise for Vattel, it seems impossible to interpret it as a critique of natural law, given that the subtitle of the *Droit des gens* was 'ou Principes de la Loi naturelle appliqués à la conduite et aux affaires des Nations et des Souverains'. The fundamental point seems to me to be the contraposition between the 'human heart as it is' and 'as we might wish it to be'. As the essay on Carneades and Grotius shows, as do other writings of the members of the Academy of Fists, the anthropology of utility looks at the motives behind human action, bringing them back to a single principle, that of self-love, the pursuit of pleasure and escape from pain, pro-

45 Ibid., 736.
46 Ibid., 736.

vided, however, that utility does not only mean material or present interests. The concept of utility included, for Vattel and for Pietro Verri in *Meditazioni sulla felicità*, otherworldly goods, long-term goods, of which compassion and an easy conscience are a part.

Following the tradition of well-understood self-love, the Verri brothers and Beccaria rejected a double position in matters of moral justice: the hard-line one that sees virtue as self-renunciation[47] and the dualist one, which identifies in compassion a principle of sociality distinct from self-love and therefore draws a distinction between duties performed for oneself and those performed for others. On the opposite side, we find the critique of amoral realism embodied in Machiavelli, who, according to Verri, legitimized both tyranny and wickedness, choosing to forget that 'men have hearts and are capable of terrible remorse'. The theoretical vice of Machiavellianism ran parallel to that committed by those who based moral principles on reason: 'you establish the principles of righteousness as if men did not feel, as if there were no painful feelings in the soul, as well as in human limbs'.[48]

The proposal made by Alessandro Verri – as well as by other members of the Academy of Fists – was for a rational science of public law, construed as part of a broader science of ethics and politics, namely that of the 'science of humanity' that had evolved since ancient times[49] and ultimately consisted of a doctrine of legislation and duties. As a science, the determination of its first principles and the deduction of its consequences belonged to reason, and competence in it resided with the 'humane philosopher'. The raw material of the science is human nature, but not all men are able to understand themselves and the motives for their actions: 'It is certain that man is constantly in search of his utility. Let us therefore base the system on this. Only the man

47 It is in this sense that we should interpret Beccaria's passage in *Dei delitti e delle pene*, ch. 2: 'No man has made a gift of part of his freedom with the common good in mind; that kind of fantasy exists only in novels' (CPO, 10). An analogous position, in a transcendent key, can be found in Alessandro Verri, *Saggio di Morale cristiana* (1763), ed. Pierre Musitelli (2016), http://illuminismolombardo.it/testo/saggio-di-morale-cristiana/?tipo=1.

48 *Caffè*, vol. 2, 738–739. However, it should be remembered that the relationship between the members of the Academy of Fists and Machiavelli is far from one of pure opposition, as evidenced by the letter from Beccaria to Morellet dated 26 January 1766: 'Nello scrivere l'opera mia ho avuto innanzi gli occhi Galileo, Machiavello e Giannone. Ho sentito scuotere le catene della superstizione e gli urli del fanatismo soffocare i gemiti della verità', EN, vol. 4, 221; 'But I can say that, in writing my work, I had before me the examples of Machiavelli, Galileo, and Giannone. I could hear the rattling chains of superstition and the howls of fanaticism stifling the faint moans of truth', CPO, 121.

49 *Caffè*, vol. 2, 728: 'la scienza dell'uomo è vecchia'.

who thinks about them, sees utility relationships: everyone seeks happiness, desires it, and has a confused notion of it'.[50]

The rationalism of the moderns, whose principal representative was considered to be Pufendorf, produced a science of duties predicated on the false assumption that all men are rational and therefore guilty when they ignore the right standard of moral action. This system translated into a circular logic and an injustice: on the one hand, it considered natural law only as a rational science, forgetting that not everyone was capable of developing reason to the point of being aware of these standards. On the other hand, by wrongly presupposing that such standards were clear and knowable by everyone, it did not recognize ignorance as an extenuating factor. Modern moral rationalism was therefore impaired by its erroneous conception of responsibility and the imputability of human actions, and thus failed to distinguish the guilty from the innocent.[51]

4 The Ignorant Citizen and the Citizen Philosopher

Alessandro Verri's texts help to clarify the dual anthropological and epistemological level on which the philosophical and political project pursued by the 'Milanese school' proceeded, and the particular articulation of passions and reason, of particularism linked to historical context and the universality of principles of justice. While there is only one human nature and the science of man is ancient, there are different gradations in which the elements of human nature, passions and reason combine, depending on the individual and the level of development of nations. Human nature is at the same time variable and immutable. An enormous interval was considered to separate savage nations from civilized ones and to divide the 'common rustic' from the 'sublime philosopher'.[52] This contrast can be found in Beccaria's manuscript of *On Crimes and Punishments*, which in fact aimed to demonstrate how public legislation should account for the fact that its intended beneficiaries are not only rational beings, but also others, of all conditions, thus assuming that men animated by the desire for personal happiness may have a limited ability to weigh up 'utility relationships'.

---

50 Ibid., 738.

51 Ibid., 732–733; see in addition the article, also by Alessandro Verri, 'Alcune idee sulla filosofia morale', which begins: 'Most men understand themselves the least'; ibid., 685.

52 *EN*, vol. 1, 143.

In the revised version of the work by Pietro Verri, the latter changed the terms, reducing to a common denominator the differences, which lose the social and individual absoluteness of the first version: 'the ignorant citizen and the citizen philosopher'[53] are both members of society and their differences do not cancel out their common traits as 'citizens'. But the terms of the question do not change: the human material that is the object of politics is identical to that of the science of man and concerns a being endowed with a mixture of reason and passions. Man's freedom consists in the possibility of choice, and the ability to choose is reduced the greater the grip of the passions is. Torture is the perfect example of how the domination of pain can become unnatural by annihilating freedom of choice and using the individual's desire for self-preservation to bring about self-destruction, through forced confession.

The law and the government – as long as they are not tyrannical – must intervene in this space of liberty in order to transform individual interests into public happiness. Far from presupposing a spontaneous or natural harmony of interests, the members of the 'Milanese school' considered the legislative sphere crucial to correct the 'confusion' of the 'ignorant citizens', starting by administering a judicious dose of incentives and disincentives. Given these premises, the sphere of politics depended on the broader one of moral justice, of which it was a part, but at the same time must disregard any consideration that was not properly linked to the goal of preserving political society. The exclusion of religious motives did not simply respond to an editorial strategy of self-protection from censorship but was based on a distinction rooted in the tradition of natural law. Having said that, the preservation of society did not exclude religion from matters of relevance to government and legislation.[54]

The fundamental point, however, was the role attributed to the 'citizen philosophers' or to the 'philosopher jurisconsults'. While the 'ignorant citizens' were the targets and beneficiaries of social laws, the philosopher citizens, *qua* citizens, were like the ignorant citizens, but, as philosophers, were the experts who must develop the science of legislation and therefore instruct sovereigns

53 Ibid., vol. 1, 38. On Pietro Verri's changes to Beccaria's manuscript, see Gianni Francioni, 'Confronto tra la prima e la seconda redazione', ibid., 267.

54 See § XXXIX of *Dei delitti* and the difficulties Beccaria had in writing it, with the related notes by Gianni Francioni and his textual commentary, *EN*, vol. 1, 117–119, 268–270. We can only recall that the self-censorship exercised here by Beccaria relates to a fear of the ecclesiastical authorities, not of the Habsburg government, which aimed to control the religious sphere as much as possible: see Ettore Passerin d'Entrèves, 'Le premesse del riformismo di Maria Teresa e di Giuseppe II nel campo ecclesiastico, in Austria e in Lombardia', in *Economia, istituzioni, cultura in Lombardia*, vol. 2, 729–740.

on the reforms to be undertaken, as did those citizens who aspired, through higher education, to become part of the ruling class.

So we see that the conception of law and economy elaborated by members of the 'Milanese school' was aimed at redefining the hierarchies of power and knowledge in a way that largely coincided with the reformist politics of the Austrian government. In the new 'Piano scientifico per l'Università di Pavia' of 1773, the first of the newly established faculties was that of philosophy, whose subject is the science of man, who 'must know himself, other things, their different relationships, and the alterations they have undergone, in order to benefit from them for his own education and happiness. All this is the purpose of Philosophy, the most important of all the studies'.[55] In first position among the proposed courses we find logic and metaphysics, understood as the study of knowledge and its progress, and of the language and method relating to the discovery of truth. After this comes moral philosophy, which combined natural law with utilitarianism and sensualism, similarly to the 'pugilists'. The foundation of obligation refers back to the existence of God, who is known through sentiments inspired by the 'spectacle of nature'.[56] This is therefore a natural law independent from revelation, whose precepts are derived from a sociability based on self-love: 'Man is weak, he needs the help of others: he recognizes in them their similar shape, actions, and needs; He recognizes them as his equals; This is the source of all social duties, of that love of one's Neighbour founded on the first Laws of sociability and on properly understood self-love'.[57]

It is not possible to follow in detail the contents of the plan, but the references to first principles, to a method of instruction aimed at creating debate and not erudition, emerge repeatedly. History is the continuation of morals and the person called to teach it must be a 'Philosophical Man', who knows how to 'unfold its causes, deduce its effects, and investigate its circumstances, thus weaving a genuine essay of Philosophical History and of the human heart'.[58] As such, there is a strict connection between moral philosophy, natural law and the teaching of jurisprudence in the broadest sense as a science of society: 'The security, property, peace and harmony of society are the most essential and precious things. The task of procuring and preserving them falls

55 'Piano scientifico per l'Università di Pavia', in *Statuti e ordinamenti della Università di Pavia dall'anno 1361 all'anno 1859. Raccolti e pubblicati nell'XI centenario dell'Ateneo* (Pavia: Tipografia cooperativa, 1925), 228–255, at 228.

56 Note here the evocation of Noël-Antoine Pluche's famous work *Le spectacle de la nature* (1732–1750) and of 'La confession de foi du vicaire Savoyard' in Book IV of Rousseau's *Émile*.

57 'Piano scientifico per l'Università di Pavia', 229.

58 Ibid., 230–231.

to Jurisprudence and the more noble Philosophy, founded on the intimate understanding of the human heart'.[59] Particularly with regard to the teaching of law, the objective was to establish a new 'model of the jurist', and thus 'in time producing a Philosophical Jurisconsult and a Legislator',[60] as Senator Pecci wrote in the 'Plan of Legal Studies' from 1767, in full agreement with Alessandro Verri's proposal in *Il Caffè*.

In short, there was a clear convergence between the reform plans and the pugilists' battle to overthrow the existing hierarchies of knowledge and power. Both ascribed primacy to the legislative philosopher, as the one responsible for recovering the true principles of natural and political law and serving as a true adviser to the prince. The new hierarchy reduced and then swept away the intermediary bodies and common law, but it did not translate into a form of omnipotence for legislative power and positive law; rather, it meant a despotism of laws derived not from the will of the legislator, but from the principles of philosophy.[61] The clearest example is the teaching of criminal law, which Beccaria gave a new foundation by tracing its principles to those of public law and the theory of the social contract.

5 The Principles of Criminal Law: On Crimes and Punishments

Even though the contribution to the history of economic thought made by the 'Milanese school' has been widely recognized, it cannot be denied that its biggest breakthrough and most original work was Beccaria's famous treatise, *Dei delitti e delle pene*. The work represented a methodological revolution in the field of criminal law.[62] With the education reform, the Austrian government also aimed to introduce criminal law as an independent subject of study.

---

59 Ibid., 255, also cited by Elisabetta Fiocchi in the previous chapter.

60 Archivio di Stato di Milano, Studi, p.a., cart. 375, fasc. 3, Nicola Pecci, 'Piano legale degli studi', fol. 10. The Archive stores two copies of Pecci's 'Plan', the first described as complete and the other as an incomplete version. I could verify that both manuscripts are incomplete, as we will see below. On the new 'model of the jurist', see Maria Carla Zorzoli, 'La formazione dei giuristi lombardi nell'età di Maria Teresa: il ruolo dell'Università', in *Economia, istituzioni, cultura in Lombardia*, vol. 3, 743–769, at 767.

61 On the despotism of law, see Christof Dipper, '*Despotie* und *Verfassung*: Zwei Freiheitskonzepte der Mailänder Aufklärung', in *Beiträge zur Begriffsgeschichte der Italienischen Aufklärung im Europäischen Kontext*, ed. Helmut C. Jacobs and Gisela Schlüter (Frankfurt am Main: Peter Lang, 2000), 23–58.

62 In relation to previous criminalists and judicial practice, Beccaria's work is certainly an 'epistemological' revolution. Compared with the works of preceding contractualist authors, it is a methodological revolution due to the extension of the deductive method from the 'principles of public law' to the 'principles of criminal law'.

In traditional curricula it had been included either in the final part of the Justinian *Institutes*, dedicated to obligations that originated *ex delicto*, as shown by the treatise of Venanzio de Mays, or else in lessons on local law. In treatises of politics and the law of nature and nations, from Pufendorf to Burlamaqui and Vattel, the power to punish was considered a prerogative of sovereignty and consequently constituted one of the most important parts of political or civil law, once again defined, in the language of the Verri brothers, as 'particular public law', which, together with universal public law – in other words the law of nations – was one of the two branches of public law.[63]

At the very time Beccaria was working on the first draft of his masterpiece, the original title of which was *Delle pene, e delitti*, the Milanese Senate published, on 5 October 1763, a call for professorships to be filled in the Palatine School of Milan and in the University of Pavia in accordance with a reformed study plan instead of the traditional one. Among the disciplines included was that 'Of criminal practice, or of crimes and punishments'.[64] If we are right to surmise that among the members of the Senate who had issued the call was the father of the Verri brothers, it seems hard to believe that the members of the Academy of Fists, at the very time they were beginning their implacable fight against the Senate and local jurisprudence, ignored the title of that chair and that the decision to rethink the order of the title of Beccaria's work was not partly inspired by it. The plan for the French translation of *Dei delitti e delle pene*, launched and then abandoned by Pietro Verri in 1764, appears to have been the counterpoint to that course of studies: *Des délits et des peines, ou Principes de la jurisprudence criminelle*.[65] The title opposes principles against practice, against the claims of sovereignty by a Senate acting as judge and legislator and resorting to arbitrary judgements, torture and the death penalty.

The radical innovation of Beccaria's text consisted precisely in the rigorous deduction of the principles of the power to punish from the theory of

63 For this distinction in the plan by Nicola Pecci, see Elisabetta Fiocchi Malaspina in Chapter 3 of the present volume. On the power to punish and the right to life and death in modern natural law, see Gabriella Silvestrini, 'Fra diritto di guerra e potere di punire: il diritto di vita e di morte nel *Contratto sociale*', *Rivista di Storia della filosofia* 70 (2015): 125–141; Dieter Hüning, '"Is not the power to punish essentially a power that pertains to the state?" The Different Foundations of the Right to Punish in Early Modern Natural Law Doctrines', *Politisches Denken Jahrbuch* 14 (2004): 43–60.

64 Archivio di Stato di Milano, Studi, p.a., cart. 296. The call is reproduced in Maria Gigliola di Renzo Villata, '1740–1765: un declino inarrestabile? Il Senato milanese "recalcitrante" tra misure riformistiche di ripiego e modesti segni di rinnovamento dell'Ateneo pavese', in *Almum Studium Papiense*, vol. 2.1, 63–82, at 77.

65 *ENPV*, vol. 1, 795–800.

the social contract, thus filling a gap in eighteenth-century moral and political science, which had already developed, through Rousseau and Vattel, 'the true relations between the sovereign and the subjects, and between the nations'.[66] However, this genuine theoretical originality cannot be interpreted as being opposed to natural law, since public law presupposes natural law and the science of politics depends on moral science.

The tripartition of 'revelation, natural law and the conventions arrived at by society' seen as the three main sources of the 'moral and political' principles 'regulating mankind' was not a mere screen erected to protect the work from religious censorship.[67] Pietro Verri had already made mention of this tripartition in his *Meditazioni sulla felicità*, which he found in Protestant theories of natural law that had distanced themselves from revelation. The tripartition also inspired the plans for the reform of the university, which aimed to bring the teaching of theology under state control, albeit while seeking mediation with the ecclesiastical institutions. Theology found itself in fourth place in the list of faculties proposed by the various reform projects, reflecting the marginalization of revelation and the Catholic religion in contrast to natural law, which remained central, but was nevertheless inscribed in the 'heart' of man, and had principles which could be discovered rationally.

The separation of religion and politics, of sin and crime, that is clearly established in Beccaria's work can also be found in the more cautious but no less decisive reform plans. In lessons on criminal law, professors had to demonstrate 'What is the nature and essence of crime, and the difference between the moral and political order in this matter'. In consequence, the principle of proportionality between crimes and punishment and the purpose of penal laws, namely 'the wellbeing of the Public', were affirmed. From these premises a three-part division of 'criminal law' was established: (1) the nature of crimes and punishments, (2) the judicial authority, termed the executor, and (3) criminal procedure.[68]

From this perspective, and in particular in the Milanese context, bracketing revealed religion – another of *Il Caffè*'s defensive editorial strategies – did not mean abandonment of natural law. Correctly understood, the latter continued

66 On Beccaria's introduction to *Dei delitti e delle pene*, see Gabriella Silvestrini, 'Cesare Beccaria: "Il Rousseau degli Italiani"?', in *Nell'officina dei Lumi. Studi in onore di Gianni Francioni*, ed. Giuseppe Cospito and Emilio Mazza (Como-Pavia: Ibis, 2021), 179–194.

67 *On Crimes and Punishment*, 'To the Reader', CPO, 4.

68 See Pecci's 1767 'Piano legale', Archivio di Stato di Milano, p.a., cart. 375, fasc. 3, copy 1, fols 12v–13r. See also the 'Piano scientifico per l'Università di Pavia', 239–240.

to constitute the boundaries of what was conceivable within the social and political science proposed by members of the Academy of Fists.

The reference to the inalienable right to self-defence that appears in the various editions of *Dei delitti*, in other words to the 'rights of man', is repeated in Pietro Verri's *Osservazioni sulla tortura*. And in chapter 16 of the *Ricerche intorno alla natura dello stile*, which remained unpublished, Beccaria, musing on the origin of the idea of justice, wrote: 'right can be defined as a necessary consequence of the use of our faculties, and justice as not preventing others from using the same faculties; just as duty may be defined as that which is necessary for us to do to ensure that the necessary use of the faculties of others is not impeded'.[69]

Therefore, if any difference can be discerned between the reform projects and the works of the 'pugilists', the most important one is that the former make no reference to inalienable rights of man nor to the possibility of finding a discrepancy between the duties of man and the duties of the citizen established by positive law. The 'pugilists' obviously thought that such discrepancy must be judged by the individual, who might then exercise a legitimate right to disobedience, if not outright resistance.[70]

6 Conclusions: The 'Pugilists' in the University Reform and the 'Imbroglio' of the Chairs

As is well known, on 9 January 1769 Beccaria delivered his inaugural lecture as professor of cameral sciences, a discipline later renamed 'public economy'.[71]

69 *EN*, vol. 2, 205. When having to express an opinion on the 'punishment of the nobles', beginning with the distinction between criminal and political offences, Beccaria defined criminal offences as those which, apart from leading towards the destruction of society, 'violate natural law'; see *EN*, vol. 9, 481–482.

70 Pietro Verri, *Meditazioni sulla felicità*, 748: 'I don't know if religion allows us to obey the prince's proclamations when they call on us to betray or kill a criminal, but if religion allowed it, it would be better to calculate whether the good that is done to men by freeing them from one judged to be a danger to public peace is greater than the evil of authorizing by example cold-hearted treason and legitimate murder'. In the correspondence of the Verri brothers there is an undeniably positive view of the execution of Charles I of England. See the letter from Alessandro Verri to Gian Rinaldo Carli, 20 June 1767, in *Lettere e scritti inediti di Pietro e Alessandro Verri*, vols 4, ed. Carlo Casati (Milano: Giuseppe Galli, 1879–1881), vol. 2, 265–274, at 270. See also Gianni Francioni, '"Ius" e "potestas". Beccaria e la pena di morte', *Beccaria. Revue d'histoire du pouvoir de punir* 2 (2016): 13–49, at 47–48.

71 On Beccaria's lecture, see Wolfgang Rother, 'The Beginning of Higher Education in Political Economy in Milan and Modena: Cesare Beccaria, Alfonso Longo, Agostino Paradisi', *History of Universities* 19(2) (2004): 119–158.

Rather than an intentional choice, the creation of this position appears to have been the result of a series of circumstances that dramatically altered the original plan to give the author of the *Delitti* the chair of public law in the Palatine School of Milan.

On 25 June 1765 Beccaria wrote to the chancellor, Prince Welzel Anton Kaunitz, requesting his support for his application for a post. The reform of the university was at a turning point, the Senate had been deprived of its educational competences, and the new delegation appointed by Vienna had begun its work. The wording of the message does not appear to leave any doubt: by sending the prince the 'two little books' he had published up to then, *Del disordine e de' rimedi delle monete nello Stato di Milano* and the third edition of the *Delitti*, the young marquis explained that he had no interest in 'forensic studies' and the 'career of the gown'. This was therefore a clear rejection of forensic jurisprudence and judicial practice, but not of the law in general. In fact, the text continues, 'I have always made my delight and my occupation those sciences that pertain to the regulation and economy of a state'.

The first version of this sentence had read 'of politics and the public jus, of the finances, of commerce and of that which belongs to the [...]'.[72] Beccaria was not requesting just any position, but a professorship in the political sciences, which included public law and public economy. The 'jurisconsult philosopher' was writing to offer his knowledge in the context of the reform of the institutions and of the education system theorized by the 'pugilists'. A few months later Vienna revoked responsibility for trade matters from the Milanese Senate and with a royal dispatch dated 20 November 1765 established the Supreme Council of Public Economy, which Gian Rinaldo Carli and Pietro Verri joined.[73] In October 1765 the marquis repeated his request, this time asking for a position in the same council, but was once more made to wait.[74]

In the meantime, the fame of his book spread like wildfire. The French translation brought him an invitation to Paris and led to his famous journey to the capital of the *philosophes* in the autumn of 1766, accompanied by Alessandro Verri, who had been encouraged to go by his brother Pietro, whose work commitments did not allow him to leave Milan. The trip, though, was marked by conflict between Beccaria and Alessandro, which resulted in the end of the intellectual and personal solidarity of the members of the Academy of Fists. But it did not disrupt the strong network of relations between Milan

72 *EN*, vol. 4, 101.

73 Carlo Capra, *I progressi della ragione. Vita di Pietro Verri* (Bologna: Il Mulino, 2002), 247–250.

74 *EN*, vol. 4, 263.

and Vienna that helped to find an 'annexation' (*annicchiamento*) in the Viennese administration for the pugilists and their friends.

Meanwhile, Catherine the Great of Russia had discovered the young Italian's work and invited him to Moscow. Beccaria used the invitation by the Russian sovereign to ask Vienna for a position at home. In this he was helped by friends who were preparing the plan to reform the university, in particular Gian Rinaldo Carli and Nicola Pecci. The latter, when drafting the 'Piano di studi legale', proposed, apart from the chair in public law at the University of Pavia held by Venanzio de Mays, the introduction at the Palatine School of Milan of a course in public law which, in an initial plan, covered, within 'particular public law', also the 'Rules of public Economy, of luxury, of Sumptuary Laws, exportation and importation of goods, the procedures for civil and criminal judgments, and of testamentary dispositions'.[75] Intended for a wider audience than that of students preparing to embark on a career in courts, as judges, lawyers and notaries, the course at the Palatine School was conceived as part of the general training of citizens who aspired to play a part in public administration. The right person for the role was Beccaria, who was the subject of correspondence in the spring of 1767 between the Count of Firmian and Prince Kaunitz, who declared himself in favour of introducing the chair in Milan and of assigning it to a young man who, unlike many Italians, intended to dedicate himself to the study of philosophy and not 'merely to the trivial jurisprudence of the court, deprived of any erudition, or to frivolous studies'.[76]

A dramatic change occurred during the autumn of 1767: Beccaria's name had become attached to a different chair – still at the Palatine School in Milan – that in cameral sciences. Was this destiny or chance? We know for certain that the first version of the 'Piano degli studi legale' written by Nicola Pecci and sent to Vienna on 10 September 1767 did not include a chair in economics or cameral sciences. This professorship was instead proposed in the documents accompanying the plan, and for this very reason Prince Kaunitz, in his response to the plan of 16 November 1767, which was very critical of the project but enthusiastic about introducing to Milan a course in cameral

75 Nicola Pecci, 'Piano', Archivio di Stato di Milano, p.a., cart. 375, fasc. 3, copy 2, fol. 10 verso. In the copy 1 of the manuscript there is an evident gap between fol. 19 verso and fol. 20 recto: the folio 19 verso stops with 'Sumptuary Laws' and folio 20 recto begins with 'del Feudo rimangono al Vassallo'. It is therefore impossible, on the basis of copy 1, to understand what Pecci originally included in the course on public law.

76 Letter from Kaunitz to Firmian, 21 May 1767, in Angelo Mauri, 'La cattedra di Cesare Beccaria', *Archivio storico italiano* 91 (1933): 199–262, at 211.

sciences like the one held by Sonnenfels in Vienna, expressed his disappointment that the description of the course had not been included in the academic plan.[77]

We might therefore presume that the idea of *doubling* the Milanese chair of public law and creating a parallel one in cameral sciences had come to the members of the Deputation only belatedly, when it was no longer possible to alter the plan before sending it to Vienna. What had happened in the meantime?

Perhaps the answer lies in the correspondence between Pietro and Alessandro Verri. The latter, when Beccaria returned to Milan in November 1766, left for London, where he remained a couple of months. He then returned via Paris to Italy where, without passing through Milan, he headed for Tuscany and eventually ended up in Rome. The letters between Alessandro and his brother gradually reveal a desire on Alessandro's part to turn his temporary journey into a permanent abandonment of the city of his birth, while Pietro, hoping for his brother's return, made strong arguments against. And in this crescendo of emotions, Pietro sought to entice Alessandro back to Milan with promises of employment, thanks to the support of Firmian and of Carli.

However, Alessandro made plans to establish himself elsewhere, as he feared a return to his family. At a certain point he dreamed of a chair in Pisa, hoping for the support of Pompeo Neri:

> I have an idea that is not yet mature, about which I will do what you advise. There are many empty chairs in Pisa: it is up to President Neri whether I might get one. I find that I enjoy some esteem for the work I have published. Logic, metaphysics, ethics, public and private and criminal law suit me, and I can keep my word. One cannot live with Father in Milan, there would be constant anger, an immortal desire to do harm: perpetual and cruel war! Waiting for a position is a long antechamber, and then I feel positively oppressed by the idea of a type of slavery that takes me away from letters, towards which I feel enraptured by yearning.[78]

---

77 Archivio di Stato di Milano, *Studi*, p.a., cart. 375, fasc. 1, Letter from Kaunitz of 16 November 1767, fol. 8: 'I therefore do not know why the plan for the chair in Cameral Sciences has been omitted from the other projects and plans for the respective sciences and chairs to be established in Milan. Is this not a chair which, considering the circumstances of the time, must be one of the most important and most useful to the nation?'

78 Alessandro Verri to Pietro Verri, 20 April 1767, in *Viaggio a Parigi e Londra (1766–1767). Carteggio di Pietro e Alessandro Verri*, ed. Gianmarco Gaspari (Milano: Adelphi, 1980), 405–406.

Pietro, disconsolate, dissuaded him, just as he stated his opposition to Alessandro journeying to Vienna to ingratiate himself with the Habsburg authorities. At a certain point, however, the situation came to a head in an alarming manner. In Rome Alessandro fell in love with a married woman and risked never returning to Milan. Pietro first attempted to 'disillusion him' by casting severe doubts on the respectability of his lover. Then, when Alessandro confessed his genuine love, the unexpected 'imbroglio' of a chair in public law appeared. In a famous letter of 17 October 1767 a distraught Pietro informed his brother that, through no fault of his own or of his father, Gabriele, the request for the creation of a chair of public law at the Palatine School had been sent to Vienna on Alessandro's behalf. By a series of circumstances and misunderstandings, Count Gabriele Verri, urged by Paolo Frisi, Nicola Pecci and Gian Rinaldo Carli, had already made a formal commitment to the Viennese authorities on behalf of his son. What, in the end, would it cost him to commute between Milan and Rome, the older brother asked, probably in league with his father. It would be too difficult to turn back now.[79] But Alessandro, indignant, asked his brother not to interfere further in his personal pursuit of happiness and firmly rejected the proposal.[80]

We can only imagine how things went. Faced with the threat of a permanent estrangement from Alessandro and a romantic attachment that would have been difficult for the family to swallow, Pietro and Gabriele Verri increased their pressure on their friends to find Alessandro not just any position, and one that he probably would not want, but a 'niche' in the reform of the university, thus indulging his passion for 'letters'. The main protagonists, the Verri family, Carli, Firmian and Pecci, hurriedly found a solution in the idea of doubling up the chair in public law and offering Beccaria the equivalent position in economics as compensation. This explains the unexpected appearance, in the presentation of the plans sent to Vienna in September 1767, of the course in cameral sciences.

Alessandro's refusal to return to Milan and renounce his happiness, and Kaunitz's enthusiasm for the proposal of a course in the cameral sciences led

79 *Carteggio di Pietro e di Alessandro Verri*, ed. Emanuele Greppi and Alessandro Giulini (Milano: Cogliati, 1926), vol. 1, II, 90–92.

80 As attested in the copy, written by Pietro Verri's copyist, conserved in Fondazione Mattioli, Milan, Italy, Archivio Verri, 279, fol. 418, Alessandro's letter dates to 23 October 1767; I would like to express my gratitude to Sara Rosini, Fondazione Mattioli, who helped me to decipher the handwriting of Pietro Verri's copyist; in the *Carteggio di Pietro e di Alessandro Verri*, vol. 2, this letter from Alessandro is attributed to 13 October, following the copyist of the Società Storica Lombarda; it is conserved at Biblioteca Nazionale Braidense, Milan, Italy, Carteggio Verri, 2, fol. 856.

to a modification of the initial project. The course in public law in the Palatine School of Milan would be dropped and Alfonso Longo would be given the task of presenting lectures in ecclesiastical public law. Beccaria would instead find himself hurriedly compiling, for Gian Rinaldo Carli, the plan for the chair in cameral sciences and his course. This, launched at the start of 1769, would be the first step in the reform that would be fully enacted only in 1773, when Beccaria, despite the success of his lectures, having already obtained a position as an 'employee' in the Council of Cameral Sciences, abandoned the university post.

These were the crossed destinies and dreams that resulted in the less than 'triumphal' entry of economic science into the Palatine School of Milan. Far from being an autonomous science, to Beccaria's mind as well as to others involved in the reforms, while public economy was indeed a fundamental branch of knowledge, it was not the backbone of a political science, but instead remained firmly anchored in morality and the law of nature and of nations.

Archival Sources

Archivio di Stato di Milano, Milan, Italy, Studi, p.a., cart. 269, 375.
Biblioteca Nazionale Braidense, Milan, Italy, Carteggio Verri, 2.
Fondazione Mattioli, Milan, Italy, Archivio Verri, 279.

Bibliography

Audegean, Philippe, 'Droit naturel et droit à la vie. Beccaria lecteur de Hobbes', *Diciottesimo secolo* 4 (2019): 33–45.

Audegean, Philippe, *La philosophie de Beccaria: savoir punir, savoir écrire, savoir produire* (Paris: Vrin, 2010).

Bazzoli, Maurizio, 'Aspetti della recezione di Pufendorf nel Settecento italiano', in *Dal* De Jure naturae et gentium *di Samuel Pufendorf alla codificazione prussiana del 1794*, ed. Marta Ferronato (Padova: Cedam, 2005), 41–60.

Beccaria, Cesare, *Edizione Nazionale delle Opere di Cesare Beccaria*, ed. Luigi Firpo and Gianni Francioni, 16 vols (Milano: Mediobanca, 1984–2014).

Beccaria, Cesare, *On Crimes and Punishments and Other Writings*, ed. Richard Bellamy (Cambridge: Cambridge University Press, 1995).

Bessler, John, *The Celebrated Marquis: An Italian Noble and the Making of the Modern World* (Durham, NC: Carolina Academic Press, 2018).

Bondolfi, Alberto, 'Beccaria et la religion: la réaction de Facchinei et du Saint-Office', in *Le moment Beccaria: naissance du droit pénal moderne (1764–1810)*, ed. Philippe Audegean and Luigi Delia (Liverpool: Liverpool University Press/Voltaire Foundation, 2018), 33–42.

Capra, Carlo, *I progressi della ragione. Vita di Pietro Verri* (Bologna: Il Mulino, 2002).

Capra, Carlo, *La Lombardia austriaca nell'età delle riforme, 1706–1796* (Torino: Utet, 1987).

Capra, Carlo, 'Longo, Alfonso', in *Dizionario Biografico degli Italiani* (Roma: Istituto dell'Enciclopedia Italiana, 2005), vol. 65, 687–692.

Carteggio di Pietro e di Alessandro Verri, ed. Emanuele Greppi and Alessandro Giulini (Milano: Cogliati, 1923).

Cavanna, Adriano, 'La codificazione del diritto nella Lombardia austriaca', in *Economia, istituzioni, cultura in Lombardia nell'età di Maria Teresa*, 3 vols, ed. Aldo De Maddalena, Ettore Rotelli and Gennaro Barbarisi (Bologna: Il Mulino, 1982), vol. 3, 611–657.

Cesare Beccaria. La controverse pénale XVIIIe–XXIe siècle, ed. Michel Porret and Élisabeth Salvi (Rennes: Presses Universitaires de Rennes, 2015).

Cléro, Jean-Pierre, 'Un tournant dans la conception du droit pénal: Beccaria and Bentham', in *Entre droit et morale: la finalité de la peine*, ed. Annette Sousa Costa (Bern: Peter Lang, 2010), 63–98.

Concepts and Contexts of Vattel's Political and Legal Thought, ed. Peter Schröder (Cambridge: Cambridge University Press, 2021).

de Champs, Emmanuelle, 'Bentham et l'héritage de Beccaria: du *Projet d'un corps complet de législation* aux *Traités des législation civile et pénale*', in *Cesare Beccaria. La controverse pénale XVIIIe–XXIe siècle*, ed. Michel Porret and Élisabeth Salvi (Rennes: Presses Universitaires de Rennes, 2015), 99–110.

Diderot, Denis, 'Droit naturel', in *Encyclopédie, ou dictionnaire raisonné des sciences, des arts et des métiers, etc.*, ed. Denis Diderot and Jean le Rond d'Alembert, University of Chicago ARTFL Encyclopédie Project (autumn 2022 edition), ed. Robert Morrissey and Glenn Roe, https://encyclopedie.uchicago.edu (accessed on 14 January 2023).

Diderot, Denis, *Political Writings*, ed. and trans. John Hope Mason and Robert Wokler (Cambridge: Cambridge University Press, 1992).

Dipper, Christof, '*Despotie* und *Verfassung*: Zwei Freiheitskonzepte der Mailänder Aufklärung', in *Beiträge zur Begriffsgeschichte der Italienischen Aufklärung im Europäischen Kontext*, ed. Helmut C. Jacobs and Gisela Schlüter (Frankfurt am Main: Peter Lang, 2000), 23–58.

di Renzo Villata, Maria Gigliola, '1740–1765: un declino inarrestabile? Il Senato milanese "recalcitrante" tra misure riformistiche di ripiego e modesti segni di rinnovamento dell'Ateneo pavese', in *Almum Studium Papiense. Storia dell'Università di Pavia*, vol. 2.1, *Dall'età austriaca alla nuova Italia*, ed. Dario Mantovani (Milano: Cisalpino Istituto Editoriale Universitario, 2015), 63–82.

di Renzo Villata, Maria Gigliola, '1765–1771: Gli anni decisivi per la riforma. Dall'incubazione ai risultati', in *Almum Studium Papiense. Storia dell'Università di Pavia*, vol. 2.1, *Dall'età austriaca alla nuova Italia*, ed. Dario Mantovani (Milano: Cisalpino Istituto Editoriale Universitario, 2015), 83–114.

di Renzo Villata, Maria Gigliola, 'Avant Beccaria. La culture juridique à l'épreuve du temps', in *Le bonheur du plus grand nombre. Beccaria et les Lumières*, ed. Philippe Audegean et al. (Lyon: ENS, 2017), 47–61.

di Renzo Villata, Maria Gigliola, 'Cesare Beccaria (1738–1794)', in *Law and the Christian Tradition in Italy: The Legacy of the Great Jurists*, ed. Orazio Condorelli and Rafael Domingo (London: Routledge, 2021), 331–347.

di Renzo Villata, Maria Gigliola, 'Introduzione. La formazione del giurista in Italia e l'influenza culturale europea tra Sette e Ottocento: il caso della Lombardia', in *Formare il giurista. Esperienze nell'area lombarda tra Sette e Ottocento*, ed. di Renzo Villata (Milano: Giuffrè, 2004), 1–106.

Duke Georg, George, Robert P., 'Introduction', in *The Cambridge Companion to Natural Jurisprudence*, ed. George Duke and Robert P. George (Cambridge: Cambridge University Press, 2017), 1–13.

Ferrajoli, Luigi, 'Beccaria e Bentham', *Diciottesimo secolo* 4 (2019): 75–84.

Ferrand, Jérôme, 'La nécessité, passager clandestin de l'abolitionnisme beccarien', in *Le bonheur du plus grand nombre. Beccaria et les Lumières*, ed. Philippe Audegean et al. (Lyon: ENS, 2017), 127–138.

Fiocchi, Elisabetta, 'De Mays, Venanzio', https://naturallawdatabase.thulb.uni-jena.de/item/natlaw_196.

Francioni, Gianni, 'Beccaria, philosophe utilitariste' (first Italian edition 1990), in *Le bonheur du plus grand nombre. Beccaria et les Lumières*, ed. Philippe Audegean et al. (Lyon: ENS, 2017), 23–44.

Francioni, Gianni, 'Censura e autocensura nella rivista "Il Caffè"', in *Varianti politiche d'autore. Da Verri a Manzoni*, ed. Beatrice Nava (Bologna: Pàtron, 2019), 15–57.

Francioni, Gianni, '"Ius" e "potestas". Beccaria e la pena di morte', *Beccaria. Revue d'histoire du pouvoir de punir* 2 (2016): 13–49.

Francioni, Gianni, 'Nota introduttiva', in Pietro Verri, *Meditazioni sulla felicità* (1763), in *Edizione Nazionale delle Opere di Pietro Verri*, vol. 1, *Scritti letterari, filosofici e satirici*, ed. Gianni Francioni (Roma: Edizioni di Storia e Letteratura, 2014), 685–687.

Gallotti, Carla Federica, 'Diffusione dei lumi e crisi delle riforme in Spagna nella testimonianza di Pietro Paolo Giusti (1772–1781)', *Studi Settecenteschi* 11–12 (1988–1989): 237–303.

Garlati, Loredana, 'Beccaria: Filosofo acclamato del passato e giurista misconosciuto del futuro', in *Dialogando con Beccaria. Le stagioni del processo penale italiano*, ed. Giovanni Chiodi and Loredana Garlati (Torino: Giappichelli, 2015), 1–30.

Garlati, Loredana, 'Tradition et réformisme. Les inspirateurs culturels du Beccaria processualiste', in *Le bonheur du plus grand nombre. Beccaria et les Lumières*, ed. Philippe Audegean et al. (Lyon: ENS, 2017), 63–77.

Garnsey, Peter, *Against the Death Penalty: Writings from the First Abolitionists – Giuseppe Pelli and Cesare Beccaria*, texts translated and with historical commentary by Peter Garnsey (Princeton, NJ: Princeton University Press, 2020).

Guderzo, Giulio, 'La riforma dell'università di Pavia', in *Economia, istituzioni, cultura in Lombardia nell'età di Maria Teresa*, 3 vols, ed. Aldo De Maddalena, Ettore Rotelli and Gennaro Barbarisi (Bologna: Il Mulino, 1982), vol. 3, 854–861.

Haakonssen, Knud, 'Early Modern Natural Law Theories', in *The Cambridge Companion to Natural Jurisprudence*, ed. George Duke and Robert P. George (Cambridge: Cambridge University Press, 2017), 76–102.

Hart, Herbert L. A., 'Bentham and Beccaria', in idem, *Essays on Bentham: Studies in Jurisprudence and Political Theory* (Oxford: Clarendon Press, 1982), 40–52.

Helvétius, C[laude]-A[drien], *De l'esprit, or, Essays on the mind, and its several faculties* (London: Albion Press, 1810).

Hochstrasser, Tim, *Natural Law Theories in the Early Enlightenment* (Cambridge: Cambridge University Press, 2000).

Hüning, Dieter, '"Is not the power to punish essentially a power that pertains to the state?" The Different Foundations of the Right to Punish in Early Modern Natural Law Doctrines', *Politisches Denken Jahrbuch* 14 (2004): 43–60.

Hutcheson, Francis, *Recherches sur l'origine des idées que nous avons de la beauté et de la vertu*, 2 vols, French trans. by Marc-Antoine Eidous (Amsterdam [i.e. Paris], 1749).

'Il Caffè' 1764–1766, 2nd edition revised, ed. Gianni Francioni and Sergio Romagnoli (Torino: Bollati Boringhieri, 1998).

Il caso Beccaria. A 250 anni dalla pubblicazione del 'Dei delitti e delle pene', ed. Vincenzo Ferrone and Giuseppe Ricuperati (Bologna: Il Mulino, 2016).

Ippolito, Dario, 'Contrat social et peine capitale. Beccaria contre Rousseau', in *Rousseau et l'Italie. Littérature, morale et politique*, ed. Philippe Audegean, Magda Campanini and Barbara Carnevali (Paris: Harmattan, 2017), 147–176.

Le bonheur du plus grand nombre. Beccaria et les Lumières, ed. Philippe Audegean et al. (Lyon: ENS, 2017).

Lettere e scritti inediti di Pietro e Alessandro Verri, 4 vols, ed. Carlo Casati (Milano: Giuseppe Galli, 1879–1881).

Mauri, Angelo, 'La cattedra di Cesare Beccaria', *Archivio storico italiano* 91 (1933): 199–262.

Muceni, Elena, *Apologia della virtù sociale. L'ascesa dell'amor proprio nella crisi della coscienza europea* (Milano: Mimesis, 2018).

Musitelli, Pierre, *Le flambeau et les ombres: Alessandro Verri, des Lumières à la Restauration (1741–1816)* (Paris: École française de Rome, 2016).

Passerin d'Entrèves, Ettore, 'Le premesse del riformismo di Maria Teresa e di Giuseppe II nel campo ecclesiastico, in Austria e in Lombardia', in *Economia, istituzioni, cultura in Lombardia nell'età di Maria Teresa*, 3 vols, ed. Aldo De Maddalena, Ettore Rotelli and Gennaro Barbarisi (Bologna: il Mulino, 1982), vol. 2, 729–740.

Petronio, Ugo, *Il Senato di Milano: istituzioni giuridiche ed esercizio del potere nel ducato di Milano da Carlo V a Giuseppe II* (Milano: Giuffrè, 1969).

Preto, Paolo, 'Facchinei, Ferdinando', in *Dizionario Biografico degli Italiani* (Roma: Istituto dell'Enciclopedia Italiana, 1994), vol. 44, 29–31.

Reinert, Sophus A., *The Academy of Fisticuffs: Political Economy and Commercial Society in Enlightenment Italy* (Cambridge, MA: Harvard University Press, 2018).

Rother, Wolfgang, 'The Beginning of Higher Education in Political Economy in Milan and Modena: Cesare Beccaria, Alfonso Longo, Agostino Paradisi', *History of Universities* 19(2) (2004): 119–158.

Schröder, Peter, 'Natural Law and Enlightenment in France and Scotland – A Comparative Perspective', in *Early Modern Natural Law Theories: Contexts and Strategies in the Early Enlightenment*, ed. Tim J. Hochstrasser and Peter Schröder (Dordrecht: Springer, 2003), 297–317.

Shackleton, Robert, 'The Greatest Happiness of the Greatest Number: The History of Bentham's Phrase', *Studies on Voltaire and the Eighteenth Century* 90 (1972): 1641–1682.

Silvestrini, Gabriella, 'Cesare Beccaria: "Il Rousseau degli Italiani"?', in *Nell'officina dei Lumi. Studi in onore di Gianni Francioni*, ed. Giuseppe Cospito and Emilio Mazza (Como-Pavia: Ibis, 2021), 179–194.

Silvestrini, Gabriella, 'Fra diritto di guerra e potere di punire: il diritto di vita e di morte nel *Contratto sociale*', *Rivista di Storia della filosofia* 70 (2015): 125–141.

Spector, Céline, *Éloges de l'injustice. La philosophie face à la déraison* (Paris: Seuil, 2016).

Statuti e ordinamenti della Università di Pavia dall'anno 1361 all'anno 1859. Raccolti e pubblicati nell'XI centenario dell'Ateneo (Pavia: Tipografia cooperativa, 1925).

Thomson, Ann, 'French Eighteenth-Century Materialists and Natural Law', *History of European Ideas* 42 (2016): 243–255.

Turchetti, Maria Francesca, 'Alfonso Longo e l'Accademia dei Pugni (con quattro lettere inedite)', *Archivio storico lombardo* 140 (2014): 152–185.

Verri, Pietro, *Edizione Nazionale delle Opere di Pietro Verri*, vol. 1, *Scritti letterari, filosofici e satirici*, ed. Gianni Francioni (Roma: Edizioni di Storia e Letteratura, 2014).

Verri, Alessandro, *Saggio di Morale cristiana* (1763), ed. Pierre Musitelli (2016), http://illuminismolombardo.it/testo/saggio-di-morale-cristiana/?tipo=1.

Viaggio a Parigi e Londra (1766–1767). Carteggio di Pietro e Alessandro Verri, ed. Gianmarco Gaspari (Milano: Adelphi, 1980).

Wootton, David, 'Helvétius: From Radical Enlightenment to Revolution', *Political Theory* 28 (2000): 307–336.

Zorzoli, Maria Carla, 'La formazione dei giuristi lombardi nell'età di Maria Teresa: il ruolo dell'Università', in *Economia, istituzioni, cultura in Lombardia nell'età di Maria Teresa*, 3 vols, ed. Aldo De Maddalena, Ettore Rotelli and Gennaro Barbarisi (Bologna: Il Mulino, 1982), vol. 3, 743–769.

PART 2

Recoveries and Criticisms of Natural Law

CHAPTER 5

Natural Ethics and History: Antonio Genovesi and Mario Pagano

Girolamo Imbruglia

1 Introduction

In the 1750s, with the appearance of the *Encyclopédie*, the two *Discours* of Rousseau, the *Code de la Nature* by Morelly and finally, in 1758, *De l'Esprit* by Helvétius, thinking around natural law was experiencing a radical change. It was debated whether natural law could be an instrument of political transformation. Already in his article '*Autorité politique', which appeared in the first volume of the *Encyclopédie*, Diderot had taken up the theme of Locke's *Two Treatises of Government* – of the right to appeal to abstract reason in a situation of crisis and breakdown in society. In 'Fanatisme' Alexandre Deleyre also followed this line of reasoning and showed that politics unsupported by natural reason were a cause of social ruin. Theocratic politics, guided by superstition and fanaticism, or Hobbesian Leviathan, with its maxim *Salus populi suprema lex esto*, as expression of utilitarianism and conventionalism, paved the way to despotism. For Deleyre, the only way to avoid these two dangers was to follow Voltaire and his theorization of natural law, which managed to curb irrational and violent passions and ensured *bienveillance*. Criticism of the principle of *Salus populi* in the name of natural law was also at the centre of Rousseau's article 'Economie politique'. For Rousseau, that principle concealed the wish of those in government to assert themselves, who by that deception forced citizens to sacrifice themselves not for the general good but in the interests of power. Uniting government and sovereignty so that the latter could direct and restrain the power of the 'police' (the executive power) had been a problem that no legislator had ever been able to solve – but this was answered in the *Contrat social* (1762). The wise lawgiver had to be able to transform the natural rights of men in the duties of the citizens.[1]

1 Jean-Jacques Rousseau, *Of the Social Contract*, IV, 8, in idem, *Of the Social Contract and Other Political Writings*, Engl. transl. Quintin Hoare, ed. Christopher Bertram (London: Penguin Books, 2012), 131: 'So there is a purely civil profession of faith whose article it is the Sovereign's

Helvétius took the opposite position, and in *De l'Esprit* rejected these theories of natural law and presented a complete system of utilitarian politics.[2] Both the platonic metaphysics of Shaftesbury and the scepticism of Montaigne had been unable to understand 'the history of the world', where 'time must necessarily produce, in the physical and moral worlds, revolutions that change the face of empires', and where therefore 'the same actions may successively become useful and prejudicial, and consequently, by turns, assume the name of virtuous and vicious'. Moral virtue was the relation between individual interest and public interest: it was 'a desire of general happiness', and 'consequently, the public welfare is the object of virtue'.[3] Two paths could lead towards the creation of a happy society for as many citizens as possible: 'either an extraordinary education, or an excellent legislation'[4] – the route of administrative reforms, or a republican utopia. But Helvétius realized the difficulties and, in this work, seemed to discard both solutions. 'I should perhaps try to lay out the plan of a good education [...] If I renounce this task it is because, even supposing that I can actually explain the means of making men better, it is evident that in our present customs it would be almost impossible to make use of these means'.[5]

Such were also the themes of the debate that developed in Naples, but with a relevant, specific difference caused by the circulation of the ideas of the Neapolitan philosopher Giambattista Vico (1668–1744). Vico had discussed the relationship between *jus naturale gentium* and political authority in his *Scienza nuova* (Naples, 1725, 1730, 1744), where he criticized Grotius, Hobbes

---

province to determine, not precisely like dogmas of Religion, but as feelings of sociability, without which it is impossible to be a good Citizen or a loyal subject'.

2 Ann Thomson, 'French Eighteenth-Century Materialists and Natural Law', *History of European Ideas* 42(2) (2016): 243–255, at 253, acknowledges that 'Helvétius therefore adopted a position influenced by Hobbesian voluntarism', but according to her, Helvétius's position is not a complete juxtaposition to jusnaturalism. On the question of enlightened utilitarianism and jusnaturalism, see likewise Sophie Audidière, *Passions de l'intérêt* (Paris: Honoré Champion, 2022) and Gabriella Silvestrini's discussion of Beccaria in Chapter 4 of the present volume.

3 Claude-Adrien Helvétius, *De l'Esprit*, II, 13 (Londres [i.e. Liège]: [Clement Plomteux], 1776), vol. 1, 172–173 (the English text in Helvétius, *De l'Esprit or Essays on Mind and its several faculties*, ed. William Mudford (London: M. Jones, 1807). See David Wootton, 'Laughing at Helvétius', in *Etica e religione nella tradizione repubblicana. Aspetti storici e teorici*, ed. Maurizio Viroli et al. (Torino: Fondazione Agnelli, 1996), 95–124.

4 Helvétius, *Esprit*, III, 23, vol. 2, 546.

5 Ibid., IV, 16, vol. 2, 206–207.

and the theories of natural law of the seventeenth century.[6] According to him, the *jus gentium* had not an a priori foundation and was originated within history; it was *natural* because it was the answer to the natural sentiments and need of society.[7] Among these theories, against Vico, Antonio Genovesi stayed true to Grotian jusnaturalism[8] and opted decisively for education, paying less attention to the centrality of sovereignty in the 1750s.[9] He believed that in modern Europe public education was an essential instrument for training the citizen in civic humanism, and proposed projects for reform, fighting corruption and halting the drift towards despotism. Genovesi's most outstanding disciple, Mario Pagano, overturned this idea of politics. He followed Rousseau and Vico and for him the basic issue of enlightenment was the political critique of legislation. At the centre of these trends, Genovesi and his school enlarged the theory of natural law through a new reflection on history, both the natural history of mankind and the national history of their kingdom.

2 Antonio Genovesi

After having been ordained priest in Salerno, in 1743 Antonio Genovesi (1713–1769) arrived in Naples, where he immediately abandoned his theological studies to commit himself to the study of moral philosophy.[10] In 1746 he

---

6 See Isaiah Berlin, 'The Philosophical Ideas of Giambattista Vico', in idem, *Vico and Herder: Two Studies in the History of Ideas* (New York: Viking Press, 1976), 3–98, at 34: 'Vico attacks the great jurists Grotius, Selden, Pufendorf […] for their blindness to the idea of development, *nascimento*, coming to birth, from which *natura* is derived, whereby one generation, or culture, grows into another'.

7 Felix Waldmann, 'Natural Law and the Chair of Ethics in the University of Naples, 1703–1769', *Modern Intellectual History* 19 (2022): 54–80, and John Robertson, 'Sociability in Sacred Historical Perspective, 1650–1800', in *Markets, Morals, Politics: Jealousy of Trade and the History of Political Thought*, ed. Béla Kapossy, Isaac Nakhimovsky and Sophus A. Reinert (Cambridge, MA: Harvard University Press, 2018), 53–81.

8 Richard Tuck, 'The "Modern" Theory of Natural Law', in *The Languages of Political Theory in Early-Modern Europe*, ed. Anthony Pagden (Cambridge: Cambridge University Press, 1987), 99–119.

9 'Government is an entity made up of the legislative and executive power. It is created by families coming together. Therefore, there can be as many types of government as the ways in which peoples have wished to be governed'. Antonio Genovesi, *Spirito delle leggi del signore di Montesquieu con le note dell'abate Antonio Genovesi* (1777) (Napoli: Gennaro Reale, 1820), vol. 1, 100 [ad *Esprit des lois*, II, 1].

10 As Galanti put it, 'Abbot Genovesi was of enlightened piety and for the honour of humanity ardently desired that Theology be abolished'. Giuseppe Maria Galanti, *Elogio storico del signor abate Antonio Genovesi* (1772) (Napoli: Bibliopolis, 1977), 66.

was engaged to teach ethics at the University of Naples[11] and became a university professor, which no French intellectual was. He was convinced that he could create a new public ethos through the circulation of his thought and through teaching. In 1753 he was appointed to the chair of commerce and mechanics at the same university. For over ten years his teaching continued to be of extraordinary importance, on account of the enormous impact of the approximately sixty books he published and of his great academic success. 'Here, in his books of immortal character / He speaks, he teaches, and will teach forever'.[12] One of his pupils (whom we shall meet soon again), Carlo Pecchia, said that thousands of students had been instructed by Genovesi in 'every species of knowledge', not out of 'vile interest' but out of generosity. Felix Waldmann has accurately reconstructed Genovesi's academic activity, coming to the conclusion that between 1746 and 1769 his students numbered around 3,000, when also taking account of the private school: an amazing number. The average age of the students attending lectures was between seventeen and twenty-three, and it should be noted that these students came from all regions of the continental kingdom (therefore, excluding Sicily). This is of prime importance, since it meant that Genovesi's ideas were not the exclusive prerogative of the Neapolitan elite, but had an incisive and broad circulation throughout the Kingdom of Naples, creating a widespread awareness of the need for reforms and of their main goals. Waldman has succeeded in naming about eighty of this anonymous mass of listeners, who more or less directly made up part of the Genovesi 'school'.[13] In the reconstruction of their subsequent careers we can grasp the general and most profound meaning of Genovesi's teaching in Neapolitan society: namely, the formation of the ethos of the southern ruling class.

His courses usually lasted two years and we may conjecture that they brought together three main theoretical areas, corresponding to the three phases into which Genovesi himself divided his own work as a *philosophe*. The first was metaphysical and moral philosophy, followed in the 1750s by the study of economics, until finally, in 1767, he changed 'from a merchant to a decretal-

11 Raffaele Iovine, 'Una cattedra per Genovesi nella crisi della cultura moderna a Napoli, 1744–1754', *Frontiera d'Europa* 7 (2001): 359–532.

12 'Quaggiù ne' libri d'immortali tempre; / E parla, e insegna, e insegnerà per sempre'. Carlo Pecchia, *Elogio dell'abate Antonio Genovesi* (Napoli, 1769), xv, cited by Felix Waldmann, *Antonio Genovesi, the 'Scuola Genovesiana', and Philosophy in the Kingdom of Naples, 1743–1792* (unpublished Cambridge PhD dissertation,, 2015–2016), 38. I could read this important work owing to the courtesy of the author, whom I thank.

13 Waldmann, *Antonio Genovesi*, 42–53.

ist'.[14] With this ironic definition of himself, Genovesi emphasized his polemics as jurist against the ecclesiastical tradition. It is true that these 'figures' – philosopher, economist, jurist – corresponded to particular political and cultural situations for which Genovesi wanted to furnish specific responses; nevertheless, in his reflections their perspectives entwine without ever cancelling each other out. Tracing the publication of his works chronologically, it is not possible to identify any particular group of works that corresponds thematically and temporally to one of the three phases. Genovesi created his own original 'plan of ethics', which was the common line of his new research. The theory of the laws of nature[15] is connected with natural jurisprudence but not confused with it and in the construction of civil society the 'duties' of man conceived in the wake of Pufendorf are combined with the theory of Grotian natural sociability and rights.

At the end of his life, in his last work of jurisprudence and duties written for his students, the *Diceosina, o sia, della filosofia del giusto e dell'onesto* (1766) (from the Greek δικαιοσύνη), Genovesi based his theory of morality upon the separation of theology from moral and political life.[16] In order to explain his 'science of ethics' he followed Grotius, Pufendorf and Locke, and embraced the enlightened approach to natural law theories. The book was composed of two parts: the theory of the natural right to happiness and the theory of duties,[17] which put human natural sociability in practice. The a priori norms of the good and just were to be followed in the institutions of human life. In the rational ontology of the world there was reciprocity between natural rights and social duties, and therefore in the civil structure the relationship between power (paternal and political) and obedience was a protection against usurpation and violence. In order to achieve not an arithmetical equality, but the

14 Antonio Genovesi, *L'affare delle Decretali* (this includes seventeen works written between 1766 and 1769], in idem, *Dialoghi e altri scritti. Intorno alle* Lezioni di commercio, ed. Eluggero Pii (Napoli: Istituto Italiano per gli Studi filosofici, 2008), 497.

15 Antonio Genovesi, *Elementa metaphysicae*, vol. 4, *Principia Legis naturalis, et officiorum humanorum* (Neapoli: Ex Typographia Benedecti Gessari, 1756). See Waldmann, 'Natural Law', *passim.*

16 Antonio Genovesi, *Diceosina, o sia, della filosofia del giusto e dell'onesto* (1766–1771), ed. Niccolò Guasti (Venezia: Centro di studi sull'illuminismo G. Stiffoni-Edizioni della Laguna, 2008). Its Latin edition had the title *De jure et officiis in usum tironum* (Neapoli: Ex typographia Simoniana, 1767). See Antonio Genovesi, *Autobiografia e Lettere*, ed. G. Savarese (Milano: Feltrinelli, 1962), 19.

17 According to Genovesi, *Diceosina*, I, ch. 5, § 1, 75, duty is the execution of the eternal rule of the honest and of the just. On the 'true, compelling, divine norm for human life', see *Diceosina*, I, ch. 4, § 20, 67.

legal equality of natural rights, society had to acknowledge both private property but also a social control of luxury. The book had great success because of its energy, but from another point of view the pages look faded.[18] Genovesi tried to unite two languages, those of the theories of human rights and of civic republicanism,[19] but he did not succeed. His abstract consideration of human nature was not able to bring forth a real description of institutions and manners. Following the Christian humanistic interpretation of Cicero,[20] Genovesi's models were Inca Peru, Jesuit missions of Paraguay and the Quakers' Pennsylvania. More than devise a strategy to project actual reforms, his jusnaturalism drove him to dwell on archaic models of utopia.

Perhaps Genovesi's case shows the difficulty for jusnaturalism to answer the political and social problems of a European society at the middle of the century. The synthesis of those two perspectives was indeed a difficult task. Locke himself had shown that politics 'contains two parts, very different the one from the other'. One part dealt with the science of sovereignty, 'the origin of societies, and the rise and extent of political power'; the other taught 'the art of governing men in society'. This 'is best to be learned by experience and history, especially that of a man's own country'. It was policing: namely, the government's technique for maintaining order in society and ensuring that laws and duties are respected. It was possible to address the theory of sovereignty while placing the police in the background, as Locke, Sydney and others had done; but it was not possible to speak of the police without sovereignty because this would have justified despotic power.[21]

At the end of his career also Genovesi became aware of the weakness of jusnaturalism and felt the need to be 'learned by experience and history, especially that of a man's own country'.

The importance of a critical knowledge of the history of the nation in order to think of a radical and proper strategy of reform arose in 1768, when Genovesi was involved by Bernardo Tanucci in the design of a new position – l'Avvocato della Corona (the Crown Attorney) – intended to defend the royal prerogatives

---

18 Franco Venturi, 'Antonio Genovesi', in *Illuministi italiani*, vol. 5, *Riformatori napoletani* (Milano-Napoli: Ricciardi, 1962), 4–46, at 33.

19 Niccolò Guasti, 'Introduzione', in Genovesi, *Diceosina*, xxv.

20 See for instance Cicero, *De republica*, I, 2, 2, and *De Officiis*, III, 5, 23. On the presence of Cicero's stoicism in Grotius, see Knud Haakonssen, 'Early Modern Natural Law Theories', in *The Cambridge Companion to Natural Law Jurisprudence*, ed. George Duke and Robert George (Cambridge: Cambridge University Press, 2017), 76–102, at 80.

21 John Locke, *Some thoughts concerning Reading and Study for a Gentleman* (1703), in idem, *Political Essays*, ed. Mark Goldie (Cambridge: Cambridge University Press, 1997), 348–355, at 351.

(regalism) against the Church. Tanucci had been a key minister since Charles III Bourbon had founded the new Kingdom of Naples in 1734.[22] Loyal to the political ideal of absolute monarchy, Tanucci considered the feudal power of the barons and the claims of power of the Roman Church over the Neapolitan kingdom as the two main dangers for the authority of the king. In this sense, Tanucci was near to the jurisdictionalist ideology of the *ceto togato*, the equivalent of the French *robe*, who claimed political control over the Church. Neapolitan jurisdictionalism had had its principal exponent in Pietro Giannone, whose *Istoria civile del regno di Napoli* (1723) had defended the history of Neapolitan institutions as independent from ecclesiastical intrusion.[23]

In the second half of the 1760s Tanucci found an ally in Genovesi. But the violence of latter's polemic against the Church drove the *philosophe* to distance himself from Giannone's jurisdictionalism. He indicated certain readings for the '*brevarium* of this Attorney', comprising many late-seventeenth-century French Gallican and Jansenist texts,[24] the works by Giannone and Paolo Sarpi, the *Science du gouvernement* by Réal de Courban and a collection of eighteenth-century petitions and remonstrances made by the king's attorneys and lawyers in the parliaments of Paris and Rouen.[25] But these legalist and jurisdictionalist works were not enough. The required philosophical spirit had to be fuelled by two works of a different kind that were symbolic of the Age of Enlightenment: Montesquieu's *Spirit of the Laws* and Cosimo Amidei's *La Chiesa e la Repubblica dentro i loro limiti*.[26] The recommendation

---

22 Girolamo Imbruglia, 'Tanucci, Bernardo', *Dizionario Biografico degli Italiani* (Roma: Istituto dell'Enciclopedia Italiana, 2019), vol. 94, 830–834.

23 See Giuseppe Ricuperati, *L'affaire Giannone face à l'Europe: Vie de Pietro Giannone, Profession de foi et Abjuration*, ed. Gisela Schlüter and Giuseppe Ricuperati (Paris: Honoré Champion, 2019).

24 Jacques Bénigne Bossuet, *Défense de la Déclaration de l'Assemblée générale du Clergé de France de 1682 touchant la puissance ecclésiastique* (Amsterdam: aux dépenses de la Compagnie, 1745); Roland Le Vayer de Boutigny, *Traité de l'autorité des rois touchant l'administration de l'Eglise*, better known as the *Traité de la Régale* (A Cologne: chez Pierre Marteau, 1682); Ellies Dupin, *Traité de la puissance ecclésiastique et temporelle* (s.l., 1707); and Jean Levesque de Burigny, *Traité de l'autorité du pape, dans le quel ses droits sont établis et réduits à leurs justes bornes et les principes de l'Eglise gallicane justifiez* (La Haye: A. de Rogissart,1720).

25 Antonio Genovesi, *Istruzioni per l'Avvocato della Real Corona*, in *Dialoghi e altri scritti. Intorno alle Lezioni di commercio*, 549–551. See Girolamo Imbruglia, 'L'ultimo Genovesi. Tra Kaunitz e Montesquieu', in *Antonio Genovesi. Economia e Morale*, ed. Anna Maria Rao (Napoli: Giannini, 2018), 113–129.

26 Cosimo Amidei, *La Chiesa e la Repubblica dentro i loro limiti*, ed. Antonio Rotondò (Torino: Utet, 1980).

of these texts ousted the action of the crown attorney from the narrow confines of the relation between State and Church.[27] It was impossible to reconcile Montesquieu and Amidei with the *Traité de la Régale*, Giannone's jurisdictionalism with Locke's natural law. What separated them was the different foundation of sovereignty, which for Montesquieu and Amidei – as now for Genovesi – resided in the people, not in the sovereign, and their different aims: namely the civil liberty of the citizens and not obedience. Enlightenment culture demanded that reforms go beyond mere administrative structures.[28] A new perspective was needed.

3 Late Genovesi: A Historian?

This theme appeared in the second edition of the *Lezioni di Economia* (1768–1770). Alongside the emphasis on the antifeudal polemic, Genovesi defended the free market and the freedom of work, trade and the ownership of land, attacking the tax measures that favoured the privileges of the aristocracy and ecclesiastical properties that were cut off from the market.[29] At a time of crisis in the kingdom, following the terrible famine of 1763–1764[30] and after the expulsion of the Jesuits, Genovesi had to address the question of the essential fusion of the reforms with a force that had not been so dramatic earlier.[31] It was pointless to propose changes 'without thinking of bringing together the forces that have been kept asunder for eight centuries. These forces [have to be] yoked to a moving hub to ensure that they all push together driven by a common spirit'.[32] Change could not merely be proposed; it had to become social force. This goal, which brought together the reflections on natural law economics and ethics, had been absent in Naples

27 Imbruglia, 'L'ultimo Genovesi'.

28 Girolamo Imbruglia, 'Jansenist Jurisdictionalism and Enlightenment: Two Ways of Thinking Politics in Mid-Eighteenth-Century Naples', in *Monarchism and Absolutism in Early Modern Europe*, ed. Cesare Cuttica and Glenn Burgess (London: Pickering and Chatto, 2014), 101–116.

29 John Robertson, 'Political Economy and the "Feudal System" in Enlightenment Naples: Outline of a Problem', in *Peripheries of Enlightenment*, ed. Richard Butterwick, Simon Davies and Gabriel Sánchez Espinosa (Oxford: Voltaire Foundation, 2008), 65–86.

30 Franco Venturi, *Settecento riformatore*, vol. 5:1, *L'Italia dei lumi (1764–1790): La rivoluzione di Corsica. Le grandi carestie degli anni sessanta. La Lombardia delle riforme* (Torino: Einaudi, 1987), 221–305.

31 Franco Venturi, 'Church and Reform in Enlightenment Italy: The Sixties of the Eighteenth Century', *Journal of Modern History* 48 (1976): 215–232.

32 Antonio Genovesi, *Delle Lezioni di commercio o sia di Economia civile*, ed. Maria Luisa Perna (Napoli: Istituto Italiano per gli Studi Filosofici, 2005), 617.

for cultural reasons too, since there had been no reflection on the nature of the Neapolitan State. The jurisdictionalist doctrine of Giannone and his disciples had defended the State against the prevarications of the Church but had not defined the identity of the kingdom. Giannone's followers had no answer to it. It was a problem which – starting from the *Esprit des lois* – called for an enlightened historiographic approach, of the kind provided by Hume and Voltaire.[33] In the *Lezioni* Genovesi complained of the lack of a good history of the Kingdom of Naples. Inspired by Montesquieu and by Beccaria, Genovesi polemicized openly against the local historic-juridical tradition that glorified the immutability of civil and juridical relations which confirmed the unity of the state above individual conflicts.

In the middle of the 1760s Genovesi drafted a commentary on the *Esprit des lois*, which was to be published posthumously in 1777.[34] His focus on the actual conditions of life in the kingdom brought to light the mutability of social and political structures as opposed to the false positive of the endurance of juridical constructs. What ought to be the hub of the historic reflection was the *philosophique* awareness that societies are driven by conflicting interests that determine the various forms of their possible integration. Within the kingdom, the development of the 'middle class' had to be fostered; in the cities this was represented by the intellectual professions and in the countryside by small and medium-size landowners. This was the middle class that Hume had spoken of, on which the nation could rely for its reform. From this perspective, the utopian model was not *Diceosina*'s Inca Peru or Jesuit missions, but the United Kingdom. In order to grasp in depth the nature of the Neapolitan monarchy and to devise realistic reforms, a history of social conflicts – especially feudal and those with the Church – was necessary. It was true that particular histories were not lacking; but the lack of 'general' histories was serious, as he pointed out in a note to the second edition of the *Lezioni*:

> The least bad is that by Giannone [...] But he was not a true philosopher and a historian who is not a philosopher cannot be useful in enlightened ages; and he was interested in other problems; he neither wanted nor could write an accomplished general history of our Kingdom. Now the time is ripe for it.[35]

33 Girolamo Imbruglia, 'Antonio Genovesi lecteur de Voltaire et de Montesquieu', *Revue Voltaire* 13 (2013): 267–279.

34 See Venturi, *Settecento riformatore*, vol. 1, 566–567.

35 Genovesi, *Delle Lezioni di commercio*, 629, n. *u.*, which is missing in the first edition (1765–1767).

Perhaps, just to posit an impossible conjecture, after having been a metaphysician, an economist and a jurist, Genovesi's fourth identity could have been that of historian.

4 Genovesi's School: Natural Right Theories, History and Reform

That note opened up new perspectives. The seed of the *Lezioni di Economia* was not lost. In the 1770s and 1780s the long history of the Kingdom of Naples became the central theme of the Neapolitan Enlightenment, and the tradition of both Vico and Giannone was judged not sufficient. Giuseppe Maria Galanti, one of Genovesi's most ardent disciples, argued that despite his 'highest wisdom, deep research, enormous erudition', Vico had not explained 'the progress of nations'; and that Giannone's *Civil history* had been admired 'for want of a better model'.[36] These were the words and the ideas of Genovesi's *Lezioni di Economia*.

Rather than taking up his economic teaching, Genovesi's disciples reconsidered the issue of natural law and natural jurisprudence, while linking it up to the new historiographical reflection at European level. This is what Carlo Pecchia (1715–1784), Giacinto Dragonetti (1738–1818), Francescantonio Grimaldi (1741–1784) and Gaetano Filangieri (1752–1788) did. The question they all addressed was the nature of the Neapolitan monarchy, which Genovesi had placed at the top of the agenda in his last years, albeit remaining hesitant about it. His commentary on the *Esprit des lois* had stopped at book XXI, so that he had not dealt with the feudal issue. This was the issue that everyone was most interested in.[37] These historians were split into two groups.

One group adopted an approach that could be defined as historic-administrative, loyal to Giannonian tradition. Carlo Pecchia, who, as we have seen, had been among the disciples of Genovesi, in the *Storia civile e politica del Regno di Napoli* [...] *da servire di supplimento a quella di Pietro Giannone* (1778–1783) studied the 'feudal political system', upholding the Germanic presence in the south as positive. He praised its system of anti-ecclesiastical laws, while acknowledging that the civil laws were deficient and in need of reform. This was a compromise interpretation intended to commend the Norman and Swabian struggles against the Church and attack the vast acquisition of undue privileges and royal prerogatives (*regalie*) by the barons and ecclesiastics. In

36 Galanti, *Elogio storico*, 23.

37 Salvatore Rotta, 'Montesquieu nel Settecento italiano: note e ricerche', *Materiali per una storia della cultura giuridica* 1 (1971): 55–209, at 128–131, http://www.eliohs.unifi.it/testi/900/rotta/rotta_montesettit.html (accessed 30 September 2022).

Pecchia's opinion – later also taken up by Dragonetti[38] – in the first half of the thirteenth century Frederick II had indeed yoked the civil structure to the political construct of the feu. The feu was an ordering principle ordained by the sovereign and it could not be legitimately eliminated since it was an inherent pilaster of royalty: only reform of abuse was possible. The feudal history of the Kingdom of Naples was different from that of the rest of Europe since it displayed fundamental juridical and institutional features of stability and law rather than of anarchy and licence. Pecchia's and Dragonetti's return to Giannone served to consecrate the institution of monarchy through the condemnation of ecclesiastical power, which was the sole cause of the degeneration and poverty of the state. However, for Galanti and another enlightened intellectual disciple of Genovesi, Melchiorre Delfico, who were far from this tradition of jurisdictionalism, the original structure of the state was that of monarchy, which then degenerated under the baronial prevarications. Conceiving feudalism as an element of order within the monarchy, these intellectuals believed it possible to envisage an end to the feudal system almost like a form of euthanasia. It was wishful thinking.

The other group of Neapolitan *philosophes* saw the history of the Kingdom of Naples as similar to that of the rest of Europe, and believed that to understand it one also needed to know the works by Hume and Chastellux, Raynal, Voltaire and Robertson. Galanti's publishing house printed many works by European Enlightenment thinkers; he also translated and printed Hume's *History of England*, which had been so extensively used by Genovesi in his *Lezioni* and was now published in Italian along with Robertson's works. Hume's appendix on feudalism to the *History* enjoyed wide circulation. 'The feudal law is the chief foundation both of the political government and of the jurisprudence established by the Normans in England'.[39] Neapolitan readers could not but feel concerned by this story. This was Mario Pagano's horizon.

5 Mario Pagano's Philosophic History of the Kingdom of Naples

Mario Pagano (1748–1799) was not one of Genovesi's university students, but he was a greatly appreciated disciple. In his first work, the *Disegno del sistema*

---

38 Giacinto Dragonetti, *Origine dei feudi nei regni di Napoli e Sicilia* (Napoli: Nella Stamperia Regale, 1788). See also, along the same lines but later, Nicola Vivenzio, *Storia del regno di Napoli e suo governo dalla decadenza dell'Impero romano al re Ferdinando IV* (Napoli: Nel Gabinetto letterario, 1811).

39 David Hume, 'The Feudal and Anglo-Norman Government and Manners', in idem, *The History of England*, appendix II (Indianapolis, IN: Liberty Fund, 1983), vol. 1, 455–488.

della scienza degli Uffizi (1769),[40] Pagano gratefully recalls the encouragement he received from Genovesi to write on this argument, which was characteristic of the latter's teaching.[41] In this book Pagano took his cue from Genovesi's *Diceosina* in order to define 'offices',[42] but developed the ethical argument beyond the coordinates of early eighteenth-century natural law.[43] A consideration of natural jurisprudence entailed a non-abstract consideration of the regeneration of a political state, and called for the definition of its nature.[44] As Genovesi had taught in his last years, the kingdom's history needed to be written. But this theme was also a way to reconsider Vico's natural law theory. In the *Diceosina* Genovesi had distinguished the natural rights from the norms and rules which were essential to the conservation of society; for Vico there was not a distinction, but a necessary relationship between the *jus naturale gentium* and the historical forms of authority, between the fundamental principles and the ethical and political practice, between the universal form (the *verum*) and its possible implementation in specific historical and political situations (the *certum*).[45] Between Genovesi and Vico, Pagano was taking his own path to think about history and society.

The history of the Neapolitan kingdom was the focus of the *Saggi politici*, which appeared in two editions, in 1783–1785 and in 1791–1792.[46] As we shall

---

40 Pagano's text is presented in Francesco Berti, 'Nota introduttiva a Mario Pagano, Disegno del sistema della scienza degli uffizj', *Archivio Storico del Sannio* 15 (2010): 153–174. The *Disegno* was written to support the candidature of Trojano Odazi, one of Genovesi's pupils, for the chair of ethics at the Nunziatella military college. Shortly afterwards Pagano himself made an unsuccessful application for the chair of ethics at the University of Naples, where he later became an 'extraordinary lecturer'.

41 In 1768 Genovesi was asked to supply the names of teachers for the Scuola del Salvatore, which the Jesuits had left when they were expelled from the kingdom. Genovesi provided about thirty names for various disciplines, including philology and history, and also for the 'Offizi' (offices), for which he proposed Giacinto Dragonetti, Francescantonio Grimaldi and Tommaso Cervone. See Waldmann, *Antonio Genovesi*, 43.

42 Office is a 'human action, decided after the idea of the just and honest', in Berti, 'Nota', 159.

43 Franco Venturi, 'Mario Pagano', in *Illuministi italiani*, vol. 5, *Riformatori napoletani*, ed. Franco Venturi (Milano: Ricciardi, 1962), 785–833, at 786.

44 See Dario Ippolito, *Mario Pagano: il pensiero giuspolitico di un illuminista* (Torino: Giappichelli, 2008).

45 See Fabrizio Lomonaco, 'Appunti sul "diritto naturale delle genti" nel *De uno*', *Laboratorio dell'ISPF* 13 (2016), http://www.ispf-lab.cnr.it/2016_LMF.pdf (accessed 30 September 2022).

46 Francesco Mario Pagano, *Saggi politici* (Napoli: Gennaro Verriento, 1783; Napoli: Vincenzo Flauto, 1785) (henceforth *IS*); Francesco Mario Pagano, *Saggi politici* (Napoli: Filippo Raimondi, 1791–1792), ed. Luigi Firpo and Laura Salvetti Firpo (Napoli: Vivarium, 1993) (henceforth *IIS*).

see, the latter, being produced after 1789, presents a different political interpretation but the historiographical framework is the same.

For Pagano, as for Montesquieu, human societies were systems determined by the environment, by entrenched anthropological history and by political and constitutional conflicts. To develop his own model of philosophical history Pagano turned to conjectural history, both French – in particular Rousseau, Raynal and Boulanger – and Scottish, in particular William Robertson. He mapped the history of Naples like a history not only of institutions, but of civilization. Civilization was a category already present in the first edition of the *Saggi politici*, indicating the way society had been formed and the meaning of its movement.[47] He brought to light how the violence of reality and the 'right of strength' had been transformed into a 'moral order, a justice opposed to force'.[48] Enlightenment conjectural history was reconceived in the light of Vico's theories as a history of 'social progress' within which feudalism was acknowledged as having a crucial place in both political history and social theory.

Pagano asked himself, 'are men all equal in moral faculties by nature?',[49] and asserted that men had lived in conditions of natural community prior to the formation of the states of the 'general society of human species'.[50] He, too, took his cue from Scottish anthropology. He recalls Adam Ferguson and his theory of the original division of powers: '[Men] have always been united in society, according to their natural instinct, and have had from the beginning the exercise, if imperfect, of their properties and the constitution of a government, in which a valiant man was granted executive power, a board of elders was in charge of the public council and the whole ensemble of the people unfolded public will, according to Ferguson'.[51]

Precisely because it is original, this government is found everywhere. 'This government […] does not depend on the customs of particular northern nations, as for a long time it was falsely believed due to learned men; […] but it is universally good for all peoples, when found in the same circumstances'.[52] Pagano therefore accepted the Scottish historian's correction of Montesquieu, who believed that feudalism was a specifically European phenomenon.

---

47 *IS*, 41; *IIS*, 77.

48 *IIS*, 15.

49 *IIS*, 28.

50 *IIS*, 20.

51 *IIS*, 29. See Adam Ferguson, *An Essay on the History of Civil Society*, II, 2–3 (1767), ed. Duncan Forbes (Edinburgh: Edinburgh University Press, 1966), 81 ff.

52 *IS*, vol. 2, 245.

Support for the controversy with Montesquieu was combined with Pagano's reading of Guillaume-Thomas Raynal's *Histoire philosophique et politique des Établissements et du commerce des Européens dans les deux Indes*, in which he found new echoes of Scottish historiography, especially John Millar.[53] Pagano read the second edition of the *Histoire* (1774) and very probably also the third (1780)[54] – much more extensive than the first two, of 1770 and 1774. According to the *Histoire*, the emergence from the savage world takes place when a theocratic or monarchic power is established:

> As soon as a multitude of small nations had destroyed a large one, many chiefs or tyrants divided each vast monarchy into several fiefs. The people, who gained no advantage by the government of one, or of several men, were always oppressed and trampled upon from these dismemberings of the feudal anarchy.[55]

Through the barbarian invasions, the nations of Europe were plunged a second time, by slavery and despair, into that state of insensibility and indolence which must for many ages have been the primary state of the human race, and derived little advantage from the fertility of their soil.[56] Feudalism, without 'police intérieure, ni jurisprudence, ni luxe, ni beaux-arts', was a system of anarchy and tyranny dominated by the principle of contempt for useful work, which is the ruin of all societies.[57] It was nevertheless a 'political system', in which despotism was broken down into as many tyrants as there are vassals.[58] In turn, it produced also irrational and fanatical beliefs.[59] In

53 See Girolamo Imbruglia, 'Tra Anquetil Duperron e l'*Histoire des deux Indes*: libertà, dispotismo e feudalesimo', *Rivista storica italiana* 106 (1994): 140–193.

54 Guillaume-Thomas Raynal, *Histoire philosophique et politique des Établissements et du commerce des Européens dans les deux Indes* (A Geneve: Chez Jean-Leonard Pellet, 1780) (henceforth *HDD*). On the *Histoire*, see the editors' introduction to their edition, Guillaume-Thomas Raynal, *Histoire philosophique et politique des Établissements et du commerce des Européens dans les deux Indes*, ed. Anthony Strugnell et al. (Ferney-Voltaire: Centre international d'étude du XVIIIe siècle, 2010–2020), vol. 1, xxvii–lxxx. See also *Autour de l'abbé Raynal: genèse et enjeux politiques de l'Histoire des deux Indes*, ed. Antonella Alimento and Gianluigi Goggi (Ferney-Voltaire: Centre international d'étude du XVIIIe siècle, 2018).

55 *HDD*, XIX, 2, vol. 4, 475.

56 *HDD*, 'Introduction', I, 19, 14, 11.

57 *HDD*, XIII, 50, vol. 3, 464.

58 *HDD*, I, 16, vol. 1, 89.

59 *HDD*, XIX, 9, vol. 4, 632. 'The nations groaning under the tyranny of the feudal government, wished for, and still believed in, the end of the world', vol. 6, 407.

Java, the feudal system had made men degenerate: 'Here men were wolves to each other'.[60] In Europe, rather than having been imposed by the barbarian conquerors, feudalism had been preordained by the Romans through their despotism and their 'gouvernement militaire'. In these pages Pagano could discern a late-eighteenth-century species of Vico-like return to barbarism. If Pagano accepted the expansion of the category of feudalism to a global dimension made by European historiography, in the analysis of its political nature he was not in agreement with Montesquieu, and still less with Filangieri and Robertson.

For Montesquieu, the original form of government had been that of the heroic monarchy,[61] in which sovereignty belongs to the people while the sovereign manages the other two powers. Conversely, for Pagano the original form of government had been the 'aristocratic feudal' system. The long period of the 'social chaos' of savagery ended with the appearance in power of the assembly of nobles, which had emerged as far back as the age of hunting. This marked the advent of sovereignty.[62] When society passed from the pre-political to the political state, the nobles consolidated their power over the weaker and more defenceless individuals by offering or imposing protection in conflicts during wartime and protection of agricultural labour in peacetime. The result was the 'despotic feudal aristocracy' or the 'aristocratic feudal government'[63] in which power is entirely in the hands of the aristocracy. The people did not exist[64] and the king had a purely military function: the three powers resided in the aristocratic 'public assembly'.

This theory was proposed not only against Montesquieu, but also against Robertson and Filangieri. According to Robertson, feudalism had represented a degeneration of monarchy, which, after being progressively weakened, had been defeated by a 'military establishment'. 'The genius of the feudal government was purely aristocratic'. It had been 'gothic' but not monstrous, since there were 'the first rudiments of the policy and laws now established in Europe'.[65] The new division of property was the result of conquest by free men. Although the judgement of feudalism was certainly negative, Robertson had established a continuity between the feudal world and the modern.

60 *HDD*, II, 19, vol. 1, 214.

61 Montesquieu, *Esprit des lois*, XI, 11.

62 *IS*, appendix to ch. 4, vol. 5, 11 = *IIS*, III, 15, 243.

63 *IIS*, III, 10, 225 and 240.

64 *IIS*, V, 10, 323.

65 William Robertson, 'View of the Progress of Society in Europe, from the Subversion of the Roman Empire to the Beginning of the Sixteenth Century', in *The History of the Reign of Charles V*, in idem, *Works* (London: Cadell, 1831), 336.

The continuity between feudalism and modern monarchy was also found in Filangieri's *La scienza della legislazione*. Feudalism had emerged through the barons' usurpation of royal power,[66] which the monarchs had to accept in view of the crisis of the economic system. This usurpation of the monarchy could have been opposed and a renewed monarchy could have led to a renewal of civil society, which Scottish historiography had shown to be the key ally of sovereignty against the barons.[67] Therefore Filangieri's proposal to end feudalism was not the jurisdictional control of the lands returning to the Crown with the extinction of the lineage (as 'Giannonian' jurists of the second half of eighteenth century proposed), but putting the lands which had been deprived of feudal privilege on the market.[68] The barons had to relinquish jurisdiction and restore the power to the sovereign. Recognizing this monarchic right was a display of trust in absolute monarchy within which Filangieri, like Genovesi, envisaged the policy of reform. For instance, in the 1788 *Parere* (*Opinion*) on the reform projects for the Tavoliere della Puglia, Filangieri – as observed by Galanti – accepted a compromise between the gradualist reform method and the desire to make way for the social forces.

For Pagano, royal power had been consolidated not through the mediation of the aristocracy but against the aristocracy, by using the military, and this also enabled it to take over the legislative and judiciary functions. Hence there was discontinuity between the feudal system and that of the monarchy. However, although he agreed with the universal extension of the category of feudalism that characterized the second half of the seventeenth century, at a later stage Pagano went back to Montesquieu,[69] in outright disagreement with the readings of Robertson and Filangieri: 'Feudal jurisdiction arose with feudal government. The eminent president Montesquieu introduced this idea, which others refuted with weak arguments. Sharp-witted Robertson [...] voiced the contrary opinion, namely that jurisdictions were slowly usurped by the barons'.[70] Pagano saw no temporal distinction between the institutions of feudalism and the feudal nobility. The notion of a feudal monarchy was an absurd hypothesis devised to explain how feudalism derived from monarchy,

66 Gaetano Filangieri, *La scienza della legislazione*, III, 17, ed. Vincenzo Ferrone (Venezia: Centro di studi sull'illuminismo G. Stiffoni-Edizioni della Laguna, 2003–2004), vol. 3, 170.

67 Filangieri, *La scienza della legislazione*, II, 37, vol. 2, 245 ff.

68 Anna Maria Rao, *L'amaro della feudalità* (Napoli: Guida, 1984), *passim*.

69 Girolamo Imbruglia, 'Rivoluzione e civilizzazione: Pagano, Montesquieu e il feudalesimo', in *Poteri, democrazia, virtù: Montesquieu nei movimenti repubblicani all'epoca della Rivoluzione francese*, ed. Domenico Felice (Milano: FrancoAngeli, 2000), 99–122.

70 *IIS*, VII, 8, vol. 2, 252–253.

which was an institution of the opposite kind. Feudal monarchy was a fanciful notion, which Montesquieu had never entertained, because it was pointless: in a feudal government aristocracy is in command from the very beginning. But Montesquieu himself was also wrong in believing that the aristocracy was necessary in a monarchy, in view of its anti-despotic function. The opposite was true. It was the nobility that hampered any reforming action by the monarchy, turning it instead to despotism.[71] The radical difference between monarchy and feudalism was that in the latter a constitution was impossible.

Pagano consequently rejected both Giannone's interpretation of feudal monarchy, in which the monarchy had found an ordering principle in the feud, and the Scottish one, which characterized it as the product of degeneration, because these theories had in common the idea that in the beginning there had been a monarchical structure. The Scottish argument helped to explain not how the feudal system had arisen but how it had been defeated, in Great Britain but not in Naples. The Neapolitan feudal system was not analogous to that of Europe, as Filangieri had claimed; it was one of a kind in Europe, albeit not on account of the positivity of the feud envisaged by Pecchia and Dragonetti but, on the contrary, because it was under the control of the aristocratic feudal system. A modern monarchy had never emerged in Naples, neither of the absolute kind on the model of Louis XIV, nor on the British model.[72]

6 The Kingdom of Naples: History and Revolution

Pagano drew a political consequence from this stance on the nature of the feudal system. Reforms were possible only in the case of a politically strong power. In the first edition of the *Saggi* he still displayed trust in the Bourbon monarchy. It was the last spark of Genovesi's teaching. By the second edition his conclusion was already different: reform was inconceivable.

'What national public force can be recognized in such a state?' None. In the Kingdom of Naples there were no civil forces that felt the need to claim the respect of rights. Agriculture, trade and the arts were lacking in this 'miserable state'.[73] On one side was the immense wealth of the aristocracy and the clergy; on the other, 'the servile populace'. Frederick II of Swabia, the hero of southern jurisdictionalism and the model of the wise king, had not put an end

71 *IIS*, III, 11, 232.3.

72 See David Hume's 'Idea of a Perfect Commonwealth', in idem, *Political Discourses* (Edinburgh: Printed by R. Fleming, for A. Kincaid and A. Donaldson, 1752), 282–283.

73 *IIS*, I, 30, 259.

to the 'monstrous confusion' of the feudal world; he had created a state on the model of Byzantine monarchy, where the laws were those of the 'fierceness of despotism and of a declined nation'.[74] Feudalism, subordination to the Church, corruption and the slavery of the Byzantine world forged Neapolitan monarchy: 'a feudal and dependent kingdom, in which the institutions and customs of barbaric decline were merged with the original barbarism brought by our conquerors: a servile nature and fierce independence, ignorance, and fraud, superstition and shallowness'.[75]

But the story could have been different. A third social group had developed in the course of the Spanish viceroyalty, especially in the seventeenth century: that of the magistrates and lawyers ('togati'). Loyal to the state, they positioned themselves 'between the rich and powerful and the miserable populace', and they had been responsible for some positive changes in the constitution of the kingdom. This social group created a 'proportional mean' between luxury and poverty, between power and servitude. Through them it might have been possible to open a breach in the government, but the feudal nature of the state thwarted this evolution, because they made alliances with the feudatories. The parlous state of the kingdom was due not to baronial resistance to monarchical action – which was an understandable power struggle – but to the corruption that the monster of feudalism had generated. In the Neapolitan kingdom 'the legal clique, monasticism [...] the feudal spirit shaped the national character, so that neither public education nor public interest nor national spirit ever existed among us':[76]

> Just as the feudal institutions that transfer ownership of people and personal rights destroy civil liberty and the natural and civil laws, so prohibitive rights cancel the ownership, the nature of which implies the use of one's things as and how one wishes [...] An ownership that destroys the nature of ownership, a right that annuls the right, is a civil monster and something which at once is and is not.[77]

In this society the legal class, which could have opened a new path towards reformist policy, allowed itself to be swallowed up by the monarchical feudal system. It betrayed its very function, which was that of ensuring justice. A monstrous system had been created, since privilege, licence and violence

74 *IIS*, I, 30, 255.
75 *IIS*, I, 30, 254–255.
76 *IIS*, I, 30, 261–262.
77 *IIS*, V, 21, 348–349.

found protection in the law and the institutions. Genovesi's enlightened impatience with the legal class was transformed by Pagano into an unprecedentedly radical social denouncement.

This society betrayed 'its own purpose', which was 'the preservation of man's natural rights'.[78] There are two kinds of needs, physical and moral: society does not aim simply at the fulfilment of basic needs, but also at establishing 'the moral communion of our souls'. Perfectibility brings about the dual conversion of physical need into moral dynamic, and of fact into right. In the history of southern Italy this conversion of civilization was not accomplished. The institutional powers did not seem capable of producing the fundamental change taught by the Scots, namely the strengthening of the middle class. Pagano stressed the issue of the creation of the middle class, which Genovesi had already discussed as the crucial theme of reform policy in Neapolitan society.[79] In the last edition of the *Saggi politici* the two last chapters of the final essay, on the 'General View of the History of the Kingdom', were cut. Pagano was driven to abandon any project for reform. The model of civilization from below was impossible. All that remained was action from above, to hope for a Neapolitan Tsar Peter who would plan a constitutional reform, destroy the feudal world and establish new institutions of liberty. But it was difficult to have such trust in the Neapolitan king Ferdinand Bourbon and in his court.[80]

The *philosophe* was increasingly isolated. Pagano had 'extraordinary' success and 'much glory' in his university lectures[81] but he was aware that he was addressing only public opinion and that he was by now far removed from the official intellectual world. He did not share the trust in the monarchy. The case of the French revolution unveiled a new perspective from which to think about politics, history and natural rights.[82] Perhaps Pagano had in mind one of the most radical passages of the *Histoire philosophique et politique des deux Indes*, which we know to be by Diderot:

---

78 *IS*, vol. 2, 158.

79 Melissa Calaresu, 'Searching for a "Middle Class"? Francesco Mario Pagano and the Public for Reform in Late Eighteenth-Century Naples', in *Enlightened Reform in Southern Europe and Its Atlantic Colonies, c. 1750–1830*, ed. Gabriel Paquette (Farnham: Ashgate, 2009), 63–82.

80 For a clear description of the corruption of Bourbon's court at the end of the century see Raffaele Ajello, 'I filosofi e la regina: il governo delle Due Sicilie da Tanucci a Caracciolo (1776–1786)', *Rivista storica italiana* 103 (1991): 398–454.

81 Waldmann, *Antonio Genovesi*, 87, n. 116; and Gioele Solari, *Studi su Francesco Mario Pagano*, ed. Luigi Firpo (Torino: Giappichelli, 1963), 34–35.

82 Marcel Gauchet, *La Révolution des droits de l'homme* (Paris: Gallimard, 1989).

> The situation of the restorer of a corrupted nation is very different [...] A nation is only regenerated in a sea of blood. It is the image of old Eson, whose youth Medea could renew by no other mode, except that of cutting him to pieces and boiling him. It is not in the power of one man to raise a fallen nation. It appears that this must be the result of a long series of revolutions. The man of genius doth not live long enough, and leaves no successors.[83]

To guide the historical dynamics of his nation the *philosophe* appears to have returned to natural ethics. 'The philosopher is by reason what natural man is by feeling',[84] and has to draw on the atemporal realm of justice, which legitimizes the necessary recourse to change and, if necessary, to violence. As a revolutionary he accepted Rousseau's ideas that he had rejected as a disciple of Vico.

On 29 October 1799, he confronted with a noble moral conscience the death to which the Bourbon had condemned him.

Bibliography

Ajello, Raffaele, 'I filosofi e la regina: il governo delle Due Sicilie da Tanucci a Caracciolo (1776–1786)', *Rivista storica italiana* 103 (1991): 398–454.

Amidei, Cosimo, *La Chiesa e la Repubblica dentro i loro limiti*, ed. Antonio Rotondò (Torino: Utet, 1980).

Audidière, Sophie, *Passions de l'intérêt* (Paris: Honoré Champion, 2022).

Autour de l'abbé Raynal: genèse et enjeux politiques de l'Histoire des deux Indes, ed. Antonella Alimento and Gianluigi Goggi (Ferney-Voltaire: Centre international d'étude du XVIIIe siècle, 2018).

Berlin, Isaiah, 'The Philosophical Ideas of Giambattista Vico', in idem, *Vico and Herder: Two Studies in the History of Ideas* (New York: Viking Press, 1976), 3–98.

Berti, Francesco, 'Nota introduttiva a Mario Pagano, Disegno del sistema della scienza degli uffizj', *Archivio Storico del Sannio* 15 (2010): 153–174.

Bossuet, Jacques Bénigne, *Défense de la Déclaration de l'Assemblée générale du Clergé de France de 1682 touchant la puissance ecclésiastique* (Amsterdam: aux dépenses de la Compagnie, 1745).

83 *HDD*, XI, 4, vol. 2, 103.

84 *IS*, vol. 2, 308.

Calaresu, Melissa, 'Searching for a "Middle Class"? Francesco Mario Pagano and the Public for Reform in Late Eighteenth-Century Naples', in *Enlightened Reform in Southern Europe and Its Atlantic Colonies, c. 1750–1830*, ed. Gabriel Paquette (Farnham: Ashgate, 2009), 63–82.

Dragonetti, Giacinto, *Origine dei feudi nei regni di Napoli e Sicilia* (Napoli: Nella Stamperia Regale, 1788).

Dupin, Ellies, *Traité de la puissance ecclésiastique et temporelle* (s.l., 1707).

Ferguson, Adam, *An Essay on the History of Civil Society* (1767), ed. Duncan Forbes (Edinburgh: Edinburgh University Press, 1966).

Filangieri, Gaetano, *La scienza della legislazione*, ed. Vincenzo Ferrone (Venezia: Centro di studi sull'illuminismo G. Stiffoni-Edizioni della Laguna, 2003–2004).

Galanti, Giuseppe Maria, *Elogio storico del signor abate Antonio Genovesi* (1772) (Napoli: Bibliopolis, 1977).

Gauchet, Marcel, *La Révolution des droits de l'homme* (Paris: Gallimard, 1989).

Genovesi, Antonio, *Autobiografia e Lettere*, ed. Gennaro Savarese (Milano: Feltrinelli, 1962).

Genovesi, Antonio, *De jure et officiis in usum tironum* (Neapoli: Ex typographia Simoniana, 1767).

Genovesi, Antonio, *Delle Lezioni di commercio o sia di Economia civile*, ed. Maria Luisa Perna (Napoli: Istituto Italiano per gli Studi Filosofici, 2005).

Genovesi, Antonio, *Diceosina, o sia, della filosofia del giusto e dell'onesto* (1766–1771), ed. Niccolò Guasti (Venezia: Centro di studi sull'illuminismo G. Stiffoni-Edizioni della Laguna, 2008).

Genovesi, Antonio, *Elementa metaphysicae*, vol. 4: *Principia Legis naturalis, et officiorum humanorum* (Neapoli: Ex Typographia Benedecti Gessari, 1756).

Genovesi, Antonio, *L'affare delle Decretali*, in idem, *Dialoghi e altri scritti. Intorno alle* Lezioni di commercio, ed. Eluggero Pii (Napoli: Istituto Italiano per gli Studi filosofici, 2008).

Genovesi, Antonio, *Spirito delle leggi del signore di Montesquieu con le note dell'abate Antonio Genovesi* (1777) (Napoli: Gennaro Reale, 1820).

Haakonssen, Knud, 'Early Modern Natural Law Theories', in *The Cambridge Companion to Natural Law Jurisprudence*, ed. George Duke and Robert George (Cambridge: Cambridge University Press, 2017), 76–102.

Helvétius, Claude Adrien, *De l'Esprit* (Londres [i.e. Liège]: [Clement Plomteux], 1776).

Helvétius, Claude Adrien, *De l'Esprit or Essays on Mind and its several faculties*, ed. William Mudford (London: M. Jones, 1807).

Hume, David, 'Idea of a Perfect Commonwealth', in idem, *Political Discourses* (Edinburgh: Printed by R. Fleming, for A. Kincaid and A. Donaldson, 1752), 282–283. See also its modern edition, ed. Knud Haakonssen (Cambridge: Cambridge University Press, 2012).

Hume, David, 'The Feudal and Anglo-Norman Government and Manners', in idem, *The History of England*, appendix II (Indianapolis, IN: Liberty Fund, 1983).

Imbruglia, Girolamo, 'Antonio Genovesi lecteur de Voltaire et de Montesquieu', *Revue Voltaire* 13 (2013): 267–279.

Imbruglia, Girolamo, 'Jansenist Jurisdictionalism and Enlightenment: Two Ways of Thinking Politics in Mid-Eighteenth-Century Naples', in *Monarchism and Absolutism in Early Modern Europe*, ed. Cesare Cuttica and Glenn Burgess (London: Pickering and Chatto, 2014), 101–116.

Imbruglia, Girolamo, 'L'ultimo Genovesi. Tra Kaunitz e Montesquieu', in *Antonio Genovesi. Economia e Morale*, ed. Anna Maria Rao (Napoli: Giannini, 2018), 113–129.

Imbruglia, Girolamo, 'Rivoluzione e civilizzazione: Pagano, Montesquieu e il feudalesimo', in *Poteri, democrazia, virtù: Montesquieu nei movimenti repubblicani all'epoca della Rivoluzione francese*, ed. Domenico Felice (Milano: FrancoAngeli, 2000), 99–122.

Imbruglia, Girolamo, 'Tanucci, Bernardo', in *Dizionario Biografico degli Italiani* (Roma: Istituto dell'Enciclopedia Italiana, 2019), vol. 94, 830–834.

Imbruglia, Girolamo, 'Tra Anquetil Duperron e l'*Histoire des deux Indes*: libertà, dispotismo e feudalesimo', *Rivista storica italiana* 106 (1994): 140–193.

Iovine, Raffaele, 'Una cattedra per Genovesi nella crisi della cultura moderna a Napoli, 1744–1754', *Frontiera d'Europa* 7 (2001): 359–532.

Ippolito, Dario, *Mario Pagano: il pensiero giuspolitico di un illuminista* (Torino: Giappichelli, 2008).

Kapossy, Béla, *Iselin contra Rousseau: Sociable Patriotism and the History of Mankind* (Basel: Schwabe Verlag, 2006).

Le Vayer de Boutigny, Roland, *Traité de l'autorité des rois touchant l'administration de l'Eglise*. [*Dissertations Sur l'Autorité légitime des Rois, En matiére de Regale*.] (A Cologne: chez Pierre Marteau, 1682)].

Levesque de Burigny, Jean, *Traité de l'autorité du pape dans le quel ses droits sont établis et réduits à leurs justes bornes et les principes de l'Eglise gallicane justifiez* (La Haye: A. de Rogissart, 1720).

Locke, John, *Some Thoughts concerning Reading and Study for a Gentleman* (1703), in idem, *Political Essays*, ed. Mark Goldie (Cambridge: Cambridge University Press, 1997), 348–355.

Lomonaco, Fabrizio, 'Appunti sul "diritto naturale delle genti" nel *De uno*', *Laboratorio dell'ISPF* 13 (2016), http://www.ispf-lab.cnr.it/2016_LMF.pdf (accessed 30 September 2022).

Pagano, Francesco Mario, *Disegno del sistema della scienza degli uffizi*, in Francesco Berti, 'Nota introduttiva a Mario Pagano, Disegno del sistema della scienza degli uffizj', *Archivio Storico del Sannio* 15 (2010): 153–174.

Pagano, Francesco Mario, *Saggi politici* (Napoli: Gennaro Verriento, 1783; Napoli: Vincenzo Flauto, 1785).

Pagano, Francesco Mario, *Saggi politici* (Napoli: Filippo Raimondi, 1791–1792), ed. Luigi Firpo and Laura Salvetti Firpo (Napoli: Vivarium, 1993).

Pecchia, Carlo, *Elogio dell'abate Antonio Genovesi* (Napoli, 1769).

Rao, Anna Maria, *L'amaro della feudalità* (Napoli: Guida, 1984).

Raynal, Guillaume-Thomas, *Histoire philosophique et politique des Établissements et du commerce des Européens dans les deux Indes* (A Geneve: Chez Jean-Leonard Pellet, 1780).

Raynal, Guillaume-Thomas, *Histoire philosophique et politique des Établissements et du commerce des Européens dans les deux Indes*, ed. Anthony Strugnell et al. (Ferney-Voltaire: Centre international d'étude du XVIIIe siècle, 2010–2022).

Ricuperati, Giuseppe, *L'affaire Giannone face à l'Europe: Vie de Pietro Giannone, Profession de foi et Abjuration*, ed. Gisela Schlüter and Giuseppe Ricuperati (Paris: Honoré Champion, 2019).

Robertson, John, 'Political Economy and the "Feudal System" in Enlightenment Naples: Outline of a Problem', in *Peripheries of Enlightenment*, ed. Richard Butterwick, Simon Davies and Gabriel Sánchez Espinosa (Oxford: Voltaire Foundation, 2008), 65–86.

Robertson, John, 'Sociability in Sacred Historical Perspective, 1650–1800', in *Markets, Morals, Politics: Jealousy of Trade and the History of Political Thought*, ed. Béla Kapossy, Isaac Nakhimovsky and Sophus A. Reinert (Cambridge, MA: Harvard University Press, 2018), 53–81.

Robertson, William, 'View of the Progress of Society in Europe, from the Subversion of the Roman Empire to the Beginning of the Sixteenth Century', in *The History of the Reign of Charles V*, in idem, *Works* (London: Cadell, 1831).

Rotta, Salvatore, 'Montesquieu nel Settecento italiano: note e ricerche', *Materiali per una storia della cultura giuridica* 1 (1971): 55–209, http://www.eliohs.unifi.it/testi/900/rotta/rotta_montesettit.html (accessed 30 September 2022).

Rousseau, Jean-Jacques, *Of the Social Contract and Other Political Writings*, Engl. transl. Quintin Hoare, ed. Christopher Bertram (London: Penguin Books, 2012).

Solari, Gioele, *Studi su Francesco Mario Pagano*, ed. Luigi Firpo (Torino: Giappichelli, 1963).

Thomson, Ann, 'French Eighteenth-Century Materialists and Natural Law', *History of European Ideas* 42(2) (2016): 243–255.

Tuck, Richard, 'The "Modern" Theory of Natural Law', in *The Languages of Political Theory in Early-Modern Europe*, ed. Anthony Pagden (Cambridge: Cambridge University Press, 1987), 99–119.

Venturi, Franco, 'Antonio Genovesi', in *Illuministi italiani*, vol. 5, *Riformatori napoletani* (Milano: Ricciardi, 1962), 4–46.

Venturi, Franco, 'Church and Reform in Enlightenment Italy: The Sixties of the Eighteenth Century', *Journal of Modern History* 49 (1976): 215–232.

Venturi, Franco, 'Mario Pagano', in *Illuministi italiani*, vol. 5, *Riformatori napoletani* (Milano: Ricciardi, 1972), 785–833.

Venturi, Franco, *Settecento riformatore*, vol. 5.1, *L'Italia dei lumi* (*1764–1790*)*: La rivoluzione di Corsica. Le grandi carestie degli anni sessanta. La Lombardia delle riforme* (Torino: Einaudi, 1987).

Vivenzio, Nicola, *Storia del regno di Napoli e suo governo dalla decadenza dell'Impero romano al re Ferdinando IV* (Napoli: Nel Gabinetto letterario, 1811).

Waldmann, Felix, *Antonio Genovesi, the 'Scuola Genovesiana', and Philosophy in the Kingdom of Naples, 1743–1792* (Junior Research Fellowship diss., Trinity College, Cambridge, 2015–2016).

Waldmann, Felix, 'Natural Law and the Chair of Ethics in the University of Naples, 1703–1769', *Modern Intellectual History* 19 (2022): 54–80.

Wootton, David, 'Laughing at Helvétius', in *Etica e religione nella tradizione repubblicana. Aspetti storici e teorici*, ed. Maurizio Viroli et al. (Torino: Fondazione Agnelli, 1996), 95–124.

CHAPTER 6

Pufendorf and Hutcheson in the Alps: Variations on Natural Law in Eighteenth-Century Italy

Serena Luzzi

1 Making It a Duty to Translate Pufendorf: Almici's Project

If we look at the works brought to press in mid-eighteenth-century Venice, which at the time was the capital of Italian publishing, we would be led to conclude that a major cultural and confessional taboo had been overcome. For it is here that, in response to the demands of an increasingly growing clientele, a series of re-editions and translations began to appear that made it possible for the wider public to gain access to the foundational works of Protestant natural law. Samuel Pufendorf, Hugo Grotius, John Locke and Christian Wolff thus became household names; their works left the close confines of richly stocked private libraries and began to circulate, gaining a wider readership, even if all these works were at the time censored by the Roman Catholic Church; meanwhile, literary periodicals began to feature the first articles devoted to modern natural law. For the print shops in Venice, sensitive to trends in the market, it was now becoming easier to obtain the secular authorizations needed to publish those books, though they did have to resort to false place-names so as to avoid tensions with Church hierarchies.[1] What was happening in Venice was not extraordinary; we now know that the reception of natural law up and down the Italian peninsula had already been underway; in fact, the works of Grotius, Pufendorf and Hobbes were familiar, and were used as textbooks in the universities.[2] The publishing market in Venice therefore reflected a broad

1 See Mario Infelise, *L'editoria veneziana nel '700* (Milano: FrancoAngeli, 1989), 87–88, at 94. See also Patrizia Bravetti and Orfea Granzotto, *False date: Repertorio delle licenze di stampa veneziane con falso luogo di edizione (1740–1797)* (Firenze: Firenze University Press, 2008), 113 (no. 279, 27 February 1757, Hugo Grotius, *De jure belli, ac pacis*), 116 (no. 290, 14 September 1757, Samuel von Pufendorf, *De officio hominis et civis*), 116 (no. 291, 12 January 1758, John Locke, *De intellectu humano*), 120 (no. 305, 27 May 1758, Samuel Pufendorf, *De iure naturae et gentium*), 125 (no. 324, 11 February 1759, Christian Wolff, *Philosophia moralis*).

2 See Chapter 1 of the present volume, by Emanuele Salerno, and Chapter 2, by Alberto Clerici.

and widespread trend both in Italy and beyond. And yet, perhaps ahead of anywhere else and more forcefully, there emerged out of Venice a sense of restless innovation involving the approach to Protestant natural law in the Italian cultural and confessional context. It was not a settled matter that the works of Protestant authors should be able to circulate. And even less uncontroversial was the possibility of public debate on sensitive topics in ethics or on the role of human reason, or, more to the point, on the rational foundations of natural law.

At issue, in other words, was the possibility of going to the heart of transalpine systems of natural law. An important signal was sent out when Pufendorf's 1672 *De iure naturae et gentium* received its first Italian translation.[3] The translator was Giambattista Almici (1717–1793), a lawyer from Brescia, a wealthy town in the subalpine belt that was subject to the Republic of Venice.[4] The first two volumes appeared in Venice in 1757, and only in 1759 was the work completed – four volumes in all, the translation based on Jean Barbeyrac's French edition, possibly the second one (1712) but more probably the later ones (1732, 1740, 1750).[5] It should be underlined that this is a selective translation: in many passages, Pufendorf's text undergoes major reworking and 'corrections', as Almici calls them. And Almici follows Barbeyrac's notes only in part, to leave plenty of room for his own reasoning. Nevertheless, despite the many rearrangements, Almici's work still represents a significant moment, because it is the first attempt to render into Italian the work of the prince of Protestant natural law. The initiative drew great interest. In fact, it had been preceded by a well-conducted promotional effort,[6] and all along

3 Samuel Pufendorf, *Il diritto della natura e delle genti o sia sistema generale de' principii li più importanti di morale, giurisprudenza e politica, rettificato, accresciuto, e illustrato da Giovambattista Almici* (Venezia: Pietro Valvasense, vols 1 and 2 1757, vol. 3 1758, vol. 4 1759).

4 See Stefania Stoffella, 'Almici, Giovambattista', in *Dizionario biografico dei giuristi italiani (XII–XX secolo)*, ed. Italo Birocchi et al. (Bologna: Il Mulino, 2013), vol. 1, 45; and Maurizio Bazzoli, 'Giambattista Almici e la diffusione di Pufendorf nel Settecento italiano', *Critica storica* 16 (1979): 3–100, at 17 and n. 55.

5 It is not possible to say which edition was used by Almici but he certainly did not use the first: Almici's translation refers to a note by Barbeyrac that was not present in the first edition (1706), whereas it is present from the second edition (1712) onwards. Pufendorf, *Il diritto della natura e delle genti*, 6, n. 1; Samuel Pufendorf, *Le droit de la nature et des gens, ou Système général des Principes les plus importans de la morale, de la jurisprudence, et de la politique*, 2 vols (Amsterdam: Pierre De Coup, 1712), vol. 1, 8, n. 6. Public libraries in Padua and in Venice suggest a greater circulation of the later editions, especially the fourth edition (1732), which Almici may also have used. I owe this information to the courtesy of Gabriella Silvestrini.

6 Bazzoli, 'Giambattista Almici e la diffusione di Pufendorf'.

the peninsula, from Turin to Naples, from Venice to Palermo, it gained many orders – at least 206 – from lawyers, literati, booksellers and the clergy.[7]

What had driven Almici to embark on such a venture, in defiance of the veto and censorship it could well be expected to face? What was his project? In the preface to the translation, Almici describes his enterprise as a scientific and cultural 'duty';[8] every language barrier had to be taken down to give Pufendorf's masterwork the widest circulation. The first goal was to narrow the gap with the rest of European culture, where this work was so important that it had already been made available in several languages. Almici was driven by a sense of esteem even greater than that which he describes in the preface, which was written so that the book might pass the censorship screening by either the state or the Church – two ever-present entities capable of shaping the writing and choices of an author. The first part of the preface is therefore mainly a long *pars destruens* peppered with unforgiving and opinionated judgements about the work he is about to translate. That was, in reality, a strategy designed to soften the shock and scandal the book was bound to elicit in some circles.[9] It falls to the reader to slog through the boredom of these presumptuous and aggressive pages before finally grasping the translator's true feelings about Pufendorf, described later in the preface as the most compelling and accurate of the 'philosophical natural lawyers', this work being the best in the entire landscape of natural law.[10] From the reader Almici expects

7 The list of subscribers can be found in the back matter of the second volume (1757) and it is published in Diego Quaglioni, 'Pufendorf in Italia: Appunti e notizie sulla prima diffusione della traduzione italiana del *De iure naturae et gentium*', *Il Pensiero politico* 32 (1999): 235–250, at 246–250.

8 He states: 'It was squarely a matter of duty that a work of such great merit, and of such importance […], should also make its entry into the Italian Republic of Letters, which in no respect falls behind the others of Europe'. The Italian original reads: 'Era ben di dovere che un'opera di tanto merito e di tanta importanza […] vedesse anche la Repubblica Letteraria d'Italia, che in nulla cede all'altre d'Europa'. Almici's preface to his translation of Pufendorf, *Il diritto della natura e delle genti*, vol. 1, i, § I, 'Prefazione'.

9 Backing up this claim is a letter of April 29, 1756, in which Camillo Almici – Giambattista's brother and a priest – writing to Giovanni Battista Chiaramonti comments that the 'book's very title, and to an even greater extent its preface, will serve to avert the scandal the book attracts: through the former and the latter, both, the work will come out self-corrected, and all but rewritten in many of its parts'. The Italian original: 'Il titolo istesso del libro, e molto più la prefazione servirà ad ovviare allo scandalo preteso del libro: mentre sì dell'uno, come dell'altra risulterà essersi l'opera corretta, e quasi rifatta in molte sue parti'. Quoted in Bazzoli, 'Giambattista Almici e la diffusione di Pufendorf', 25.

10 See Almici, 'Prefazione', in Pufendorf, *Il diritto della natura e delle genti*, xvii and following, but see also vii, § VI.

an unbiased mind, free of 'scholastic cavilling' and 'misconceived ideas',[11] in short, an emancipated reader. These innuendos are aimed at those who are intent on waging battle against natural law of a Protestant stripe, unwavering in their allegiance to Scholasticism – well-known and highly regarded personalities such as the theologian Daniele Concina (1687–1756), who in his writings associated natural law with atheism, forging a violent and dangerous identification, as well as the Bavarian monk Anselm Desing (1699–1772), the Jesuit Ignaz Schwarz (1690–1740)[12] and many other more or less influential figures, all engaged against heretical thinkers and their theories, regarded as fatal to the mind and the soul.

Almici had previously staked out a position against those who took exception to transalpine natural law theories, in a 1750 article titled 'Saggio sopra la Ragione umana, o sia la Natural legge contro i disapprovatori di un tale studio' (Essay on human reason, or natural law, *contra* those who disapprove of such inquiries).[13] This is testimony of his prior interest in a topic that was increasingly attracting attention and controversy, but also shows his short patience with naysayers who were unwilling to engage in open debate. The article announces the project of the translation and should be seen as the initial trailblazing text on the difficult path to the introduction of modern natural law theory in Italy's cultural and confessional environment. Almici was all but unknown when his article appeared in the authoritative journal edited by the abbot Angelo Calogerà, a learned man of science. In running with this eulogy

11 Ibid., xix–xx.

12 See specifically Daniele Concina, *Della religione rivelata contro gli ateisti, deisti, materialisti, indifferentisti* (Venezia: Presso Simone Occhi, 1754), but examples are legion. On Concina, see Antonella Barzazi, *Gli affanni dell'erudizione: Studi e organizzazione culturale degli ordini religiosi a Venezia tra Sei e Settecento* (Venezia: Istituto Veneto di Scienze, Lettere ed Arti, 2004); Ignaz Schwarz, *Institutiones juris universalis, naturae et gentium, ad normam moralistarum nostri temporis, maxime protestantium Hugonis Grotii, Puffendorfii, Thomasii, Vitriarii, Heineccii aliorumque ex recentissimis adornatae et ad crisin revocatis eorum principiis, primum fusiore, tum succinctiore methodo pro Studio Academico, praesertim catholico accommodatae*, 2 vols (Augustae: sumptibus Francisci Antonii Strötter, typis Antonii Maximiliani Heiss, Typographi Catholici, 1743); Anselm Desing, *Diatribe circa methodum Wolffianam, in philosophia practica universali, hoc est in principiis juris naturae statuendis adhibitam, quam non esse methodum, nec esse scientificam, ostenditur* (Pedeponti, vulgo Stadt am Hof bey Regenspurg: sumtibus Joannis Gastl, Bibliopolae, 1752).

13 Giambattista Almici, 'Saggio sopra la Ragione umana, o sia la Natural Legge, contro i disapprovatori d'un tale studio', *Raccolta d'opuscoli scientifici e filologici* 44 (1750): 141–212. The journal was edited by Angelo Calogerà from 1728 to 1754. It ran to fifty-one volumes and was published in Venice by Simone Occhi.

of natural law, Calogerà let pass some vehemently accusatory language. This was, after all, consistent with his cultural programme, which made it a priority to foster cultural renewal. The journal served as a forum through which new debates and projects could flourish.[14]

From the outset, the article takes issue with the short-sightedness of those who ensconce themselves in traditional models that have become sterile, and Almici cites John Locke's recommendation of Grotius and Pufendorf as foundational reading for young men as soon as they are able to assimilate them.[15] These were useful and indeed essential readings, ready to be brought to a wider readership, with whom they could spark fresh debates. Protestant publishing was making its way into the Catholic universities of the Habsburg lands, insofar as this was considered politically useful, and in the new faculties established in Pavia, in Austrian Lombardy, even the theology course was to include a study of Protestant thinkers and 'pagan' ones,[16] regardless of the fact that the ecclesiastical authorities in Rome did not take kindly to such a development in the curriculum.

In a renewed *querelle* couched in terms of philosophy and natural law, Almici confidently listed the modern thinkers whose philosophy surpassed that of the ancients, paying little regard to the prohibitions which censorship, both ecclesiastical and secular, placed on Protestant authors and their books: Hugo Grotius, Samuel Pufendorf, Richard Cumberland, Jean Barbeyrac, William Wollaston, Johann Gottlieb Heineccius and others were all intro-

14 On Calogerà's cultural profile, see Barzazi, *Gli affanni dell'erudizione* and Scipione Maffei, *Le lettere di Scipione Maffei ad Angelo Calogerà*, ed. Antonio Fallico, Corrado Viola and Fabio Forner (Verona: Cierre Grafica, 2016).

15 Almici, 'Saggio sopra la Ragione umana', 200. See John Locke, *Some Thoughts concerning Education* (1693), ed. John W. Yolton and Jean S. Yolton (Oxford: Clarendon Press, 1989), 239, § 186: 'When he has pretty well digested Tully's *Offices*, it may be seasonable to set him upon Grotius *de Jure Belli & Pacis*, or which I think, is the better of the two, Pufendorf *de Jure naturali & Gentium*; wherein he will be instructed in the natural Rights of Men, and the Original and Foundations of Society, and the Duties resulting from thence'. An education in politics, Locke comments elsewhere, requires a reading of his *Two Treatises of Government* (1690), among other works: 'To these one may adde Puffendorfe *De Officio Hominis et civis*, and *De Iure Naturali et Gentium*, which last, is the best book of that kind'. Quoted from 'Some Thoughts concerning Reading and Study for a Gentleman' (or: 'Mr. Locke's extempore Advice &c'.) (1703), in Locke, *Some Thoughts concerning Education*, 319–327, at 322.

16 See Chapter 3 of the present volume, by Elisabetta Fiocchi Malaspina, and Chapter 4, by Gabriella Silvestrini. See also Marco Bernuzzi, *La Facoltà teologica dell'Università di Pavia nel periodo delle riforme (1767–1797)* (Milano: Istituto Editoriale Cisalpino–La Goliardica, 1982), 84, n. 94.

duced by Almici, it is worth noting, as 'ours',[17] which implies that they were regarded by him as part of a shared cultural and scientific space. Almici's admiration for these thinkers, coupled with his open-mindedness, led him to suggest a compromise that would make it possible to proceed with intellectual debate despite the confessional barrier: the philosophical and the confessional spheres had to be kept separate. Almici condenses all his arguments in this regard into the rhetorical question: Are we perhaps to rid ourselves of Aristotle and Plato because of their 'misguided, impious, and untenable notions',[18] or, in short, because of their convictions as pagans? Similar questions had been floating around for some time, to be sure, but had never been given an unqualified 'no' in response.[19]

Once all the 'errors' of the Protestant philosophers have been pointed out and censured, Almici comments, it will be possible to extract much benefit from their works. The article closes with a comment that is more provocative than liberal in tone, being aimed at young men who should set out on a course of study based on a syllabus of solid readings. Let them ignore those who want to keep them away 'from such a fecund and valuable study', and let them apply themselves to such readings 'with full vim and vigour'.[20] Almici was gearing up for a proper culture war, advocating Protestant natural law and calling for a renewal of Italian culture at large. A new opportunity came his way when a fellow countryman, the theologian Carlo Polini, published *De juris divini et naturalis origine*, which sought to discredit rationalism and which reaffirmed Scripture rather than natural law as foundational.[21] Polini's was not just *any* book; the pope himself had promoted it in response to a new and feared cultural movement. Almici's fastidious and no less bellicose review of the work reflects the dogged aversion that writings on natural law still attracted, and it speaks to what was at stake.[22] It is in this context that Almici undertook the

17 Almici, 'Saggio sopra la Ragione umana', 199.

18 Ibid., 207.

19 As early as 1714, for example, Ludovico Antonio Muratori, writing under the protection of a pseudonym, had asked that question publicly in the preface to his *De ingeniorum moderatione*: 'At mihi impia quidem haereticorum dogmata perpetuo displiceant; sed numquam displiceat veritas vel in haereticorum ore. Numquid enim quaecumquae ab heterodoxis dicuntur, ea omnia continuo pro falsis ac impiis habenda?' Lamindi Pritanii [Ludovico Antonio Muratori], *De ingeniorum moderatione in religionis negotio* (Lutetiae Parisiorum: apud Carolum Robustel, 1714), 'Praefatio'.

20 Almici, 'Saggio sopra la Ragione umana', 209.

21 Carlo Polini, *De juris divini et naturalis origine* (Brixiae: Jacobus Turlinus, 1750).

22 [Giambattista Almici], letter of 2 August 1756, Brescia, in *Memorie per servire all'istoria letteraria* (Venezia: Pietro Valvasense, 1756), vol. 8, part II, 42–48 and 49–52 (text in Latin).

translation of Pufendorf's *De iure naturae et gentium* into vernacular Italian, from one of the editions with Barbeyrac's commentary.

The original manuscript of the translation has been lost. It is therefore impossible for us to assess the impact of the censors, who granted Almici a placet with the proviso that he corrects the contents of the text; nor is it possible to gauge the extent to which Almici in fact had qualms of a confessional nature. What we do know is that on multiple occasions in the published translation, Pufendorf's text gets doctored to grave effect. Even so, some of the core features of Pufendorf's thought are firmly kept in place, starting from the rationalistic approach he takes in developing a conception of society and of man and his representation of the state. The break from Scholasticism is clear-cut. Almici's engagement with Pufendorf and Barbeyrac is to the point and tightly woven, complete with numerous footnotes that often draw inspiration or are derived from Emer de Vattel's quite recent *Droit des gens*.[23]

Almici's makeover of the text met with criticism from knowledgeable and exacting readers, such as Clemente Baroni Cavalcabò, who was based in Italian-speaking Tyrol, under the Habsburg monarchy, and devoted himself to the study of natural law. As he saw it, this was 'among the most important' subjects of study, yet it was quite neglected in Italy, whose culture was prone to 'losing itself in minutiae'.[24] Baroni Cavalcabò, however, decided not

---

23 On Almici as a reader of Vattel, see Elisabetta Fiocchi Malaspina, *L'eterno ritorno del* Droit des gens *di Emer de Vattel (secc. XVIII–XIX): L'impatto della cultura giuridica in prospettiva globale* (Frankfurt am Main: Max Planck Institute for European Legal History, 2017), 55–57.

24 Clemente Baroni Cavalcabò, letter to Amedeo Svajer, 5 February 1763, quoted in Serena Luzzi, 'Percorsi secolarizzati nell'Italia del Settecento, tra diritto naturale ed etica scozzese', in *Illuminismo e protestantesimo*, ed. Giulia Cantarutti and Stefano Ferrari (Milano: FrancoAngeli, 2010), 149–170, at 152. There is to date no full consideration of Clemente Baroni Cavalcabò (1726–1796), or at least none that accounts for the depth of his inquiries into natural law, but see Stefania Stoffella, 'Il diritto naturale nella corrispondenza e negli scritti di Giovanni Battista Graser e di Clemente Baroni Cavalcabò', in *Aufklärung cattolica ed età delle Riforme: Giovanni Battista Graser nella cultura europea del Settecento*, ed. Serena Luzzi (Rovereto: Accademia Roveretana degli Agiati, 2004), 191–206. But see also Riccarda Suitner, 'Introduzione', in Clemente Baroni Cavalcabò, *L'impotenza del demonio di trasportare a talento per l'aria da un luogo all'altro i corpi umani dimostrata da Clemente Baroni delli Marchesi Cavalcabò accademico di Rovereto, dove anche si dimostra l'impossibilità di volare con artifizio umano* (Rovereto, 1753, repr. Bologna: Forni, 2013); Riccarda Suitner, 'The powerlessness of the devil. Scientific knowledge and demonology in Clemente Baroni Cavalcabò (1726–96)', in *Knowledge and Profanation: Transgressing the Boundaries of Religion in Ancient and Premodern Scholarship* (Leiden: Brill, 2019), 330–356; Christian Zendri, 'Clemente Baroni Cavalcabò e la stregoneria' and Antonio Trampus, 'Religione e superstizione: Gianrinaldo Carli, Clemente Baroni

to take an active role. Prudence advised him against publishing his own writings devoted to natural law and to Grotius and Hobbes, both of whom he held in high esteem. His role in giving currency to the themes of natural law therefore remained by and large confined to the private spaces of correspondence and the meetings held in the Accademia roveretana degli Agiati, a progressive society devoted to promoting cultural mediation, with an interest in Germanic culture (a pursuit facilitated by a familiarity with the German language, with which the rest of the Italian peninsula was much less conversant), and the activities of which were guided by a supra-confessional principle.[25] From this academy the journals in Venice and Florence would receive news and reviews of books published in German (but not in Latin). It was at one of the meetings of the academy that Baroni Cavalcabò read a dissertation devoted to Grotius, mounting an argument in favour of the validity of his *etsi Deus non daretur* (as if God did not exist).[26]

It is no surprise that Almici's translation was not to Baroni's liking. Baroni was so upset by the remaking of Pufendorf's original, by the 'admixture' (*mescolanza*) and the edits the text underwent in Almici's hands, that he cancelled his order and refused to buy the subsequent volumes.[27] More than that, for once setting aside his usual caution, he publicly responded with an article objecting to what, in his view, was the wrong interpretation that Almici gave to Pufendorf's position on the right of resistance. Baroni criticizes the erroneous logical path whereby the right to resistance is upheld on the one

---

Cavalcabò e il tramonto del dibatto su magia e stregoneria in Italia', in *Gli illuministi e i demoni. La disputa su magia e stregoneria dal Trentino all'Europa*, ed. Riccarda Suitner (Roma: Edizioni di Storia e Letteratura, 2019), 127–143, 23–36.

25 Stefano Ferrari, 'L'Accademia roveretana degli Agiati e la cultura di lingua tedesca (1750–1795)', in *La cultura tedesca in Italia 1750–1850*, ed. Alberto Destro and Paola Maria Filippi (Bologna: Patron, 1995), 217–276.

26 The text, which remained unpublished, was read in public at a meeting of the Accademia roveretana degli Agiati held in 1755. In a letter to a friend who was a priest, Baroni Cavalcabò underscored that the issue was sensitive (*delicato*) and 'apt to elicit scandal', and with conviction he explained that 'man can know natural law and is duty-bound to observe it even without assuming the existence of God'. Clemente Baroni Cavalcabò, letter to Giovanni Battista Graser, Sacco/Rovereto, 23 August 1755, quoted in Stoffella, 'Il diritto naturale nella corrispondenza', 195, 198–199 (the original reads: 'L'uomo può conoscere la legge naturale e ha l'obbligo d'osservarla anche senza supporre l'esistenza di Dio').

27 Giuseppe Valeriano Vannetti, letter to Giambattista Chiaramonti, Rovereto, 5 April 1758, in *Discorrere per lettera: Carteggio Giuseppe Valeriano Vannetti–Giambattista Chiaramonti (1755–1764)*, ed. Liliana de Venuto (Trento: Civis, 2007), 244.

hand and the obligation to comply with a sanction is upheld on the other.[28] In his learned article, Grotius, Hobbes and Pufendorf are depicted as 'heroes of civil science' (*eroi della scienza civile*) and repeatedly mentioned as authoritative masters.[29] The debate sparked by Almici's translation, in which he himself often took part,[30] once more offers evidence of a public readership interested in the issues raised by natural law and ready to weigh in by contributing to academic-literary periodicals, which at the time served as the main tool for communicating ideas and moving the cultural conversation forward.

If Almici's objective was to give currency to Pufendorf's work, the ensuing debates and publishing initiatives crowned it with success. Indeed, a few years later, in 1761, Pufendorf's compendium of the work, *De officio hominis et civis* (1673), was published in an Italian translation based on Barbeyrac's French edition.[31] The translator, Michele Grandi (1718–1786), was a clergyman in Padua who held a degree in law. Explicit in his intent to preserve a line of continuity with Almici's translation of Pufendorf's *De iure naturae et gentium*, as well as with Barbeyrac's earlier (1707) translation of its compendium, Grandi offered his work to readers who had not yet had a chance to read the unabridged work (*Opera grande*) or who might not be fluent in French.[32] Even so, Grandi strayed away from Almici's style and promised a complete and undoctored equivalent of Barbeyrac's edition, considering that readers were asking to engage with 'these celebrated writers' views' as they had been published. Here, then, was evidence of a pool of readers large enough not to be neglected, and they not only took an interest in the classics of Protestant natural law but also wanted to access these texts in versions as close as possible to the original. True to that

28 The dispute was over the proper interpretation of Pufendorf's *De jure naturae et gentium*, vol. 8, iii, § 1. On Baroni's criticism, see Stefania Stoffella, 'Il diritto di resistenza nel Settecento italiano. Documenti per la storia della traduzione del *De iure naturae et gentium* di Pufendorf', *Laboratoire italien: Politique et société* 2 (2001): 173–199.

29 [Clemente Baroni Cavalcabò], Rovereto, 10 October 1757, in *Memorie per servire all'istoria letteraria* (Venezia: Pietro Valvasense, 1757), vol. 10, 313–328. Even though the article is anonymous, Almici knew its authorship, as can be gathered from the fact that in his reply a direct reference is made to Baroni.

30 [Giambattista Almici], letter of 13 January 1759, Brescia, in *Nuove Memorie per servire all'istoria letteraria* (Venezia: Silvestro Marsini, 1759), vol. 1, 123–133.

31 Samuel Pufendorf, *I doveri dell'uomo e del cittadino: Tali che a lui dalla legge naturale sono prescritti, dalla versione francese di Giovanni Barbeyrac tradotti, e con molte aggiunte corretti, ed illustrati da Michele Grandi accademico di Udine* (Venezia: Francesco Pitteri, vols 1 and 2 1761, vol. 3 1767). The translator, Michele Grandi, tells us that his translation reflects the work he did comparing several earlier translations: see 'Avvertimento sopra questa traduzione italiana', x and n. 3.

32 Ibid., x–xi.

idea, Grandi took care to place his own extensive commentary in notes set apart from Pufendorf's text, which could thus be appreciated in its integrity. Here, too, it is impossible for us to gain a proper sense of the effect that censorship might have had on the notes, but we can observe that, even with all the confessional safeguards packed into the text, Grandi did on the whole adhere to Pufendorf's system. It is no accident that he insisted on bringing young people into the conversation; it was the more recent generations who formed the ideal audience for the translation[33] as a contribution to a much-anticipated renewal.

2 Bogeymen and Witches, or: Moving toward a Catholic System

In the landscape of the Italian debate surrounding natural law, it took much toil for any Catholic alternative to emerge. An initial important effort in this direction came in 1764, with a book published in Venice by the Dominican friar Bonifazio Finetti. An earlier version of it had been so battered by his superiors in the monastic order that its publication was prohibited.[34] Finetti was anything but subversive in his intentions. What he wanted to do was to provide a counterweight to the worrisome spread and encroachment of Protestant works on natural law,[35] while the 'good' books grounded in sound doctrine were rare or non-existent. It was no longer enough to lament the sorry situation and spread blame for it; it was necessary to provide at once a book on natural law cast in a Catholic mould, something that had yet to be seen in Italy.[36] In his dedication to Maria Theresa, of whom he was a subject, Finetti claimed (rightfully) a historical first for himself, having preceded anyone else in Italy in putting out a work capable of offering an updated overview of nat-

33 Ibid., xiii.

34 Giovanni Francesco [Bonifazio] Finetti, *De principiis juris naturae et gentium adversus Hobbesium, Pufendorfium, Thomasium, Wolfium et alios*, 2 vols (Venetiis: apud Thomam Bettinelli, 1764). On Finetti (1705–1782), see Barzazi, *Gli affanni dell'erudizione*, 249–253; Silvano Cavazza, 'Finetti, Bonifazio', in *Dizionario Biografico degli Italiani* (Roma: Istituto dell'Enciclopedia Italiana Treccani, 1997), vol. 48, 40–42. See also Chapter 2 of the present volume, by Alberto Clerici.

35 '[…] accuratiusque dici posse crediderim, libros quidem malos immane nimiam in copiam excrevisse; at bonorum numerum multo minorem adhuc esset; ut idcirco aut de illis minuendis, aut de istis augendis hodie laborandum videatur […]'. Finetti, *De principiis juris naturae et gentium*, vol. 1, 'Praefatio', xi.

36 Ibid., xii.

ural law.[37] Despite Finetti's stated principle, however, his translation was not meant to reach a broad audience, considering it was written in Latin. The book is the outcome of a difficult compromise, attempting as it did to 'at once reject and accept'[38] Germanic natural law and to set Scholastic doctrine within a coherent framework – or, in short, to adopt the solid Protestant model. The book was a compromise even in relation to the expectations of the Dominican order, which (as mentioned) had rejected (and thus censored) the original manuscript and imposed a substantial revision of it. In a sort of critical anthology, Finetti brought together the finest minds of modern natural law: Hobbes, Pufendorf, Thomasius, Wolff – all quoted in the book – as well as Grotius, Selden, Barbeyrac, Buddeus, Burlamaqui and Heineccius. Their works are presented and discussed following the template of the Scholastic tradition and under the strictures of a confessional framework. Finetti's confessional circumspection was targeted by a reader who was anything but charitable to him, Carlantonio Pilati, who would soon champion a wide-ranging reform project in Italy. At the time, Pilati was teaching law in Trento, the capital of an ecclesiastical principality in the Alps, an area where the Italian world interfaced with the Germanic one.[39]

Before we get to Pilati himself, it is worth considering his assessment of Finetti's work. In a letter to Finetti, Pilati recognizes his merits – being up to date on the subject matter – but takes a negative view of the work itself, on account of the apologetic aim by which it is informed.[40] The Italians, Pilati commented, are 'extraordinarily wary' of natural law and moral science, recoiling from them like children do 'from bogeymen and witches'.[41] Italian books with all their biases were worthless. The reason why Italian culture was slow to catch up lay entirely in its resistance to Protestant culture, and this delay was

37 Ibid., ii, 'Mariae Theresiae Augustae': 'profecto cum opus istuc sit in hoc genere primum, quod ex Italia prodeat'.

38 Merio Scattola, 'Protestantesimo e diritto naturale cattolico nel XVIII secolo', in *Illuminismo e protestantesimo*, ed. Giulia Cantarutti and Stefano Ferrari (Milano: FrancoAngeli, 2010), 131–148, at 139, which is a good source on the development of a Catholic system of natural law in the nineteenth century. See also Chapter 10 in the present volume, by Francesca Iurlaro.

39 On the Italian reformer, see note 47, below.

40 Carlantonio Pilati wrote two letters to Giovanni Bonifazio Finetti, the first dated 16 July and the second 30 September 1766. The letters are published in Giovanni Francesco [Giovanni Bonifazio] Finetti, *Apologia del genere umano accusato d'essere stato una volta bestia*, 3 vols (Venezia: Vincenzo Radici, 1768), vol. 1, xxxviii, xxxix–xliii.

41 Carlantonio Pilati to Giovanni Giacomo Cresseri, February 1763. See Luzzi, 'Percorsi secolarizzati nell'Italia del Settecento', 152.

especially dire and manifest when it came to the study of natural law. Finetti had therefore not broken the taboo. But would Pilati do so?

Pilati himself devoted two works to natural law that signal an entirely different orientation and argumentative style. He used his sharp quill to call for an intellectual rejuvenation through which to dismantle and finally break free from the dominant system of thought, which had been shaped by confessional concerns and was an expression of a clerical power that needed to be limited.

The occasion for this call to action was the publication in 1765 of a textbook on traditional natural law by a doctor of theology, under the name Giovanni di Dio, whose real name was Francesco Staidel, a Franciscan friar, also from Trento.[42] Pilati unleashed a cutting satire against Staidel and his book[43] because of its charge of heresy against Protestant natural lawyers without reflecting on their merits.[44] And in fact the arguments Staidel puts forward against natural law are incoherent; as Pilati comments, any author, no matter how pagan or heretic, could do better.[45] Staidel's performance was nothing but a dogmatic provocation.

3 Natural Law Does Not Exist: What Then?

Of all the conceptions of natural law to come out of Italy in the early 1760s, perhaps none was more confessionally unbeholden and radical than the one put forward by Carlantonio Pilati, intent as he was on overcoming the taboo and the accompanying impasse that was holding back the development of philosophy all along the peninsula.

On several occasions Pilati can be seen to have had little patience with confessional strictures because they could so heavily impair the quality of

42 Joanne de Deo Staidelio (1732–1777), *Lex naturæ propugnata* (Tridenti: ex typographia episcopali Monauniana, 1765).

43 Lapi Coraliti [Carlantonio Pilati], *Judicium de duobus P. Joannis De Deo Staidelii Libris, quorum alter lex naturalis propugnata, alter Enchiridium theologiae inscriptus est* (Lugani: typis Agnelli, 1766).

44 Ibid. A few examples: 'Nonne Grotius, Cumberlandius, Pufendorfius, Cudworthius, Wollastonius, aliique ad manus erant, ex quibus optima potuisses pro lege naturali tuenda argumenta sumere? Aut si haereticos odis', 8; 'Itaque fidem mihi in hoc, quod dicam, adhibeas, velim: Purus putus Theologus non est idoneus ad Jus naturae ita ut oportet, tractandum', 18; 'possunt te Grotius, Pufendorfius, Barbeiracius, Heineccius, quos tu viros ludibrio habere soles, multo meliora docere', 32.

45 Ibid., 'Ego mallem auctor esse cuicunque, ut de iis rebus, quae ad hominum officia pertinent, quemlibet potius Auctorem paganum, aut haereticum, quam opera tua, Staidelj, consuleret', 32.

philosophical reflection in Italy. An enterprising character, not too compunctious, and in fact irreverent, he was willing to resort to the shrewdest means to remove obstacles preventing him from fulfilling his needs and interests.[46] Thus, in pursuit of his interest in the Protestant world, he declared himself ready to convert. This was a lie but it allowed Pilati to closely observe the Protestant world. With his lies, and thanks to his bilingualism (he had studied in Salzburg), he spent a semester in Helmstedt (Lower Saxony) in 1761 in the capacity of *Privatdozent*. As we will see, this was in many respects a turning point in his life. Central to his writings was the need to reshape the relation between church and state and, more to the point, to secularize politics and culture in Italy. His work of greatest acclaim in this vein was *Di una riforma d'Italia*, published in Chur (Canton of Grisons) in 1767. This lays out a sweeping programme for an urgent modernization that would even earn the praise of Voltaire.[47] It was necessary to change the Italian outlook, imbued as it was with specious values, and to free that culture of its clerical and confessional shackles. In *Di una riforma d'Italia*, Catholic and Protestant authors and titles take turns and any confessional force is neutered. The style is aggressive and so is the anticlericalism by which it is informed. Among other things, Pilati went so far as to advocate an across-the-board policy of tolerance.

We should not be surprised, then, that Pilati was also the author of a work in which natural law is treated from a provocative perspective that had no precedent in Italian culture: *L'esistenza della legge naturale impugnata e sostenuta* (The existence of natural law, challenged and sustained), published in Italian in Venice in 1764 and then in German in 1767.[48] Its title is misleading, for the author's actual intent was not to weigh the pros and cons of natural law but

---

46 See Serena Luzzi, 'Pilati, Carlantonio', in *Dizionario Biografico degli Italiani* (Rome: Istituto dell'Enciclopedia Italiana Treccani, 2015), vol. 83, 660–663.

47 Carlantonio Pilati, *Di una riforma d'Italia ossia dei mezzi di riformare i più cattivi costumi, e le più perniciose leggi d'Italia*, ed. Serena Luzzi (Roma: Edizioni di Storia e Letteratura, 2018). The work was translated into French in two separate editions, both dated 1769 (Amsterdam: Marc-Michel Rey; Rimini [Paris]: F.lli Albertini [false date]), and subsequently also into German, in 1775 (Zürich: Orell, Gessner, Füssli & Comp.). See Serena Luzzi, 'Der exportierte Antiklerikalismus: Europäische Stationen eines italienischen Reformprojekts im 18. Jahrhundert', in *Italien in Europa: Die Zirkulation der Ideen im Zeitalter der Aufklärung*, ed. Frank Jung and Thomas Kroll (Paderborn: Fink, 2014), 161–184. In general about secularization, see Irene Gaddo and Edoardo Tortarolo, *Secolarizzazione e modernità. Un quadro storico* (Roma: Carocci, 2017).

48 Carlantonio Pilati, *L'esistenza della legge naturale impugnata e sostenuta* (Venezia: Antonio Zatta, 1764). The work is organized as two parts, the first (1–106) laying out the arguments against the existence of natural law, the second (107–196) surveying the ones for its existence. On this book, see Luzzi, 'Percorsi secolarizzati nell'Italia del Settecento'.

outright to deny its existence. It was the prospect of censorship and the prodding of friends that persuaded him to add a second, contrarian part to his book that camouflaged his real thinking through this rhetorical illusion: the camouflage made it possible to publish the work in Venice without having to use a false place of publication.[49] He thus chose this two-headed structure for the book in order to ward off any doubt about his orthodoxy and thus keep up appearances (for Pilati had by this time turned deist). But to no avail: the book was placed on the *Index Librorum Prohibitorum*, precisely on account of its Janus-faced organization and its ready recourse to heretical authors. It is worth mentioning, in this connection, that the decree of condemnation betrays the Roman censors' ignorance of the philosophical sources and ideas referenced in the text.[50] But the arguments presented in the book were problematic even for Wilhelm Heinrich Winning, the Protestant pastor in Chur who translated it into German and who had forged a bond of friendship with the author.[51] Indeed, there was no doubt in Winning's mind about the existence of natural laws.

To demonstrate the non-existence of natural law was definitely a challenge. How had Pilati arrived at such a conviction? What were his models? It is not difficult to see the influence of Michel de Montaigne's *Essais*, and in particular his 'Apology for Raymond Sebond' and 'Of Cannibals'.[52] It is against the background of these famous texts that Pilati takes up anew the problem of cultural variety across human societies. The next step was to call into question the purported existence of a natural law of universal validity, thus taking issue with Barbeyrac, who on several occasions in translating Pufendorf challenged Montaigne's position in this regard.[53] However, Pilati's anti-universalism ended up rejecting the very idea of natural law. 'This pur-

49 Venetian authorities had given permission to print the manuscript if it falsely indicated Lucca as its place of publication. See Bravetti and Granzotto, *False date*, 191 (no. 524, 22 December 1763).

50 Luzzi, 'Percorsi secolarizzati nell'Italia del Settecento', 166.

51 Wilhelm Heinrich Winning, 'Vorrede des Uebersetzers', in *Des Herrn Pilati bestrittene und verfochtene Wirklichkeit des natürlichen Gesetzes, aus dem Italiaenischen übersetzt, und mit einer Vorrede begleitet von Wilhelm Heinrich Winning* (Lindau: Jacob Otto, 1767).

52 Michel de Montaigne, *Essais*, editio princeps (Bordeaux: S. Millanges, 1580), vol. 2, ch. 12 ('Apology'); vol. 1, ch. 31 [misnumbered in the book as trentième] ('Of Cannibals'). On the debate on human diversity, see Daniel Carey, *Locke, Shaftesbury, and Hutcheson: Contesting Diversity in the Enlightenment and Beyond* (Cambridge: Cambridge University Press, 2006), 44–45, 49–50.

53 See, for example, Jean Barbeyrac, 'Préface du Traducteur', in Pufendorf, *Le droit de la nature*, vol. 1, i–xcii, at xiv–xv. Cf. Carey, *Locke, Shaftesbury, and Hutcheson*, 67–68.

ported natural law', he comments in his work on the existence – or, rather, the *non-existence* – of natural law, 'is pure fiction' – 'a fantasy'; 'it does not exist'; it is 'a fanciful notion conceived by subtle but vain ratiocinators'.[54] The theme of the weakness of reason runs through the entire book.[55] Even so, Pilati does not follow Montaigne all the way to scepticism, but rather finds a positive solution in the moral sense theory developed by the Scottish philosopher Francis Hutcheson: universality can be ascribed only to the natural instinct.[56] It is worth pointing out that in *L'esistenza della legge naturale* the connection made with Scottish philosophy is not entirely clear, considering that, in an effort to avoid censorship, the original text was tampered with in such a way that its argumentative coherence is broken up, and the author's position is thus made ambiguous and elusive. Suffice it to note that the book closes with an eccentric eulogy to Thomas Aquinas (and implicitly to Scholasticism) – and nothing could be further from Pilati's thinking.[57]

The conceptual framing in which his thinking is actually set can instead be garnered from a quick and apparently marginal comment he makes whose key terms are *moral sentiment* (*sentimento morale*) and *instinct* (*istinto*), and from the note to that comment, in which Pilati makes reference to Hutcheson and his *Inquiry into the Original of Our Ideas of Beauty and Virtue*.[58] That this is not to be accounted as a piece of marginalia squeezed in as an afterthought is borne out by Pilati's subsequent correspondence and writings, from which we learn, on the contrary, that this passage is what survives of an entire framework of thought in which the author's anti-rationalist convictions combine with Hutcheson's philosophical system. Among the readers of Pilati's book there was one who did not fail to notice that the author was familiar with 'works that in Italy were perhaps little known',[59] and among these were certainly the works of Hutcheson. In the early 1760s, when Pilati published his book, Hutcheson's philosophy does not seem to have had much recognition in Italy. To be sure, Cesare Beccaria was a reader of Hutcheson, whose work he

54 Pilati, *L'esistenza della legge naturale*, 6, 17, 27, 44, 76, 94 (the original reads: 'un ghiribizzo di sottili, ma vani raziocinatori').

55 Ibid., 6, 8–10, 12, 14–16, 17, 24, 44.

56 Knud Haakonssen, *Natural Law and Moral Philosophy: From Grotius to the Scottish Enlightenment* (Cambridge: Cambridge University Press, 1996), 63–84; Carey, *Locke, Shaftesbury, and Hutcheson*, 150–199.

57 Pilati, *L'esistenza della legge naturale*, 196.

58 Ibid., 128 and note b.

59 Giuseppe Valeriano Vannetti, letter to Giambattista Chiaramonti, Rovereto, 19 May 1764, in *Discorrere per lettera*, 599.

studied in French translation,[60] but we can only speculate as to the full significance of this fact, for we are missing a systematic study of the state of affairs at the time. As for Pilati, his encounter with moral sense philosophy took place during the months he spent in 1761 in Lower Saxony at the Protestant University of Helmstedt, as mentioned above. Pilati could reap the benefits of a cultural process of broad scope that in Germany fostered the reception of English works in the Germanic lands through their translations and through their reviews in academic journals.

In Helmstedt, Pilati was keeping an eye on Francophone journals that offered an up-to-date overview of Anglophone culture for those unacquainted with English, and in particular he was reading the *Bibliothèque britannique*, which is mentioned in his work.[61] But Pilati's appreciation of Hutcheson's *Inquiry* comes from other, more direct sources, too; indeed, from Lower Saxony he came back not only with the complete *Bibliothèque britannique* but also with a German translation of the *Inquiry*,[62] giving us further evidence of his interest in philosophical systems which had been developed on the other side of the Channel and which he had hitherto been unaware of. Instinct is the decisive alternative in support of an anti-rationalistic and radically relativistic *Weltanschauung* that Pilati would never veer away from – a conception we find expressly stated in his works. It ought to be underscored here that Hutcheson himself does not deny the existence of natural law,[63] as Pilati seems to interpret him, if we are to judge by the logical connections made in the text. It

60 See Cesare Beccaria, *Des délits et des peines / Dei delitti e delle pene*, ed. Philippe Audégean (Lyon: ENS Editions, 2009), 307–308, 328, 226, 423; cf. Philippe Audégean, *La philosophie de Beccaria: Savoir punir, savoir écrire, savoir produire* (Paris: Libraire Philosophique J. Vrin, 2010), 203; Maria Francesca Turchetti, 'Libri e "nuove idee". Appunti sulla biblioteca illuministica di Cesare Beccaria', *Archivio storico lombardo* 139 (2013): 183–236.

61 See Pilati, *L'esistenza della legge naturale*, 24. Cf. *Bibliothèque britannique, ou Histoire des ouvrages des savans de la Grande-Bretagne* (A La Haye: Pierre de Hondt, 1733–1747). A complete collection of the *Bibliothèque britannique* is held at the Biblioteca Comunale in Trento, one of the few libraries in Italy with a copy of this journal. It is quite plausible that the collection was part of Pilati's library. Pilati could have bought it when he was in Helmstedt. On the journal, see Hans Bots, 'Pierre de Hondt, éditeur de la *Bibliothèque britannique* (1733–1743), et ses soucis à propos de la qualité de ce journal', in *Studies in de achttiende eeuw voor Uta Janssens*, ed. Franciscus Korsten and Jos Blom (Nijmegen: Katholieke Universiteit Nijmegen, Afdeling Engelse Taal en Cultuur, 2002), 39–54.

62 Francis Hutcheson, *Untersuchung unsrer Begriffe von Schönheit und Tugend, in zwo Abhandlungen* [...] *aus dem Englischen übersetzt*, [trans. Johann Heinrich Merck] (Frankfurt und Leipzig: in der Fleischerischen Buchhandlung, 1762). Pilati's copy is held in Trento at the Biblioteca Ufficio Beni Archivistici Librari e Archivio Provinciale, *Fondo Thun*.

63 Haakonssen, *Natural Law and Moral Philosophy*, 63–84.

is also worth noting that Pilati's adherence to moral sense philosophy does not come with any probing scrutiny of Hutcheson's more problematic axioms, first among these the universality of the moral sense and the origins of the dramatic cultural diversity that exists among human groups.[64]

A combination of censorship and self-censorship thus stifled the potential of Pilati's *L'esistenza della legge naturale*, in such a way that the principles of moral sense philosophy, still little known south of the Alps, would be hampered in finding their place in the Italian context. It is no surprise, then, that Pilati should have disowned his first work, choosing to instead point to his later writings, where his moral system is expounded with greater clarity and regains the coherence it had lost.

4 Natural Law, the Big Cheat, or: A Searing Indictment by an African Student

Pilati's conception of natural law is expounded without dissimulation in his later *Ragionamenti intorno alla legge naturale e civile* (Discussions on natural and civil law), printed in 1766,[65] two years after his *L'esistenza*. The question of the universality of instinct and the anti-rationalist polemic are present from the outset, in the first of the book's three Discussions, which Pilati dedicates to his friend Dietrich Lichtenstein, Bürgermeister of Helmstedt.[66] That Discussion reveals itself to be all the more significant if we consider how firmly rooted in natural law the thinking and culture were at the University of Helmstedt, and how difficult it had been for moral sense philosophy to gain any influence in the Lutheran environment, in part owing to the optimistic

64 See Carey, 'The Dilemma of Diversity', in Carey, *Locke, Shaftesbury, and Hutcheson*, 172–184.

65 See Carlantonio Pilati, 'Della legge naturale' ('Of natural law'), in Carlantonio Pilati, *Ragionamenti intorno alla legge naturale e civile* (Venezia: Antonio Zatta, 1766), 25–43.

66 Pilati, *Ragionamenti*, 3–24: 'Carolus Antonius Pilatus Joachimo Theodoro Lichtensteinio Serenissimo Brunsvicensium Duci A Consiliis S.P.D'. On Pilati's experience as a teacher in Helmstedt and the cultural context, see Serena Luzzi, 'Fehler und Vorzüge der deutschen Universitäten: Ansichten eines italienischen Privatdozent in Helmstedt (1761)', *Braunschweigisches Jahrbuch für Landesgeschichte* 99 (2018): 185–201. Lichtenstein had a copy of Pilati's *Ragionamenti*, but it remains unknown if he offered a reply. See the catalogue of Lichtenstein's library, sold at a public sale after his death: *Verzeichniß einer Sammlung von juristischen, historischen und theologischen Büchern des sel. Herrn Hofrath Lichtensteins … zu Helmstädt in dem Lichtensteinischen Hause an die Meistbietenden öffentlich verkauft werden soll* (1775), 99, no. 467, 'Ragionamenti intorno alla legge naturale et civile di C. A. Pilati, in Venez. 766 br. pp'.

anthropology by which that philosophy is underpinned.[67] In *Ragionamenti*, Lichtenstein is invited by Pilati to engage with him on this philosophical alternative fleshed out in the book and to give a forthright assessment of it.[68]

Pilati's *Ragionamenti* in effect rejected the foundations of natural law: natural law is a chimera, as Montaigne and others taught; reason was uncertain and hesitant, but the moral sense autonomous, as Hutcheson argued.[69]

The position Pilati stakes out against modern natural law is expressed in scathing tones through the voice of a young African student in Europe, scornful of the philosophical principles that have been imparted to him, and resentful of the prejudices that qualify non-European peoples as 'barbarous'.[70] Pilati

67 Jens Bruning, *Innovation in Forschung und Lehre: Die Philosophische Fakultät der Universität Helmstedt in der Frühaufklärung 1680–1740* (Wiesbaden: Harrassowitz, 2012); Jennifer Willenberg, *Distribution und Übersetzung englischen Schrifttums im Deutschland des 18. Jahrhunderts* (München: Saur, 2008); Fania Oz-Salzberger, *Translating the Enlightenment: Scottish Civic Discourse in Eighteenth-Century Germany* (Oxford: Oxford University Press, 1995), 77–85.

68 Pilati, *Ragionamenti*, 15–16: 'Quum igitur et Ratio fallax, impotens, dubia, incertaque plerumque sit, et hominum, ut et gentium opiniones variae sint, atque discordes, et Lex Revelata a plerisque vel ignoretur, vel impie despiciatur, nulla jam alia Legum Naturalium cognoscendarum via, atque ratio, quae quidem tam certa, quam communis omnium hominum sit, superesse potest, quam Instinctus ille naturali, quem omnes homines eodem modo sentiunt, et per quem non modo Legem aliquam Naturae existere generatim cognoscimus, verum etiam praecipua, atque summa ejus Principia deprehendimus [...]. Haec ego ad te, Lichtensteine, perscribere volui, non quo tibi praescriberem quid deinceps in Jure Naturae sequaris, sed quo sententiam explorarem hac de re tuam. Nam aut meum amplecteris judicium, si probaveris, aut tuo stabis, et mecum illud communicabis, si aliud quoddam est tuum'.

69 In a section headed 'Moral Sense Not from Reflection', Hutcheson argues that, 'Notwithstanding the mighty Reason we boast of above other Animals, its Processes are too slow, too full of doubt and hesitation, to serve us in every Exigency'. Francis Hutcheson, *Inquiry into the Original of Our Ideas of Beauty and Virtue in Two Treatises*, 2nd edition (London: J. Darby et al., 1726), treatise II, section VII, 271.

70 Pilati, 'Della legge naturale', in *Ragionamenti*, 25–43. Pilati writes: 'I was there [in London] when these men began to impart to him the first lesson on Natural Law [...] and then proceeded to drill into his head the idea that unfailing means lies in the Natural Reason which is common to all men' (ibid., 26). The Italian original reads: 'Io fui presente [a Londra], quando costoro presero a dargli la prima lezione sopra la Legge Naturale [...] e poi passarono a fargli concepire che la naturale ed a tutti gli uomini comune Ragione è quel mezzo sicuro'. Shortly thereafter, he refers to 'Entire Nations that you call barbarous' (ibid., 29; the original reads 'Intere Nazioni che voi chiamate barbare'). This part of the book was translated into German by Wilhelm Heinrich Winning, who had previously translated Pilati's *Esistenza della legge naturale*: Carlantonio Pilati, *Gedanken eines Afrikaners über das Gesetz der Natur: Als ein Anhang zu dem Werke des Hernn Pilati von der Wirklichkeit des natürlichen Gesetzes, aus dem Wälschen übersetzt von W. H. W.* (Zürich und Chur: Orell, Gessner, Walser und Compagnie, 1767).

is not taking issue with any theory in particular, nor is he drawing a distinction between Catholics and Protestants or between ancient and modern traditions; rather, his attack is aimed at all the 'schools' and books that the 'learned men of Europe' have brought into being in addressing the question of natural law.[71] Rationalist philosophers, the African student says, are 'big liars' and 'frauds', whose principles he rejects out of hand as 'inventions', 'eccentricities', 'pipe dreams', 'falsehood'.[72]

The argumentative scheme is still modelled on the one hand on Montaigne – with regard to relativism – and on the other hand on Hutcheson – regarding the idea of a universal innate morality. There is no contradiction, according to Pilati: the universality of moral sense is accompanied by the relativism of reason.[73]

The gulf and hierarchy between 'savages' and the civilized cease to be, no matter the latitude. The purportedly barbarous non-Europeans share the same ethical norms with the Europeans, and under the same standards pursue the good and condemn what is morally bad. Do the European travellers' accounts depict peoples committed to merciless cruelty? These reports are false, the African student declares, as did Hutcheson before him.[74]

Even if Hutcheson is not mentioned in these pages, Pilati's dependence on the Scottish philosopher is evident as the *Inquiry* clearly provided Pilati with both the lexicon and the concepts.[75] Thus we have 'istinto naturale' (where the *Inquiry* has 'natural Instinct'); 'istinto che ci rende umani, giusti, misericordiosi, benevoli, amici l'uno dell'altro' ('benevolent universal Instinct'); 'sentimento morale' ('moral Sentiment'); 'sentimento interiore' ('internal sense'); 'passioni' ('passions', 'violent passions', 'affections'); 'amore' or 'affetto naturale' toward our fellow beings ('love', 'natural affection'), 'costituzione naturale' ('Constitution of Human Nature', 'Constitution of Nature').

The worst of the natural lawyers' failures was their inability to recognize instinct as the prime mover of moral actions – 'a folly'[76] that made them woefully inadequate to the task of accounting for the variety of human customs.

71 Pilati, *Ragionamenti*, 30, 33.

72 Ibid., 27–28, 31, 36.

73 Ibid., 37; and, in the same vein: 'Reason, that is, the Intellect, differs and varies with the diversity of nations, time periods, climates, and the heads of men'. The original reads: 'La ragione, ossia l'Intelletto, è diverso, e vario secondo la diversità delle nazioni, de' tempi, de' climi, e delle teste degli uomini'.

74 Ibid., 29, 31; Hutcheson, *Inquiry*, treatise II, section IV, 'Travellers Accounts of Barbarous Customs', 202–204; Carey, *Locke, Shaftesbury, and Hutcheson*, 172–192.

75 Pilati, *Ragionamenti*, 30–31, 33–37, 39–43.

76 Ibid., 37.

There follows a breakdown of the whole theoretical construction, including its natural laws.[77] However, Pilati's polemical stance does leave room for ambiguity, because at one point, after vehemently denying the existence of natural law, he appears to concede that it does in fact exist. For, he speculates, if we were to introspect, we would find just the scarcest trace of a natural law ('pochissime tracce di quella legge')[78] – and this implicit admission turns *explicit* when he asserts that 'the first principles of natural law come from instinct' ('i primi principii della Legge naturale vengono dallo Istinto').[79] Although his vocabulary is not patterned after Hutcheson's *Inquiry* here, it is very likely that his derivation of natural law from instinct comes from a close reading of that work.[80]

Hutcheson's *Inquiry* seems even to inform what is perhaps the most delicate passage in *Ragionamenti*, where Pilati reprises the argument that our morality is independent of religion.[81] In Pilati's version, the argument is that it is possible and even necessary to proceed independently of revealed truth, and that the moral principle by which we are all bound is that of instinct.[82] This is a crucial point that we find reiterated in the *Giornale letterario*, a literary journal which Pilati founded in 1768 in Chur,[83] and through which he intended

77 Ibid. 38: 'It is either the case that [reason] is uniform in everyone or the Law which you call natural and common to the whole of humankind does not obligate everyone'. The original reads: 'O ella [la ragione] deve essere uniforme in tutti, o la Legge, che voi chiamate naturale, e comune di tutto il genere umano, non obbliga tutti'. And, in the same vein, at p. 37: 'Reason, that is, the Intellect, differs and varies with the diversity of nations, time periods, climates, and the heads of men'. The original reads: 'La ragione, ossia l'Intelletto, è diverso, e vario secondo la diversità delle nazioni, de' tempi, de' climi, e delle teste degli uomini'.

78 Ibid., 27.

79 Ibid., 39.

80 On Hutcheson's conception of the moral sense as the foundation of natural law, see Haakonssen, *Natural Law and Moral Philosophy*, 77–78.

81 Hutcheson, *Inquiry*, treatise II, section I: 'Our Moral Sense Not Founded on Religion', 128.

82 Pilati, *Ragionamenti*, 42–43: 'The African was unacquainted with Revelation, but he was right to say that the Natural Instinct is in this regard the true and proper teacher of man. […] The conclusion of this reasoning is that when it is desirable or even necessary to proceed independently of Revelation, there remains only one other principle by which to know and find Natural Law, and that is the Natural Instinct alone, namely, the moral sense'. The Italian original reads: 'L'Affricano, che non conosceva la Rivelazione, disse però bene, che l'Istinto naturale è in questo punto il vero, e proprio istruttore dell'uomo. […] La Conchiusione di questo ragionamento si è che quando si voglia o si debba prescindere dalla Rivelazione, allora niun altro principio per conoscere e rintracciare la Legge naturale rimane, che il solo naturale Istinto, ossia sentimento morale'.

83 Only five volumes of the journal were published. *Giornale letterario* [ed. Carlantonio Pilati] (A Coira: Stampatore Walser e Comp., 1768).

to keep Italian readers abreast of developments in international publishing. The occasion for setting out a different point of view was offered by the recent publication in Yverdon of Jean-Jacques Burlamaqui's *Principes du droit de la nature et des gens* in an edition annotated by the professor and publisher Fortunato Bartolomeo de Felice.[84] Burlamaqui's works were known in Italy, but they were not easy to get hold of. The first translations of his *Principes* did not appear until 1780, in Venice, and then in Siena in 1781/1782. In 1772 in Florence a similar initiative was prohibited for political reasons.[85]

Writing from Chur, Pilati expressed his disagreement with both Burlamaqui and de Felice.[86] Burlamaqui did recognize a universal moral instinct inherent in human nature, but he understood this instinct to be dependent on reason; and de Felice, worse still, argued that it is impossible to reason independently of God's will.[87] In direct contrast to that view, Pilati reiterated the need for the question of natural law to be considered independently of revelation, insisting on the universality of instinct and on its primacy over reason, relative to which it retained its own autonomy.

Pilati's adherence to moral sense philosophy is also present in his best-known work, *Di una riforma d'Italia*. This is only a matter of passing reference, but it is always with a view to delegitimizing natural law theory relative to moral sense theory, from which he will never depart.[88]

---

84 Jean-Jacques Burlamaqui, *Les Principes du droit de la nature et des gens* [...], *avec la suite du droit de la nature qui n'avait point encore paru: Le tout considérablement augmenté par M. le Professeur de Felice*, 8 vols (Yverdon, 1766–1768). On the Yverdon edition, see Gabriella Silvestrini, 'Tra Burlamaqui e Beccaria: Il diritto di vita e di morte nel modello giusnaturalistico di Fortunato Bartolomeo de Felice', in *Fortunato Bartolomeo de Felice: Un intellettuale cosmopolita nell'Europa dei Lumi*, ed. Stefano Ferrari (Milano: FrancoAngeli, 2016), 53–80, at 53–62.

85 See Sandro Landi, *Il governo delle opinioni: Censura e formazione del consenso nella Toscana del Settecento* (Bologna: Il Mulino, 2000), 254–256, 284–286; and Fiocchi Malaspina, *L'eterno ritorno del* Droit des gens *di Emer de Vattel*, 59–60. The translator of the Venice edition, based on the editio princeps, is Benedetto Crispi (Venezia: Giovanni Gatti, 1780); the Tuscan translation is based on the version edited by de Felice (Siena: Luigi e Benedetto Bindi, 1780–1782).

86 Carlantonio Pilati, review of *Les principes du droit de la nature et des gens*, by Jean-Jacques Burlamaqui, *Giornale letterario* 2 (1768): 64–74; see esp. 68–72.

87 On de Felice in this regard, see Edoardo Tortarolo, 'Dimorfismo imperfetto: Secolarizzazione e cristianesimo', in *Fortunato Bartolomeo de Felice. Un intellettuale cosmopolita nell'Europa dei Lumi, ed. Stefano Ferrari* (Milano: FrancoAngeli, 2016), 35–51.

88 Pilati, *Di una riforma d'Italia*: 'Our Natural Lawyers', Pilati comments, 'have sold us a bill of goods', 291; The Italian original reads: 'I nostri Scrittori del Diritto Naturale ci hanno venduto lucciuole per lanterne'.

5 The Difficult Path of Natural Law in Eighteenth-Century Italy

Modern doctrines of natural law are known to have been circulating in Italy as early as the late seventeenth century. However, it was only within the closed confines of libraries and universities that they could be dissected and debated. And even here the discussion was confined to a selection of topics.

Half a century later, a new cultural climate took shape that approached natural law with fresh priorities – with a willingness to reflect on its underlying assumptions and moral principles – and in arenas of discussion and exchange that were more open. In the mid-eighteenth century, there was a widespread perception among scholars in Italy that, culturally, the peninsula had fallen behind Europe – a gap, they reasoned, owing to the historical resistance to take up the seminal works of Protestant natural law. Various and significant initiatives testifying to the changes underway in Italy came in particular from Venice and from the borderlands between the Italian and German worlds.

As we have seen, an important role is to be attributed to Giambattista Almici, the first author to provide an Italian translation of Pufendorf's *De iure naturae et gentium*, using Barbeyrac's annotated edition. Almici was conspicuously the driving force behind the revitalization programme that sought to break free of confessional strictures, and at whose core lay the study of the masters of Protestant natural law.

To be sure, this revived interest was hindered in its progress, and even muffled, by confessional concerns coupled with the conditioning of the censorship brought to bear by both church and state, but the new scene was nonetheless lively.

In effect, the debate on natural law in many respects mirrored the difficult secularization process that marked the eighteenth century in Italy. This was a process in large part sustained by elites seeking to limit the inordinate power of the church and to advance political cultures not informed by religious or confessional values. The interest in Protestant natural law that visibly took hold in the mid-eighteenth century is therefore an important part of a broader push for secularization that was at least attempted. For much of the Italian peninsula's Catholic culture this was an unacceptable risk; for most people, the trusted texts remained those of the Scholastics.

No authoritative, compelling reply to Protestant doctrines had come out of Italy. An implicit admission of this came, as we have seen, from a religious thinker, Giovanni Bonifacio Finetti, whose book provided a survey of natural law. It was certainly not an answer to the problem (and it was also subjected to heavy censorship), but it did provide materials for new solutions in a process that would take a full century to run its course, attesting to the challenges the

Catholic world was facing in its effort to grapple with transalpine natural law and its underlying principles.

This cultural renaissance also spurred others on to make radical proposals unlike anything that had appeared hitherto in Italy, our example being the initiative of Carlantonio Pilati, the jurist from Trento who had the advantage of being familiar with the Germanic world. His deist position is fully coherent with his aggressive plan to secularize Italy as it was in 1760. It is no accident, then, that he should have been among the first outspoken critics to denounce the delay with which natural law in Italy could become even a subject of reasoned discussion.

Nevertheless, Pilati was dissatisfied also with natural law and went so far as to deny its existence, unreservedly embracing Francis Hutcheson's moral sense philosophy. Pilati discovered the Scottish philosopher during the few months he spent at the Protestant University of Helmstedt, in Lower Saxony – an encounter made possible by the fact that much literature from the other side of the Channel was conveyed to the Continent by being translated and reviewed. Pilati himself, then, benefited from cultural mediation and himself took on a similar role through his own work.

From the mid-eighteenth century, there began to circulate translations, articles and discussions in academic journals, as well as essays that sometimes entertained radical ideas of natural law, but at the same time all of them offered alternatives to the classics of modern natural law. This activity set in motion a process of significant renewal. This rejuvenating force, however, came up against the resistance of confessional, cultural and political forces pushing in the opposite direction. It was in this polarity that transalpine natural law had to make its long way through Italy.

Bibliography

[Almici, Giambattista], letter of 2 August 1756, Brescia, in *Memorie per servire all'istoria letteraria* (Venezia: Pietro Valvasense, 1756), vol. 8, part II, 42–48 and 49–52.

[Almici, Giambattista], letter of 13 January 1759, Brescia, in *Nuove Memorie per servire all'istoria letteraria* (Venezia: Silvestro Marsini, 1759), vol. 1, 123–133.

Almici, Giambattista, 'Saggio sopra la Ragione umana, o sia la Natural Legge, contro i disapprovatori d'un tale studio', *Raccolta d'opuscoli scientifici e filologici* 44 (1750): 141–212.

Audégean, Philippe, *La philosophie de Beccaria: Savoir punir, savoir écrire, savoir produire* (Paris: Libraire Philosophique J. Vrin, 2010).

Barbeyrac, Jean, 'Préface du Traducteur', in Samuel Pufendorf, *Le droit de la nature et des gens, ou Système général des Principes les plus importans de la morale, de la jurisprudence, et de la politique*, 2 vols (Amsterdam: Gerard Kuyper, 1706), vol. 1, pp. i–xcii.

[Baroni Cavalcabò, Clemente], Rovereto, 10 October 1757, in *Memorie per servire all'istoria letteraria* 10 (Venezia: Pietro Valvasense, 1757), 313–328.

Barzazi, Antonella, *Gli affanni dell'erudizione: Studi e organizzazione culturale degli ordini religiosi a Venezia tra Sei e Settecento* (Venezia: Istituto Veneto di Scienze, Lettere ed Arti, 2004).

Bazzoli, Maurizio, 'Giambattista Almici e la diffusione di Pufendorf nel Settecento italiano', *Critica storica* 16 (1979): 3–100.

Beccaria, Cesare, *Des délits et des peines / Dei delitti e delle pene*, ed. Philippe Audégean (Lyon: ENS Editions, 2009).

Bernuzzi, Marco, *La Facoltà teologica dell'Università di Pavia nel periodo delle riforme (1767–1797)* (Milano: Istituto Editoriale Cisalpino–La Goliardica, 1982).

Bibliothèque britannique, ou Histoire des ouvrages des savans de la Grande-Bretagne (A La Haye: Pierre de Hondt, 1733–1747).

Bots, Hans, 'Pierre de Hondt, éditeur de la *Bibliothèque britannique* (1733–1743), et ses soucis à propos de la qualité de ce journal', in *Studies in de achttiende eeuw voor Uta Janssens*, ed. Franciscus Korsten and Jos Blom (Nijmegen: Katholieke Universiteit Nijmegen, Afdeling Engelse Taal en Cultuur, 2002), 39–54.

Bravetti, Patrizia and Orfea Granzotto, *False date: Repertorio delle licenze di stampa veneziane con falso luogo di edizione (1740–1797)* (Firenze: Firenze University Press, 2008).

Bruning, Jens, *Innovation in Forschung und Lehre: Die Philosophische Fakultät der Universität Helmstedt in der Frühaufklärung 1680–1740* (Wiesbaden: Harrassowitz, 2012).

Burlamaqui, Jean-Jacques, *Les principes du droit de la nature et des gens …, avec la Suite du droit de la nature qui n'avait point encore paru: Le tout considérablement augmenté par M. le Professeur de Felice*, 8 vols (Yverdon: 1766–1768).

Carey, Daniel, *Locke, Shaftesbury, and Hutcheson: Contesting Diversity in the Enlightenment and Beyond* (Cambridge: Cambridge University Press, 2006).

Cavazza, Silvano, 'Finetti, Bonifazio', in *Dizionario Biografico degli Italiani* (Roma: Istituto dell'Enciclopedia Italiana Treccani, 1997), vol. 48, 40–42.

Concina, Daniele, *Della religione rivelata contro gli ateisti, deisti, materialisti, indifferentisti* (Venezia: Presso Simone Occhi, 1754).

Desing, Anselm, *Diatribe circa methodum Wolffianam, in philosophia practica universali, hoc est in principiis juris naturae statuendis adhibitam, quam non esse methodum, necesse scientificam, ostenditur* (Pedeponti, vulgo Stadt am Hof bey Regenspurg: sumtibus Joannis Gastl, Bibliopolae, 1752).

Discorrere per lettera: Carteggio Giuseppe Valeriano Vannetti–Giambattista Chiaramonti (1755–1764), ed. Liliana de Venuto (Trento: Civis, 2007).

Ferrari, Stefano, 'L'Accademia roveretana degli Agiati e la cultura di lingua tedesca (1750–1795)', in *La cultura tedesca in Italia 1750–1850*, ed. Alberto Destro and Paola Maria Filippi (Bologna: Patron, 1995), 217–276.

Finetti, Giovanni Francesco [Bonifazio], *Apologia del genere umano accusato d'essere stato una volta bestia*, 3 vols (Venezia: Vincenzo Radici, 1768).

Finetti, Giovanni Francesco [Bonifazio], *De principiis juris naturae et gentium adversus Hobbesium, Pufendorfium, Thomasium, Wolfium et alios*, 2 vols (Venetiis: apud Thomam Bettinelli, 1764).

Fiocchi Malaspina, Elisabetta, *L'eterno ritorno del* Droit des gens *di Emer de Vattel (secc. XVIII–XIX): L'impatto della cultura giuridica in prospettiva globale* (Frankfurt am Main: Max Planck Institute for European Legal History, 2017).

Gaddo, Irene and Edoardo Tortarolo, *Secolarizzazione e modernità. Un quadro storico* (Roma: Carocci, 2017).

Giornale letterario, 6 vols [ed. Carlantonio Pilati] (A Coira: Stampatore Walser e Comp., 1768).

Haakonssen, Knud, *Natural Law and Moral Philosophy: From Grotius to the Scottish Enlightenment* (Cambridge: Cambridge University Press, 1996).

Hutcheson, Francis, *Inquiry into the Original of Our Ideas of Beauty and Virtue in Two Treatises*, 2nd edition (London: J. Darby et al., 1726).

Hutcheson, Francis, *Untersuchung unsrer Begriffe von Schönheit und Tugend, in zwo Abhandlungen ... aus dem Englischen übersetzt* [trans. Johann Heinrich Merck] (Frankfurt and Leipzig: in der Fleischerischen Buchhandlung, 1762).

Infelise, Mario, *L'editoria veneziana nel '700* (Milano: FrancoAngeli, 1989).

Lamindi Pritanii [Ludovico Antonio Muratori], *De ingeniorum moderatione in religionis negotio* (Lutetiae Parisiorum: apud Carolum Robustel, 1714).

Landi, Sandro, *Il governo delle opinioni: Censura e formazione del consenso nella Toscana del Settecento* (Bologna: Il Mulino, 2000).

Lapi Coraliti [Carlantonio Pilati], *Judicium de duobus P. Joannis De Deo Staidelii Libris, quorum alter lex naturalis propugnata, alter Enchiridium theologiae inscriptus est* (Lugani: typis Agnelli, 1766).

Locke, John, *Some Thoughts concerning Education* (1693), ed. John W. Yolton and Jean S. Yolton (Oxford: Clarendon Press, 1989).

Luzzi, Serena, 'Der exportierte Antiklerikalismus: Europäische Stationen eines italienischen Reformprojekts im 18. Jahrhundert', in *Italien in Europa: Die Zirkulation der Ideen im Zeitalter der Aufklärung*, ed. Frank Jung and Thomas Kroll (Paderborn: Fink, 2014), 161–184.

Luzzi, Serena, 'Fehler und Vorzüge der deutschen Universitäten: Ansichten eines italienischen Privatdozent in Helmstedt (1761)', *Braunschweigisches Jahrbuch für Landesgeschichte* 99 (2018): 85–102.

Luzzi, Serena, 'Percorsi secolarizzati nell'Italia del Settecento, tra diritto naturale ed etica scozzese', in *Illuminismo e protestantesimo*, ed. Giulia Cantarutti and Stefano Ferrari (Milano: FrancoAngeli, 2010), 149–170

Luzzi, Serena, 'Pilati, Carlantonio', in *Dizionario Biografico degli Italiani* (Roma: Istituto dell'Enciclopedia Italiana Treccani, 2015), vol. 83, 660–663.

Maffei, Scipione, *Le lettere di Scipione Maffei ad Angelo Calogerà*, ed. Antonio Fallico, Corrado Viola and Fabio Forner (Verona: Cierre Grafica, 2016).

Montaigne, Michel de, *Essais*, editio princeps (Bordeaux: S. Millanges, 1580).

Oz-Salzberger, Fania, *Translating the Enlightenment: Scottish Civic Discourse in Eighteenth-Century Germany* (Oxford: Oxford University Press, 1995).

Pilati, Carlantonio, *Di una riforma d'Italia ossia dei mezzi di riformare i più cattivi costumi, e le più perniciose leggi d'Italia*, ed. Serena Luzzi (Roma: Edizioni di Storia e Letteratura, 2018).

Pilati, Carlantonio, *Gedanken eines Afrikaners über das Gesetz der Natur: Als ein Anhang zu dem Werke des Hernn Pilati von der Wirklichkeit des natürlichen Gesetzes, aus dem Wälschen übersetzt von W. H. W.* (Zürich und Chur: Orell, Gessner, Walser und Compagnie, 1767).

Pilati, Carlantonio, *L'esistenza della legge naturale impugnata e sostenuta* (Venezia: Antonio Zatta, 1764).

Pilati, Carlantonio, *Ragionamenti intorno alla legge naturale e civile* (Venezia: Antonio Zatta, 1766).

Polini, Carlo, *De juris divini et naturalis origine* (Brixiae: Jacobus Turlinus, 1750).

Pufendorf, Samuel, *I doveri dell'uomo e del cittadino: Tali che a lui dalla legge naturale sono prescritti, dalla versione francese di Giovanni Barbeyrac tradotti, e con molte aggiunte corretti, ed illustrati da Michele Grandi accademico di Udine* (Venice: Francesco Pitteri, vols 1 and 2 1761, vol. 3 1767).

Pufendorf, Samuel, *Il diritto della natura e delle genti o sia sistema generale de' principii li più importanti di morale, giurisprudenza e politica, rettificato, accresciuto, e illustrato da Giovambattista Almici* (Venezia: Pietro Valvasense, vols 1 and 2 1757, vol. 3 1758, vol. 4 1759).

Pufendorf, Samuel, *Le droit de la nature et des gens, ou Système général des Principes les plus importans de la morale, de la jurisprudence, et de la politique*, 2 vols (Amsterdam: Gerard Kuyper, 1706).

Quaglioni, Diego, 'Pufendorf in Italia: Appunti e notizie sulla prima diffusione della traduzione italiana del *De iure naturae et gentium*', *Il Pensiero politico* 32 (1999): 235–250.

Scattola, Merio, 'Protestantesimo e diritto naturale cattolico nel XVIII secolo', in *Illuminismo e protestantesimo*, ed. Giulia Cantarutti and Stefano Ferrari (Milano: FrancoAngeli, 2010), 131–148.

Schwarz, Ignaz, *Institutiones juris universalis, naturae et gentium, ad normam moralistarum nostri temporis, maxime protestantium Hugonis Grotii, Puffendorfii, Thomasii, Vitriarii, Heineccii aliorumque ex recentissimis adornatae et ad crisin revocatis eorum principiis, primum fusiore, tum succinctiore methodo pro Studio Academico, praesertim catholico accommodatae*, 2 vols (Augustae: sumptibus Francisci Antonii Strötter, typis Antonii Maximiliani Heiss, Typographi Catholici, 1743).

Silvestrini, Gabriella, 'Tra Burlamaqui e Beccaria: Il diritto di vita e di morte nel modello giusnaturalistico di Fortunato Bartolomeo de Felice', in *Fortunato Bartolomeo de Felice: Un intellettuale cosmopolita nell'Europa dei Lumi*, ed. Stefano Ferrari (Milano: FrancoAngeli, 2016), 53–80.

Staidelio, Joanne de Deo, *Lex naturæ propugnata* (Tridenti: ex typographia episcopali Monauniana, 1765).

Stoffella, Stefania, 'Almici, Giovambattista', in *Dizionario biografico dei giuristi italiani (XII–XX secolo)*, ed. Italo Birocchi et al. (Bologna: Il Mulino, 2013), vol. 1, 45.

Stoffella, Stefania, 'Il diritto di resistenza nel Settecento italiano. Documenti per la storia della traduzione del *De iure naturae et gentium* di Pufendorf', *Laboratoire italien: Politique et société* 2 (2001): 173–199.

Stoffella, Stefania, 'Il diritto naturale nella corrispondenza e negli scritti di Giovanni Battista Graser e di Clemente Baroni Cavalcabò', in *Aufklärung cattolica ed età delle Riforme: Giovanni Battista Graser nella cultura europea del Settecento*, ed. Serena Luzzi (Rovereto: Accademia Roveretana degli Agiati, 2004), 191–206.

Suitner, Riccarda, 'Introduzione', in Clemente Baroni Cavalcabò, *L'impotenza del demonio di trasportare a talento per l'aria da un luogo all'altro i corpi umani dimostrata da Clemente Baroni delli Marchesi Cavalcabò accademico di Rovereto, dove anche si dimostra l'impossibilità di volare con artifizio umano* (Rovereto, 1753, repr. Bologna: Forni, 2013).

Suitner, Riccarda, 'The powerlessness of the devil. Scientific knowledge and demonology in Clemente Baroni Cavalcabò (1726–96)', in *Knowledge and Profanation: Transgressing the Boundaries of Religion in Ancient and Premodern Scholarship* (Leiden: Brill, 2019), 330–356.

Tortarolo, Edoardo, 'Dimorfismo imperfetto: Secolarizzazione e cristianesimo', in *Fortunato Bartolomeo de Felice. Un intellettuale cosmopolita nell'Europa dei Lumi*, ed. Stefano Ferrari (Milano: FrancoAngeli, 2016), 35–51.

Trampus, Antonio, 'Religione e superstizione: Gianrinaldo Carli, Clemente Baroni Cavalcabò e il tramonto del dibatto su magia e stregoneria in Italia', in *Gli illuministi e i demoni. La disputa su magia e stregoneria dal Trentino all'Europa*, ed. Riccarda Suitner (Roma: Edizioni di Storia e Letteratura, 2019), 23–36.

Turchetti, Maria Francesca, 'Libri e "nuove idee". Appunti sulla biblioteca illuministica di Cesare Beccaria', *Archivio storico lombardo* 139 (2013): 183–236.

Verzeichniß einer Sammlung von juristischen, historischen und theologischen Büchern des sel. Herrn Hofrath Lichtensteins ... zu Helmstädt in dem Lichtensteinischen Hause an die Meistbietenden öffentlich verkauft werden soll (1775).

Willenberg, Jennifer, *Distribution und Übersetzung englischen Schrifttums im Deutschland des 18. Jahrhunderts* (München: Saur, 2008).

Winning, Wilhelm Heinrich, *Des Herrn Pilati bestrittene und verfochtene Wirklichkeit des natürlichen Gesetzes, aus dem Italiaenischen übersetzt, und mit einer Vorrede begleitet von Wilhelm Heinrich Winning* (Lindau: Jacob Otto, 1767).

Zendri, Christian, 'Clemente Baroni Cavalcabò e la stregoneria', in *Gli illuministi e i demoni. La disputa su magia e stregoneria dal Trentino all'Europa*, ed. Riccarda Suitner (Roma: Edizioni di Storia e Letteratura, 2019), 127–143.

CHAPTER 7

The Transformation of Eighteenth-Century *Jus gentium* into Nineteenth-Century Law of Nations: An Italian Debate

Antonio Trampus

This chapter surveys the nineteenth-century Italian debate on natural law through an analysis of the Venetian context and of the impact of the Venetian situation – after the end of the Republic (1797) – on the historical tradition of the law of nations as a political tool for legitimization of the European state system. The main argument is twofold: first, that in the Venetian Republic natural law was a tool supporting the role of the small state in the international system; second, that the disappearance of the Venetian Republic in the new post-Restoration European context transformed the use of natural law in university teaching and the very perception of natural law and the law of nations until it was reduced to an outdated source.

The use of natural public law in the late eighteenth and early nineteenth century allows us to open a window on how the law of nations influenced the generation of scholars and law practitioners as well as international politics during the years of the Napoleonic Empire and then the culture of the Restoration.[1] This was a context profoundly different from that of the initial spread and discussion of natural law in the eighteenth century. Emer de Vattel's *Droit des gens* (1758) was at the centre of this debate,[2] and Göttingen was the place where one of the scholars who most influenced the law of nations and the theory of diplomacy in the early nineteenth century was undertaking studies: Georg Friedrich von (de) Martens (1756–1821). Moreover, his father, Conrad, had been the Danish consul to Venice from 1739 until his death in 1786, and his brother Wilhelm Conrad (1748–1828) remained in Venice as Danish consul, founding the Venetian branch of the family. The study manual that de Martens

1 Throughout this chapter, 'Restoration' is used in the 'continental' sense to refer to the period from 1814 to the 1840s.

2 Elisabetta Fiocchi Malaspina, *L'eterno ritorno del* Droit des gens *di Emer de Vattel* (*secc. XVIII–XIX*). *L'impatto sulla cultura giuridica in prospettiva globale* (Frankfurt am Main: Max Planck Institute for European Legal History, 2017); *The Legacy of Vattel's* Droit des gens, ed. Koen Stapelbroek and Antonio Trampus (Cham: Palgrave Macmillan, 2019).

 | DOI:10.1163/9789004685130_009

published in 1785 (*Primae lineae iuris gentium Europaearum practici in usum auditorum adumbratae*) gave early evidence of his indebtedness to the work of Vattel and this was consolidated by further reflection on the importance of the voluntary element in the sources of international law.

This cultural heritage was collected by Georg Friedrich de Martens' nephew Charles (or Karl). When Charles de Martens started publishing *Causes célèbres du droit des gens* (1827), Vattel's work may have seemed outdated. In reality, the collection of cases recorded by Charles de Martens to prove the birth and the codification of a modern international law had strong roots in natural law and in Vattel's *Droit des gens*, considered not only as a theory but also as a practical tool for the solution of international disputes. Through some of these cases, in particular that of the diplomatic crisis between the Republic of the United Provinces and the Republic of Venice in 1771–1785, we will show some aspects of the fortune of Vattel's work in nineteenth-century Europe.

1 Natural Law and the Law of Nations in the University of the Venetian Republic

The emergence of the modern 'civilized monarchies'[3] in eighteenth-century Europe presented great challenges to the old trade Republic of Venice and to much of the old Europe in general. If the old Europe was like Christian Wolff's 'civitas maxima'[4] or Voltaire's 'great republic',[5] that is, a state in its own right, the new Europe threatened to fall apart because of commercial rivalries and needed to be reformed. Different explanations were provided for the phenomenon of 'jealousy of trade' and for the perishing of republics in the new inter-state system.[6]

The response to these challenges by the University of Padua, the only university in the Republic of Venice in which the leading classes of the Serenissima were formed, was not adequate. In particular, during the second half of

3 See David Hume, 'Of Civil Liberty', in *Political Essays*, ed. Knud Haakonssen (Cambridge: Cambridge University Press, 1994), 51–57.

4 Nicholas Greenwood Onuf, 'Civitas Maxima: Wolff, Vattel, and the Fate of Republicanism', *American Journal of International Law* 88(2) (1994): 280–303.

5 J. G. A. Pocock, *Barbarism and Religion*, vol. 2, *Narratives of Civil Government* (Cambridge: Cambridge University Press, 1999), 72–162.

6 Istvan Hont, *Jealousy of Trade: International Competition and the Nation-State in Historical Perspective* (Cambridge, MA: Harvard University Press, 2005), 1–156; Koen Stapelbroek and Antonio Trampus, 'Commercial Reform Against the Tide: Reapproaching the Eighteenth-Century Decline of the Republics of Venice and the United Provinces', *History of European Ideas* 36 (2010): 192–202.

the eighteenth century, natural law was mainly taught as private, not public law, thus completely obscuring the relevance of *jus gentium*. The University of Padua had a monopoly on the teaching of law; the only exception was a chair of civil and criminal law established in Venice in 1575 and reactivated in 1765 to educate the nobles in government responsibilities. In the 1760s, the teaching of natural law at the University of Padua was essentially a novelty. The first tuition of natural law took place in 1760, and from 1764 the abbot Giovanni Battista Bilesimo, a specialist in feudal law, was the first teacher in natural law and the law of nations.[7]

In this context, the teaching of natural law was always kept within the limits of a rigid Catholic orthodoxy and great care was taken to avoid authors suspected of ideas that could be dangerous for religion and for the government. As the historian Vettor Sandi wrote in 1769, it was necessary to defend the Republic from the 'poisonous theory spread all over Europe' and in particular from natural law and the law of nations.[8] As a consequence, the teaching of natural law did not go beyond the use of Wolff's works and in particular his *Institutiones juris naturae et gentium*.[9]

However, the city of Venice was an important centre for spreading the culture of natural law thanks to its printers and the editions and the translations of many important eighteenth-century texts. The debate on natural law had been intense since the 1730s, in particular through the comparison between Catholic and 'modern' Protestant natural law.[10] In 1757–1758, Giambattista Almici published the first complete translation of Pufendorf's masterpiece on natural law and the law of nations in Venice, and Heineccius' texts were often reprinted in Venice.[11] The use of Vattel's *Droit des gens* was carefully avoided, as this text above all was considered dangerous as source for a new theory

7 Giorgio Zordan, 'L'insegnamento del diritto naturale nell'ateneo patavino e i suoi titolari (1764–1855)', *Rivista di Storia del diritto italiano* 72 (1999): 5–76, at 9–24.

8 Vettor Sandi, *Principj di storia civile della Repubblica di Venezia. Dall'anno di N. S. 1700 sino all'anno 1767*, 3 vols (Venezia: presso Sebastiano Coletti, 1769–1772), vol. 1, 292.

9 Zordan, 'L'insegnamento del diritto naturale', 24–30; Maria Rosa Di Simone, 'L'influenza di Christian Wolff sul giusnaturalismo dell'area asburgica e italiana', in *Dal* De Jure Naturae et Gentium *di Samuel Pufendorf alla Codificazione prussiana del 1794*, ed. Marta Ferronato (Padova: Cedam, 2005), 221–267.

10 Merio Scattola, 'Protestantesimo e diritto naturale cattolico nel XVIII secolo', in *Illuminismo e protestantesimo*, ed. Giulia Cantarutti and Stefano Ferrari (Milano: FrancoAngeli, 2010), 131–148.

11 On Almici's translation, see Chapter 6 of the present volume, by Serenna Luzzi. On natural law in Italy and the Venetian printers, see Diego Panizza, 'La traduzione italiana del *De iure naturae* di Pufendorf: giusnaturalismo moderno e cultura cattolica nel Settecento italiano', *Studi Veneziani* 11 (1969): 483–528; Diego Quaglioni, 'Pufendorf in Italia. Appunti

of sovereignty and the state,[12] but in 1780 it was translated into Italian by Ludovico Antonio Loschi.[13] This situation did not change with the Restoration. The territory of the Republic of Venice came under the control of Austria and the teaching of private natural law was based on the work of Franz Zeiller, and that of public natural law on the work of Carl Anton von Martini, in a neo-absolutist framework.[14] Even Wolff's work was shelved because of his idea of the natural origin of private law, which questioned the prince's positive sanction. So Wolff was considered too anti-absolutist and enlightened.[15]

Following the Restoration, the political culture of Italy made use of Emer de Vattel's *Droit des gens* while viewing it from two different but complementary standpoints. On the one hand, there were those who read the text as it had been written by Vattel, with his typically eighteenth-century language and concepts attached to interpretative systems belonging to the culture of natural law and the Enlightenment.[16] On the other hand, the intellectuals of the Restoration were well aware also of the interpretations that had been made of Vattel's work in the age of the Atlantic revolutions, in particular the readings (in Naples, Rome, Bologna) that had transformed it into a dangerous and 'revolutionary' text, when it had been invoked to call into question the sovereignty and principles of authority that supported the *ancien régime*.[17]

---

e notizie sulla prima diffusione della traduzione italiana del *De iure naturae et gentium*', *Il Pensiero Politico* 32 (1999): 235–250; Stefania Stoffella, 'Assolutismo e diritto naturale in Italia nel Settecento', *Annali dell'Istituto Storico Italo-Germanico in Trento* 26 (2000): 137–175; ead., 'Il diritto di resistenza nel Settecento Italiano. Documenti per la storia della traduzione del *De iure naturae et gentium* di Pufendorf', *Laboratoire italien: Politique et société* 2 (2001): 173–199; Maurizio Bazzoli, 'Aspetti della ricezione di Pufendorf nel Settecento italiano', in *Dal* De Jure Nnaturae et Ggentium *di Samuel Pufendorf*, 41–60.

12 Antonio Trampus, *Emer de Vattel and the Politics of Good Government: Constitutionalism, Small States and the International System* (Cham: Palgrave Macmillan, 2020).

13 Antonio Trampus, 'Il ruolo del traduttore nel tardo Illuminismo: Lodovico Antonio Loschi e la versione italiana del *Droit des gens* di Emer de Vattel', in *Il linguaggio del tardo Illuminismo. Politica, diritto e società civile*, ed. Antonio Trampus (Roma: Edizioni di Storia e Letteratura, 2011), 81–108.

14 Zordan, 'L'insegnamento del diritto naturale', 6.

15 Giampietro Berti, *Censura e circolazione delle idee nel Veneto della Restaurazione* (Venezia: Deputazione di Storia patria per le Venezie, 1989), 386.

16 For a complete history of editions and list of translations of Vattel's *Droit des gens*, see Fiocchi Malaspina, *L'eterno ritorno del* Droit des gens, 262–272; a new edition of the 1797 English translation (the first of several had appeared in 1760) is *Law of Nations, or, Principles of the Law of Nature, Applied to the Conduct and Affairs of Nations and Sovereigns, with Three Early Essays on the Origin and Nature of Natural Law and on Luxury*, ed. Béla Kapossy and Richard Whatmore (Indianapolis, IN: Liberty Fund, 2008).

17 See Trampus, *Emer de Vattel and the Politics of Good Government*, 176–182.

At the beginning of the nineteenth century and especially after the Restoration, the profound changes in the meaning of words like 'homeland', 'nation', 'constitution' and 'representation' (keywords in Vattel's text) made it clear that it was no longer possible to read the *Droit des gens* with eighteenth-century eyes. To be sure, the parts of the work dealing with international relations between the states could still be useful in the new contexts of nineteenth-century diplomacy, but the first book, on the internal constitution of states, had to be radically reinterpreted in order to avoid arguments that might prove dangerous to supporters of liberal constitutions and democratic revolutions. The Italian culture of the Restoration thus set in motion a multifaceted operation aimed both at divesting the *Droit des gens* of its character as a philosophical and political work, and thereby of its potential political project, and at transforming it into a simple university textbook of international law.[18]

At the same time, European scholars and commentators, mostly in Germany, Italy and Portugal, initiated a radical critique of the first book of the *Droit des gens*, which in some cases actually involved revising and reworking the text. There remained some interpreters who still tried to use Vattel's work in a subversive sense, that is, to defend the freedoms and rights of nations and individuals, as happened in the political trials of mid-nineteenth-century Italy. Others used it to question the idea that the positive laws of the state could prevail over the natural law of communities and over individual safeguards. But among the majority of interpreters the idea prevailed that the *Droit des gens* was a historical document of a bygone age, a text that was no longer relevant, and a source that was simply technical, which presented basic concepts of international law but was not enough to elucidate political and international reality. This 'renaissance' of the *Droit des gens* as a manual for use in universities and in diplomacy was, however, destined to produce greater divergence between the culture of the Enlightenment and the culture of the Restoration.

A large part of the new Italian editions and studies of the *Droit des gens* in the first half of the nineteenth century were therefore devoted to commenting on and criticizing Vattel's text.[19] As a result, in the climate of the Congress of Vienna, of the Restoration and then of the liberal revolutions, it became more and more necessary to explain, clarify and define the ideas of the Swiss author. What is more, increasingly commentators realized that a serious campaign was needed to neutralize the political use of this text but, in the opinion

18 See Luigi Nuzzo, *Origini di una Scienza. Diritto internazionale e colonialismo nel XIX secolo* (Frankfurt am Main: Klostermann, 2012).

19 Fiocchi Malaspina, *L'eterno ritorno del* Droit des gens, 167 ff.

of contemporaries, there were only two ways in which this could be done effectively: by historicizing the *Droit des gens*, in other words, by delimiting its value to the historical period in which it was written; and by relegating it from the status of a politico-philosophical text to that of a practical juridical manual.

2 The Role of Venice from de Martens to Ranke: Large States versus Small States in the New Power Politics

The large number of new editions and translations of the *Droit des gens* published during the nineteenth century are, therefore, only a partial indication of the real success of Vattel's work. It was not a desire to disseminate the text that brought about that success, but, paradoxically, an ever more pressing need to circumscribe and curb it. While keeping this in mind, we must first reflect on the cultures and geographical and political areas from which most of the new editions and commentaries came. During the course of the eighteenth century, the bulk of the readings, commentaries and translations of the *Droit des gens* appeared – as we have already seen – in the small European states, which had found that Vattel's work provided them with the toolkit they needed to assert their dignity and sovereignty within the system of balances that ensued from the Treaty of Utrecht (1713). Now, however, the new editions and commentaries came mostly from the cultural circles of the great powers, that is, from the protagonists and arbiters of the new system of European balances established by the strategy of Metternich. Thus France was at the forefront of the criticism of Vattel which, without disclaiming the relevance of the work, emphasized the need to update it and explain it in a context completely different from the one in which it had been written. But even in the German Empire, which had begun to take form as the German Confederation, the approach was similar. In all these cases, the operation was carried out not by intellectuals and men of letters interested in debating the relevance of the *Droit des gens* in support of internal social reforms and the arrangement of their states, but rather by diplomats and statesmen concerned with observing the foreign policy guidelines of their countries on the international stage.

The de Martens dynasty played a key role in the transformation of the *Droit des gens* from a work of political philosophy to a practical manual, and also in the neutralization of Vattel's theories of *constitution*, *state* and *nation*. Originally, as many biographers have noted, Georg Friedrich de Martens had been formed intellectually and academically in the second half of the eighteenth century, learning from Vattel both as the author of a classic of the law of nations and as a councillor to the court of Saxony.[20] His indebtedness to Vattel can be discerned in many pages of his *Primae lineae iuris gentium Europaearum practici in usum auditorum adumbratae* (1785),[21] which later became the *Précis du droit des gens moderne de l'Europe* (first edition 1788),[22] as well as in his *Einleitung in das positive europäische Völkerrecht* (1796).[23]

It has been observed that the position of de Martens does not appear to have been against natural law but instead represented an evolution of it.[24] But his cultural orientation – of admiration for but also criticism of the natural law tradition – is evident from the moment that he entitled his work *Das positive europäische Völkerrecht* and then in French *Droit des gens* moderne *de l'Europe*. In his opinion, the law of nations was relevant as a positive and modern system, not as an expression of an older tradition. De Martens was more interested in the law of nations in force – the one actually implemented by laws and international treaties – than the philosophical system of natural law. The adjective 'modern' – which has only a vague and circumstantial connection with the German 'positive' – was clearly used as the antonym of 'ancient', thus marking a clear break with the tradition that preceded Vattel.[25]

The de Martens family is the missing link that allows us to understand how the historicization of the *Droit des gens* took its place in the new international context of the power politics inaugurated by Metternich. As well as their villa in the countryside of Mira, the family had a house in Venice, in Rio di san Cancian, from the time of Conrad's and then Wilhelm Conrad's service as Danish consuls to Venice in the final years of the Republic. These connections

20 Robert Figge, *Georg Friedrich von Martens, sein Leben und seine Werke. Ein Beitrag zur Geschichte der Völkerrechtswissenschaft* (Gleiwitz: Hill, 1914), 19.

21 Georg Friedrich von Martens, *Primae lineae iuris gentium Europaearum practici in usum auditorum adumbratae* (Göttingen: Dieterich, 1785), 7, 138, 188, 242.

22 Georg Friedrich von Martens, *Précis du droit des gens moderne de l'Europe: fondé sur les traités et l'usage. Pour servir d'introduction à un cours politique et diplomatique* (Göttingen: Dieterich, 1788), 83, 97, 140, 160, 211, 283, 333, 392, 401, 425–430. The work was then constantly reprinted until the 1820s.

23 Georg Friedrich von Martens, *Einleitung in das positive europäische Völkerrecht: auf Verträge und Herkommen gegründet* (Göttingen: Dieterich, 1796), 54, 260, 273, 300, 306, 339. On Martens' handbook in Italy, see Maria Rosa Di Simone, 'I curricula giuridici prima di Napoleone', in *Le università napoleoniche. Uno spartiacque nella storia italiana ed europea dell'istruzione superiore*, ed. Piero Del Negro and Luigi Pepe (Bologna: Clueb, 2008), 145–167.

24 Martti Koskenniemi, 'Into Positivism: Georg Friedrich von Martens (1756–1821) and Modern International Law', *Constellations* 15:2 (2008): 189–207, at 190.

25 Wilhelm G. Grewe, *The Epochs of International Law*, trans. and rev. Michael Byers (Berlin-New York: De Gruyter, 2000), 291, 358, 410.

between the de Martens and Venice, between the historical function of natural law and the history of Venice, as well as among the de Martens and Leopold von Ranke (see below), have never been studied. The grandson of Conrad and son of Wilhelm Conrad (and thus the nephew of Georg Friedrich), Karl de Martens was a significant figure who eventually took up his uncle's work and played host to Leopold von Ranke in Venice. The approach taken by Karl (or Charles, as he signed his name from the 1820s onwards) to the law of nations would, as we shall see, partly reflect his sensitivity to history and the commitment he shared with Ranke to the recovery of diplomatic sources in the Venetian archives.[26]

Charles de Martens made two key contributions to the reception of the *Droit des gens*. It was he who received and administered the legacy of Georg Friedrich through the re-editions and summaries of his writings. In addition, by virtue of his diplomatic work – he became foreign commissioner to the King of Prussia – he promoted the use of Vattel's work as a simple depository of historical-diplomatic information rather than as an international politico-philosophical project. His friendship with Leopold von Ranke was conducive to this approach. The link between the two has never been closely studied despite its importance not only for the transformation of the *Droit des gens* into a source of historical-diplomatic information, but also for how a series of cultural connections that would be used during the nineteenth century was activated. In this way Vattel became a source, for example, for the historical role of the Church of Rome in the early-modern architecture of alliances and, in the drafting of treaties, to fathom the system of Westphalia, and to evaluate the historical function performed by the Catholic Church and the pope.[27]

To understand how Ranke's work intersected with readings of Vattel, it is necessary to return to the German historian's early education. As we know, his interest in the past was not the mere curiosity of an erudite man and the years of his education in the philological school of Leipzig should be read in relation to his later studies in Berlin. History, for Ranke, was an 'ideal' story, that is, one full of cultural and spiritual tensions. The study of antiquity illuminated the modern era, just as the study of great empires of the past threw light on the history of recent great 'empires', such as the German one or the papacy.

---

26 Philipp Mueller, 'Archives and History: Towards a History of "the Use of State Archives" in the 19th Century', *History of the Human Sciences* 26 (2013): 27–49, https://journals.sagepub.com/doi/full/10.1177/0952695113502483 (accessed January 2023).

27 Henry Thomas Buckle, *History of Civilization in England* (London: Longmans Green and Co., 1873), vol. 2, 41, refers to a comparison between Vattel, *Droit des gens*, and Ranke, *Geschichte der Päpste*.

In the years after the Restoration, when Ranke applied the philological method to historical criticism, he witnessed the emergence of the Europe of nations and of new great powers, which appeared to him the manifestation of the absolute in the finite individual. He believed the study of the history of nations, and of Germany in particular, to be essential in order to understand the history of humanity, of the generations and peoples. It must be recognized that 'the particular holds within itself the universal' and thus every nation must be traced back to a time that is both absolute and finite, irrational and earthly, arbitrary and necessary.[28]

It was against this background that Ranke laid the foundations for his essay on the great powers (*Die grossen Mächte*, 1833), which contained a radical reformulation of the concept of the 'great power', and which would have a significant influence on the culture of the nineteenth and twentieth centuries. As with most statesmen of the time, Ranke held that the only great powers were those that – thanks to their economic and military strength – were able to create a sphere of influence with which the other states had to maintain a simple *droit de regard*. Ranke's distance from the work of Vattel, and from eighteenth-century culture in general, became unbridgeable from this point. For Vattel, power (*puissance*) was a quality commensurate with the exercise of political power, with its effectiveness and interest. It was much closer to the idea of the reason of state than to the actual measure of influence exerted at the interstate level.[29] For Vattel, all states, irrespective of size, operated in a framework of formal equality and could therefore play a role within the logic of exercising their power to maintain interstate balance. For Ranke, however, this vision was no longer possible, for the great powers in their historical mission were incompatible with the pluralism of Vattel's international system.[30]

This reasoning could also be used to analyse the historical events of the pre-Restoration states and in particular of the Republic of Venice. In the second half of the eighteenth century, Venice, as we saw above, had wanted to use the *Droit des gens* to establish the opposite principle. This principle was that even as a small republican state Venice – now without effective military or economic power – could have the dignity to place itself in the international forum

28 Santi Di Bella, *Leopold von Ranke. Gli anni della formazione* (Soveria Mannelli: Rubbettino, 2005), 61, 89.

29 Fiocchi Malaspina, *L'eterno ritorno del* Droit des gens, 28, 111.

30 On this point, with a specific comparison between Ranke and Vattel, see Iver B. Neumann, 'Status Is Cultural: Durkheimian Poles and Weberian Russians Seek Great-Power Status', in *Status and World Politics*, ed. T. V. Paul, Deborah Welch Larson and William C. Wohlforth (Cambridge: Cambridge University Press, 2014), 85–114, at 89.

on the same level as a great power. It was the internal organization and good government that satisfied the criteria for a constitutional state and thereby allowed formal equality between nations. Ranke had been fascinated by Venetian history since his youth, and in order to grasp the greatness and decline of the Republic he was among the first to take advantage of the opening of the Serenissima's archives, which was made possible by the Austrian government after the definitive cession of Veneto to Austria. In 1828, he first went to Vienna, where Friedrich von Gentz facilitated an audience with Prince Metternich, and then, with the necessary permissions to access the Venetian archives,[31] he arrived in Venice, where he was welcomed by the de Martens family. His study of these archives and of the history of the Republic led to a long series of publications, starting in 1831, and convinced him that Venice could have been a power in the sense intended by Vattel, but not a 'great power' in the international political sense, especially after it had ceased to be faithful to its own institutions and tried instead to imitate those of others.

3 Venetian Politics and Natural Law by Charles de Martens

As we have seen, there was a direct link between the de Martens family and Venice and between Ranke and the de Martens family. And the course of events affecting Vattel's work during the nineteenth century and its new function as a practical tool for the study of diplomatic history were linked to these actors.

From the time of the *Précis du droit moderne de l'Europe* (translated into English in 1795) Georg Friedrich de Martens had engaged in direct dialogue with the leading authors of public and natural law of the eighteenth century, from Burlamaqui to Mably and Vattel himself. Indeed, the *Droit des gens* was one of the main sources used in the *Précis* for documentary and interpretative purposes.[32] After the *Précis*, which enjoyed an uninterrupted period of success lasting several decades, de Martens had written another two volumes which contained a collection of well-known cases of modern international law selected for explanatory reasons to cover about fifty years, from the War of the Austrian Succession to 1799.[33]

31 Theodore H. von Laue, *Leopold von Ranke: The Formative Years* (Princeton, NJ: Princeton University Press, 1950), 34–38.

32 Fiocchi Malaspina, *L'eterno ritorno del* Droit des gens, 51.

33 Georg Friedrich von Martens, *Erzählungen merkwürdiger Fälle des neueren Europäischen Völkerrechts*, 2 vols (Göttingen: Schröder, 1800 and1802).

As the formulation of the project and the introduction to the collection of cases made clear, this work and the *Précis* were complementary and should be read together; the *Précis*, which still followed Vattel's approach, provided the key to the case work. In the new context of the Restoration this connection was, however, no longer useful and the separation of the case studies from their eighteenth-century and natural law interpretative matrix gained impetus when Georg Friedrich died in 1821, only a few years after having been appointed representative of the King of Hanover to the diet of the German Confederation in Frankfurt.

Charles de Martens, Georg Friedrich's nephew, was resident minister of the Grand Duchy of Weimar in Dresden. Shortly after his uncle's death, he began to rework his entire corpus, first publishing a *Manuel diplomatique* (1823) and then, shortly after, two volumes of *Causes célèbres du droit des gens* (1827).[34]

With the *Manuel diplomatique* de Martens shifted the public's attention from the eighteenth-century primacy of natural law and the law of nations, understood as foundational rights of the state and as a set of natural principles to be used in harmonizing the conduct of nations. Instead, he focused on international law conceived as a living and positive law that was composed of cases and modified through practical explanations. At the same time, he launched another project, namely that of reworking and transforming the two volumes of his uncle's *Erzählungen*. The resulting *Causes célèbres du droit des gens*, co-published by the printers Brockhaus of Leipzig and Ponthieu of Paris, was in fact an update of his uncle's work in appearance only. Although the introduction stated that the author had taken up his uncle's ideas,[35] the work was actually profoundly different in approach. The cases presented twenty years earlier were reduced in number and abridged, while the timespan under review was extended to more than a century, beginning in 1703. The selected cases were therefore no longer representative of a 'modern' law of nations, in the current sense, but of a historical conception of law and diplomacy. Moreover, the two volumes were dedicated, significantly, to the leader of a great power, Nicolas I, Emperor of Russia and King of Poland, and the great majority of the chosen cases were examples of competition and confrontation between small and large states, and old and new powers: Savoy against France, Sweden against Great Britain, Spain against Great Britain, Portugal against Spain, the United Provinces against France, and so on. The references to Vattel were

34 The editorial history is provided by Oke Manning, *Commentaries on the Law of Nations* (London: S. Sweet et al., 1839), 52–53.

35 Charles de Martens [Karl von Martens], 'Avant-propos', in idem, *Causes célèbres du droit des gens* (Leipzig: Brockhaus; Paris: Ponthieu, 1827), vol. 1, ix–xviii, at xvi.

reduced to a few irrelevant citations, which completely weakened the importance and value which had been attached to the *Droit des gens* in the previous century.

The two de Martens constituted a point of reference for other authors who explicitly associated the criticism of Vattel's incompleteness and generality with the problem of the nation, such as the philosopher and politician Silvestre Pinheiro Ferreira (1769–1846). His annotated edition of Vattel's *Droit des gens* was also destined to be successful in Venice.[36] According to Pinheiro, in order to make use of the *Droit des gens* it was no longer enough to create a commentary but, rather, a thorough revision of Vattel's text and theories was necessary. The points given most attention should be those relating to the relationship between state and nation and the wrong definition of what a state was, because, according to Pinheiro, the nation was such only when it had the strength to respect and be respected by other nations and states. Another point for discussion was state sovereignty over diplomatic agents – with a specific reference to the old practices of the Venetian Republic[37] – and the vagueness with which Vattel, in 1758, had defined the constitution as a fundamental regulation of the state.

Bibliography

Bazzoli, Maurizio, 'Aspetti della ricezione di Pufendorf nel Settecento italiano', in *Dal* De jure naturae et gentium *di Samuel Pufendorf alla Codificazione prussiana del 1794*, ed. Marta Ferronato (Padova: Cedam, 2005), 41–60.

Berti, Giampietro, *Censura e circolazione delle idee nel Veneto della Restaurazione* (Venezia: Deputazione di Storia patria per le Venezie, 1989).

Birocchi, Italo, 'Traduzioni e cultura giuridica nell'Italia dell'Ottocento', in *Justement traduire. Les enjeux de la traduction juridique* (*Histoire du droit, droit comparé*), ed.

36 Italo Birocchi, 'Traduzioni e cultura giuridica nell'Italia dell'Ottocento', in *Justement traduire. Les enjeux de la traduction juridique* (*Histoire du droit, droit comparé*), ed. Marie Bassano and Wanda Mastor (Toulouse: Presses de l'Université de Toulouse, 2020), 31–55; Niccolò Tommaseo and Gino Capponi, *Carteggio inedito dal 1833 al 1874*, ed. Isidoro Del Lungo and Paolo Prunas (Bologna: Zanichelli, 1911–1932), vol. 2, 788; Niccolò Tommaseo, *Venezia negli anni 1848 e 1849: memorie storiche inedite*, ed. Giovanni Gambarin (Firenze: Le Monnier, 1950), vol. 2, 173.

37 See the notes by Charles Vergé in Georg Friedrich von Martens, *Précis du droit des gens moderne de l'Europe augmentée des notes de Pinheiro-Ferreira*, 2nd edition (Paris: Guillaumin et al., 1864), vol. 2, especially 32, 56, 151–152.

Marie Bassano and Wanda Mastor (Toulouse: Presses de l'Université de Toulouse, 2020), 31–55.

Buckle, Henry Thomas, *History of Civilization in England* (London: Longmans Green and Co., 1873), vol. 2.

Di Bella, Santi, *Leopold von Ranke. Gli anni della formazione* (Soveria Mannelli: Rubbettino, 2005).

Di Simone, Maria Rosa, 'I curricula giuridici prima di Napoleone', in *Le università napoleoniche. Uno spartiacque nella storia italiana ed europea dell'istruzione superiore*, ed. Piero Del Negro and Luigi Pepe (Bologna: Clueb, 2008), 145–167.

Di Simone, Maria Rosa, 'L'influenza di Christian Wolff sul giusnaturalismo dell'area asburgica e italiana', in *Dal* De iure naturae et gentium *di Samuel Pufendorf alla Codificazione prussiana del 1794*, ed. Marta Ferronato (Padova: Cedam, 2005), 221–267.

Figge, Robert, *Georg Friedrich von Martens, sein Leben und seine Werke. Ein Beitrag zur Geschichte der Völkerrechtswissenschaft* (Gleiwitz: Hill, 1914).

Fiocchi Malaspina, Elisabetta, *L'eterno ritorno del* Droit des gens *di Emer de Vattel (secc. XVIII–XIX). L'impatto sulla cultura giuridica in prospettiva globale* (Frankfurt am Main: Max Planck Institute for European Legal History, 2017).

Grewe, Wilhelm G., *The Epochs of International Law*, trans. and rev. Michael Byers (Berlin: De Gruyter, 2000).

Hont, Istvan, *Jealousy of Trade: International Competition and the Nation-State in Historical Perspective* (Cambridge, MA: Harvard University Press, 2005).

Hume, David, 'Of Civil Liberty', in *Political Essays*, ed. Knud Haakonssen (Cambridge: Cambridge University Press, 1994), 51–57.

Koskenniemi, Martti, 'Into Positivism: Georg Friedrich von Martens (1756–1821) and Modern International Law', *Constellations* 15(2) (2008): 189–207.

Laue, Theodore H. von, *Leopold von Ranke: The Formative Years* (Princeton, NJ: Princeton University Press, 1950).

Manning, Oke, *Commentaries on the Law of Nations* (London: S. Sweet et al., 1839).

Martens, Karl von, 'Avant-propos', in idem, *Causes célèbres du droit des gens* (Leipzig: Brockhaus; Paris: Ponthieu, 1827), vol. 1, ix–xviii.

Martens, Georg Friedrich von, *Einleitung in das positive europäische Völkerrecht: auf Verträge und Herkommen gegründet* (Göttingen: Dieterich, 1796).

Martens, Georg Friedrich von, *Erzählungen merkwürdiger Fälle des neueren Europäischen Völkerrechts*, 2 vols (Göttingen: Schröder, 1800 and 1802).

Martens, Georg Friedrich von, *Précis du droit des gens moderne de l'Europe: fondé sur les traités et l'usage. Pour servir d'introduction à un cours politique et diplomatique* (Göttingen: Dieterich, 1801).

Martens, Georg Friedrich von, *Précis du droit des gens moderne de l'Europe augmentée des notes de Pinheiro-Ferreira*, 2nd edition (Paris: Guillaumin et al., 1864), vol. 2.

Martens, Georg Friedrich von, *Primae lineae iuris gentium Europaearum practici in usum auditorum adumbratae* (Göttingen: Dieterich, 1785).

Mueller, Philipp, 'Archives and History: Towards a History of "the Use of State Archives" in the 19th Century', *History of the Human Sciences* 26 (2013): 27–49, https://journals.sagepub.com/doi/full/10.1177/0952695113502483 (accessed January 2023).

Neumann, Iver B., 'Status Is Cultural: Durkheimian Poles and Weberian Russians Seek Great-Power Status', in *Status and World Politics*, ed. T. V. Paul, Deborah Welch Larson and William C. Wohlforth (Cambridge: Cambridge University Press, 2014), 85–114.

Nuzzo, Luigi, *Origini di una Scienza. Diritto internazionale e colonialismo nel XIX secolo* (Frankfurt am Main: Klostermann, 2012).

Onuf, Nicholas Greenwood, 'Civitas Maxima: Wolff, Vattel, and the Fate of Republicanism', *American Journal of International Law* 88(2) (1994): 280–303.

Panizza, Diego, 'La traduzione italiana del *De iure naturae* di Pufendorf. Giusnaturalismo moderno e cultura cattolica nel Settecento italiano', *Studi Veneziani* 11 (1969): 483–528.

Pocock, J. G. A., *Barbarism and Religion*, vol. 2, *Narratives of Civil Government* (Cambridge: Cambridge University Press, 1999).

Quaglioni, Diego, 'Pufendorf in Italia. Appunti e notizie sulla prima diffusione della traduzione italiana del *De iure naturae et gentium*', *Il Pensiero Politico* 32 (1999): 235–250.

Sandi, Vettor, *Principj di storia civile della Repubblica di Venezia. Dall'anno di N. S. 1700 sino all'anno 1767*, 3 vols (Venezia: presso Sebastiano Coletti, 1769–1772).

Scattola, Merio, 'Protestantesimo e diritto naturale cattolico nel XVIII secolo', in *Illuminismo e protestantesimo*, ed. Giulia Cantarutti and Stefano Ferrari (Milano: FrancoAngeli, 2010), 131–148.

Stapelbroek, Koen, and Antonio Trampus, 'Commercial Reform Against the Tide: Reapproaching the Eighteenth-Century Decline of the Republics of Venice and the United Provinces', *History of European Ideas* 36 (2010): 192–202.

Stoffella, Stefania, 'Assolutismo e diritto naturale inItalia nel Settecento', *Annali dell'Istituto Storico Italo-Germanico in Trento* 26 (2000): 137–175.

Stoffella, Stefania, 'Il diritto di resistenza nel Settecento Italiano. Documenti per la storia della traduzione del *De iure naturae et gentium* di Pufendorf', *Laboratoire italien: Politique et société* 2 (2001): 173–199.

The Legacy of Vattel's Droit des gens, ed. Koen Stapelbroek and Antonio Trampus (Cham: Palgrave Macmillan, 2019).

Tommaseo, Niccolò, *Venezia negli anni 1848 e 1849: memorie storiche inedite*, ed. Giovanni Gambarin (Firenze: Le Monnier, 1950), vol. 2.

Tommaseo, Niccolò, and Gino Capponi, *Carteggio inedito dal 1833 al 1874*, ed. Isidoro Del Lungo and Paolo Prunas (Bologna: Zanichelli, 1911–1932), vol. 2.

Trampus, Antonio, *Emer de Vattel and the Politics of Good Government: Constitutionalism, Small States and the International System* (Cham: Palgrave Macmillan, 2020).

Trampus, Antonio, 'Il ruolo del traduttore nel tardo Illuminismo: Lodovico Antonio Loschi e la versione italiana del *Droit des gens* di Emer de Vattel', in *Il linguaggio del tardo Illuminismo. Politica, diritto e società civile*, ed. Antonio Trampus (Roma: Edizioni di Storia e Letteratura, 2011), 81–108.

Vattel, Emer de, *Law of Nations, or, Principles of the Law of Nature, Applied to the Conduct and Affairs of Nations and Sovereigns, with Three Early Essays on the Origin and Nature of Natural Law and on Luxury*, ed. Béla Kapossy and Richard Whatmore (Indianapolis, IN: Liberty Fund, 2008).

Zordan, Giorgio, 'L'insegnamento del diritto naturale nell'ateneo patavino e i suoi titolari (1764–1855)', *Rivista di Storia del diritto italiano* 72 (1999): 5–76.

PART 3

From Natural Law and the Law of Nations to International Law

CHAPTER 8

The Political Science of Natural Law: The Case of Perugia

Vittor Ivo Comparato

1 The Perugian University's Reforms and Natural Law

At the universities of the Papal States, the teaching of natural law had a more recent history than at other Italian *studia*, the subject being particularly controversial. This was mainly due to the ecclesiastical authorities' mistrust of the Protestant natural law schools, whose theories circulated across Europe. Thus, the Perugian case not only reflects the long and bitter struggle that conservative Catholicism put up against Enlightenment and modern culture, but it also highlights the reformers' choices in pursuing interesting intellectual avenues and combinations closely tied up with the political developments of the period. Natural law theory in Perugia wound up representing the symbolic site of every modernizing trend, and for this reason the subject always drew from conservatives the suspicion of acting as a seedbed of more or less revolutionary and liberal sentiments.[1]

In fact, the first formal course on natural law (*Diritto naturale*) was made possible only by the proclamation of the Roman Republic in 1798. At that time the course was introduced as part of the general university reform plan envisioned by a highly respected professor at the medical school, Annibale Mariotti. For a long time, Mariotti had been an intellectual lodestar for the progressive learned class adhering to the Jacobin Republic. Mariotti had travelled and spent a formative period in Rome under the papacy of Benedict XIV, as well as in Bologna, and particularly in Parma, where he came into contact with the duchy's francizing culture.[2] It was not accidental, then, that he should

1 For a detailed bibliography, see Vittor Ivo Comparato, 'Il diritto di natura a Perugia tra la Repubblica romana e l'Unità', *Annali di storia delle università italiane* 18 (2014): 221–241. See also Chapter 2 of the present volume, by Alberto Clerici. I would like to thank Regina Lupi for her unvaluable help in finalizing the English version of this chapter.

2 Serena Innamorati, 'Profilo bio-bibliografico di Annibale Mariotti', in *Annibale Mariotti, 1738–1801: Cultura scientifica, storica e politica nell'Umbria di fine Settecento*, ed. M. Roncetti (Perugia: Deputazione di Storia Patria, 2002), 11–23.

© VITTOR IVO COMPARATO, 2024 | DOI:10.1163/9789004685130_010

have kept the essential texts of the Enlightenment philosophers in his library.[3] On the basis of Mariotti's university reform plan, the interior minister in Rome, Antonio Franceschi, approved the establishment of the natural law course at the Perugian law school, citing these grounds:

> All the moral ideas of virtue, duty, etc., that once were the object of vague ethical treatments will now be included in the Law of Nature and of Nations [*Diritto di natura e delle genti*], and with much greater profit, since these ideas will no longer be learned abstractly, but always in connection with the relations among men and among nations.[4]

What this pedagogical function of natural law recalls is not a form of Jacobin radicalism but, rather, an eighteenth-century reformist spirit, like that of Antonio Genovesi. In fact, in 1767, in requesting minister Bernardo Tanucci to authorize the establishment of the course on natural law in Naples, Genovesi pointed out both the utility of the chair in training administrative personnel and the fact that the course 'would serve to teach youths the science of duties insofar as these are founded on the law and on the law of nations [*ius delle genti*]'.[5] Genovesi's influence on Perugian culture is also attested by the quotations from his works by later professors. It is necessary to clarify 'later', because with the fall of the Roman Republic, the natural law course established in March 1799 was abolished as soon as August of the same year, and its first professor, Bernardino Mezzanotte, a man of letters, left no record of his teaching. The same thing happened with the courses on public law, constitutional law, civil law and criminal law, which in 1800 were likewise brought to a stop.[6] As for Annibale Mariotti, he was imprisoned and died in 1801.

Before moving on with this reconstruction of the tortuous succession of natural law courses from the Roman Republic to the Revolution of 1848, we should consider that the intellectual climate of the Umbrian province at the end of the eighteenth century was anything but static. The curial faction – first

3 Maria Alessandra Panzanelli Fratoni, 'La biblioteca di Annibale Mariotti', in *Annibale Mariotti, 1738–1801*, 95–116.

4 Raffaele Belforti, 'La riforma repubblicana dell'Università di Perugia nel 1799', *Rassegna storica del Risorgimento* 27 (1940): 969.

5 Antonio Genovesi, 'Lettera a Deodato Targianni', in idem, *Dialoghi ed altri scritti intorno alle lezioni di commercio*, ed. Eluggero Pii (Napoli: Istituto Italiano per gli Studi Filosofici, 2008), 418. On Genovesi and Naples, see Chapter 5 of the present volume, by Girolamo Imbruglia.

6 Letizia Giovagnoni, *I professori dell'Università degli studi di Perugia tra la Repubblica Romana e l'Unità* (PhD diss., University of Perugia, 2012), 194 ff.

serving an anti-Enlightenment and anti-Jansenist function, and then an anti-revolutionary one – had its standard bearers precisely in Umbria: the printers Ottavio Sgariglia and Giovanni Tomassini, of Assisi and Foligno, specialized in publishing anti-modern literature.[7] The attack on Protestant natural law schools, too, had been underway for some time, becoming intertwined with the polemic against the Enlightenment. In Perugia, in 1789, the publisher Carlo Baduel received a commission from an unnamed 'prelate, who is outstanding by virtue of his birth, intellect, doctrine, and study, and who sits sovereignly on one of the most august Tribunals of the world in virtue of his practice and for the glory of the true laws'.[8] Under this commission, Baduel published a critical history of natural law theory – from Grotius to Vattel and Burlamaqui – extracted from Appiano Buonafede's *Della restaurazione di ogni filosofia nei secoli XVI, XVII e XVIII* (On the restoration of every philosophy), with its well-known antimodern verve.[9] This suggests – albeit ambiguously – that natural law was a topic of debate, and the circulation of natural law texts both in their Latin editions and in their French and Italian translations is evidenced by the library holdings in Umbria.

One may speculate, too, that resistance to the introduction of natural law teaching also came from the Perugian law school. A historian of the University of Perugia, Giuseppe Ermini, has assessed that by the end of the eighteenth century the law school had gone into a deep decline under a conservative stranglehold. The Perugian law school was indeed still proud of the lineage it could trace from Bartolus de Saxoferrato and was unwilling to open itself to modern European law schools.[10] After all, the *studium* was still based on the rules set forth in the 1625 papal brief of Urban VIII. By this act, the pope had formed an alliance between the Curia and the Perugian oligarchy through the episcopal control over the *studium*; moreover, the brief stated that all lecturers were required to be citizens of Perugia with a doctoral degree awarded by the same university, thereby ensuring a local hereditary succession for all chairs.

7 Mario Tosti, 'La fucina dell'antigiansenismo italiano: I gesuiti iberici espulsi e la tipografia di Ottavio Sgariglia di Assisi', in *La presenza in Italia dei gesuiti iberici espulsi: Aspetti religiosi, politici, culturali*, ed. Ugo Baldini and Gian Paolo Brizzi (Bologna: Clueb, 2010), 355–365.

8 'Avvertimento dell'editore', in Agatopisto Cromaziano, *Della storia critica del moderno diritto di natura e di genti: Discorsi raccolti dalla Restaurazione di ogni filosofia Agatopisto Cromaziano* (Perugia: Carlo Baduel, con le dovute licenze, 1789), xiv–xv. This person is thought to be Giovanni Maria Riminaldi, of Ferrara, dean of the Roman Rota.

9 Appiano Buonafede's work was originally published in Venice in 1786–1789.

10 Giuseppe Ermini, *Storia dell'Università di Perugia*, 2 vols (Firenze: Olschki, 1971), vol. 1, 541.

Indeed, none of the attempts at reform by archbishops Marsili and De Buoi in the seventeenth and eighteenth centuries had proved successful.[11] With the first Restoration, under the imperial regency (1799–1800), a 'Plan to reopen the University of Perugia' was drawn up. This plan could have preserved at least some of the Jacobin reforms, if Cardinal Consalvi had not intervened with a negative opinion. At that point, only a regime change could liberalize the system.

And indeed, the second opportunity to introduce the teaching of natural law came with the return of the French and the new Napoleonic regime. In the period from 1809 to 1811 a university reform plan was again drawn up, this time mainly thanks to the role of the Roman Barnabite Giuseppe Colizzi. In 1799, Colizzi had been summoned to Perugia by the republican government to teach a course entitled 'Analisi dell'intendimento umano' (Analysis of human understanding), a title that leaves no doubt as to its derivation from Lockean sensualism. Colizzi was a scientist and had already gained a wide reputation for his studies in chemistry and for having been a versatile professor of philosophy, theology, mathematics and physics at several Barnabite schools.[12] Then, in 1810, the departmental government recalled Colizzi – recommending him to the Consulta straordinaria degli Stati Romani[13] as university inspector – and assigned the office of university rector to Giuseppe Antinori, another professor who had supported to the Roman Republic. Colizzi and Antinori were then entrusted not only with administrative and financial responsibilities, but also with the task of designing a new reform plan, formally completed only in 1812.[14] Meanwhile, two new courses were launched for the 1811/1812 academic year: Italian literature, assigned to Antinori, and chemistry, to Colizzi, who was also appointed for the course on natural law, now renamed 'Diritto naturale e sociale' (Natural and social law). Then, in 1812, the official course 'Natural and social law' was assigned to the jurist and humanist Pietro Antonio Magalotti, a patrician from Terni,[15] who had earned his law degree at the Sapienza Uni-

---

11 Regina Lupi, *Gli studia del papa: Nuova cultura e tentativi di riforma tra Sei e Settecento* (Firenze: Centro Editoriale Toscano, 2005), 30.

12 See Letizia Giovagnoni, 'P. Giuseppe Colizzi all'Università degli Studi di Perugia', *Barnabiti studi* 27 (2010): 7–83.

13 In Napoleonic times, the lands of the Papal States occupied by the French were initially governed by the Consulta straordinaria per gli Stati Romani; they were divided into departments and Perugia was part of the Dipartimento del Trasimeno.

14 Ermini, *Storia dell'Università di Perugia*, vol. 2, 653 ff.

15 See Andrea Giardi and Vincenzo Pirro, *Pietro Antonio Magalotti (1757–1829): Erudito, giureconsulto, docente di diritto* (Arrone: Thyrus, 2008).

versity of Rome and had been recommended for this position by the imperial vice prefect of Perugia, Giovanni Spada (himself a member of Terni's nobility). Colizzi succeeded Magalotti from 1816 to 1825, that is, until the course was once more suppressed, now under the papal bull *Quod divina sapientia* of Leo XII (1824). Not accidentally, the new pope's anti-reformist policy applied to that course, which had always been suspected of being a medium for liberal ideas. In reality, the papacy's concern was about the student unrest in the pontifical area of Emilia and Romagna, a movement that would also express itself openly in Perugia in the upheavals of 1831.

The course on the law of nature and nations would not be reintroduced until 1847. At that time the course was entrusted to Colizzi's pupil Emilio Barbanera, who would teach it until 1851. But this long hiatus should not be regarded as a total eclipse of natural law theory, since Colizzi continued to have a relevant political and intellectual role, in his capacity both as president of the Perugian Collegio Pio della Sapienza and as a scholar. After retirement, he worked for ten years on his six-volume work *Saggio analitico di giurisprudenza naturale e sociale* (Analytical essay on natural and social jurisprudence).[16]

2 Recovering the European Intellectual Debate of the Seventeenth and Eighteenth Centuries

We thus have two main figures as teachers of natural law, Magalotti and Colizzi, neither of whom was a citizen of Perugia or held a doctoral degree from its university. Both had supported to the Roman Republic, and later to the imperial government, and both were involved in the project to modernize the university. Political developments pushed them to collaborate with the regime of the period and to maintain the uneasy balance between the necessity to update the university programmes and to respect orthodoxy. But even in the activity of teaching there gave rise to the difficulty of choosing texts and reference points, which were subject to control by the local inquisitor and the Roman Congregation of Studia.

In the intellectual development of the first formally appointed professor, Magalotti, it bears underscoring that he was trained at the Roman law school,

16 Giuseppe Colizzi, *Saggio analitico di giurisprudenza naturale e sociale* (Perugia: tipografia Baduel – da Vincenzo Bartelli, con superiore permesso, 1833–1836).

and that he most likely was in touch with the circles of the Catholic *Aufklärung*.[17] His first work had been an erudite book on the history of Terni in Roman antiquity.[18] But in 1806–1807 he published his own translation of Grotius's *De veritate religionis christianae*. This Italian translation (printed in Foligno by the episcopal publisher Tomassini) was undertaken because nothing of that kind existed, apart from a series of Latin editions dating to the eighteenth century. Magalotti's choice to translate this text reveals his long practice in exploring Grotius's thought, and a specific interest in the first two books of *De veritate* (the only ones with a translator's commentary). Magalotti's presentation is for the most part a defence of Grotius against the charge of Socinianism that had been advanced by a string of critical commentators from Bossuet to Faure, Balthus, Houtteville and Valsecchi. However, as Maurizio Bazzoli has shown, in the second half of the eighteenth century, the Catholic attitude toward Grotius took a positive turn, also with an anti-Pufendorfian function.[19] Still, in Grotius's *De veritate* the apologists saw a text whose *consensus gentium* and theological rationalism could hide the germ of natural religion, and the idea that moral principles and natural law could be accessed by 'right reason', as these were imprinted into human nature directly by God. The translator's commentary seems to move in this direction when, from the very beginning, he recalls Rousseau's *Émile* to confirm the Grotian view on God as the creator of every regularity in the universe, and of natural society and civil society, both based on human reason.

A few years after translating Grotius, as we saw, Magalotti was teaching the course 'Natural and social law' at the University of Perugia. From the manuscripts held by municipal libraries of Terni and Perugia[20] we can understand how much his approach depended on Grotius. Magalotti's 'Brief prelimi-

---

17 Marina Caffiero, 'Le "Efemeridi letterarie" di Roma (1772–1798): Reti intellettuali, evoluzione professionale e apprendistato politico', in *Dall'erudizione alla politica: Giornali, giornalisti ed editori a Roma, tra XVII e XX secolo*, ed. Marina Caffiero and Giuseppe Monsagrati (Milano: FrancoAngeli, 1997), 63–101.

18 Pietro Antonio Magalotti, *Terni ossia l'antica Interamna Nahartium non già colonia, ma municipio de' Romani: Dissertazione offerta da Pietro Antonio Magalotti al pubblico di detta città* (Fuligno: Giovanni Tomassini stampator vescovile, 1795).

19 Maurizio Bazzoli, 'Grozio nel Settecento italiano', in *La recezione di Grozio a Napoli nel Settecento*, ed. Vittorio Conti (Firenze: Centro Editoriale Toscano, 2002), 43–65, at 57–59.

20 The Terni Municipal Library holds in the Fondo Magalotti both the texts of his lectures and the sources he drew on, such as the works of Jean-Jacques Burlamaqui and a draft of the lectures of Lampredi ('Minuta delle lezioni del prof. Lampredi di Pisa sul diritto delle genti e del commercio'). The Biblioteca Augusta of Perugia (hereinafter BAP) holds the manuscript of the 1812/1813 course on natural and social law (BAP, MS 1149, fols 1–308), whose incipit is 'Breve Discorso preliminare ai Principj del Diritto di Natura, e delle Genti'.

nary speech on the principles of the Law of Nature and of Nations' opens with the statement that 'Natural Law is nothing but the collection of Laws which right reason demonstrates to be consonant with human nature. These Laws are laid down by the Author of Nature himself. Hence, Natural Law could also be properly called the Code of God, the Code of the Author of Nature'. Grotius, 'that sublime genius', as Magalotti goes on to comment, was certainly the modern author who wrote about natural law more extensively and elegantly than anyone else. Natural law must be the foundation of all legislation: this law is universal and is binding not only on citizens but on all men, kings, peoples, and nations. It is perpetual and immutable, for it descends from nature and 'from its wisest Author'. Natural law doctrines 'are the worthiest for Man and the Citizen', and without them there would be no notion of what is fair and honest. This science 'holds within itself the principles of Morality, Jurisprudence, and Politics'.[21]

Grotius was thus Magalotti's main reference point, but the above presentation is based directly upon the *Principes du droit de la nature et de gens* by the Genevan jurist Jean-Jacques Burlamaqui.[22] Burlamaqui's *Principes*, which Magalotti used as a sort of textbook, was a model of synthesis that did not separate the beloved Grotian natural law from Pufendorfian utilitarianism, thus enabling Magalotti to tread the middle path, which was suitable for the time. Another quality of Burlamaqui's work consists in its being primarily a philosophy of law. And so, apart from the mandatory preamble on the divine origin of natural law, in reality, both Burlamaqui and Magalotti founded natural law on right reason. And on this subject, both of Pufendorf's works, *De jure* and *De officio*, were extensively mentioned, being available in the French translation – enriched with a long 'Préface' – by Barbeyrac, who was also quoted on several occasions (on which Almici's Italian translation of the *De jure* was also based).[23]

---

21 Magalotti, 'Breve Discorso preliminare', BAP, MS 1149, fols 1r–4v.

22 Jean-Jacques Burlamaqui, *Principii del diritto naturale di G. G. Burlamachi consigliere di Stato: Traduzione dal francese del C.B.C.* (Venice: Giovanni Gatti, 1780), pt II, ch. 14, § 16, 317. On the Italian translation, and its translator, Count Benedetto Crispi, of Ferrara, see Antonio Trampus, 'Il ruolo del traduttore nel tardo illuminismo: Lodovico Antonio Loschi e la versione italiana del *Droit des gens* di Emer de Vattel', in *Il linguaggio del tardo illuminismo. Politica, diritto e società civile*, ed. Antonio Trampus (Roma: Edizioni di Storia e Letteratura, 2011), 81–108, at 94 ff.

23 Samuel Pufendorf, *Le droit de la nature et des gens, ou systeme general des principes les plus importans de la morale, de la iurisprudence, et de la politique, traduit du Latin* [...] *par Jean Barbeyrac* (Amsterdam: Henri Schelte, 1706), vol. 1, 'Préface du traducteur'; idem, *Les devoirs de l'homme, et du citoien, tels qu'ils lui sont prescrits par la loi naturelle, traduits*

Magalotti was very familiar with Italian Catholic natural law scholars, such as Finetti, Lascaris and Lampredi, but also very clear is the influence exerted on him by Genovesi. The Neapolitan philosopher and economist held that, by nature, man is first and foremost a moral being, and principles – i.e., the original trait that distinguishes humans from animals – are the condition for the establishment of human societies. Natural law is essentially firm and immutable, just like the laws and forces that govern the earth, which 'in their essence never vary'. Even more clearly, Genovesi stated that the 'World's physical laws are the foundation of Moral laws': 'from this it follows that the law of nature is always felt by all men, in every time, every place, every state, and across all the differences that education introduces among men'.[24]

At this late stage, after a long history of different phases and political-philosophical controversies about natural law, the newly appointed professors of the Perugian *studium* resorted to those authors who favoured the traditional identity between morality, law and politics – an identity that could still secure the firmness and universality of natural law.[25] However, the rationalism informing Magalotti's course was bound to face the theological question of the primacy of revelation and Church over the rational foundation of moral principles, albeit of divine origin. This is the point where the rationalist current of Catholic natural law theory established a compromise: revelation was to be considered the confirmation of the principles inscribed *ab origine* into human nature, as was evidenced by the fact that such principles essentially coincided with Christianity. In the end, though, it cannot be ascribed to Grotius, who, in the prolegomena of his *De jure*, distinguishes natural law from evangelical ethics, the latter being morally much more exacting.[26]

The part of the course devoted to the practical and political import of natural law principles is quite limited. Prudence would make this advisable to anyone preparing to teach for two years under the Napoleonic regime and then two more under the pontifical regime. Without taking up the political problem of the best historical forms of government, Magalotti argued that good government rests on legislation containing both the moral principle –

du latin […] *par Jean Barbeyrac* (Amsterdam: Henri Schelte, 1707). See Chapter 6 of the present volume, by Serena Luzzi.

24 Antonio Genovesi, *Della diceosina o sia della filosofia del giusto e dell'onesto* (1766) (Napoli: Saverio Giordano, 1830), vol. 1, 67–68.

25 See Paolo Comanducci, *Settecento conservatore: Lampredi e il diritto naturale* (Milano: Giuffrè, 1981), 171 ff.

26 Hugo Grotius, *The Rights of War and Peace*, ed. R. Tuck (Indianapolis, IN: Liberty Fund, 2005), I, 126.

essential to law – and the utilitarian principle of the common happiness.[27] Magalotti's tendency was to bring together – without critical scrutiny – all the most convincing theses on the state of nature and the origins of society, so long as they converged towards universalism and ethical rationalism. This suggests that he belonged to the generic *scuola giusnaturalistica*, as Norberto Bobbio called the modern natural law school once it survived into the Restoration period, even if its ambition to explain the actual nature of society and the state in philosophical terms had been exhausted.[28]

Magalotti's approach was primarily philosophical, but since natural law theory was considered so generic and comprehensive, in 1814 the professor was entrusted with the course 'Diritto di commercio' (Commercial law), which he then published under the title *Principj politico-filosofico-legali del diritto di commercio* (Politico-philosophico-legal principles of commercial law, 1819).[29] By reading this work, we can understand – right from the premise – that Magalotti's main sources on civil society, besides Grotius, were Pufendorf, Barbeyrac, Montesquieu and Heineccius. But he also drew on Hobbes, Locke and Le Clerc. In treating on commerce, he essentially relied on Jean-François Melon and on the 'exceptionally clear Genovesi', referring to his *Diceosina* and *Lezioni di commercio*. But then he also used the French translation of Adam Smith's *Wealth of Nations*. Ultimately, the connection between this course and the course on natural law lies in Magalotti's attribution to manufacture and commerce of the decisive role for founding and enabling civil society to pursue its aim, that is, the *pubblica felicità*.[30]

By the 1810s, mentioning natural law and quoting from the classics of modern natural law theory seem to have passed the threshold for trust. In fact, these classics made their way into other courses held at the University of Perugia, and this practice was even considered an indispensable update. In the manuscript of Silvestro Bruschi's 'Prolegomena' to his course 'Istituzioni criminali' (First principles of criminal law), introduced in 1812, the professor dealt with the same problem that was concerning his colleagues in their teaching of natural law – that of ensuring 'unity, certainty, and perpetuity' for the moral

27 Magalotti, 'Breve Discorso preliminare', fols 81r ff.

28 Norberto Bobbio, 'Il giusnaturalismo', in *Storia delle idee politiche, economiche e sociali*, ed. L. Firpo (Torino: UTET, 1980), vol. 4, I, 491–558, see esp. 548–551.

29 Pietro Antonio Magalotti, *Principj politico-filosofico-legali del diritto di commercio compilati l'anno 1814 da Pietro Antonio Magalotti Pubblico Professore di Diritto Naturale e Sociale nell'Università di Perugia per uso della sua Scuola: Con annotazioni in fine* (Spoleto: Bassoni e Bossi, con approvazione, 1819).

30 Ibid., 12.

rule.[31] Bruschi's argument essentially followed the same line of reasoning; because the pursuit of one's own happiness has its correlative in the happiness of others, it follows that men are obliged by nature to cooperate with one another. In reality, when man introspects, he recognizes that 'a universal principle, indubitable and speaking to each man's heart, can only be found in desiring the good, toward which we are all inclined and destined by nature'. Thus, the search for the good (understood as the moral good) stands before man as an obligatory precept, that is, it stands as law.[32] Ultimately, Bruschi was interested in demonstrating the truth of the fundamental tenet, common to all the anti-voluntaristic natural lawyers, that 'only the power of reasoning (with which all men are endowed) can make clear to each person what the true norm of free actions is, by teaching us to distinguish the true good from the false'.[33] God has written all this into human nature; thus it responds to the finalism of creative omnipotence.

3 From Natural Law to Political Science: A Metaphysical Principle for a Realistic Investigation of Civil Society

The courses established under the 1810 reform, which Ermini has observed to have been wisely kept in place after the 1814 Restoration,[34] served clearly as a sort of seminar for modernization. The teaching of natural and social law – since its beginning a symbol of this new trend – retained the original function of providing the best arena for applying universal reason to civil society, as this kind of exercise remained at once philosophical and theological. Nevertheless, this teaching also offered many useful analytical tools for all sectors of the civil societies. In this regard, the abbot Colizzi was an important interpreter; he succeeded Magalotti in the chair, now renamed 'Diritto naturale ed economia pubblica' (Natural law and public economics), from 1816 to 1825. Although Colizzi has been largely neglected by historians, he pioneered a very interesting path, owing not only to the sources he used, but also to his gradual transition from metaphysics to political science. In comparison with Magalotti, Colizzi embraced a more ambitious philosophical strategy and a different gnoseology, referring to a Catholic anti-Enlightenment philosopher.

31 Silvestro Bruschi, 'Prolegomeni da anteporsi alle Istituzioni Criminali del Chiar. Prof. Dott. Silvestro Bruschi', MS at the Historical Archive of the University of Perugia, fols 1–66.

32 Ibid., 12 ff.

33 Ibid., 16–17.

34 Ermini, Storia dell'Università di Perugia, vol. 2, 660.

These conceptual tools initiated a novel natural law development in the nineteenth century. It was elaborated by a professor with remarkable knowledge not only of philosophy, but also of political science and economics.

Colizzi's courses are very well documented. Indeed, we have the manuscript of the 1824 course, compiled by a student;[35] and, even more importantly, we have the six-volume edition of his previous courses – much expanded and reworked for publication under the title *Saggio analitico di giurisprudenza naturale e sociale* (1833–1836).[36] The first part of the manuscript course – corresponding to the first volume of the published *Analytical essay on natural and social jurisprudence* – contains the core elements of Colizzi's philosophy, which we can summarize in these terms: natural law is 'eternal and invariable'.[37] Its horizon is not convenience, but the truth. 'Metaphysical truth' leads to 'moral truth'. The model of metaphysical truth is geometric and mathematical truth. Immutability, universality and mathematical certainty 'pertain to the order of essential relations among things'.[38] These relations hold for both numerical series and moral rules, and serve to define what is beautiful, honest, just and decorous.[39]

What we can observe here is a mental universe whose origin is not legal but philosophic-scientific, and with some unexpected reference points. First, Colizzi's theory of knowledge was meant to reconcile the scientists' experimental sensualism with the purity of geometric truth. In taking this approach, Colizzi referred to the *ideologisti*'s common conception that all ideas originate from sensations produced by external objects' impulses on the nerve fibres up to the brain.[40] At this final point, Colizzi argued that an active principle, an 'immaterial substance', intervenes to convert sensations into ideas and

35 Giuseppe Colizzi, 'Corso analitico di Giurisprudenza Naturale dettato dal Sig. Don Giuseppe Colizzi nell'anno scolastico 1824 Professore della medesima nella Pubblica Università di Perugia: Ad uso di me Francesco Paolotti', in BAP, MS 3218.

36 If we compare the six volumes of *Saggio analitico* against the 1824 lectures ('Corso analitico'), we find that the sequence of chapters and theses in the first three volumes correspond to the first three parts of the manuscript course. We cannot establish whether the remaining three volumes correspond to any other courses by Colizzi or whether they are the outcome of his project for a complete textbook on the law of nature and of nations.

37 Colizzi, 'Corso analitico', ch. 11, 67.

38 Ibid., 68. Colizzi provides a list of these essential relations, between: (1) a principle and its cause, (2) a cause and its effect, (3) a means and its end, (4) what is of greater perfection over what is of less, and (5) the part and the whole. Ibid., 20; cf. *Saggio analitico*, vol. 1, 113.

39 Colizzi, 'Corso analitico', ch. 10; cf. *Saggio analitico*, vol. 1, ch. 10, 273.

40 For the French *idéologues* and their important reception in Italy, see Sergio Moravia, *Il pensiero degli idéologues* (Firenze: La Nuova Italia, 1974).

notions (ideas or feelings that, as Locke said, would suppose a moral object).[41] Nevertheless, the automatic extension of scientific truth into the moral truth remained highly doubtful. On this subject, indeed, Colizzi referred not to Lockean philosophy, but to the philosophy of his Barnabite brother, the cardinal Sigismondo Gerdil, who was the author of a whole series of works that had just been republished in fifteen volumes in Rome (1806–1809). Gerdil, a Savoyard philosopher and theologian, was an anti-Enlightenment polemicist who looked to Malebranche as his philosophical reference point and had acquired from him the idea of 'Order'. For the Oratorian philosopher Malebranche, the immutable order of perfections – which the creatures of God partake of – is the inviolable rule by divine will, thus corresponding to the eternal law, but a law that is also natural and necessary, for all kind of spirits.[42] The notion of the just and unjust comes, through reason, from God. For Malebranche, the comprehension of this Order is associated with a natural inclination, as an aspect of the spontaneous tendency of man to seek happiness and perfection, which is one of the constant themes of Gerdil,[43] and also of Colizzi.

Thus, Malebranche's conception of Order came – through Gerdil – to Colizzi, who used it in the first place as the foundation of natural law's rationality and immutability; even God cannot change the law of nature, being himself the source of the Order.[44] For man, this order is 'the Norm without which he could not give to his operations any imprint of the true, just, honest. Therefore, this norm is *obligatory* for him; it's a *real Law*'.[45] It follows that the moral being – the same one who gives origin to civil society – is such insofar as he is a rational being.

An anonymous reviewer of the first volume of Colizzi's *Saggio analitico* was concerned that the author based the idea of an eternal and immutable norm on the order perceived by reason, when reason cannot elaborate anything that did not previously exist in the senses (*quod prius non fuerit in sensu*).[46] This could make the reader run the risk of identifying the supreme Being with nature itself as absolute intelligence, thereby paving the way for ideal-

41 Colizzi, *Saggio analitico*, vol. 1, 36, 43, 45–46.

42 Nicolas Malebranche, *Trattato dell'amore di Dio: Lettere e risposta al R. P. Lamy*, ed. A. Stile (Napoli: Guida, 1999), 57–59.

43 Sigismondo Gerdil, *Philosophiae moralis institutiones*, Disputatio III, ch. 1, 'Juris naturalis definitio', in idem, *Opere edite ed inedite* (Roma: Vincenzo Poggioli, 1806), vol. 6, 212.

44 Colizzi, *Saggio analitico*, vol. 1, appendix to ch. 13, 369–377.

45 Ibid., 372–373.

46 Review signed by C., in the section titled 'Rivista critica italiana' of the *Ricoglitore italiano e straniero* 4 (1837, February): 275–280.

ism or pantheism.[47] Indeed, similar doubts had already occurred to suspicious Roman censors,[48] and the inquisitor in Perugia informed Colizzi of other passages that were 'disliked' or considered 'dangerous' in Rome.[49] In the end, the ecclesiastical authorities did not forget either the 'Jacobin' past or the Lockean and *idéologique* inclinations of Colizzi.

In the following five books, the transition from the logico-metaphysical enquiry to applied natural jurisprudence unfolds in four parts, taking the following as their subjects: human actions in general; man in natural society; man in civil society; and states, with their relations.[50] The second volume thus enters into a meticulous analysis of the moral quality, and quantity, of just and unjust actions, also examining the factors – such as climate – by which actions are conditioned,[51] as well as the imputability of actions in the sphere of positive law, that is, criminal law.[52] In this first declension of natural law, the author constantly deals with the theses of Hobbes, and especially of Pufendorf, both his *De jure* and his *De officio*. Indeed, these were the authors on which both the dichotomous philosophical model of the origin of civil society and the utilitarian element of societies' real foundation were based.[53] In his judgement on the main natural lawyers Colizzi does not consider Grotius, endorses Cumberland's and Pufendorf's systems (albeit with reservations), and criticizes Hobbes's and Christian Thomasius's arguments.[54]

The entire third volume deals with the question of man in the state of nature, starting with the analysis of the 'original rights of man'. These are essentially two: the right to personhood and the right to liberty. Both are dictated by the law of nature, but they are also necessarily regulated by the same law; thus – as Colizzi observed referring to Montesquieu – man cannot want

47 The Congregation of Studia had developed patterns for theological dissertations against atheists, pantheists and sceptics. On this, see Sandra Scaletti, *Scuole e università a Perugia tra insurrezione e restaurazione, 1831–1835* (Perugia: Galeno, 1984), 153–56.

48 Stanislao da Campagnola, 'La censura "romana" di un "Saggio" di Giuseppe Colizzi', *Bollettino della Deputazione di Storia Patria per l'Umbria* 78 (1981): 285–296; Scaletti, *Scuole e università*, 159–162.

49 See the letter of censorship by the Congregation, 23 November 1833, reproduced in Scaletti, *Scuole e università*, 242–243. As a prudential measure, control over the rest of Colizzi's work was entrusted directly to the imprimatur of the Master of the Sacred Palace, the Dominican friar Domenico Buttaoni (ibid., 246).

50 Colizzi, *Saggio analitico*, vol. 1, 5.

51 Ibid., vol. 2, 68–69. His source here was Jean-Charles de Lavie's *Abregé de la République de Jean Bodin* (Paris: Cailleau, 1793).

52 Colizzi, *Saggio analitico*, vol. 2, ch. 3 ff.

53 Bobbio, 'Il giusnaturalismo', 508–512.

54 Colizzi, *Saggio analitico*, vol. 2, ch. 14, 278–432.

what he wants, but only what he has to (want).[55] We are not yet in the political sphere, but in the pre-political one that has to be considered not as a 'stage' (a real transition which humanity actually passes through), but as an analytical step that Colizzi undertakes to verify the binding processes of natural law. Thus, for example, he locates equality as a 'natural' dimension of being human, and even if in the 'social' dimension – in society – there is inequality (power relations), equality will be effective there as a moral principle that induces man to recognize humanity in all persons, regardless of their condition.

This type of argument shows that the absolute rigour of the law of nature must then be consistent with actual reality, and that means that natural law is confined to the sphere of 'the ought'. Thus, in the state of nature – in addition to the original and derivative rights here located by Colizzi's analysis – we can already find not an idealized happiness[56] but, rather, humanity's real nature in action, with human freedom to choose between good and evil, man's natural tendency to live in society and form families, and with the duties that accompany rights.

Duties form the subject of the entire second chapter of the third volume,[57] a moral treatise culminating in the universal rules 'Do not do to others what you would not have them do to you' and 'Do to others what you would have them do to you'.[58] This is the law of humanity and benevolence,[59] which is not only a voluntary act, but a preliminary duty – derived from the 'essential relations' – that requires each member of the human species to place the good of his species ahead of his own particular interest.[60] Therefore, it is not surprising to find in Colizzi's philosophy quotations from Seneca, Aristotle, Cicero, Hobbes, Pufendorf and Kant (even if only to criticize some of their judgements), but no mention of revelation, for the author conceives the law of nature as being inscribed in the Order. According to Colizzi, it is within this theoretical framework that moral parameters must be located, in order to let them be the basis of positive law. Indeed, Colizzi also deals with the *principles* of criminal law, family law and legal obligations, in this pre-political sphere. It is here, in this hypostasis of natural society, that the author compares the Order of essential relations with the variables regarding human nature itself, and the circumstances that can divert or affect human nature. Natural law is

55 Ibid., vol. 3, chs 7–8.
56 Ibid., 127ff., criticizing Rousseau's *Discours sur les origines de l'inégalité parmi les hommes*.
57 Ibid., 59–119.
58 Ibid., 113.
59 Ibid., 94 ff.
60 Ibid., 112.

the Order, and cannot vary; by contrast, circumstances do vary, depending on individuals and on the influences they experience in civil society.

Colizzi always relies on the essential Order as his instrument of analysis, but civil society is not a philosophic-legal fiction. It is an actual organization with legal constants, and historical and political variables. Volume 4, devoted to humanity in the condition of civil society, thus marks a clear passage to political science, and consequently to other sources and texts. Colizzi advises – from the very first footnote in volume 4 – that he is reading Benjamin Constant's 1822 commentary on Filangieri's work on the science of legislation.[61] And in fact, the normative chain that started from the essential Order had its conclusion in the civil legislation of individual states. Civil societies are formed by conferring sovereignty on one person, a few individuals, or the entire social body, in order to guarantee their own 'security and prosperity'. The exercise of sovereignty unfolds in four parts, namely, the legislative, judicial, 'conservative' and executive powers, headed by separate officers, or moral bodies. The historical forms of civil society are listed in this sequence: 'pure' primigenial monarchy; absolute monarchy; temperate, hereditary or elective monarchy; national monarchy; aristo-popular monarchy; democracy; and federal government. In each form of government, all of the four functions mentioned above are present, and placed in relation to natural law, by both general and specific connections with empirical realities.

At this point, accompanying, if not prevailing over, the natural lawyer, the political scientist is fully aware that in contemporary civil life only 'mixed' forms of government exist. The subjects that compose them also provide 'conventions or pacts to fix the functions of power and the limits on its exercise'. This set of regulations or 'organic laws', laid down 'by common agreement', is called the 'Constitution of the State'.[62]

Generally, we can say that for Colizzi governments operate according to natural law principles when the institutions in each of their main functions act consistently with the principles of the essential Order, the same order that presided over the formation of civil society for guaranteeing the primary aims of security and prosperity. The law of nature thus becomes an obligatory horizon for the institutional bodies, that is, the four parts of sovereign power. It is evident that when Colizzi turns from ethics and philosophy of law to applied

61 Benjamin Constant, *Commentaire sur l'ouvrage de Filangieri par Benjamin Constant*, 4 vols (Paris: P. Dufart, P. Didot l'ainé, 1822–1824); Gaetano Filangieri, *Scienza della legislazione*, 8 vols (Napoli, 1780–1788).

62 Colizzi, *Saggio analitico*, vol. 4, c. 1, 'Origine delle società civili', 3–26.

government policies, he keeps sliding deeper and deeper into political realism, even if he continues to use the Order as the standard. In concrete terms, in addressing legislative power, and listing its functions – which override those of any other power – Colizzi lays out all the subjects of competence entrusted to the legislator, from public order and national defence to the economy. In relation to the aim of public interest, the resulting rights also carry duties. And, consistently with this reasoning, Colizzi mainly deals with public economy, which occupies about 270 pages of volume 4.

As usual, he does not name his sources, but merely says that they are 'modern publicists'. There are, however, two footnotes that indicate important reference points for the part on government: two classics of Enlightenment political science in Germany and Austria, namely, Jakob Friedrich von Bielfeld's *Institutions politiques*[63] and Joseph von Sonnenfels's *La scienza del buon governo*.[64] Colizzi could not have missed Bielfeld's statement that 'while natural law tells us what is right, politics teaches us what is useful'.[65] Colizzi's conception of natural law implied that everything which is consistent with the aim of ensuring the security and prosperity of society is useful and thus, in principle, also just. This enabled him to move into the political sphere with his own ideas about the science of government. Among these ideas, the ones that show his marked modernizing tendency (the source of the censors' concerns) are, first, those on economics. Indeed, these ideas disclose that Colizzi relied not only on the late mercantilists, such as Bielfeld and Sonnenfels, but also on the classical economists, such as Adam Smith, Jean-Baptiste Say and James Mill. In politics, Colizzi was a utilitarian and liberal, favourable to the emerging industrial economy. From his recurrent evocation of the 'Order of essential relations', it is clear that this order was nothing more and nothing less than the rational pursuit of public and private good through good government based on competence. Other decidedly reformist attitudes concerned, for example, censorship, which he generally approved but not for texts dealing with science, letters and the arts. Private worship of confessions other than Catholicism was also accepted. Moreover, Colizzi advocated a radical reform of education, proposing public schools, for boys and girls, and he was against Latin and in favour of courses useful to society at large.[66]

---

63 Jakob Friedrich von Bielfeld, *Institutions politiques par Monsieur le Baron de Bielfeld* (Leiden: J. F. Bassompierre, 1768–1774) (1st editon The Hague, 1760).

64 Joseph von Sonnenfels, *La scienza del buon governo* (Venezia: Giovanni Vitto, con pubblica approvazione, 1785; revised edition Milano: Giovanni Silvestri, 1832). Originally *Grundsätze der Polizei, Handlung und Finanzwissenschaft* (Vienna, 1765–1767).

65 Bielfeld, *Institutions*, vol. 1, ch. 6, § 7, 141.

66 Colizzi, *Saggio analitico*, vol. 4, ch. 5, § 1, 209–222.

The volume ends – or rather is completed in terms of political science – with an examination of state 'constitutions', selected as models of the main forms of government. Colizzi starts out by making three disclaimers: he does not wish to discuss the quality of individual forms of government; he restricts his sources to a few authors, such as Hobbes, Constant's commentary on Filangieri, and Destutt de Tracy's commentary on Montesquieu, while the others are collectively mentioned simply as 'modern publicists'. Regarding each form of government, Colizzi chooses to describe the legal system of some contemporary states: for explaining absolute monarchy he selects Denmark; for national monarchy, Sweden; for aristo-popular monarchy, the United Kingdom and France; for representative democracy, the constitution of Pennsylvania;[67] and for the federal state, the systems of the United States and the German Confederation.[68]

Volume 5 turns to the other perspective of post-revolutionary political science: the rights of man and of the citizen. Are they inalienable? Certainly they are, because according to natural law they are a property of each person as a human being; but in society, they can only partly be enjoyed: by choosing to enter into the civil condition, man agrees to limit his liberty (submitting himself to laws) and his equality (submitting himself to government and accepting social ranks, inevitably connected with the different functions of the social Order), even though man never renounces natural equality, which is therefore protected by law. It is clear that here Colizzi moved far away from political Jacobinism.

The last volume is devoted to the law of nations, distinguishing an 'internal' law of nations (i.e., public law) from an 'external' law of nations (i.e., international relations). In the internal law of nations, we find indications concerning the reciprocal rights and duties of sovereign and subjects, which had been addressed by an almost endless political literature. Nevertheless, in the internal law of nations, the reference to natural law still retained its acknowledged function of judging the state's practical choices (especially territorial) to be licit or illicit. With regard to the external law of nations, the intention of applying the Order theory to relations among states, considering them as individuals in the state of nature, would have been useless because purely formal.[69] However, Colizzi did not intend to forsake the continuity between

67 He is thus choosing the most radically democratic constitution in the landscape of the period, containing a bill of rights that, not incidentally, Mario Pagano had taken as his model in drafting a constitution for the Parthenopean (Neapolitan) Republic of 1799.

68 Colizzi, *Saggio analitico*, vol. 4, chap. 8, 513–626.

69 Ibid., vol. 6, pt II, pp. 116 ff.

morality, natural law and the law of nations. Thus, for example, in Martens's introduction to his *Précis du Droit des gens moderne de l'Europe* (one of the main sources for Colizzi), he finds the claim that each state as a moral person – and also each of its members as a man – retains a 'natural' relation to foreigners, other communities, or peoples; therefore, natural law can apply to any kind of international relations, except to those stated in individual states' agreements.[70] That a common legal sphere was in point of fact born as a shared form of civilization did not, however, mean that Europe was to be thought of as a single civil society, bound by a positive and universal *ius gentium*.[71] In the law of nations, universal principles of humanity apply alongside *de facto* conventions, customs, treaties and international practices, which have to be considered through states' actual behaviours. The specialized literature and the publication of treaties (and collections of them) had been profuse in the late eighteenth century,[72] but to access them *in extenso* was not possible for an author confined in remote Perugia. Still, the volume does contain many references to recent specialized works by Bielfeld, Martens, Lampredi, Klüber, Schmalz and Vattel.[73] Colizzi chose the best authors available in Italian or French and drew inspiration from them in treating specific problems on which he thought they had valuable insights to offer (neutrality, commerce, navigation, rankings and embassies), even if he followed his own educational scheme.

70 Georg Friedrich von Martens, *Précis du Droit des gens moderne de l'Europe: fondé sur les traités et l'usage* (A Gottingue: dans la librairie de Dieterich, 1801), vol. 1, 'Introduction', § 4, 5.

71 Ibid., § 7–8, 10–14.

72 An inventory can be found, for example, in Martens's *Manuel diplomatique*, published in Paris in 1822. For histories and bibliographies of the European law of nations as they looked at the time, see Johann Ludwig Klüber, *Droit de gens moderne de l'Europe* (Stuttgart: J. G. Cotta, 1819), ch. 2; and Theodor Anton Schmalz, *Le droit de gens européen*, trans. L. de Bohm (Paris: N. Maze, 1823), 298–303. See in the present volume Chapter 7, by Antonio Trampus.

73 Bielfeld, *Institutions politiques*; Giovanni Maria Lampredi, *Del commercio dei popoli neutrali in tempo di guerra* (Florence, n.p., con approvazione dei superiori, 1788); Klüber, *Droit de gens moderne de l'Europe*; Schmalz, *Le droit de gens européen*; Emer de Vattel, *Le droit des gens, ou Principes de la loi naturelle appliqués à la conduite et aux affaires des nations et des souverains* (London [Neuchâtel]: Société typographique, 1758). On Vattel and the European states' new scenario after the mid-eighteenth century, see Giovanni Tarello, *Storia della cultura giuridica moderna* (Bologna: il Mulino, 1976), 151–153; and Elisabetta Fiocchi Malaspina, *L'eterno ritorno del Droit des gens di Emer de Vattel* (*secc.* XVII–XIX) (Frankfurt: Max Planck Institute for European Legal History, 2017), chs 3 and 4, 228–234.

The journey that started out from an abstract philosophy of natural law and which was not always well received by censors and critics thus reached its end station in the practical problems of a world that was rapidly changing, and full of revolutionary ferment. The work's fortune was certainly compromised by its size, which made it unsuitable as a textbook (even though a 144-page extract was published in 1836).[74] Colizzi's work can still be found in the main Umbrian libraries and in many Italian law libraries, but it does not seem to have had a noteworthy international echo. While Giulio Bartolini did recently include Colizzi among those who had had an international influence, in connection with the relationship between the local/national contexts and international legal rules and doctrines, that was largely because his work was done in a place and at a time that saw important political events.[75]

4 Conclusion: From the 1848 Revolution to Italian Unification

As a highly esteemed professor in Perugia,[76] Colizzi had students who would approach the Risorgimento uprising with serious commitment. One of his students, Emilio Barbanera, was appointed to the chair in the law of nature and of nations in 1847, when the course was reopened during the political phase that led to the new Roman Republic. Although we do not have his writings, we must suppose him to have been much more involved in political life than in teaching. Barbanera had been among the organizers in Perugia behind the Neo-Guelphist movement to unify Italy as a monarchy under the pope,[77] but later, as a committed exponent of the Perugian popular circle, he clearly supported the ending of the clerical government and was incriminated for an article published in the *Osservatore del Trasimeno*.[78] Obviously, with the third Restoration, he could no longer hold the chair. This time, the Roman Congregation decided not to abolish the course, but to assign it to trusted

74 Ferdinando Speroni, *Estratto ragionato del saggio analitico di giurisprudenza naturale e sociale del prof. d. Giuseppe Colizzi* (Perugia: Baduel, 1836).

75 Giulio Bartolini, 'What Is a History of International Law in Italy For? International Law Through the Prism of National Perspectives', in *A History of International Law in Italy*, ed. Giulio Bartolini (Oxford: Oxford University Press, 2020), 3 ff.

76 Francesco Bartoli, 'Biografia dell'Abate prof. D. Giuseppe Colizzi', *Giornale scientifico-letterario di Perugia* 86 (1846): 171–187.

77 Ferdinando Treggiari, 'Avvocati umbri', in *Avvocati che fecero l'Italia*, ed. Stefano Borsacchi and Gian Savino Pene Vidari (Bologna: il Mulino, 2011), 542–544.

78 Idem, 'Emilio Barbanera (1799–1876)', in *Avvocati che fecero l'Italia*,, 544–551, at 545.

people: thus, for the 1853 course the position was given to the Servite friar Bonfiglio Mura.[79] He held the chair until Unification (1861), with the task of restoring anti-modern natural law, and so to demolish the heritage of his predecessors, despite their moderation. In his inaugural lecture in 1853,[80] Mura singled out Martin Luther, Rousseau, Pufendorf, Thomasius and Burlamaqui as the thinkers responsible for separating natural law from theology, and for leaving humanity prey to utilitarianism and unrestrained freedom. He then listed Helvétius, d'Holbach, Bentham, Genovesi, Melchiorre Gioia and Gian Domenico Romagnosi as basically followers of Epicurus's 'abject morality'.[81] There is an explicit reference to Colizzi's theses, most significantly the thesis that excluded revelation as the direct source of natural law and placed it in the 'order', that is, in the universal reason instilled by God in man. To Mura, this seemed to be the typical error of unbelievers, of many Protestants and of those 'modernizing Catholics who consider it necessary entirely to exclude Revelation when treating of reason'.[82] So, in addition to Protestants and the 'friends of constitutions', the 'modernizing Catholics' also seemed to the theologian of intransigence, Bonfiglio Mura, a great danger to the education of young people.

The cycle of Perugian natural law theory can thus be considered to have been concluded by mid-century, having played a very significant role in the troubled and confused time that passed between two revolutions, a time that had essentially both affected and tested the intrinsic political nature of natural law.

Archival Sources

Biblioteca Augusta of Perugia (BAP), Perugia, Italy, MS 1149, MS 3218.
Historical Archive of the University of Perugia, Perugia, Italy.
Municipal Library, Terni, Italy, Fondo Magalotti.

79 See Carla Frova, 'Bonfiglio Mura (1810–1882) docente e rettore nell'Università di Perugia', in *Scritti sullo* Studium perusinum, ed. Erika Bellini and Maria Alessandra Panzanelli Fratoni (Perugia: Deputazione di storia patria per l'Umbria, 2011), 201–220.

80 The lecture was published as Bonfiglio Mura, *Sull'importanza del diritto di natura e delle genti* (Perugia: tipografia Bartelli, 1854).

81 Ibid., 20.

82 Ibid., 27.

Bibliography

Bartoli, Francesco, 'Biografia dell'Abate prof. D. Giuseppe Colizzi', *Giornale scientifico-letterario di Perugia* 86 (1846): 171–187.

Bartolini, Giulio, 'What Is a History of International Law in Italy For? International Law Through the Prism of National Perspectives', in *A History of International Law in Italy*, ed. G. Bartolini (Oxford: Oxford University Press, 2020), 3–15.

Bazzoli, Maurizio, 'Grozio nel Settecento italiano', in *La recezione di Grozio a Napoli nel Settecento*, ed. Vittorio Conti (Firenze: Centro Editoriale Toscano, 2002), 43–65.

Belforti, Raffaele, 'La riforma repubblicana dell'Università di Perugia nel 1799', *Rassegna storica del Risorgimento* 27 (1940): 959–976.

Bielfeld, Jakob Friedrich von, *Institutions politiques par Monsieur le Baron de Bielfeld* (Leiden: J. F. Bassompierre, 1768–1774) (1st edition The Hague, 1760).

Bobbio, Norberto, 'Il giusnaturalismo', in *Storia delle idee politiche, economiche e sociali*, ed. L. Firpo (Torino: UTET, 1980), vol. 4, I, 491–558.

Burlamaqui, Jean-Jacques, *Principii del diritto naturale di G. G. Burlamachi consigliere di Stato. Traduzione dal francese del C.B.C.* (Venezia: Giovanni Gatti, 1780).

'C.', in 'Rivista critica italiana', *Ricoglitore italiano e straniero* 4 (1837, February): 275–280.

Caffiero, Marina, 'Le "Efemeridi letterarie" di Roma (1772–1798): Reti intellettuali, evoluzione professionale e apprendistato politico', in *Dall'erudizione alla politica: Giornali, giornalisti ed editori a Roma, tra XVII e XX secolo*, ed. Marina Caffiero and Giuseppe Monsagrati (Milano: FrancoAngeli, 1997), 63–101.

Colizzi, Giuseppe, *Saggio analitico di giurisprudenza naturale e sociale* (Perugia: tipografia Baduel – da Vincenzo Bartelli, con superiore permesso, 1833–1836).

Comanducci, Paolo, *Settecento conservatore: Lampredi e il diritto naturale* (Milano: Giuffrè, 1981).

Comparato, Vittor Ivo, 'Il diritto di natura a Perugia tra la Repubblica romana e l'Unità', *Annali di storia delle università italiane* 18 (2014): 221–241.

Comparato, Vittor Ivo, 'La prima traduzione italiana del *De veritate* di Grozio', *Bollettino della Deputazione di Storia Patria per l'Umbria* 113 (2016): 229–264.

Constant, Benjamin, *Commentaire sur l'ouvrage de Filangieri par Benjamin Constant* (Paris: P. Dufart, P. Didot l'ainé, 1822–1824).

Cromaziano, Agatopisto, *Della storia critica del moderno diritto di natura e di genti: Discorsi raccolti dalla Restaurazione di ogni filosofia di* (Perugia: Carlo Baduel, con le dovute licenze, 1789).

da Campagnola, Stanislao, 'La censura "romana" di un "Saggio" di Giuseppe Colizzi', *Bollettino della Deputazione di Storia Patria per l'Umbria* 78 (1981): 285–296.

de Lavie, Jean-Charles, *Abregé de la République de Jean Bodin* (Paris: Cailleau, 1793).

Ermini, Giuseppe, *Storia dell'Università di Perugia*, 2 vols (Firenze: Olschki, 1971).

Filangieri, Gaetano, *Scienza della legislazione*, 8 vols (Napoli, 1780–1788).

Fiocchi Malaspina, Elisabetta, *L'eterno ritorno del Droit des gens di Emer de Vattel (secc. XVII–XIX)* (Frankfurt: Max Planck Institute for European Legal History, 2017).

Frova, Carla, 'Bonfiglio Mura (1810–1882) docente e rettore nell'Università di Perugia', in *Scritti sullo* Studium perusinum, ed. Erika Bellini and Maria Alessandra Panzanelli Fratoni (Perugia: Deputazione di storia patria per l'Umbria, 2011), 201–219.

Genovesi, Antonio, *Della diceosina o sia della filosofia del giusto e dell'onesto* (1766) (Napoli: Giordano, 1830).

Genovesi, Antonio, 'Lettera a Deodato Targianni', in idem, *Dialoghi ed altri scritti intorno alle lezioni di commercio*, ed. Eluggero Pii (Napoli: Istituto Italiano per gli Studi Filosofici, 2008), 418.

Gerdil, Sigismondo, *Philosophiae moralis institutiones*, Disputatio III, ch. 1, 'Juris naturalis definitio', in idem, *Opere edite ed inedite* (Roma: Vincenzo Poggioli, 1806).

Giardi, Andrea, and Vincenzo Pirro, *Pietro Antonio Magalotti (1757–1829): Erudito, giureconsulto, docente di diritto* (Arrone: Thyrus, 2008).

Giovagnoni, Letizia, *I professori dell'Università degli studi di Perugia tra la Repubblica Romana e l'Unità* (PhD diss., University of Perugia, 2012).

Giovagnoni, Letizia, 'P. Giuseppe Colizzi all'Università degli Studi di Perugia', *Barnabiti studi* 27 (2010): 7–83.

Grotius, Hugo, *The Rights of War and Peace*, ed. R. Tuck (Indianapolis, IN: Liberty Fund, 2005).

Innamorati, Serena, 'Profilo bio-bibliografico di Annibale Mariotti', in *Annibale Mariotti, 1738–1801: Cultura scientifica, storica e politica nell'Umbria di fine Settecento*, ed. M. Roncetti (Perugia: Deputazione di Storia Patria, 2002), 11–23.

Klüber, Johann Ludwig, *Droit de gens moderne de l'Europe* (Stuttgart: J. G. Cotta, 1819).

La recezione di Grozio a Napoli nel Settecento, ed. Vittorio Conti (Firenze: Centro Editoriale Toscano, 2002).

Lampredi, Giovanni Maria, *Del commercio dei popoli neutrali in tempo di guerra* (Firenze: n.p., con approvazione dei superiori, 1788).

Lampredi, Giovanni Maria, *Joannis M.ae Lampredi Florentini in Pisana Academia antecessoris Juris publici universalis sive juris naturae et gentium theoremata quae ab eo in eadem Academia exponuntur & declarantur*, 3rd edition (Florentiae: typis Regiae Celsitudinis, 1792).

Lupi, Regina, *Gli studia del papa: Nuova cultura e tentativi di riforma tra Sei e Settecento* (Firenze: Centro Editoriale Toscano, 2005).

Magalotti, Pietro Antonio, *Principj politico-filosofico-legali del diritto di commercio compilati l'anno 1814 da Pietro Antonio Magalotti Pubblico Professore di Diritto Naturale e Sociale nell'Università di Perugia per uso della sua Scuola: Con annotazioni in fine* (Spoleto: Bassoni e Bossi, con approvazione, 1819).

Magalotti, Pietro Antonio, *Terni ossia l'antica Interamna Nahartium non già colonia, ma municipio de' Romani: Dissertazione offerta da Pietro Antonio Magalotti al pubblico di detta città* (Fuligno: Giovanni Tomassini stampator vescovile, 1795).

Malebranche, Nicolas, *Trattato sull'amore di Dio: Lettere e risposta al R. P. Lamy*, ed. A. Stile (Napoli: Guida, 1999).

Martens, Georg Friedrich von, *Précis du Droit des gens moderne de l'Europe: fondé sur les traités et l'usage* (A Gottingue: dans la librairie de Dieterich, 1801).

Moravia, Sergio, *Il pensiero degli idéologues* (Firenze: La Nuova Italia, 1974).

Mura, Bonfiglio, *Sull'importanza del diritto di natura e delle genti* (Perugia: tipografia Bartelli, 1854).

Panzanelli Fratoni, Maria Alessandra, 'La biblioteca di Annibale Mariotti', in *Annibale Mariotti, 1738–1801: Cultura scientifica, storica e politica nell'Umbria di fine Settecento*, ed. M. Roncetti (Perugia: Deputazione di Storia Patria, 2002), 95–116.

Samuel Pufendorf, *Le droit de la nature et des gens, ou systeme general des principes les plus importans de la morale, de la iurisprudence, et de la politique, traduit du Latin* [...] *par Jean Barbeyrac* (Amsterdam: Henri Schelte, 1706).

Samuel Pufendorf, *Les devoirs de l'homme, et du citoien, tels qu'ils lui sont prescrits par la loi naturelle, traduits du latin* [...] *par Jean Barbeyrac* (Amsterdam: Henri Schelte, 1707).

Scaletti, Sandra, *Scuole e università a Perugia tra insurrezione e restaurazione, 1831–1835* (Perugia: Galeno, 1984).

Schmalz, Teodor Anton, *Le droit de gens européen*, trans. L. de Bohm (Paris: Maze, 1823).

Sonnenfels, Joseph von, *La scienza del buon governo* (Venezia: Giovanni Vitto, con pubblica approvazione, 1785; revised edition, Milano: Giovanni Silvestri, 1832).

Speroni, Ferdinando, *Estratto ragionato del saggio analitico di giurisprudenza naturale e sociale del prof. d. Giuseppe Colizzi* (Perugia: Baduel, 1836).

Tarello, Giovanni, *Storia della cultura giuridica moderna* (Bologna: il Mulino, 1976).

Tosti, Mario, 'La fucina dell'antigiansenismo italiano: I gesuiti iberici espulsi e la tipografia di Ottavio Sgariglia di Assisi', in *La presenza in Italia dei gesuiti iberici espulsi: Aspetti religiosi, politici, culturali*, ed. Ugo Baldini and Gian Paolo Brizzi (Bologna: Clueb, 2010), 355–365.

Trampus, Antonio, 'Il ruolo del traduttore nel tardo illuminismo: Lodovico Antonio Loschi e la versione italiana del *Droit des gens* di Emer de Vattel', in *Il linguaggio del tardo illuminismo. Politica, diritto e società civile*, ed. Antonio Trampus (Roma: Edizioni di Storia e Letteratura, 2011), 81–108.

Treggiari, Ferdinando, 'Avvocati umbri', in *Avvocati che fecero l'Italia*, ed. Stefano Borsacchi and Gian Savino Pene Vidari (Bologna: il Mulino, 2011), 542–544.

Treggiari, Ferdinando, 'Emilio Barbanera (1799–1876), in *Avvocati che fecero l'Italia*, ed. Stefano Borsacchi and GianSavino Pene Vidari (Bologna: il Mulino, 2011), 544–551.

Vattel, Emer de, *Le droit des gens, ou Principes de la loi naturelle appliqués à la conduite et aux affaires des nations et des souverains* (London [Neuchâtel]: Société typographique, 1758).

Vattel, Emer de, *The Law of Nations, or, Principles of the Law of Nature Applied to the Conduct and Affairs of Nations and Sovereigns, with Three Early Essays on the Origin and Nature of Natural Law and on Luxury*, ed. Béla Kapossy and Richard Whatmore (Indianapolis, IN: Liberty Fund, 2008).

CHAPTER 9

The Chair of International Law and Pasquale Stanislao Mancini's Lectures in Turin

Frédéric Ieva

Pasquale Stanislao Mancini,
deputy, exile, minister, he had a most important role
in all the great battles which were fought to give us a homeland.[1]

1 The Turin Faculty of Law

From the eighteenth century, the law faculty of the University of Turin was the 'privileged training institution of the Savoy elites'.[2] Shortly after the signing of the Peace of Utrecht (1713), the university of the capital of the new kingdom was reformed by a series of measures implemented in 1720, 1723 and 1729. The aim of Victor Amadeus II, the King of Sardinia, was to give the state control over every aspect of education, in particular 'preparing fully trained public officials and loyal subjects'.[3] Several noteworthy intellectuals, such as the Sicilian Francesco d'Aguirre, and Bernardo Andrea Lama and Mario Agostino

1 Giuseppe Zanardelli, *In memoria di Pasquale Stanislao Mancini* (Napoli: Tipografia Melfi e Joele, 1911), 43. I extend my thanks to the editors of the present volume, Gabriella Silvestrini and Elisabetta Fiocchi Malaspina, for having invited me to take part in this research project on the history of the chairs of international law in Italy during the modern age, and for their observations, which have greatly improved the following pages. My deepest thanks also go to Italo Birocchi, Guido Franzinetti, Gian Savino Pene Vidari, Antonio Trampus and Adriano Viarengo, who read the first draft of this chapter.

2 Donatella Balani, *Toghe di Stato. La facoltà giuridica dell'Università di Torino e le professioni nel Piemonte del Settecento* (Torino: Deputazione Subalpina di Storia Patria, 1996), x. On this period of reform, see Guido Quazza, *Le riforme in Piemonte nella prima metà del Settecento* (Cavallermaggiore: Gribaudo, 1992), 393–398.

3 Balani, *Toghe di Stato*, 2.

Campiani from Rome, were very active in those years of reform.[4] However, this renewal process was partly hindered by the conclusion of an agreement between the government of Turin and the Roman Curia in 1727, an event that prompted the reformist intellectuals to leave the Savoy capital.[5]

Nevertheless, some of the proposals put forward by d'Aguirre[6] found their way, through the 'Costituzioni di Sua Maestà per l'Università di Torino' (1729), into the legislation of the Kingdom of Sardinia, which, among other things, removed secondary school teaching from the control of religious orders. These legal provisions also had the objective of allowing a closer watch on the education of the citizens, instilling in them respect for authority (royal and religious) and, at the same time, forging deep bonds of loyalty to the Savoy monarchy.

Without any intention of weakening religious orthodoxy, which continued to be seen as an *instrumentum regni* to support the government, the management of schools of every kind and level passed to the State, in the person of the Magistrate of the Reform, a most sensitive position for which personages of great importance were always chosen.[7]

The University of Turin was in a poor state: the increasing scarcity of financial resources allocated to teaching had brought about the departure of its most renowned teachers, and no control was exercised on the activities of the professors and the students. The appeals made by d'Aguirre and Scipione Maffei[8] for teaching staff to receive regular remuneration met with some success, progress being made with the *Regio biglietto* of 3 April 1738, which

---

4 See Giuseppe Ricuperati, 'L'Università di Torino e le polemiche contro i professori in una relazione di parte curialista del 1731', *Bollettino storico-bibliografico subalpino* 64:1 (1966): 341–374; idem, 'Bernardo Andrea Lama professore e storiografo nel Piemonte di Vittorio Amedeo II', *Bollettino storico-bibliografico subalpino* 66(1–2) (1968): 11–101; and idem, 'Campiani, Mario Agostino', in *Dizionario Biografico degli Italiani* (Roma: Istituto dell'Enciclopedia Italiana, 1974), vol. 17, 530–533.

5 On the effects of the 1727 concordat, see Maria Teresa Silvestrini, *La politica della religione. Il governo ecclesiastico nello Stato sabaudo del XVIII secolo* (Firenze: Olschki, 1997), 89–102.

6 See Regina Lupi, *Francesco D'Aguirre. Riforme e resistenze nell'Italia del primo settecento* (Firenze: Centro Editoriale Toscano, 2011); Dino Carpanetto and Giuseppe Ricuperati, *L'Italia del settecento* (1st edition 1986; Roma: Laterza, 2008), 181–183. Geoffrey Symcox, *Victor Amadeus II: Absolutism in the Savoyard State 1675–1730* (Berkeley, CA: University of California Press, 1983) remains a worthwhile resource.

7 See Alessandra Bourlot, *Il Magistrato della Riforma dell'Università di Torino nel Settecento* (MA diss., Università degli Studi di Torino, 1991–1992).

8 In 1718 Scipione Maffei had sent to the government of Turin his *Parere sul migliore ordinamento della Regia Università di Torino alla Sua Maestà Vittorio Amedeo II*, about which, see Balani, *Toghe di Stato*, 23, n. 47. More generally on Maffei see: *Scipione Maffei nell'Europa del Settecento*, ed. Gianpaolo Romagnani (Verona: Cierre, 1998); Gianpaolo Romagnani, 'Maffei, Scipione', in *Dizionario Biografico degli Italiani* (Roma: Istituto dell'Enciclopedia Italiana,

established 'a single system of pay, divided into salary bands',[9] which largely remained in force throughout the eighteenth century.

Despite its various difficulties, the period of reform enabled the university to establish better working principles, with the institution structured into four faculties (theology, law, medicine and, from 1721, surgery) with a total of twenty teachers. The selection of professors was left to the Magistrate of the Reform, who drew up a shortlist of candidates, one of whom would be appointed by the sovereign. The faculty of law was organised into five chairs: two professorships of civil law, one of canon law and two of institutional law (civil and canonical, established in 1731).

The reforms left the law faculty somewhat smaller, despite a number of suggestions made by d'Aguirre, who had proposed the foundation of a chair of 'de jure naturali, gentium et civili'.[10] None of his proposals were accepted, least of all that calling for the establishment of teaching in public law, which was considered too thorny a subject. The situation would remain largely unchanged until the end of the century, and the new charters of 1772 merely confirmed the previous ones. The course curricula were left unchanged, giving the impression that, in contrast to the innovations that were being introduced in other universities in the Italian peninsula, stagnation prevailed in Turin. Among the examples of innovations that could be cited it is worth mentioning the creation of the chair of natural law and the law of nations established on a permanent basis by the University of Pisa in 1738 and that of public law created in Modena in 1767.[11] An attempt was made in the early 1730s to establish a chair in *jus gentium* in Turin, but this was thwarted by strong opposition from the Curialist faction, essentially because they feared that such teaching might call into question the prince's authority in fiscal matters.[12]

In fact, the '*jus naturale et gentium* was never introduced in the university, although it was conceded that the fundamental principles of this science

---

2006), vol. 67, 256–263; and Paolo Ulvioni, *'Riformar il mondo'. Il pensiero civile di Scipione Maffei*, with a new edition of the 'Consiglio Politico' (Alessandria: Edizioni dell'Orso, 2008).

9 Cf. Balani, *Toghe di Stato*, 24.

10 Francesco D'Aguirre, *Della fondazione e ristabilimento degli studi generali in Torino*, ed. Municipio di Salemi (Palermo: Tip. Giannitrapani, 1901), book II, chs 3 and 4. The plan had been presented in 1717. The course of studies required four years for the bachelor's degree; five for the master's degree; and six for entry into the College of Teachers.

11 See Danilo Marrara, 'Pompeo Neri e la cattedra pisana di "diritto pubblico" nel XVIII secolo', *Rivista di storia del diritto italiano* 59 (1986): 173–202. On the case of Modena, see Carlo Guido Mor, *Storia dell'Università di Modena* (Modena: STEM, 1963), 91 ff., 160 ff.; and Chapter 1 of the present volume, by Emanuele Salerno.

12 See Giuseppe Ricuperati, 'L'Università di Torino e le polemiche contro i professori'.

would become part of the curricula of philosophical disciplines',[13] and it was therefore dealt with by teachers of moral philosophy, such as Michele Casati and Sigismondo Gerdil, both of whom were of an anti-Enlightenment persuasion.[14]

Later, between 1792 and 1798, the university was closed, and then in the Napoleonic era it was reformed several times, while in the early years of the Empire the Faculty of Law saw the number of its students increase significantly.[15] After the first liberal uprisings, the university was partially reopened following a closure that lasted from 1821 to 1823, albeit under the rigid control of the Piedmontese government.[16] From that point on it lived in a 'state of mediocrity'[17] until the winds of change that began to blow in the early 1830s; in 1832, the famous French mathematician Augustin-Louis Cauchy was called to the chair of sublime physics (but in fact mathematical physics in general) in the Faculty of Sciences.[18] Of greater pertinence to our discussion, however, was the speech delivered in the Senate by Federigo Sclopis in 1844, in which he underlined the need to improve the teaching of law.[19] The king, Charles Albert, was convinced that the kingdom's bureaucratic-administrative cadres should be educated in the Faculty of Law and initiated a reform plan aimed at updating the subjects and methods of teaching, relying on people of great prestige and experience. For this reason, in 1844 he appointed Cesare Alfieri di Sostegno, a member of the Council of State since its establishment in 1837,

---

13 Balani, *Toghe di Stato*, 61.

14 On these academics, see Pietro Stella, 'Casati, Michele', in *Dizionario Biografico degli Italiani* (Roma: Istituto dell'Enciclopedia Italiana, 1978), vol. 21, 262–265; Roberto Valabrega, *Un anti-illuminista dalla cattedra alla porpora: Giacinto Sigismondo Gerdil professore, precettore a corte e cardinale* (Torino: Deputazione Subalpina di Storia Patria, 2004).

15 For some notes on the Piedmontese university in this period, see Giampaolo Romagnani, 'L'età napolenica', in *L'Università di Torino. Profilo storico e istituzionale*, ed. Francesco Traniello (Torino: Pluriverso, 1993), 28–32, at 31.

16 See Narciso Nada, 'La Restaurazione', in *L'Università di Torino*, 34–39, at 37.

17 Ida Ferrero, *Innovazione nella facoltà giuridica torinese. Didattica e docenti di metà Ottocento* (Torino: Deputazione Subalpina di Storia Patria, 2018), 7.

18 See Paola Dealbertis, 'I manoscritti di Augustin Cauchy dell'Archivio Faà di Bruno', in *Francesco Faà di Bruno. Ricerca scientifica, insegnamento e divulgazione*, ed. Livia Giacardi (Torino: Deputazione Subalpina di Storia Patria, 2004), 627–638.

19 See Federigo Sclopis, *Dello studio e dell'applicazione delle leggi. Discorso detto dianzi all'eccellentissimo R. Senato di Piemonte nella solenne apertura dell'anno giuridico il dì 16 di novembre 1844* (Torino: Bocca, 1845), 33. Gian Savino Pene Vidari, 'Sclopis, Federigo', in *Dizionario Biografico degli Italiani* (Roma: Istituto dell'Enciclopedia Italiana, 2018), vol. 91, 575–578.

as Magistrate for the Reform.[20] Evidence of this royal support for reform was shortly after seen in the establishment of chairs of mechanics and mechanical chemistry on the eve of the establishment of the Faculty of Physical and Mathematical Sciences in 1848 and, above all, through the *Regio biglietto* of 6 December 1845, of the Faculty of Political Economy. This subject had previously been introduced during the period of French rule and was confirmed in 1817 but abolished after the uprisings of 1821.[21] The Neapolitan economist Antonio Scialoja,[22] who was very close to Pasquale Stanislao Mancini, was appointed head of this faculty to lead the teaching of the subject. Mancini followed closely Scialoja's incorporation into Savoy society, writing both to Sclopis himself[23] and, especially, to Carlo Ilarione Petitti di Roreto: 'tell me *frankly* what impact he [Scialoja] has had on the *chair* and in private *society*, I am hoping for good news'.[24]

Scialoja's lessons, which began in January 1846,[25] were a great success, being warmly received by the public and often attended by many subalpine intellectuals, such as Cesare Balbo,[26] Cesare Alfieri, Count Camillo Benso di Cavour,[27]

20 See Maria Teresa Pichetto, 'Cesare Alfieri di Sostegno e le riforme politiche e sociali nel Piemonte Carloalbertino', in *Alfieri di Sostegno tra Torino e Firenze*, ed. Cristina Vernizzi (Torino: Museo Nazionale del Risorgimento Italiano, 1997), 31–56. See also Simonetta Polenghi, *La politica universitaria italiana nell'età della Destra storica (1848–1876)* (Brescia: La Scuola, 1993), 17, 19, 31, 68, 70–72.

21 See Gian Savino Pene Vidari, 'Prospettive e contributi della facoltà giuridica per l'Unità', in *Dall'università di Torino all'Italia unita. Contributi dei docenti al Risorgimento e all'Unità*, ed. Clara Silvia Roero (Torino: Deputazione Subalpina di Storia Patria, 2013), 1–58, at 2.

22 Cf. Domenicantonio Fausto, 'Scialoja, Antonio', in *Dizionario Biografico degli Italiani* (Roma: Istituto dell'Enciclopedia Italiana, 2018), vol. 91, 526–530.

23 Cf. Archivio Accademia delle Scienze di Torino (AAST), Turin, Italy, Fondo Carteggi, 26985, Pasquale Stanislao Mancini to Federico Sclopis, Naples, 2 April 1846.

24 Archivio Museo Nazionale del Risorgimento di Torino (AMNRIT), Turin, Italy, Archivi Storici, Fondo Petitti, 1080 (typed copy of n. 761), Pasquale Stanislao Mancini to Carlo Ilarione Petitti di Roreto, Naples, 15 May 1846.

25 See Gian Savino Pene Vidari, 'Considerazioni sul contributo degli esuli risorgimentali al rinnovamento della facoltà giuridica torinese', *Rivista di storia del diritto italiano*, 76 (2003): 1–26, at 3. This useful article considers the beginnings of the supplementary legal course. See also Ester de Fort, *Esuli e migranti nel Regno sardo. Per una storia sociale e politica del Risorgimento* (Roma: Carocci; Torino: Istituto per la storia del Risorgimento italiano, Comitato di Torino, 2022), 185–186.

26 On Cesare Balbo, see *Cesare Balbo alle origini del cattolicesimo liberale*, ed. Gabriele De Rosa and Francesco Traniello (Roma: Laterza, 1996).

27 See Adriano Viarengo, *Cavour* (Roma: Salerno, 2010), to which I refer the reader for a bibliography; Camillo Cavour, *Tutti gli scritti*, 4 vols, collected and edited by Carlo Pischedda and Giuseppe Talamo, with an introductory note by Pierangelo Gentile (Torino: Centro Studi Piemontesi, 2016, anastatic reprint of the original 1976 edition).

Ilarione Petitti[28] and Quintino Sella, who wrote enthusiastic accounts of the course delivered by the Neapolitan economist.[29]

Other professors already working for the university welcomed these signs of renewal. For example, Felice Merlo, a professor of the institutions of civil law, also spoke about natural law, explaining it in his lessons alongside the ideas of Vico, according to whom the *jus naturae* meant 'working in conformity with what one recognizes as true'.[30] Merlo's thinking had been influenced by his friend Vincenzo Gioberti, and Merlo began to promote 'Gioberti's "true theory of natural law"', according to which 'man's perception of the world and of himself is that of a continuous creation'.[31] At the root of these concepts was the belief that, on the one hand, man accepted the idea of the existence of a supreme and absolute legislator and, on the other, with the use of reason was able to deduce general legal rules, inferring from them more specific ones that would form the 'actually applicable positive law'.[32]

Another academic open to the renewal of legal studies was Pietro Luigi Albini, who in 1839 wrote *Saggio analitico sul diritto e sulla scienza e istruzione politico legale* (Analytical Essay on Law and on the Science of and Education in Politics and Law),[33] in which he attempted to provide a broad general picture of all areas of jurisprudence.

The emphasis placed on renewal was fully grasped by Cesare Alfieri di Sostegno, who set up a Senate commission to draw up a plan for the reorganization of legal studies, and it was no coincidence that this included, among others: Federico Sclopis and Giuseppe Siccardi (presidents), Felice Merlo (member) and Albini (secretary).[34] The most important novelty of the

28 See Pasquale Stanislao Mancini, 'Notizia della vita e degli studi di Carlo Ilarione Petitti', in Carlo Ilarione Petitti di Roreto, *Del giuoco del lotto considerato ne' suoi effetti morali, politici ed economici: opera postuma* (Torino: Stamperia reale, 1853), v–xix; Manfredi Alberti, 'Petitti, Carlo Ilarione', in *Dizionario Biografico degli Italiani* (Roma: Istituto dell'Enciclopedia Italiana, 2015), vol. 82, 659–662.

29 See Umberto Levra, 'Sella, Quintino', in *Dizionario Biografico degli Italiani* (Roma: Istituto dell'Enciclopedia Italiana, 2018), vol. 91, 809–814. Like Scialoja's lessons, Mancini's lessons were also attended by illustrious people like Giovanni Nepomuceno Nuytz and Terenzio Mamiani; see Eloisa Mura, *Mancini in cattedra. Le lezioni torinesi di diritto internazionale del 1850–51 e 1851–52* (Pisa: ETS, 2018), 12, 197.

30 As Ferrero's writes in *Innovazione nella facoltà giuridica torinese*, 17.

31 Ibid., 18.

32 Ibid., 19.

33 Published in Vigevano by Pietro Vitali e Comp. in 1839. On Albini, see Ferrero, *Innovazione nella facoltà giuridica tironese*, 148 ff.

34 See Claudia Storti Storchi, *Ricerche sulla condizione giuridica dello straniero in Italia: dal tardo diritto comune all'età preunitaria. Aspetti civilistici* (Milano: Giuffrè, 1989), the section entitled 'Le lezioni napoletane e torinesi del Mancini e l'istituzione della cattedra di diritto internazionale nel Regno di Sardegna', in particular at 302, n. 63.

reform was the creation of a two-year finishing course of law that was open to graduate students whose ambition was to teach or join the College of Doctors of the Faculty of Law.[35]

Emboldened by royal support, Cesare Alfieri was able to create numerous chairs: the teaching of public and international law was assigned in 1847 to Felice Merlo, but he could teach only the inaugural lecture course as he took on numerous political commitments in 1848, first the vice-presidency of the Senate, subsequently a ministerial post, and then the office of prime minister.[36]

However, in this period international law was not yet a subject in its own right but was taught as part of public law. In 1849 the course 'Public Constitutional and Institutional Law' was assigned to L. Amedeo Melegari, who, however, ended up limiting his focus to the exegesis of the articles of the constitution.[37] The subjects were split up only in 1850, with the creation of a professorship for Pasquale Stanislao Mancini, who began teaching on 22 January 1851. Thus the University of Turin became the first in Italy to offer a course in international law separate from those of internal and external public law.[38] It is therefore time to concentrate our attention on Mancini.

2 The Turin Chair of Pasquale Stanislao Mancini

As we have seen, Mancini had for some time been in correspondence with several subalpine intellectuals, whom he had met during the congresses of

35 See Paola Di Iorio, *Ricerche su Pasquale Stanislao Mancini a Torino* (PhD diss., Università di Torino, 1992–1993), 33 ff. From 1850 to 1856 the subjects included in the law course were: Constitutional Law (Melegari), External International Public Law and Private International Law (Mancini), Rational Principles of Law (Albini) and Political Economy (Ferrara). These were special chairs because they belonged to the finishing course rather than to the normal one. On Melegari, see Gian Savino Pene Vidari, 'Ideali e realismo, insegnamento e pratica giuridica: Luigi Amedeo Melegari', in *Lavorando al cantiere del 'Dizionario biografico dei giuristi italiani (XII–XX sec.)'*, ed. Maria Gigliola di Renzo Villata (Milano: Giuffrè, 2013), 275–323.

36 The course was called 'Principi razionali del Diritto, Diritto Pubblico e Diritto Internazionale'. See Gian Savino Pene Vidari, 'Merlo, Felice', in *Dizionario Biografico degli Italiani* (Roma: Istituto dell'Enciclopedia Italiana, 2009), vol. 73, 718–721.

37 See Pene Vidari, 'Considerazioni sul contributo degli esuli', 7.

38 See Elisa Mongiano, 'Pasquale Stanislao Mancini. Nazionalità e diritto internazionale all'Università di Torino', *Rivista Italiana per le scienze giuridiche* 4 (2013): 363–377, at 365. See also Eloisa Mura, 'Aperture nazionali e nuovo regolamento degli studi all'indomani del Quarantotto', in *La Facoltà di Giurisprudenza dell'Università di Cagliari*, ed. Italo Birocchi (Pisa: ETS, 2018), 325–358, at 330 ff.

scientists in which he had taken part in Naples (1845) and Genoa (1846)[39] or with whom he had made contact when working as a journalist. For a long time he had corresponded in particular with Federico Sclopis, but the Turinese archives also preserve his letters to Ilarione Petitti, Carlo Ignazio Giulio, Pier Dionigi Pinelli, Domenico Carutti and Domenico Berti, all of them prominent figures in Turin.[40] Thanks to such acquaintances and to his fame as a jurisconsult, he was able to create an important space for himself in the society of intellectuals and political figures in Savoy, giving rise in its capital to a lively salon frequented by both exiles and Piedmontese politicians.[41]

A complex figure who has not yet been the subject of an academic biography,[42] Mancini, despite having a wide-ranging curiosity that had led him to study music, literature and translation, remained essentially a jurisconsult steeped in Enlightenment culture.[43] Despite some valuable reconstruction of

---

39 Nine congresses of Italian scientists were held between 1839 and 1847. Maria Pia Casalena, *Per lo Stato, per la Nazione. I congressi degli scienziati in Francia e in Italia (1830–1914)* (Roma: Carocci, 2007); ead., 'In Europa e ritorno. I congressi degli scienziati italiani tra modelli europei e via nazionale', *Mélanges de l'École française de Rome* 130(2) (2018): 273–283; in the same special issue entitled *La fabrique transnationale de la 'science nationale' en Italie (1839–fin des années 1920)*, see also Vincent Genin, 'Pasquale S. Mancini: du laboratoire juridique national à la Fabrique du droit international (1866–1869)': 323–332.

40 The most conspicuous correspondence is that with Sclopis, preserved in AAST, a series of 35 missives from July 1842 to 1876. See for example letter 26988, undated, in which Mancini congratulated himself on the establishment of the Commission presided over by Sclopis, which improved the position of the University of Turin at a time when in Italy 'legal studies especially are in a deplorable position'. Letters sent to the other correspondents mentioned are preserved in AMNRIT, while the library Biblioteca di Storia e Cultura del Piemonte 'Giuseppe Grosso' holds the letters that Mancini wrote to Giulio.

41 This Turinese period has been widely studied. See Luigi Firpo, 'Gli anni torinesi', in *Pasquale Stanislao Mancini. L'uomo, lo studioso, il politico*, ed. Ortensio Zecchino and Giovanni Spadolini (Napoli: Guida, 1991), 139–156, and, in the same volume, Rosanna Giannandrè, 'Mancini e l'ambiente degli esuli napoletani a Torino', 157–176; Elisa Mongiano, 'Gli anni torinesi', in *Per una rilettura di Mancini. Saggi sul diritto del Risorgimento, ed. Italo Birocchi* (Pisa: ETS, 2018), 121–158; and Umberto Levra, 'L'esilio torinese di Pasquale Stanislao Mancini', in *Per la Costruzione dell'identità nazionale. Francesco De Sanctis e Pasquale Stanislao Mancini dalla provincia meridionale all'Europa*, ed. Renata De Lorenzo (Soveria Mannelli: Rubettino, 2020), 31–59.

42 Italo Birocchi, 'Presentazione', in *Per una rilettura di Mancini*, 11–17, at 11.

43 The Enlightenment culture resurfaced in Mancini through suggestions he took from Giambattista Vico and Pietro Giannone. In fact, he often claimed to feel 'Neapolitan and Giannonian'; see Lorenzo Frugiuele, *La Sinistra e i cattolici. Pasquale Stanislao Mancini giurisdizionalista anticlericale* (Milano: Vita e Pensiero, 1985), 11. On Mancini as a student of Giannone, see Pietro Giannone, *L'affaire Giannone face à l'Europe. Vie de Pietro*

his biography there is a lack of in-depth study of his internationalist thinking, and so it is possible only to highlight some of the most significant moments of his life here,[44] before examining the first two university courses that he taught in Turin in order to ascertain which sources he used to support his arguments.

Born in 1817 in Castel Baronia, in the province of Avellino, Mancini was educated in the seminary of Ariano Irpino and the Salvatore lycée in Naples, before he went on to obtain his degree in law, also in Naples, in 1835, the year of his first appearance in court.

His debut on the political scene was made in the tumultuous period of 1848 in Naples, specifically during the events of 15 May 1848, when the Bourbon army fought on the streets of Naples against insurgents who had erected barricades in defence of the Chamber that had been elected but not allowed to meet. This prohibition was a gesture that Mancini, himself a supporter of the protest signed by sixty-six deputies, called 'an act of blind and incorrigible despotism'.[45] This was a crucial moment in the history of the Italian south because it was in that very year that the 'monarchy–nation relationship' was traumatically torn apart.[46]

Giannone, Profession de foi et Abjuration, a selection of texts translated, annotated and commented by Gisela Schlüter and Giuseppe Ricuperati (Paris: Honoré Champion, 2019), 33 ff., but see also the observations on the influence of Cesare Beccaria and Gaetano Filangieri on Mancini by Enrica Di Ciommo, *La nazione possibile. Mezzogiorno e questione nazionale nel 1848* (Milano: FrancoAngeli, 1993), 105.

44 See the entry 'Mancini, Pasquale Stanislao', in *Dizionario Biografico degli Italiani* (Roma: Istituto dell'Enciclopedia Italiana, 2007), vol. 78, 537–547. See also Bartolomeo De Rinaldis, *Su la vita e le opere di Pasquale Stanislao Mancini* (Napoli: Stabilimento tipografico dell'Unione, 1876), which, despite providing a narrative with a somewhat hagiographic tone, contains certain biographical information of considerable interest. The bibliography on Mancini is very extensive; see at least *Pasquale Stanislao Mancini. L'uomo, lo studioso, il politico*, ed. Ortensio Zecchino and Giovanni Spadolini (Napoli: Guida, 1991); Eloisa Mura, *All'ombra di Mancini. La disciplina internazionalistica in Italia ai suoi albori* (Pisa: ETS, 2017); and ead., *Mancini in cattedra*. The writings by his daughter Grazia Mancini Pierantoni (of which see 'Alcune Lettere di P. S. Mancini', *Nuova Antologia* (1900), 313–328) are somewhat biased, as has been noted by Gian Savino Pene Vidari, 'Prospettive e contributi della facoltà giuridica', 15, n. 62.

45 Pasquale Stanislao Mancini, *Due scritti politici*, ed. Augusto Pierantoni (Roma: Società editrice Dante Alighieri, 1899), xxix, where the full text of the protest written by Mancini is provided. The repression by the Bourbon government aroused indignation throughout Europe, in particular from William Gladstone, who, commenting on the events in Naples, wrote: 'This is the negation of Good erected into a System of Government', in William Ewart Gladstone, *Two Letters to the Earl of Aberdeen, on the State Prosecutions of the Neapolitan Government*, 3rd edition (London: John Murray, 1851), 6.

46 Di Ciommo, *La nazione possibile*, 321.

Once Ferdinand II issued the order to dissolve the Chamber on 13 March 1849, Mancini repeatedly came to the defence of the former deputies who had been subjected to persecution by the Bourbon monarchy.[47] He himself ran the risk of being arrested but, having been warned of his imminent capture, managed to board a French ship and reached safety in Genoa before finally seeking refuge in Turin, where he arrived on 5 October 1849.[48]

According to Augusto Pierantoni,[49] in the first half of the nineteenth century three political factions were active on the Italian peninsula: the legitimists (conservatives), or those in favour of absolute governments; the reformists (liberals), supporters of freedom and independence; and the unitarian republicans (democrats or radicals), inspired by the ideas of Giuseppe Mazzini. Despite the fact that he had not given a systematic form to his political ideas, Mancini may be considered a reformist, insofar as he was the conveyor of a clear liberal project based on three points: secularism, legal rationalism and utility.[50] He was an exponent of the liberal group which maintained good relations with both moderate liberals and democratic liberals, as his cordial rapport with Lorenzo Valerio demonstrated.[51]

The Irpinian jurist soon entered the nerve centres of ministerial circles, being appointed during 1850 as a member of the commission established for the revision of civil and criminal legislation as well as that tasked with rationalizing judicial statistics. With the passing of the special 'law' of 1850 he was given a professorship in international law at the Faculty of Law, University of Turin. This moment is of particular relevance and merits closer examination.[52]

---

47 In particular he defended Carlo Poerio, Pier Silvestro Leopardi and Giuseppe Massari; see Pasquale Stanislao Mancini, 'A' giureconsulti e Pubblicisti italiani' (1851), in idem, *Due scritti politici*, 1–102; Frugiuele, *La Sinistra e i cattolici*, 16.

48 All these events are described in great detail in the preface by Pierantoni in Mancini, *Due scritti politici*, xl ff. See also De Rinaldis, *Su la vita e le opere di Pasquale Stanislao Mancini*, 27 ff.; Viviana Mellone, *Napoli 1848. Il movimento radicale e la rivoluzione* (Milano: FrancoAngeli, 2017), 223 ff.

49 Pierantoni married Mancini's daughter Grazia Sofia in 1868; see Eloisa Mura, 'Pierantoni, Augusto Francesco', in *Dizionario Biografico degli Italiani* (Roma: Istituto dell'Enciclopedia Italiana, 2015), vol. 83, 291–294.

50 See Di Ciommo, *La nazione possibile*, 115; Federico Chabod, *Storia della politica estera italiana dal 1870 al 1896. Le premesse* (Bari: Laterza, 1951), 253.

51 See Adriano Viarengo, *Lorenzo Valerio. La terza via del Risorgimento, 1810–1865* (Roma: Carocci; Torino: Istituto per la storia del Risorgimento italiano, Comitato di Torino, 2019); idem, 'Valerio, Lorenzo', in *Dizionario Biografico degli Italiani* (Roma: Istituto dell'Enciclopedia Italiana, 2020), vol. 98, 23–26.

52 Gian Savino Pene Vidari, 'Un secolo e mezzo fa (22 gennaio 1851): la lezione torinese di Pasquale Stanislao Mancini sulla nazionalità', *Studi Piemontesi* 31(2) (2002): 273–285.

On 12 April 1850 the Minister of Public Instruction, Cristoforo Mameli, presented a bill to the Senate aimed at establishing a chair that would assist young men who wished to pursue a diplomatic career. The new subject would be called 'special instruction in consular and diplomatic science' and would expound 'the principles of the modern European law of nations',[53] focusing in particular on maritime law and the history of treaties. However, access to state diplomacy was almost exclusively in the hands of the aristocracy, which would not tolerate the idea that a degree in law could become a privileged qualification for diplomatic careers. Federico Sclopis realized that the project, if formulated that way, would have aroused strong opposition from the nobility. In a report to the Senate of 7 May 1850 he therefore presented a new plan which left aside allusions to a diplomatic career and proposed the creation of a new chair of external public and international private law.[54] After debate in the Senate and in the Chamber of Deputies, the plan was passed into law in November 1850.[55] But during the Senate debate there had been no lack of objections. In particular, Ermolao Asinari of San Marzano, deeming it not appropriate to give the Faculty of Law a new course, had asked for the provision to be postponed until 1851, when discussions would take place on 'a new formation of the law course and [...] a new coordination of its chairs'.[56] Mameli rejected the objections, underlining that the subjects (modern law of nations, maritime law in relation to public law, and history of treaties) that would be taught in the new course were 'useful and necessary in any form of government to almost all orders of citizens'.[57] The draft law was approved, with thirty-three votes in favour and fifteen opposed.

Mancini, whose notoriety had grown considerably after the publication, in 1841, of his exchange of letters with Terenzio Mamiani on the right to pun-

---

53 *Atti del Parlamento subalpino*, Sessione del 1850 dal 20 dicembre al 18 dicembre 1850 (IV Legislatura), collected and enhanced with notes and unpublished documents by Galletti Giuseppe and Trompeo Paolo (Torino: Tipografia Eredi Botta, 1863), 533.

54 Cf. Ibid., 534.

55 The law can be read in *Raccolta degli atti del governo di sua Maestà il re di Sardegna*, vol. 18,, *Dal 1° gennaio a tutto dicembre 1850, dal n.° 971 al 1125 bis* (Torino: Stamperia Reale, [1850]), 745–746.

56 *Atti del Parlamento subalpino*, 332. The chairs of the Faculty of Law had indeed increased from five (1846) to fourteen (1849); on the parliamentary debate, see Pene Vidari, 'Un secolo e mezzo fa (22 gennaio 1851)', 275–279; Emilia Morelli, *Tre profili. Benedetto XIV, Pasquale Stanislao Mancini, Pietro Roselli* (Roma: Edizioni dell'Ateneo, 1955), 67–70.

57 *Atti del Parlamento subalpino*, 333.

ish,[58] had begun to take an interest in international law in 1844, when he published his essay 'Esame di un'opera di diritto internazionale pubblicata da Nicola Rocco' (Examination of a Work of International Law Published by Nicola Rocco).[59] In 1839–1840, he had opened a private law school in Naples that became one of the best in the city,[60] and in 1847 he was appointed substitute in the chair in natural law at the University of Naples. The Bourbon government removed him from this chair on 5 December 1849 following his escape to Turin.[61]

Mancini made his debut in Turin with an inaugural lecture that particularly inflamed the audience, due to its references to freedom and the 'right to nationality'.[62] The teaching of international law was part of the finishing course until the reform of 9 October 1856 which inserted the subject into the ordinary five-year course of the Faculty of Law, making it mandatory for students, who would take it for the whole of their final year.[63]

---

58 Terenzio Mamiani and Pasquale Stanislao Mancini, *Fondamenti della filosofia del diritto e singolarmente del diritto di punire. Lettere di Terenzio Mamiani e Pasquale Stanislao Mancini* (Livorno: Tipografia Vigo, 1875). Cf. Italo Birocchi, 'Pasquale Stanislao Mancini e la cultura giuridica del Risorgimento', in *Per una rilettura di Mancini*, 19–119, at 29–35.

59 'Esame di un'opera di diritto internazionale pubblicata da Nicola Rocco', *Continuazione delle Ore solitarie – Biblioteca di scienze morali, legislative ed economiche*, issue 1 (1844): 10–30. On this, see Erik Jayme, *Pasquale Stanislao Mancini. Internationales Privatrecht zwischen Risorgimento und praktischer Jurisprudenz* (Ebelsbach: Gremer, 1980). See also Yuko Nishitani, *Mancini und die Parteiautonomie im Internationalen Privatrecht: Eine Untersuchung auf der Grundlage der neu zutage gekommenen kollisionsrechtlichen Vorlesungen Mancinis* (Heidelberg: Universitätsverlag Winter, 2000).

60 De Rinaldis, *Su la vita e le opere di Pasquale Stanislao Mancini*, 18; Zanardelli, *In memoria di Pasquale Stanislao Mancini*, 71; Morelli, *Tre profili*, 55. On the private law school, see Aldo Mazzacane, 'Università e scuole private di diritto a Napoli nella prima metà dell'Ottocento', in *Università in Europa. Le istituzioni universitarie dal Medio Evo ai nostri giorni: strutture, organizzazione, funzionamento*, ed. Andrea Romano (Soveria Mannelli: Rubbettino, 1995), 549–575.

61 Frugiuele, *La Sinistra e i cattolici*, 14; 'Mancini, Pasquale Stanislao', in *Dizionario Biografico degli Italiani*, 540.

62 Pasquale Stanislao Mancini, *Della nazionalità come fondamento del diritto delle genti. Prelezione al corso di diritto internazionale e marittimo pronunziata nella R. Università di Torino* […] *nel dì 22 gennaio 1851* (Torino: Eredi Botta, 1851), 41. Cf. Gian Savino Pene Vidari, 'La prolusione di Pasquale Stanislao Mancini sul principio di nazionalità (1851)', in *Retoriche dei giuristi e costituzione dell'identità nazionale*, ed. Giovanni Cazzetta (Bologna: Il Mulino, 2013), 117–134.

63 Cf. Di Iorio, *Ricerche su Pasquale Stanislao Mancini a Torino*, 43. More generally see *Constructing International Law: The Birth of a Discipline*, ed. Luigi Nuzzo and Miloš Vec (Frankfurt am Main: Klostermann, 2012); Luigi Nuzzo, 'La storia del diritto internazionale e le sfide del presente', *Quaderni fiorentini per la storia del pensiero giuridico moderno* 42 (2013): 683–701.

3 Some of the Sources for Mancini's Turin Lectures

The importance of Mancini's inaugural lecture has been emphasized many times.[64] On the very first pages of it he stated that 'nationality, as the rational basis of the law of nations',[65] would be the 'first and cardinal idea that will dominate my course',[66] and he went on to underline that the pioneers of the discipline were two Italians, Pierino Belli d'Alba and Alberico Gentili, but 'Grotius's great work obscured and dominated all the earlier ones'.[67]

According to Mancini, in the previous century the doctrine of the law of nations had not made any great progress. Emer de Vattel, for example, had limited himself to 'making Wolff's doctrine French', offering 'a type of compendium' of it, one characterized by 'an overly superficial scientific levity' and by 'frequent oscillation and uncertainty in the application of principles'.[68] This brief quotation alone clearly demonstrates Mancini's negative view of Vattel, whose work he saw as a defective if not pejorative summary of Christian Wolff's complex ideas. More generally, however, these two thinkers 'did not go beyond Grotius's principle of a law concerning relations between states'.[69]

---

64 See for example Federico Chabod, *Idea d'Europa e civiltà moderna. Sette saggi inediti*, ed. Marco Platania (Roma: Carocci, 2010), in particular the essay 'Nazione ed Europa nel pensiero e nell'azione politica di Mazzini', 151–170; Stuart Woolf, 'Reading Federico Chabod's Storia dell'idea d'Europa Half a Century Later', *Journal of Modern Italian Studies* 7:2 (2002): 269–292.

65 Di Iorio, *Ricerche su Pasquale Stanislao Mancini a Torino*, 11–12. The text of the *Prelezione* (prolusion, or prelection) to *Della nazionalità come fondamento del diritto delle genti* had been reworked by Mancini ahead of publication, because it takes up nearly seventy printed pages.

66 Mancini, *Della nazionalità come fondamento del diritto delle genti*, 11. For an analysis of Mancini's thought on the concepts of nation and nationality, see Giuseppe Carle, 'Pasquale Stanislao Mancini e la teoria psicologica del sentimento nazionale', *La Geografia. Rivista di propaganda geografica* 5 (1917): 6–12, 50–56, 98–104; Floriana Colao, 'L'"idea di nazione" nei giuristi italiani tra Ottocento e Novecento', *Quaderni fiorentini per la storia del pensiero giuridico moderno* 30 (2001): 255–360; Luigi Nuzzo, 'Da Mazzini a Mancini: il principio di nazionalità tra politica e diritto', *Giornale di storia costituzionale* 14:2 (2007): 161–186; Alessandro Polsi, 'Nazione e cittadinanza. Pasquale Stanislao Mancini e i diritti civili degli stranieri', in *Cittadinanze nella storia dello Stato contemporaneo*, ed. Marcella Aglietti and Carmelo Calabrò (Milano: FrancoAngeli, 2017), 33–46; Carmine Pinto, *La guerra per il Mezzogiorno. Italiani, borbonici e briganti, 1860–1870* (Roma: Laterza, 2019), 14.

67 Mancini, *Della nazionalità come fondamento del diritto delle genti*, 17. On Alberico Gentili, see Italo Birocchi, 'Il *De iure belli* e l'"invenzione" del diritto internazionale', in *'Ius gentium ius communicationis ius belli': Alberico Gentili e gli orizzonti della modernità*, ed. Luigi Lacchè (Milano: Giuffrè, 2009), 101–138.

68 Mancini, *Della nazionalità come fondamento del diritto delle genti*, 19.

69 Pene Vidari, 'Prospettive e contributi', 20.

After considering the constituent elements of the nation ('reason, race, language, customs, history, laws and religions')[70] and the concept of nationality (a 'collective expression of liberty', and a 'holy and divine thing, like liberty itself')[71] Mancini concluded that when international law was born, the basic unit was the nation rather than the state, as Grotius and Vattel[72] had argued. For them the law of nations coincided with the natural law of states, whereas for Mancini it coincided with the natural law of peoples.

In the first lecture of his first course Mancini took up some of the arguments that he had set out in his inaugural lecture by once again presenting Vattel as a 'summarizer' of Wolff and underlining that both continued to enjoy great fame 'despite the superficiality of their doctrines'.[73] He therefore agreed with Pellegrino Rossi when he claimed that international relations were still governed by empirical principles.[74] However, it should be noted that in the comparison between Wolff and Vattel the German is mentioned only seven times while the Swiss is cited more than twenty times, in eighteen lectures out of the sixty-seven.[75] It might almost be argued that Mancini examined Wolff's ideas through the filter of Vattel, through which he also considered other aspects of the doctrine.

It is therefore necessary to ascertain which parts of Vattel's *Droit des gens* influenced the reflections of the Irpinian jurist. If we consider together all the quotations of Vattel in Mancini's course we note that his examination focused primarily on book III of the *Droit*, 'De la guerre'.[76] In most cases

---

70 Mancini, *Della nazionalità come fondamento del diritto delle genti*, 31.

71 Ibid., 41.

72 Ibid., 47.

73 Mura, *Mancini in cattedra*, 91; Emmanuelle Jouannet, *Emer de Vattel et l'émergence doctrinale du droit international classique* (Paris: Pedone, 1998), 10; ead., 'Les dualismes du droit des gens', in *Le droit international de Vattel vu du XXIe siècle*, ed. Vincent Chetail and Peter Haggenmacher (Leiden: M. Nijhoff, 2011), 133–150.

74 See Mura, *Mancini in cattedra*, p. 92, Pellegrino Rossi had also been mentioned in the *Prelezione*, 21. On the Tuscan intellectual and the related literature, see Luigi Lacché, 'Rossi, Pellegrino Luigi Edoardo', in *Dizionario Biografico degli Italiani* (Roma: Istituto dell'Enciclopedia Italiana, 2017), vol. 88, 696–702.

75 Among the authors most frequently cited by Mancini are: Hugo Grotius (fifty-one mentions); Henry Wheathon (nineteen); Samuel Pufendorf (fifteen); Georg Friedrich von Martens (thirteen); Montesquieu (twelve), of whom he does not appear to have a good impression, since in the *Prelezione*, at p. 51, he mentions the 'notorious book' by the Bordeaux magistrate; Friedrich Carl Savigny (eleven); Thomas Hobbes (ten); and Gian Domenico Romagnosi (ten). Surprisingly, Giambattista Vico is mentioned only four times.

76 See Emer de Vattel, *Le Droit des gens ou principes de la loi naturelle* (A Londres, s.n., 1758), vol. 2, book III, 'De la guerre', in particular the first seven chapters, which deal with topics

Mancini tended to present a doctrine set out by Grotius prior to considering how subsequent scholars took up or criticized the Dutch jurist's thesis and, as mentioned, only rarely did Mancini compare the theories of Wolff with those of Vattel. The Grotius–Pufendorf–Vattel line was more common than the Grotius–Wolff–Vattel one.[77] The impression gleaned from this is that the theories of the Swiss jurist were considered by Mancini to have been a continuation of Grotius's theses, although Vattel ultimately gave a distorted and therefore pejorative image of his doctrine.[78]

The negative evaluation of Vattel's thought, albeit only with regard to Grotius and not to Wolff, was a consequence of the fact that Mancini was very critical of the concept of just war; furthermore, negotiations aimed at consolidating the theory of political equilibrium was a practice that he despised.

The 'deceptions of mendacious diplomacy'[79] had generated the perverse mechanism of the principle of equilibrium,[80] according to which changes in territory could not be tolerated, since the increase of one state's power would be detrimental to other states. The principle of equilibrium had the shortcoming of not taking into account that of aggregation[81] and was configured only as a preventive measure based on suspicion and fear. Mancini's conclusion was clear: 'we will declare the principle of equilibrium unfair. Unjust because it is unfair to offend someone that I feared for some reason and to anticipate with a present injustice a future one'.[82]

Another interesting example is the concept of just war, which Mancini rejected, deeming it an 'absurd, immoral and prideful theory'.[83] He dedicated four lessons to the argument,[84] beginning with the theories elaborated by

---

such as offensive war, just war and the concept of balance, the declaration of war, and finally the rights to form alliances or to declare neutrality.

77 On these authors, see Maria Rosa Di Simone, *Percorsi del diritto tra Austria e Italia (secoli XVII–XX)* (Milano: Giuffrè, 2006), 80 ff.; *Grotius, Pufendorf and the Natural Law Tradition*, ed. Knud Haakonssen (Dartmouth, Dartmouth Publishing., 1998); Knud Haakonssen, 'Enlightenment and the Ubiquity of Natural Law', *Jahrbuch der Österreichischen Gesellschaft zur Erforschung des 18. Jahrhunderts* 27 (2012): 45–57.

78 See Mura, *Mancini in cattedra*, 194, in which Mancini claimed that Vattel did not change 'a syllable of his [Grotius's] doctrine if not to make it worse'. For another example, see at 249.

79 Mura, *Mancini in cattedra*, 126.

80 Cf. Vattel, *Le Droit des gens*, 39 ff.

81 The principle of aggregation concerns the acquisition of a territory by a state. It could be, as Mancini had stated, just or unjust according to whether it happened to an already powerful state or a weak one; cf. Mura, *Mancini in cattedra*, 126.

82 Mura, *Mancini in cattedra*, 126.

83 Ibid., 249.

84 Ibid., 241–255.

Grotius.[85] Grotius distinguished between justificatory and exculpatory wars; he thought that defensive conflicts were always just, as were those fought to right a wrong or to punish an injury received, and he also attempted to limit punitive wars to the latter case.[86] Vattel largely agreed with Grotius's theory, but had drawn 'worse consequences, creating a horrendous and savage theory',[87] as he had highlighted the fact that the purpose of all wars was to punish an offence already received or believed to be imminent and, moreover, that the legitimate aim of war was revenge by means of an unforgettable example that would discourage other attacks.[88]

In fact, in the aforementioned examples the polemical target was twofold, in that Mancini targeted the doctrine formulated by Vattel on the one hand, and the European political situation that came about after the Congress in Vienna on the other. While taking into account that this is a shorthand version of Mancini's lectures, and that, therefore, we are dealing with a text designed for oral rather than written dissemination,[89] the Irpinian jurist did not mince his words when expressing his opposition to the political system resulting from the agreements signed at the 1815 congress, whose overall result was defined as a 'germ of death'[90] or as an 'infamous'[91] pact of alliance between conservative forces aimed at trampling on and mortifying the principle of nationality.

The protests raised by the Austrian government against an exiled teacher who aimed to inflame subalpine youth were therefore hardly surprising. Mancini had in fact said:

---

85 The presence of Grotius in Mancini's thought deserves to be analysed more closely. But see the still useful Antonio Droetto, *Pasquale Stanislao Mancini e la scuola italiana di diritto internazionale del secolo XIX* (Milano: Giuffrè, 1954); Gian Savino Pene Vidari, *Storia del diritto in età medievale e moderna* (Torino: Giappichelli, 2019), 238–243.

86 Cf. Mura, *Mancini in cattedra*, 249.

87 Ibid.

88 Ibid. On the concept of the enemy in Vattel, see Michel Senellart, 'La qualification de l'ennemi chez Emer de Vattel', *Astérion* 2 (2004): 31–51; Gabriella Silvestrini, 'Justice, War and Inequality. The Unjust Aggressor and the Enemy of Human Race in Vattel's Theory of the Law of Nations', *Grotiana* 31 (2010): 44–68; Walter Rech, *Enemies of Mankind: Vattel's Theory of Collective Security* (Leiden: M. Nijhoff, 2013).

89 These shorthand lessons, however, are very important because they represent one of the rare testimonies of Mancini's full course; see Mura, *Mancini in cattedra*, 12. But see also Biblioteca Apostolica Vaticana, Rome, Italy, Fondo Patetta, Autografi e documenti, P. S. Mancini, 1856, which contains the texts of twenty-five lessons given by Mancini and transcribed by Di Iorio, *Ricerche su Pasquale Stanislao Mancini a Torino*, 135–431.

90 Mura, *Mancini in cattedra*, 177.

91 Ibid., 133.

> Do you believe that pity for Lombardy is the unique cause of the grudges that the peoples of all Italy feel for Austria? Or is it the continuous interventions that it has made to extinguish in them every small spark of freedom? Not only in these, but in all civilized nations a badly simulated cry and a curse against the future could arise against the thugs and dispossessors of every bad and formless government.[92]

4 By Way of Conclusion

From these brief notes it emerges how an important element of Mancini's thought, which came to the fore in the Turin lessons, was that of giving a new significance to the concept of the nation, thus counterbalancing the dominant theoretical importance that was attributed to the state. The prevalence of the concept of nation had meant that certain jurists, such as Vattel, had placed the concept of the state at the centre of their theoretical elaboration, a conceptual category also used to explain the formation of modern international law. Consequently, within these currents of thought, if the concept of the nation was defined, it appeared destined to be subordinated to that of the state and therefore in the terminological dialectic state–nation, the second was always put in the shade.[93]

Both Mancini and Vattel[94] saw the state and the nation as two distinct concepts but, whereas for the Swiss jurist the first had precedence over the second, for the Irpinian jurisconsult the idea of the nation came before that of the state. That is, Mancini completely overturned Vattel's perspective and, demonstrating that the nation would end up resolving itself legally in the state, defuse the revolutionary implications of the notion of the state.

It seems that we can exclude any influence of Giuseppe Mazzini from this discussion, since the republican option that was central to the Genoese intellectual meant that he was ignored by the 'textual circuits of the nineteenth-century jurists'.[95] As Federico Chabod pointed out, one could ask of Mazzini 'neither a treatise on the nation, nor a clear and precise plan of how to build

---

92 Ibid., 142.

93 See Colao, 'L'"idea di nazione"', 260.

94 In relation to this, see Frederick G. Whelan, 'Vattel's Doctrine of the State', *History of Political Thought* 9(1) (1988): 59–90; Ben Holland, 'The Moral Person of the State: Emer de Vattel and the Foundations of International Legal Order', *History of European Ideas* 37(4) (2011): 438–445.

95 Nuzzo, 'Da Mazzini a Mancini', 162.

[...] the United States of Europe. [...] But [...] for the nation, the ... theoretical, well-coordinated treatise, would be drafted by the jurist Pasquale Stanislao Mancini in 1851: not by Mazzini'.[96]

However, at this point some further reflections are necessary, since the conceptions of state and nation in Vattel and Mancini are divergent. The Swiss jurist became a target of Mancini because the *Droit des gens* was one of the theoretical bases of the Congress of Vienna, having been guilty of raising the concept of equilibrium to the level of a political system. The popularity that Vattel enjoyed within the major European diplomatic missions had to be discredited, by demonstrating his theoretical fragility.

But the notion that the state took precedence over the nation was actually the result of an opportunistic and subsequent interpretation of Vattel's work. Indeed, if we read the *Préliminaires* of the *Droit des gens* carefully, nation and state appear to coincide,[97] but for Mancini this equivalence, which had descended upon the nineteenth-century political scene, was not acceptable but had to be strongly criticized, since accepting it would have meant endorsing the idea that existing states should not undergo territorial changes. For him it became fundamentally important to develop a more fluid, broader concept of the nation, which is why he preferred to speak of nationality.

According to him, the nation was like a family[98] whose members, however, finding themselves scattered across several states, felt the urgent need to join together in the name of a series of characteristics that made them similar.[99] Nationality, according to Mancini, had to be transformed from a right to a 'legal duty', thus making it possible to obtain 'unity of territory'.[100] Therefore, by decontextualizing the *Droit des gens* – as indeed his political adversaries also did – he used it as an ideological tool to refute the theses of those who denied the relevance of the modern principle of nationality.[101]

These positions held by Mancini would evolve once the territorial unity of the Italian peninsula had been achieved in 1870, and would change again when he held the post of foreign minister, from 1881 to 1885. Contrary to what he had argued, he did not hesitate to sign the Triple Alliance in 1882, even though this

96 Chabod, 'Nazione ed Europa nel pensiero e nell'azione politica di Mazzini', 162; as the editor Marco Platania has clarified, at p. 7, this essay can be dated to the 1940s or 1950s.

97 Vattel, *Le Droit des gens*, 3–4.

98 Mancini, *Della nazionalità come fondamento del diritto delle genti*, 31.

99 Like origin, customs, language and above all social conscience, which are some distinctive features of nationality; see u = ibid., 41.

100 Ibid.

101 Moreover, as Italo Birocchi has written (in his essay 'Pasquale Stanislao Mancini e la cultura giuridica del Risorgimento', 59), for Mancini: 'teaching law was also doing politics'.

involved the Austro-Hungarian Empire, which had been the polemical target of his first two university courses in Turin; nor did he hesitate to drag the young Italian state into an adventurous colonial policy.[102]

Another point to emphasize is that Mancini's ideas had no utopian dimension.[103] His concept of nation was tied to a clear political objective pursued in his threefold role as a parliamentary deputy, teacher and lawyer: that of Italy's right to become a nation state. With the term 'nation', Mancini referred to a natural pre-state and pre-political society of men and to a right of peoples, whose binding elements were religion, race, language, traditions and laws, and above all the 'consciousness of nationality'.[104] These characteristics – which contributed to the creation of a profound 'commonality of law',[105] not to be found, for example, between individuals belonging to different nations – rendered superfluous the use of 'the artifices of a political pact or a social contract whose inevitable outcome was only a state subject with a strong authoritarian and oppressive purpose',[106] since, ultimately, the unity of a nation ran parallel with the unity of a state.[107]

The concept of the nation therefore stands at the centre of Mancini's reflection, the essence of which is found in the consciousness of nationality, which is expressed in a 'moral unity of a common thought, of a predominant idea that makes a society what it is, because it is realized in it'.[108] It is this 'spiritual element' that animates nationalities. Thus, following the thread of Mancini's reflections, we arrive at a fuller definition of the concept of nationality: 'a natural society of men [...] conformed to a commonality of life and social conscience'.[109] It follows that the development of nationality becomes for men not a right, but a legal duty. The Italian jurist's conclusions are of great interest since he ends up equating nationality on an individual level with human free-

102 On the idea that the Mancini of the 1850s and 1860s was very different from that of the 1880s, see Birocchi, 'Pasquale Stanislao Mancini e la cultura giuridica del Risorgimento', 26, 93–98; as well as Francesco Ruffini, 'Nel primo centenario della nascita di Pasquale Stanislao Mancini: 17 marzo 1817', *Nuova Antologia* 188 (marzo-aprile 1917), i–xvi.

103 Nuzzo, 'Da Mazzini a Mancini', 165, but see also Birocchi, 'Pasquale Stanislao Mancini e la cultura giuridica del Risorgimento', in particular 56–60.

104 Mancini, *Della nazionalità come fondamento del diritto delle genti*, 39.

105 Ibid., 32.

106 Nuzzo, 'Da Mazzini a Mancini', 165; on this negative view of the contractual solution see also the penetrating observations of Colao, 'L'"idea di nazione"', 258 ff.

107 After unification, however, in the 1870s the facts of the matter changed as the nation was depicted as depending on the state; see Colao, 'L'"idea di nazione"', 260.

108 Mancini, *Della nazionalità come fondamento del diritto delle genti*, 39.

109 Ibid., 41.

dom and, on a more general level, with the 'collective explication of freedom', it follows that nationality 'is as holy and divine a thing as freedom itself'.[110]

Archival Sources

Archivio Accademia delle Scienze di Torino (AAST), Turin, Italy, Fondo Carteggi, 26985.

Archivio Museo Nazionale del Risorgimento di Torino (AMNRIT), Turin, Italy, Archivi Storici, Fondo Petitti, 1080.

Biblioteca Apostolica Vaticana, Rome, Italy, Fondo Patetta, Autografi e documenti, P. S. Mancini, 1856.

Bibliography

Alberti, Manfredi, 'Petitti, Carlo Ilarione', *Dizionario Biografico degli Italiani* (Roma: Istituto dell'Enciclopedia Italiana, 2015), vol. 82, 659–662.

Atti del Parlamento subalpino, Sessione del 1850 dal 20 dicembre al 18 dicembre 1850 (IV Legislatura), collected and enhanced with notes and unpublished documents by Galletti Giuseppe and Trompeo Paolo (Torino: Tipografia Eredi Botta, 1863).

Balani, Donatella, *Toghe di Stato. La facoltà giuridica dell'Università di Torino e le professioni nel Piemonte del Settecento* (Torino: Deputazione Subalpina di Storia Patria, 1996).

Birocchi, Italo, 'Il *De iure belli* e l'"invenzione" del diritto internazionale, in *'Ius gentium ius communicationis ius belli': Alberico Gentili e gli orizzonti della modernità*, ed. Luigi Lacchè (Milano: Giuffrè, 2009), 101–138.

Birocchi, Italo, 'Pasquale Stanislao Mancini e la cultura giuridica del Risorgimento', in idem, *Per una rilettura di Mancini. Saggi sul diritto del Risorgimento*, ed. Italo Birocchi (Pisa: ETS, 2018), 19–119.

Birocchi, Italo, 'Presentazione', in *Per una rilettura di Mancini. Saggi sul diritto del Risorgimento*, ed. Italo Birocchi (Pisa: ETS, 2018), 11–17.

Bourlot, Alessandra, *Il Magistrato della Riforma dell'Università di Torino nel Settecento* (MA diss., Università degli Studi di Torino, 1991–1992).

Carle, Giuseppe, 'Pasquale Stanislao Mancini e la teoria psicologica del sentimento nazionale', *La Geografia. Rivista di propaganda geografica* 5 (1917).

Carpanetto, Dino, and Ricuperati Giuseppe, *L'Italia del settecento* (1st edition 1986; Roma: Laterza, 2008).

110 Ibid.

Casalena, Maria Pia, 'In Europa e ritorno. I congressi degli scienziati italiani tra modelli europei e via nazionale', *Mélanges de l'École française de Rome* 130(2) (2018): 273–283.

Casalena, Maria Pia, *Per lo Stato, per la Nazione. I congressi degli scienziati in Francia e in Italia (1830–1914)* (Roma: Carocci, 2007).

Cavour, Camillo, *Tutti gli scritti*, 4 vols, collected and edited by Carlo Pischedda and Giuseppe Talamo, with an introductory note by Pierangelo Gentile (Torino: Centro Studi Piemontesi, 2016, anastatic reprint of the original 1976 edition).

Cesare Balbo alle origini del cattolicesimo liberale, ed. Gabriele De Rosa and Francesco Traniello (Roma: Laterza, 1996).

Chabod, Federico, 'Nazione ed Europa nel pensiero e nell'azione politica di Mazzini', in idem, *Idea d'Europa e civiltà moderna. Sette saggi inediti*, ed. Marco Platania (Roma: Carocci, 2010), 151–170.

Chabod, Federico, *Storia della politica estera italiana dal 1870 al 1896. Le premesse* (Bari: Laterza, 1951).

Cittadinanze nella storia dello Stato contemporaneo, ed. Marcella Aglietti and Carmelo Calabrò (Milano: FrancoAngeli, 2017).

Colao, Floriana, 'L'"idea di nazione" nei giuristi italiani tra Ottocento e Novecento', *Quaderni fiorentini per la storia del pensiero giuridico moderno* 30 (2001): 255–360.

Constructing International Law: The Birth of a Discipline, ed. Luigi Nuzzo and Miloš Vec (Frankfurt am Main: Klostermann, 2012).

D'Aguirre, Francesco, *Della fondazione e ristabilimento degli studi generali in Torino*, ed. Municipio di Salemi (Palermo: Tip. Giannitrapani, 1901).

Dealbertis, Paola, 'I manoscritti di Augustin Cauchy dell'Archivio Faà di Bruno', in *Francesco Faà di Bruno. Ricerca scientifica insegnamento e divulgazione*, ed. Livia Giacardi (Torino: Deputazione Subalpina di Storia Patria, 2004), 627–638.

De Fort, Ester, *Esuli e migranti nel Regno sardo. Per una storia sociale e politica del Risorgimento* (Roma: Carocci; Torino: Istituto per la storia del Risorgimento italiano, Comitato di Torino, 2022).

De Rinaldis, Bartolomeo, *Su la vita e le opere di Pasquale Stanislao Mancini* (Napoli: Stabilimento tipografico dell'Unione, 1876).

Di Ciommo, Enrica, *La nazione possibile. Mezzogiorno e questione nazionale nel 1848* (Milano: FrancoAngeli, 1993).

Di Iorio, Paola, *Ricerche su Pasquale Stanislao Mancini a Torino* (PhD diss., Università di Torino, 1992–1993).

Di Simone, Maria Rosa, *Percorsi del diritto tra Austria e Italia (secoli XVII–XX)* (Milano: Giuffrè, 2006).

Droetto, Antonio, *Pasquale Stanislao Mancini e la scuola italiana di diritto internazionale del secolo XIX* (Milano: Giuffrè, 1954).

Fausto, Domenicantonio, 'Scialoja, Antonio', in *Dizionario Biografico degli Italiani* (Roma: Istituto dell'Enciclopedia Italiana, 2018), vol. 91, 526–530.

Ferrero, Ida, *Innovazione nella facoltà giuridica torinese. Didattica e docenti di metà Ottocento* (Torino: Deputazione Subalpina di Storia Patria, 2018).

Fiocchi Malaspina, Elisabetta, *L'eterno ritorno del* Droit des gens *di Emer de Vattel (secc. XVIII–XIX). L'impatto sulla cultura giuridica in prospettiva globale* (Frankfurt am Main: Max Planck Institute for European Legal History, 2017).

Firpo, Luigi, 'Gli anni torinesi', in *Pasquale Stanislao Mancini. L'uomo, lo studioso, il politico*, ed. Ortensio Zecchino and Giovanni Spadolini (Napoli: Guida, 1991), 139–156.

Frugiuele, Lorenzo, *La Sinistra e i cattolici. Pasquale Stanislao Mancini giurisdizionalista anticlericale* (Milano: Vita e Pensiero, 1985).

Genin, Vincent, 'Pasquale S. Mancini: du laboratoire juridique national à la Fabrique du droit international (1866–1869)', *Mélanges de l'École française de Rome* 130(2) (2018): 323–332.

Giannandrè, Rosanna, 'Mancini e l'ambiente degli esuli napoletani a Torino', in *Pasquale Stanislao Mancini. L'uomo, lo studioso, il politico*, ed. Ortensio Zecchino and Giovanni Spadolini (Napoli: Guida, 1991), 157–176.

Giannone, Pietro, *L'affaire Giannone face à l'Europe. Vie de Pietro Giannone, Profession de foi et Abjuration*, a selection of texts translated, annotated and commented by Gisela Schlüter and Giuseppe Ricuperati (Paris: Honoré Champion, 2019).

Gladstone, William Ewart, *Two Letters to the Earl of Aberdeen, on the State Prosecutions of the Neapolitan Government*, 3rd edition (London: John Murray, 1851).

Grotius, Pufendorf and the Natural Law Tradition, ed. Knud Haakonssen (Dartmouth: Dartmouth Publishing, 1998).

Haakonssen, Knud, 'Enlightenment and the Ubiquity of Natural Law', *Jahrbuch der Österreichischen Gesellschaft zur Erforschung des 18. Jahrhunderts* 27 (2012): 45–57.

Holland, Ben, 'The Moral Person of the State: Emer de Vattel and the Foundations of International Legal Order', *History of European Ideas* 37(4) (2011): 438–445.

Jayme, Erik, *Pasquale Stanislao Mancini. Internationales Privatrecht zwischen Risorgimento und praktischer Jurisprudenz* (Ebelsbach: Gremer, 1980).

Jouannet, Emmanuelle, *Emer de Vattel et l'émergence doctrinale du droit international classique* (Paris: Pedone, 1998).

Jouannet, Emmanuelle, 'Les dualismes du droit des gens', in *Le droit international de Vattel vu du XXIe siècle*, ed. Vincent Chetail and Peter Haggenmacher (Leiden: M. Nijhoff, 2011), 133–150.

Lacché, Luigi, 'Rossi, Pellegrino Luigi Edoardo', in *Dizionario Biografico degli Italiani* (Roma: Istituto della Enciclopedia Italiana, 2017), vol. 88, 696–702.

Levra, Umberto, 'L'esilio torinese di Pasquale Stanislao Mancini', in *Per la Costruzione dell'identità nazionale. Francesco De Sanctis e Pasquale Stanislao Mancini dalla provincia meridionale all'Europa*, ed. Renata De Lorenzo (Soveria Mannelli: Rubbettino, 2020), 31–59.

Levra, Umberto, 'Sella, Quintino', in *Dizionario Biografico degli Italiani* (Roma: Istituto dell'Enciclopedia Italiana, 2018), vol. 91, 809–814.

Lupi, Regina, *Francesco D'Aguirre. Riforme e resistenze nell'Italia del primo settecento* (Firenze: Centro Editoriale Toscano, 2011).

Mamiani, Terenzio, and Pasquale Stanislao Mancini, *Fondamenti della filosofia del diritto e singolarmente del diritto di punire. Lettere di Terenzio Mamiani e Pasquale Stanislao Mancini* (Livorno: Tipografia Vigo, 1875).

Mancini, Pasquale Stanislao, 'A' giureconsulti e Pubblicisti italiani' (1851), in idem, *Due scritti politici*, ed. Augusto Pierantoni (Roma: Società editrice Dante Alighieri, 1899), 1–102.

Mancini, Pasquale Stanislao, *Della nazionalità come fondamento del diritto delle genti. Prelezione al corso di diritto internazionale e marittimo pronunziata nella R. Università di Torino [...] nel dì 22 gennaio 1851* (Torino: Eredi Botta, 1851).

Mancini, Pasquale Stanislao, *Due scritti politici*, ed. Augusto Pierantoni (Roma: Società editrice Dante Alighieri, 1899).

Mancini, Pasquale Stanislao, 'Esame di un'opera di diritto internazionale pubblicata da Nicola Rocco', *Continuazione delle Ore solitarie – Biblioteca di scienze morali, legislative ed economiche*, issue 1 (1844): 10–30.

Mancini, Pasquale Stanislao, 'Notizia della vita e degli studi di Carlo Ilarione Petitti', in Carlo Ilarione Petitti di Roreto, *Del giuoco del lotto considerato ne' suoi effetti morali, politici ed economici: opera postuma* (Torino: Stamperia reale, 1853), v–xix.

'Mancini, Pasquale Stanislao', in *Dizionario Biografico degli Italiani* (Roma: Istituto dell'Enciclopedia Italiana, 2007), vol. 78, 537–547.

Mancini Pierantoni, Grazia, 'Alcune Lettere di P. S. Mancini', *Nuova Antologia* (1900): 313–328.

Marrara, Danilo, 'Pompeo Neri e la cattedra pisana di "diritto pubblico" nel XVIII secolo', *Rivista di storia del diritto italiano* 59 (1986): 173–202.

Mazzacane, Aldo, 'Università e scuole private di diritto a Napoli nella prima metà dell'Ottocento', in *Università in Europa. Le istituzioni universitarie dal Medio Evo ai nostri giorni: strutture, organizzazione, funzionamento*, ed. Andrea Romano (Soveria Mannelli: Rubbettino, 1995), 549–575.

Mellone, Viviana, *Napoli 1848. Il movimento radicale e la rivoluzione* (Milano: FrancoAngeli, 2017).

Mongiano, Elisa, 'Gli anni torinesi', in *Per una rilettura di Mancini. Saggi sul diritto del Risorgimento*, ed. Italo Birocchi (Pisa: ETS, 2018), 121–158.

Mongiano, Elisa, 'Pasquale Stanislao Mancini. Nazionalità e diritto internazionale all'Università di Torino', *Rivista Italiana per le scienze giuridiche* 4 (2013): 363–377.

Mor, Carlo Guido, *Storia dell'Università di Modena* (Modena: STEM, 1963).

Morelli, Emilia, *Tre profili. Benedetto XIV, Pasquale Stanislao Mancini, Pietro Roselli* (Roma: Edizioni dell'Ateneo, 1955).

Mura, Eloisa, *All'ombra di Mancini. La disciplina internazionalistica in Italia ai suoi albori* (Pisa: ETS, 2017).

Mura Eloisa, 'Aperture nazionali e nuovo regolamento degli studi all'indomani del Quarantotto', in *La Facoltà di Giurisprudenza dell'Università di Cagliari*, ed. Italo Birocchi (Pisa: ETS, 2018), 325–358.

Mura, Eloisa, *Mancini in cattedra. Le lezioni torinesi di diritto internazionale del 1850–51 e 1851–1852* (Pisa: ETS, 2018).

Mura, Eloisa, 'Pierantoni, Augusto Francesco', in *Dizionario Biografico degli Italiani* (Roma: Istituto dell'Enciclopedia Italiana, 2015), vol. 83, 291–294.

Nada, Narciso, 'La Restaurazione', in *L'Università di Torino. Profilo storico e istituzionale*, ed. Francesco Traniello (Torino: Pluriverso, 1993), 34–39.

Nishitani, Yuko, *Mancini und die Parteiautonomie im Internationalen Privatrecht: Eine Untersuchung auf der Grundlage der neu zutage gekommenen kollisionsrechtlichen Vorlesungen Mancinis* (Heidelberg: Universitätsverlag Winter, 2000).

Nuzzo, Luigi, 'Da Mazzini a Mancini: il principio di nazionalità tra politica e diritto', *Giornale di storia costituzionale* 14:2 (2007): 161–186.

Nuzzo, Luigi, 'La storia del diritto internazionale e le sfide del presente', *Quaderni fiorentini per la storia del pensiero giuridico moderno* 42 (2013): 683–701.

Pasquale Stanislao Mancini. L'uomo, lo studioso, il politico, ed. Ortensio Zecchino and Giovanni Spadolini (Napoli: Guida, 1991).

Pene Vidari, Gian Savino, 'Considerazioni sul contributo degli esuli risorgimentali al rinnovamento della facoltà giuridica torinese', *Rivista di storia del diritto italiano* 76 (2003): 1–26.

Pene Vidari, Gian Savino, 'Ideali e realismo, insegnamento e pratica giuridica: Luigi Amedeo Melegari', in *Lavorando al cantiere del 'Dizionario biografico dei giuristi italiani (XII–XX sec.)'*, ed. Maria Gigliola di Renzo Villata (Milano: Giuffrè, 2013), 275–323.

Pene Vidari, Gian Savino, 'La prolusione di Pasquale Stanislao Mancini sul principio di nazionalità (1851)', in *Retoriche dei giuristi e costituzione dell'identità nazionale*, ed. Giovanni Cazzetta (Bologna: Il Mulino, 2013), 117–134.

Pene Vidari, Gian Savino, 'Merlo, Felice', in *Dizionario Biografico degli Italiani* (Roma: Istituto dell'Enciclopedia Italiana, 2009), vol. 73, 718–721.

Pene Vidari, Gian Savino, 'Prospettive e contributi della facoltà giuridica per l'Unità', in *Dall'università di Torino all'Italia unita. Contributi dei docenti al Risorgimento e all'Unità*, ed. Clara Silvia Roero (Torino: Deputazione Subalpina di Storia Patria, 2013), 1–58.

Pene Vidari, Gian Savino, 'Sclopis, Federigo', in *Dizionario Biografico degli Italiani* (Roma: Istituto dell'Enciclopedia Italiana, 2018), vol. 91, 575–578.

Pene Vidari, Gian Savino, *Storia del diritto in età medievale e moderna* (Torino: Giappichelli, 2019).

Pene Vidari, Gian Savino, 'Un secolo e mezzo fa (22 gennaio 1851): la lezione torinese di Pasquale Stanislao Mancini sulla nazionalità', *Studi Piemontesi* 31:2 (2002): 273–285.

Pichetto, Maria Teresa, 'Cesare Alfieri di Sostegno e le riforme politiche e sociali nel Piemonte Carloalbertino', in *Alfieri di Sostegno tra Torino e Firenze*, ed. Cristina Vernizzi (Torino: Museo Nazionale del Risorgimento Italiano, 1997), 31–56.

Pinto, Carmine, *La guerra per il Mezzogiorno. Italiani, borbonici e briganti, 1860–1870* (Roma: Laterza, 2019).

Polenghi, Simonetta, *La politica universitaria italiana nell'età della Destra storica (1848–1876)* (Brescia: La Scuola, 1993).

Polsi, Alessandro, 'Nazione e cittadinanza. Pasquale Stanislao Mancini e i diritti civili degli stranieri', in *Cittadinanze nella storia dello Stato contemporaneo*, ed. Marcella Aglietti and Carmelo Calabrò (Milano: FrancoAngeli, 2017), 33–46.

Quazza, Guido, *Le riforme in Piemonte nella prima metà del Settecento* (Cavallermaggiore: Gribaudo, 1992).

Raccolta degli atti del governo di sua Maestà il re di Sardegna, vol. 18, *Dal 1° gennaio a tutto dicembre 1850, dal n.° 971 al 1125 bis* (Torino: Stamperia Reale, [1850]), 745–746.

Rech, Walter, *Enemies of Mankind: Vattel's Theory of Collective Security* (Leiden: M. Nijhoff, 2013).

Ricuperati, Giuseppe, 'Bernardo Andrea Lama professore e storiografo nel Piemonte di Vittorio Amedeo II', *Bollettino storico-bibliografico subalpino* 66(1–2) (1968): 11–101.

Ricuperati, Giuseppe, 'Campiani, Mario Agostino', in *Dizionario Biografico degli Italiani* (Roma: Istituto dell'Enciclopedia Italiana, 1974), vol. 17, 530–533.

Ricuperati, Giuseppe, 'L'Università di Torino e le polemiche contro i professori in una relazione di parte curialista del 1731', *Bollettino storico-bibliografico subalpino* 64(1) (1966), 341–374.

Romagnani, Gianpaolo, 'L'età napolenica', in *L'Università di Torino. Profilo storico e istituzionale*, ed. Francesco Traniello (Torino: Pluriverso, 1993), 28–32.

Romagnani, Gianpaolo, 'Maffei, Scipione', in *Dizionario Biografico degli Italiani* (Roma: Istituto dell'Enciclopedia Italiana, 2006), vol. 67, 256–263.

Ruffini, Francesco, 'Nel primo centenario della nascita di Pasquale Stanislao Mancini: 17 marzo 1817', *Nuova Antologia* 188 (marzo–aprile 1917), i–xvi.

Scipione Maffei nell'Europa del Settecento, ed. Gianpaolo Romagnani (Verona: Cierre, 1998).

Sclopis, Federico, *Dello studio e dell'applicazione delle leggi. Discorso detto dianzi all'eccellentissimo R. Senato di Piemonte nella solenne apertura dell'anno giuridico il dì 16 di novembre 1844* (Torino: Bocca, 1845).

Senellart, Michel, 'La qualification de l'ennemi chez Emer de Vattel', *Astérion* 2 (2004): 31–51.

Silvestrini, Gabriella, 'Justice, War and Inequality. The Unjust Aggressor and the Enemy of Human Race in Vattel's Theory of the Law of Nations', *Grotiana* 31 (2010): 44–68.

Silvestrini, Maria Teresa, *La politica della religione. Il governo ecclesiastico nello Stato sabaudo del XVIII secolo* (Firenze: Olschki, 1997).

Stella, Pietro, 'Casati, Michele', in *Dizionario Biografico degli Italiani* (Roma: Istituto dell'Enciclopedia Italiana, 1978), vol. 21, 262–265.

Storti Storchi, Claudia, *Ricerche sulla condizione giuridica dello straniero in Italia dal tardo diritto comune all'età preunitaria. Aspetti civilistici* (Milano: Giuffrè, 1989).

Symcox, Geoffrey, *Victor Amadeus II: Absolutism in the Savoyard State 1675–1730* (Berkeley, CA: University of California Press, 1983).

Ulvioni, Paolo, *'Riformar il mondo'. Il pensiero civile di Scipione Maffei*, with a new edition of the 'Consiglio Politico' (Alessandria: Edizioni dell'Orso, 2008).

Valabrega, Roberto, *Un anti-illuminista dalla cattedra alla porpora: Giacinto Sigismondo Gerdil professore, precettore a corte e cardinale* (Torino: Deputazione Subalpina di Storia Patria, 2004).

Vattel, Emer de, *Le Droit des gens ou principes de la loi naturelle* (A Londres, s.n., 1758).

Viarengo, Adriano, *Cavour* (Roma: Salerno, 2010).

Viarengo, Adriano, *Lorenzo Valerio. La terza via del Risorgimento, 1810–1865* (Roma: Carocci; Torino: Istituto per la storia del Risorgimento italiano, Comitato di Torino, 2019).

Viarengo, Adriano, 'Valerio, Lorenzo', in *Dizionario Biografico degli Italiani* (Roma: Istituto dell'Enciclopedia Italiana, 2020), vol. 98, 23–26.

Whelan, Frederick G., 'Vattel's Doctrine of the State', *History of Political Thought* 9(1) (1988): 59–90.

Woolf, Stuart, 'Reading Federico Chabod's Storia dell'idea d'Europa Half a Century Later', *Journal of Modern Italian Studies* 7(2) (2002): 269–292.

Zanardelli, Giuseppe, *In memoria di Pasquale Stanislao Mancini* (Napoli: Tipografia Melfi e Joele, 1911).

CHAPTER 10

The Law of International Love: Luigi Taparelli d'Azeglio on Catholic Natural Law and the Law of Nations

Francesca Iurlaro

1 Introduction

The Italian Jesuit Luigi Taparelli d'Azeglio (1793–1862) has been given wide and diverse scholarly attention over decades. Although his fame has been perhaps overshadowed by that of his brother, the Italian patriot Massimo d'Azeglio, Taparelli's role as a prominent intellectual of Italian Catholic conservativism, as well as his direct contribution to Catholic social thinking, has been widely acknowledged by scholars.[1]

In addition to this rather well known aspect of Taparelli's legacy, recent studies have cast a new light on his merits as a natural law theorist. According to Merio Scattola, indeed, Taparelli deserves particular notice in the history of European natural law, because of his efforts at assimilating Protestant natural law theories into Catholic thinking. It is quite odd, one might think, that a champion of Italian Catholicism resorted to Protestant doctrines of *ius naturae* to reform Catholic natural law – a branch of moral and legal reflection whose delayed development on the Italian peninsula, as Scattola observed, was striking in comparison with other European countries.[2]

1 Robert Jacquin, *Taparelli* (Paris: P. Lethielleux, 1943); *Miscellanea Taparelli. Raccolta di studi in onore di Luigi Taparelli D'Azeglio nel primo centenario della morte*, ed. Pio Cipriotti and José M. Diez Alegria (Roma: Edizioni dell'Università Gregoriana, 1964); Gianfranco Morra, *La dottrina sociale della Chiesa* (Milano: Scuola di dottrina sociale, 1988); Luigi Di Rosa, *Luigi Taparelli. L'altro d'Azeglio* (Milano: Cisalpino, 1991); Giampaolo Dianin, *Luigi Taparelli d'Azeglio (1793–1862): il significato della sua opera, al tempo del rinnovamento neoscolastico, per l'evoluzione della teologia morale* (Milano: Ed. Glossa, 2000); Thomas C. Behr, *Social Justice and Subsidiarity: Luigi Taparelli and the Origins of Modern Catholic Social Thought* (Washington, DC: Catholic University of America Press, 2019); *Catholic Social Teaching: A Volume of Scholarly Essays*, ed. Gerald V. Bradley and E. Christian Brugger (Cambridge: Cambridge University Press, 2019).

2 Merio Scattola, 'Protestantesimo e diritto naturale cattolico nel XVIII secolo', in *Illuminismo e Protestantesimo*, ed. Giulia Cantarutti and Stefano Ferrari (Milano: Angeli, 2010); Merio

DOI:10.1163/9789004685130_012

As a matter of fact, Taparelli's interpretation of Protestant natural law has a precise programmatic intent. Taparelli thought that only by engaging in a direct discussion of Protestant authors was it possible to rise to the challenge posed by the new values of liberalism. Along these lines, he believed that a modernized version of Catholic natural law (focused more on social solidarity than on its secularizing aspects) was going to provide a valuable framework to address those challenges. In fact, whereas Protestant natural law was excessively, or, rather, exclusively, relying on right reason as a source of obligation for natural law, Taparelli maintained that it was time that faith and revelation fitted into the natural law equation again. His *Saggio teoretico di diritto naturale appoggiato sul fatto* (1840–1843)[3] thus constitutes a fundamental text that bears witness to this transformation and, more generally, provides evidence of a crucial, transitional moment in the history of the reception of Protestant natural law theories in Italy.

In this chapter, I will address the question of Taparelli's reprise of the Protestant natural law tradition. Reacting against several attempts to resurrect Thomism within the Jesuit order,[4] Taparelli suggested looking at the Protestant natural law tradition instead and, as it were, fighting the enemy from within. However, while Scattola thought that Taparelli's turn to the Protestant tradition was a progressive stance to modernize the 'backwardness' of natural law on the Italian peninsula, I argue that there is more to Taparelli's enterprise than this. More specifically, in seeking to integrate Protestant sources and themes in his doctrine of natural law, Taparelli wanted to address a much more compelling issue: how could love and divine grace become the object of legal obligation, while still leaving freedom as a fundamental feature of human life and, more specifically, of the social life of Catholics?

I will address this question by looking at Taparelli's interesting reception of two crucial authors: Christian Wolff and Francisco Suárez. From this perspective, the originality of Taparelli's contribution consists in correcting Wolff's doctrine with that of a far more orthodox author of the Catholic natural law tradition, Francisco Suárez. In my view, first, Taparelli's aim is to reinvent the

---

Scattola, *Prinzip und Prinzipienfrage in der Entwicklung des modernen Naturrechts* (Stuttgart: Frommann-Holzboog, 2017), 183–238.

3 Luigi Taparelli, *Saggio teoretico di diritto naturale appoggiato sul fatto. Opera corretta ed accresciuta dall'autore*, 5 vols (Palermo: Muratori, 1840–1843; later editions Livorno 1845; Napoli 1850, 2 vols; Roma 1855, 2 vols).

4 On Taparelli and Thomism, see Francesco Dante, 'Tomismo e neotomismo a confronto nella *Rerum Novarum*', in Rerum Novarum: *Écriture, contenu, et réception d'une encyclique* (Roma: École Française, 1997), 91–105; Giovanni Vian, 'Luigi Taparelli d'Azeglio', in *Il contributo italiano alla storia del pensiero: storia e politica* (Treccani, 2013, http://www.treccani.it/enciclopedia/luigi-taparelli-d-azeglio_%28altro%29 (accessed January 2023).

language of Catholic natural law by borrowing Wolff's already existing theory and make it more appealing and authoritative to his students and readers, by directly engaging with one of the most systematic authors, and yet one that was 'easily' translatable in Catholic terms. In search for a foundation for natural law, Taparelli acknowledged that Suárez's concept of divine grace did not offer a compelling foundation for universal justice, as love is not something that can be imposed as a divine command but is only recommended by God. If there was a duty to love, people would not be free in the exercise of their will and, potentially, everything they would do 'for love' could be attributed to God. Taparelli perceives this as a problem and, instead, implicitly relies on Wolff to provide the duty to universal love (a typically Wolffian concept) as a foundation for universal justice. As I will show, however, Taparelli himself seems reluctant at times to fully acknowledge love as a foundation for legal obligation. The fact that this ambiguity could pose a threat to Catholic orthodoxy was perceived as difficult already by Taparelli's superiors. Despite these ambiguities, Taparelli managed to create a compelling doctrine of international order, by replacing the 'duty' to love, which was hardly enforceable, with a more general and passive 'debt of love' that nations have towards each other.

This chapter consists of three main parts. In the next section I assess Taparelli's scholarly and intellectual intentions. I then explain the reasons behind the choice of Christian Wolff as the main vector of Taparelli's assimilation of Protestant into Catholic natural law. I claim that Taparelli makes use of the Wolffian concepts of *perfectio*, *consensus* and *concursus* as meeting points between the two traditions of Protestantism and Catholic theology. Furthermore, he consistently adjusts Protestant natural law by adding elements of the doctrines of Francisco Suárez, the early modern champion of the Jesuit tradition of *ius naturae et gentium*. In the following section I show how these choices impact on Taparelli's reframing of international order and just war.

2 Taparelli: A Jesuit and Public Intellectual Facing the Challenges of Modernity

Prospero d'Azeglio Taparelli was born in Turin in 1793.[5] He belonged to a Piedmontese aristocratic family: his father, Cesare, was active in the Napoleonic

5 On the Piedmontese context, see Mario Riberi, 'I Taparelli d'Azeglio durante l'età napoleonica', in *'Une très-ancienne famille piémontaise'. I Taparelli negli stati Sabaudi*, Quaderni del Dipartimento di Giurisprudenza dell'Università di Torino, 13, ed. Enrico Genta, Andrea Pennini and Davide De Franco (Milano: Ledizioni, 2019), 113–138.

Wars and, once the French took Piedmont, moved with his family to Florence, where he founded *L'Ape*, one of the first Catholic magazines of the peninsula;[6] then, in 1807, a royal decree forced his family to go back to Turin. In 1809, Prospero was supposed to join, under a Napoleonic decree, the Saint Cyr military school, but he was subsequently relieved from attendance, as a result of his father's influential political connections with the pope. He then moved to Rome and in 1814 joined the recently restored Society of Jesus,[7] and changed his name to Luigi. Taparelli then became rector of the Jesuit collegium in Novara, and from 1824 to 1829 of Collegio Romano in Rome; after a period in Naples, he became a teacher at Collegio Massimo in Palermo (1833–1850). Sicily became, thus, his elective home.[8] In 1850, he founded the influential magazine *La civiltà cattolica*, which is still published today.

Taparelli witnessed the troubles the Society of Jesus was facing at the dawn of modernity: what role should Catholics have in contemporary society? How could the recently restored Jesuit order react against the dangers of individualism and liberalism?[9] Later interpreters such as Antonio Gramsci have condemned the politicization of Catholics as, paradoxically, an extreme form of secularization that was going to have a huge impact on Italian society.[10] Irrespective of the accuracy of this historical reconstruction, the Jesuits were clearly trying to fill a void in post-Restoration Italy, as witnessed by the so-called 'apostasy of masses'[11] and by the increasing absence of religion from

6 Ibid., 132–133.

7 The Society of Jesus was suppressed in Portugal, France and Spain in 1773 (in notable contrast with Russia, where the movement had unexpected growth). See *Morte e resurrezione di un Ordine religioso. Le strategie culturali ed educative della Compagnia di Gesù durante la soppressione (1759–1814)*, ed. Paolo Bianchini (Milano: Vita e Pensiero, 2006); *The Jesuit Suppression in Global Context: Causes, Events, and Consequences*, ed. Jeffrey D. Burson and Jonathan Wright (Cambridge: Cambridge University Press, 2015); Dale K. Van Kley, *Reform Catholicism and the International Suppression of the Jesuits in Enlightenment Europe* (New Haven, CT: Yale University Press, 2019). For the Italian context, see Giacomo Martina, *Storia della Compagnia di Gesù in Italia (1814–1983)* (Brescia: Morcelliana, 2003).

8 See Luigi Taparelli, *Legge fondamentale d'organizzazione nella società*, in G. De Rosa, *I gesuiti in Sicilia e la Rivoluzione del '48: con documenti sulla condotta della Compagnia di Gesù e scritti inediti di Luigi Taparelli d'Azeglio* (Roma: Edizioni di Storia e Letteratura, 1963), 169; Gabriele De Rosa, 'Luigi Taparelli d'Azeglio e i moti del '48 in Sicilia', in *Miscellanea Taparelli*, 115–128.

9 See Benedetto Croce's enduring historiographic analysis in *Storia d'Europa nel secolo decimonono* (Bari: Laterza, 1932); quoted in Fulvio de Giorgi, *Cattolici ed Educazione tra Restaurazione e Risorgimento: Ordini religiosi* (Milano: ISU Università Cattolica, 1999), 17–18.

10 Ibid., 23–24.

11 Antonio Gramsci, *Quaderni del Carcere* (Torino: Einaudi, 1975), vol. 3, 2086.

social life. As we shall see, Taparelli's reprise of natural law was instrumental in the creation of a new vocabulary of social justice capable of making sense of modernity. This vocabulary would ideally bridge the 'liberal' gap between individuals and God by acknowledging, rather, religion as the ultimate *telos* of society. Taparelli's project was a successful one, according to Scattola, precisely because it 'replied to modernity with modernity'.[12] Criticizing Johannes Messner's thesis that Catholic social thinking was born as a reaction against liberalism, Scattola has claimed that it was, rather, a reaction against Protestantism and that this was visible from the language, agendas and argumentative structures used by authors such as Taparelli.[13] This intellectual innovation, voiced by Taparelli's project of emending natural law, would eventually, after 1848, enable Catholics to participate on an equal footing in debates with liberals and socialists.[14]

But this renewed, fervid engagement of Jesuits in society's most controversial questions attracted its critics. One of the most ferocious was Vincenzo Gioberti, the Turinese clergyman, philosopher and author of *Del primato morale degli Italiani* (1843), in which he vindicated the historical importance and civilizational mission of the Italian nation. Although Taparelli was initially on good terms with Gioberti, their relationship started to creak under the weight of Gioberti's acrimonious critique of modern Jesuitism, as expressed in his long essay *Il Gesuita Moderno* (1846). Condemning any attempt at resurrecting the order, Gioberti saw Jesuits as the enemies of civilization altogether. Furthermore, Gioberti criticized the Jesuits' blind subjection to Church authority, while directly accusing Taparelli of confusing the duty to obey superiors with the general, prudential principle of agreeing with the ideas of the wisest.[15] Gioberti is here quoting a letter that Taparelli wrote to him on 15 June 1845, where he says that a peculiar trait of Jesuits is docility: this consists 'not so much in stating things one does not believe in, but rather in thinking according to the opinions of the wisest. When the Institute exhorts us to

---

12 Scattola, 'Protestantesimo e diritto naturale cattolico nel XVIII secolo', 133.

13 See also Johannes Messner, 'Die Erfahrung in der Naturrechtslehre von Taparelli', in *Miscellanea Taparelli*, 303–304.

14 Ibid.

15 Vincenzo Gioberti, *Il Gesuita Moderno* (Losanna, 1846), vol. 2, 116–117: 'e però, ottime Padre Taparelli, io non posso concedervi che l'uso inculcato ai Gesuiti e specialmente ai novizi di sottoporre l'intelletto ai superiori nelle cose che spettano alla Compagnia, e in quelle massime, che sono di maggior rilievo, e però s'intrecciano più strettamente co' suoi interessi, sia un pensare secondo il parere dei più savi, e quindi possa stimarsi un atto di perfezione'.

subject our intellect to it, it does not do so to induce us to commit an act of simulation, but, rather, an act of perfection'.[16] Furthermore, Gioberti accused the Jesuits of pantheism. By acknowledging that God actively concurs in the realization of good acts, they secured their Catholic orthodoxy; nonetheless, they also acknowledged the primacy of human reason and will when it comes to moral deliberation and, by so doing, they 'give man the dignity of a first cause'.[17] This is pivotal in Taparelli's reflection on natural law, as it calls into question the relationship between grace and freedom, as we shall see.

Apart from theological reasons, there was also political scepticism behind this hatred for Jesuits, as their conservativism was perceived as a threat to Italian liberation movements. However, as a matter of fact, Taparelli and his fellow Jesuits joined revolutionary sides during the uprisings taking place in Palermo in 1848. Gabriele De Rosa has highlighted the uniqueness of this event, which was seen as such already by contemporary observers. Nevertheless, as the liberal movement was gaining momentum on the peninsula, Gioberti criticized the Jesuit involvement in the revolutionary cause. In his view, after the order was suppressed, the Jesuits were so afraid of disappearing from the social and political scene that their involvement in revolutionary uprisings was nothing but an instance of crass political opportunism.[18]

On the other hand, one of Taparelli's fellow Jesuits in Palermo, Giuseppe Romano, vindicated the primacy of the Jesuits' pedagogical mission to voice revolutionary ideas. Interestingly, he argued, many of those ideas were made available to students precisely through the teaching of natural law. In sum, revolutionary Sicilians owe their intellectual independency to Jesuits:

> weren't the Jesuits those who, when no university was teaching natural law, in compliance with Maria Carolina's decree forbidding it, weren't they the ones that re-opened natural law chairs and invited students to discussion? If the Jesuit institution was really that retrograde and

16 Ibid., 118: '[…] non già nell'affermare ciò che non si pensa, ma nel pensare, secondo il parere dei più savi. Quando adunque l'Instituto ci esorta a sottoporre l'intelletto, ci esorta ad un atto di perfezione, non già ad un atto di simulazione'. The 'Institute' is the Society of Jesus.

17 Ibid., 459: 'Riconoscendo nell'azione di Dio il principio occasionale e cooperante dell'atto buono, evitano l'errore proscritto e si mantengono cattolici. Ma non è men vero che collocando nell'uomo il principio determinante delle sue deliberazioni virtuose, lo investono di dignità di cagion prima'. Also, Gioberti strongly criticizes Christian Wolff: having him as a pupil was the worst disgrace that could happen to Leibniz (239).

18 De Rosa, *I gesuiti in Sicilia e la rivoluzione del '48*, 10.

> conservative, how come so many of its former students nowadays have dissenting ideas?[19]

In Romano's portrait, Jesuits were teaching free thinking rather than intellectual subordination to the Church's educational, moral and social authority. Furthermore, natural law seemed to play a crucial role in providing students with such tools of intellectual emancipation. That the language of natural law was to give Catholics a new political vocabulary was very clear to Taparelli as well, and his *Saggio* rapidly became popular in Jesuit colleges and started being adopted as a textbook in many Italian universities. The question was, however, in what ways such political language was to be constructed to enhance social cohesion rather than to disrupt it. As a matter of fact, unlike Romano and his moderate attempt at modernizing the pedagogic mission of the Jesuit order and reconcile it with Gioberti's invocation to Italian independence, Taparelli, as we shall see, had a much more cautious position on the issue, and was in general less enthusiastic about the role of natural law in voicing those kinds of disruptive claims.

Indeed, Taparelli did not think of national unification as the ultimate goal nor as the starting point of society. The state is just an organism that ensures and guarantees social development,[20] as he claimed in his famous *Della nazionalità* (On Nationality), which was printed in 1847 unbeknown to Taparelli himself.[21] This short essay was supposed to be added to the new edition of the *Saggio*, and it was not meant to be published as a separate piece.

---

19 'Non furon essi che mentre le università tacevano ancora sui principi del diritto naturale proscritto dalle scuole per decreto di Maria Carolina, ne riapersero le cattedre e v'invitarono alla discussione? Se l'istituzione gesuitica fosse stata intrinsecamente conservatrice e retrograda, si troverebbero oggi in sì gran numero usciti dalle loro scuole che pensano diversamente?' Giuseppe Romano, 'La causa dei gesuiti in Sicilia', 1848, reprinted in De Rosa, *I gesuiti in Sicilia*, 259. The reference to Maria Carolina of Austria probably concerns the removal of Bernardo Tanucci from the chair of law in Pisa. See Emanuele Salerno, '*Stare pactis* and Neutrality. Grotius and Pufendorf in the Political Thought of the Early Eighteenth Century Grand Duchy of Tuscany', in *War, Trade and Neutrality: Europe and the Mediterranean in the Seventeenth and Eighteenth Centuries*, ed. Antonella Alimento (Milano: Angeli, 2011), 188–202, at 191. On teaching of natural law in the Jesuit collegia, see Emma Abbate, 'Luigi Taparelli d'Azeglio e l'istruzione nei collegi gesuitici del XIX secolo', *Archivio Storico per le Province Napoletane* 115 (1997): 467–516.

20 Gabriele De Rosa, *I gesuiti in Sicilia*, 23; 'Lettera di Taparelli a Roberto d'Azeglio', Palermo, 28 January 1847, in *Carteggi del p. Taparelli d'Azeglio*, ed. Pietro Pirri (Torino: Fratelli Bocca, 1933), 205–208.

21 Luigi Taparelli, *Della nazionalità. Breve scrittura del p. Luigi Taparelli d'Azeglio, rivista e accresciuta notabilmente dall'autore con una risposta del medesimo alle osservazioni di Vincenzo Gioberti* (Genova: Tip. F.lli Ponthenier, 1847). On the Italian debate on nation-

As a result, Taparelli's essay was misinterpreted as supporting Austrian dominion against Italian independence. In a letter to his brother, Taparelli expresses his concern that his political message is being deliberately misconstrued by his critics. He is also worried that application of natural law to concrete facts can be a double-edged sword, as general principles have different applications depending on the facts they refer to: indeed, 'national questions should be reduced to principles of universal justice, and to the facts that make those principles concrete'.[22] What are these principles of universal justice', then, and on what intellectual and religious foundations do they rest?

3 Wolff versus Suárez: Love as Law?

Taparelli often makes clear in his *Saggio*, and elsewhere, that the most fundamental aim of his book is 'to take Burlamaqui, Romagnosi and Bentham, and other similarly poisonous authors, away from the hands of young students'.[23] In the Introduction to the first edition, of 1840, Taparelli vindicates a new metaphysical foundation for the science of natural law, which he, with a distinctively Hegel-like flair, defines as 'the science of the human heart in its long and dangerous journey from the shrine of individual conscience, to the structures of the social architecture it helps to build and sustain'.[24] It is necessary to combine philosophical empiricism and spiritualism into a new metaphysics capable of including facts within theory, rather than just focusing on one or the other exclusively.

Taparelli mentions the fundamental contribution of the French philosopher Victor Cousin in elaborating what he refers to as the *novella metafisica*.[25] Such metaphysics is an eclectic amalgam of doctrines, combining English and French empiricism[26] with German spiritualism, one that perfectly reflects

---

ality, see Fabio Di Giannatale, 'Il principio di nazionalità. Un dibattito dell'Italia Risorgimentale', *Storia e Politica* 6(2) (2014): 234–269. See also Chapter 9 of the present volume, by Frédéric Ieva.

22 'Lettera di Taparelli a Massimo', 25 April 1847, in *Carteggi*, 235: 'le quistioni nazionali debbono ridursi ai principi di giustizia universale, ed ai fatti con cui questa vien concretata: né è lecito oltraggiar la giustizia nelle nazioni steaniere, come non è lecito negli individui'.

23 'Lettera di Taparelli a Roothan', Palermo, 13 February 1842, in *Carteggi*, 120. The references are to Jean-Jacques Burlamaqui, Gian Domenico Romagnosi, and Jeremy Bentham.

24 Taparelli, *Saggio teoretico di diritto naturale appoggiato sul fatto*, vol. 1, viii.

25 Ibid.

26 Taparelli writes that Locke is the father of empiricism (ibid., v). For the interpretation of Locke as the ideal predecessor of Cousin, see Pasquale Galluppi, *Lezioni di Logica e Metafisica, Prima edizione livornese* (Livorno: Mazzajoli, 1854), vol. 1, 50–51.

the inherent diversity of human nature.[27] Whereas the spiritualists insist on focusing on the primacy of human reason over passions, empiricism does the opposite. Only eclecticism can combine the two elements and, 'while acknowledging the primacy of human reason, it will neither forget nor blame human passions'. Accordingly, Taparelli concludes, 'this is the kind of moral theory we support and develop in these pages'.[28]

From this perspective, authors such as Burlamaqui and Johann Gottlieb Heineccius were potentially dangerous because their works were nothing but the expression of 'decadent sensism', according to Taparelli's evocative formulation. In his view, Protestant natural law was either thinking of human life and reason as totally detached from the life of facts and from the structures of social life, or vice versa. Additionally, it lacked a teleological orientation towards good and moral perfection – in other words, God was the great, cumbersome absence from natural law (or was, at least, declared as such) ever since Grotius's famous *etsi Deus non daretur.*

Taparelli's strategic use of Christian Wolff as a source for his *Saggio* is an interesting example of how the history of the reception of natural law theories is one of constant hybridization of sources, which are adjusted, deconstructed and reassembled to make sense of the world in a creative yet normatively meaningful way. Although Taparelli denies being a follower of any philosophical innovation or system in particular,[29] scholars have identified Wolff's impact on Taparelli's theory of natural law.[30] Wolff, however, seems to be an occasional and implicit source in Taparelli's texts – he is barely mentioned explicitly. But why precisely Wolff, and in what does the impact of his theory consist? Is it possible to retrace such influence on Taparelli or did Wolffian interpreters overemphasize the scope and significance of the German philosopher's legacy? Why would Taparelli resort to a follower of Leibniz, with all the

27 For a discussion of Cousin's eclecticism, see Michael Albrecht, *Eklektik. Eine Begriffsgechichte mit Hinweisen auf die Philosophie- und Wissenschaftsgeschichte* (Stuttgart: Frommann-Holzboog, 1994), 605–625.

28 Taparelli, *Saggio teoretico*, vol. 1, ix.

29 Ibid., vi.

30 According to Thomann, 'car à n'en pas douter Taparelli doit beaucoup à Wolff. Au point qu'il n'est guère possible de déterminer une différence doctrinale notable entre les deux auteurs'. See M. Thomann, 'Introduction', in Christian Wolff, *Gesammelte Werke*, II (Hildesheim: Olms, 1962), vol. 25, xlvii. See also Dagmar von Wille, 'La fortuna delle opere di Christian Wolff in Italia nella prima metà del Settecento: la prima edizione veronese degli *Opera Latina*', *Rivista di Storia della Filosofia* 50(2) (1995): 369–400, at 391; E. Midgley, *The Natural Law Tradition and the Theory of International Relations* (London: Elek, 1975), 202–207.

theological implications of such a choice, to rethink the foundations of natural law? Is not such a move not only counterintuitive but also distinctively anti-Catholic (think of Leibniz's doctrine of pre-established harmony)?

But before turning to the discussion of divine grace and the duty to love, it is also important to emphasize Taparelli's epistemic interest in reviving Suárez's and Wolff's philosophy, against the 'decadent sensism' of the Protestants:

> Some will find it odd that we would include the name of Suárez among those of natural law theorists. The widely shared view on the issue is, rather, that the science of natural law was created by Protestants such as Grotius, Pufendorf, etc. This blunder was generated by confusing the *creation* of this science with its *isolation*. It is true that, before these authors' contributions, the laws of natural morality where mostly taught together with Christian moral doctrines by theologians, who showed the overlap and the distinctions among the two aspects accordingly. In doing so, they used a method that was generally used back in those times. Such a method refused to isolate entirely one discipline from the other: furthermore, this system is extremely close to the nature of the truth, which is to be conceived essentially as a whole. The analytical need gradually forced interpreters to divide human knowledge into separate disciplines. Perhaps superficiality in research and disaffection for intellectual fatigue have made their way also into the heart of Catholics. Instead, for Protestants, such division was utterly necessary. In fact, since they conceded to every man the right to interpret the Gospel according to their own judgement, they were compelled to create a moral system that was independent from the Gospel, as those who judge shall not depend on those who are judged. They did this so well, that the Gospel became an unnecessary book to them. [...] Hence, the fact that Suárez was an eminent theologian does not prevent him from being admired as a profound political philosopher.[31]

For Taparelli, Suárez provided an example of epistemic unity, against the Protestant analytical tendency to separate different branches of human knowledge to construct an independent system of morality. Interestingly,

31 Taparelli, *Saggio teoretico*, vol. 2, 185–186.. Thomas Behr claims that social justice, subsidiarity and solidarity (all tenets of Taparelli's theoretical enterprise) are 'an anthropologically corrected borrowing from Pufendorf', gesturing towards the natural law tradition of *socialitas*. See Thomas C. Behr, 'Luigi Taparelli on the Dignity of Man', in *Congresso Tomista Internazionale: L'umanesimo cristiano nel terzo millennio: prospettiva di Tommaso d'Aquino* (Roma: Pontificia Accademia di San Tommaso, 2004), 1–7, at 3.

Wolff's philosophy presents a similar view of knowledge as an interconnected system held together by metaphysics. From this perspective, and against Scattola's thesis of the 'backwardness' of Catholic natural law, Taparelli does not seem to think of Suárez's doctrines as retrograde. Instead, he argues that the 'analytical' mind is a tendency to which even his contemporary fellow Catholics are falling victim ('superficiality in research and disaffection for intellectual labour have made their way also into the heart of Catholics'), one that was exogenous to Suárez's theological and political doctrines.

However, as many have observed, one of the most important innovations of Wolff consisted in the primacy he gave to psychology. Unlike Suárez, Wolff believed that 'the soul and its affections are objects of metaphysics'.[32] The importance of psychology not only to understand Wolff's system but, generally, as a crucial part of the theory of natural law is emphasized by Taparelli himself.[33] Rational and empirical psychology become fundamental tools to understand the motives behind human action and to provide a foundation for the obligation of natural law accordingly. Such a foundation relies upon the concept of *perfectio*, also explicitly deployed by Taparelli in his *Saggio*.[34]

---

32 See Christian Wolff, *Psychologia Empirica methodo scientifica pertractata, qua ea, quae de anima humana indubia experientiae fide constant, continentur et ad solidam universae philosophiae practicae ac theologiae naturalis tractationem via sternitur* (Frankfurt, 1732). Christian Leduc, 'Sources of Wolff's Philosophy: Scholastics/Leibniz', in *Handbuch Christian Wolff*, ed. Robert Theis and Alexander Aichele (Wiesbaden: Springer, 2018), 43. Leduc claims this is a rather anti-Suárezian move by Wolff. See also Carlo Fantappié, *Chiesa Romana e Modernità Giuridica*, vol. 2 (Milano: Giuffré 2008); Alexander Hollerbach, 'Das christliche Naturrecht im Zusammenhang des allgemeinen Naturrechtsdenkens', in *Naturrecht in der Kritik*, ed. Franz Böckle and Ernst-Wolfgang Böckenförde (Mainz: Grünewald, 1973), 9–38; as for Taparelli's defence of scholasticism against accusations of rationalism, see 'Lettera di Taparelli a Bonetty', Palermo, 1848, in *Carteggi*, 248–260.

33 See Taparelli, 'Introduzione', in *Saggio teoretico*, vol. 1, vi; Luigi Cataldi Madonna, 'Il connubio della ragione con l'esperienza come fondamento e scopo del programma filosofico wolffiano', in *La filosofia pratica tra metafisica e antropologia nell'età di Wolff e Vico*, ed. Giuseppe Cacciatore et al. (Napoli: Guida, 1999), 111–129; Claes Petersen, 'What Has Logic Got To Do With It? On the Use of Logic in Christian Wolff's Theory of Natural Law', *Scandinavian Studies in Law* 48 (2005): 310–320; Thomas Kleinlein, 'Christian Wolff: System as an Episode?', in *System, Order and International Law: The Early History of International Thought from Machiavelli to Hegel*, ed. Stefan Kadelbach, Thomas Kleinlein and David Roth-Isigkeit (Oxford: Oxford University Press, 2017), 216–239; Ferdinando L. Marcolungo, 'Christian Wolff e il progetto di una psicologia filosofica', in *Christian Wolff tra psicologia empirica e razionale: atti del convegno internazionale di studi Verona, 13–14 maggio 2005*, ed. idem (Hildesheim: Olms, 2007), 15–34.

34 According to Christian Leduc, in a clear departure from Leibniz, Wolff conceived of predestination as only a 'metaphysical hypothesis', in order not to endanger free will and to

In the following I will explain the importance of *perfectio* in relation to two other key concepts used by Wolff (and, later on, by Vattel)[35] and implicitly adopted by Taparelli: *consensus* and *concursus*. As far as *consensus* is concerned, Wolff claims that the aim of the intellect and the will is to be in agreement with each other, and therefore to tend towards *perfectio*, that is, moral good. The more they are in agreement with each other, the more intellect and will are *consentanei* to ('in agreement with') nature. Additionally, human beings must take care that their own actions are free and, in this respect, have an obligation 'to perform intrinsically good actions'.[36] Indeed, such harmonious agreement among faculties creates *consensus*, which is a tendency of both the sensitive and the intellectual faculty towards the same object.[37] *Perfectio*, thus, is the core of Wolff's moral and legal theory and it has multiple meanings: (1) *consensus* of different faculties, as we already pointed out; (2) the purpose of human nature; and (3) the criterion for good moral action – good is what makes us perfect.[38]

The harmonious agreement among faculties left unexplained why it is so important, and yet so difficult, as we experience from daily life, to achieve such *consensus* between reason and will. To overcome this potential dichotomy, Wolff relies on the theory of *concursus*, a multi-layered, pervasive concept used by Wolff to explain why and how we get from *consensus* to *perfectio*.

---

prevent accusations of necessitarianism (Leduc, 'Sources of Wolff's Philosophy', 49). Also, concerning Wolff's admiration of the Jesuits, see Daniel Purdy, 'Chinese Ethics within the Radical Enlightenment: Christian Wolff', in *The Radical Enlightenment in Germany: A Cultural Perspective*, ed. Carl Niekerk (Leiden: Brill, 2018), 112–130, at 123.

35 See Francesca Iurlaro, 'Vattel's Doctrine of the Customary Law of Nations between Sovereign Interests and the Principles of Natural Law', in *The Law of Nations and Natural Law 1625–1850*, ed. Simone Zurbuchen (Leiden: Brill, 2019), 278–230. Taparelli's few references to Vattel are quite critical: more specifically, Taparelli argues, Vattel wrongly considered as interference into the internal affairs of sovereigns the type of influence exercised by the pope, who does not act as a 'foreigner' but as a 'Holy Father'; thus, just like fathers are totally entitled to intervene in the life of their children, so can the pope influence sovereigns, and they in turn can be influenced by his infallible authority (Taparelli, *Saggio*, vol. 5, 208).

36 Christian Wolff, *Philosophia Practica Universalis, Pars Prior* (prostat in officina Rengeriana, 1738–1739), § 127.

37 Wolff, *Psychologia Empirica*, § 908.

38 It seems that the notion of *perfectio* is connected to the medieval concept of *bonitas transcendentalis*. Leduc suggests that Wolff borrows such notions from Suárez ('Sources of Wolff's Philosophy', at 38). See Francisco Suárez, *Disputationes Metaphysicae* I, I, 2 (Salamanticae, 1597): 'ad perfectionem ad amplitudinem huius scientiae pertinet ut haec omnia separet ac distinguat, et de universis doceat quidquid certa cognitione de his sciri potest'.

There are at least three senses in which Wolff uses the term *concursus*, and they are all interconnected. First, Wolff speaks of a 'concurrence' between God and human actions.[39] As we have pointed out, divine intervention does not precede human action but is actually co-causal and concurrent with it. This is because, as the idea of *perfectio* emphasizes, man is meant to pursue moral good (both because it makes him perfect, and because this decision concurs with the divine plan).

Second, such *concursus* happens when there is *consensus* among human faculties, as we have seen, namely when intellect and volition *concur* towards the same object (which makes it a stable desire).

The third interpretation that Wolff gives to the term *concursus* is strongly related to the previous two. Wolff uses *concursus* for our concrete engagement in other people's moral decisions (*concursus hominis ad actiones alterius*), which is something he claims often happens in reality.[40] Such engagement might produce *consensus*, in cases where we manage to convince other people to adopt behaviour to pursue perfection, or a clash of views and arguments, in which case we do not reach *consensus*.[41]

We often find echoes of Wolff's conceptual vocabulary in Taparelli's *Saggio*, despite his few direct references to the German philosopher.[42] On these rare occasions, Taparelli rejects Wolff's idea of founding natural law on the principle of perfection, arguing that there is no such thing as *perfectio* if it is limited in scope to human affairs only. For their lack of transcendent afflatus, Wolff's and other Protestant doctrines of natural law end up reducing morality to interest. A 'limited good' cannot in itself provide a valid foundation for legal obligation – a greater good is needed for that, Taparelli argues.[43]

Despite this apparent rejection of Wolff's doctrines, Taparelli engages in a silent rehash of Wolffian terminology, by toning it down with Suárez's philosophy whenever it appears too heretical, and, in turn, by re-reading Suárez in a distinctively Wolffian fashion. The fundamental metaphysical role of the law in Taparelli's project is to bridge the Protestant divide between reason and will,

39 Christian Wolff, *Vernünfftige Gedancken von Gott, der Welt und der Seele des Menschen, auch allen Dingen überhaupt: den Liebhabern der Wahrheit mitgetheilet* (prostat in officina libraria Rengeriana, 1720), § 1009. This section of the present chapter revises material from Francesca Iurlaro, *The Invention of Custom: Natural Law and The Law of Nations, ca. 1550–1750* (Oxford: Oxford University Press, 2021), 170–172.

40 Christian Wolff, *Institutiones Juris Naturae et Gentium* (Halle, 1750), § 26.

41 See Marcelo Dascal, *G. W. Leibniz: The Art of Controversies* (Dordrecht: Springer, 2008), 145.

42 See L. Taparelli, *Saggio teoretico* (Palermo, 1841), vol. 2, 176; vol. 2 (Palermo, 1843), 581.

43 Taparelli, *Saggio teoretico*, vol. 1, 40–41.

rationality and revelation.[44] As he observes: 'truth acts on intelligence, and good acts on the will; law then is a power based on truth and good. As everyone sees, such power is irresistible to the human mind, since the latter cannot but consent to the truth' (*giacché essa non può non consentire al vero*).[45] As such, Taparelli affirms, the human mind has two faculties, knowledge and will. Whereas the former is the object of logic and metaphysics, psychology deals with the study of human will (moral philosophy is, instead, the science that deals with 'establishing the rules of human action'). By stressing the importance of psychology (in the Wolffian sense of the term), Taparelli moves on to argue that natural law consists of natural principles that demonstrate how man should make moral use of the faculty of will.[46]

According to such natural principles, Taparelli observes, everything in nature tends to something, according to the will of the Creator. When someone or something achieves the purpose they tend to, they then fulfil perfection, which essentially means 'completion'. When the tendency towards which one orients his will is good, that is called rectitude.[47] This is observable not only in individuals, but also in societies and in humankind as a whole, because God has designed all of these to constantly strive for higher degrees of perfection.[48] Most importantly, such perfection can be achieved only within society, which provides human beings with the appropriate means for self-perfection. If more human wills strive for the same object (achievement of perfection), this social unity produces a 'unity of mind', which is the natural principle of 'honest living'.[49] In other words, if perfection ultimately consists in tending towards the same common good and truth (provided one knows what such things are),

44 Giovani Ambrosetti, 'Diritto come potere e diritto come ordine nel pensiero del Taparelli', in *Miscellanea Taparelli*, 1–25.

45 Ibid., 30.

46 Taparelli adds an *Epilogo ragionato del diritto naturale* to the fifth and last volume of his *Saggio*, 5–6.

47 Ibid., 8: 'Questo fine fu nella mente del Creatore che liberamente lo stabilì: esso dà il nome alla facoltà operatrice, giacché la direzione di una tendenza è determinata dallo scopo. Coroll. 2: Quando una creatura giunge a questo fine, cessa di tendervi; epperò riposa, giacché il riposo è cessazione di tendenza. Coroll. 3: Nel giungervi ella acquista una perfezione, giacché perfetto si dice ciò che è compiuto: or il giungere è compimento del tendere. [...] La perfezione della tendenza si dice rettitudine'.

48 Taparelli, *Saggio teoretico*, vol. 3, 189.

49 'Epilogo ragionato del diritto naturale', in *Saggio teoretico*, vol. 5, 61: 'la perfezione sociale consiste nell'unità di molti: or l'assenso di tutti al vero produce unità di mente: dunque produce perfezione di mente. Questa perfezione di mente è il natural principio della onestà del vivere'.

perfection lies in the folds of social consensus.[50] The Wolffian triad of concepts discussed above is operative here and evidently aimed at constructing the very fabric of Taparelli's social solidarity.

The sociological claim of observing social facts, rather than founding natural law on mere abstraction, is also reflected in Taparelli's rejection of the 'state of nature' doctrine.[51] Such doctrine is dismissed as a *fictio iuris*, 'and I don't like to build the most sacred and important aspects of human interaction on a fiction', Taparelli eloquently writes.[52] Society would only be a disconnected plurality of individuals were not they all tending towards a common goal so as to produce the social consensus that is necessary to achieve truth and goodness. Only if individuals know the truth and aim towards the same good can there be unity between them (they must share, in other words, 'unity of purpose deriving from unity of knowledge').[53] Taparelli presents an interesting and apt example of a group of papyrologists struggling to interpret the same papyrus in a coherent manner. They all know said papyrus and aim at its correct interpretation, but if they do not 'join their wills together by expressly showing their intents, so as to show that they all have a common one', their union will never amount to a proper society.[54] Human society means the 'concurrence [*cospirazione*] of many people to the achievement of the same common good, known and searched for by all of them'. The term *cospirazione* seems to hint again at another example of the typical Wolffian overlap between *consensus*, *concursus* and *perfectio*, which Taparelli explains cannot really be achieved in a state of nature: men need to know, agree and then intentionally tend towards the same actual purpose, not towards a vague, fictional one.

Taparelli argues that the proper foundation of natural law (and of social cohesion more in general) can only be a duty to love, and by so doing introducing the ideas of charity and social justice into the language of rights. This, however, is no less problematic than acknowledging such a foundational role of perfection. In this sense, the Protestant ethics of perfectibility is compatible with Catholic teleology towards common good: one could easily find in Suárez a similar general drive of *perfectio*.[55] However, the question of whether love

50 Ibid. Also, on nationality as a process towards perfection: Taparelli, *Della nazionalità*, 14.

51 On the features of Taparelli's 'realist social science', see 'Introduction', in Behr, *Social Justice and Subsidiarity*, 1–16.

52 Taparelli, *Saggio teoretico*, vol. 2, 5: 'ed io non amo fondar sopra una finzione quanto vi ha di più sacro ed importante nel commercio fra gli uomini'.

53 Ibid., 10–11.

54 Ibid., 9–10.

55 See note 38 of the present chapter.

provides a basis for legal obligation entails a discussion of grace and the role of God in human affairs that is at the exact crossroads between the two traditions of thought. Additionally, it poses a question of distributive justice, as we will see in a while.

Love is a controversial foundational principle for natural law. If we hold Wolff's doctrine of *concursus* to be true, God might be held potentially and co-causally accountable for human deeds of love. Additionally, love cannot realistically be a foundation for law because, according to the traditional dichotomies between perfect and imperfect rights and between commutative and distributive justice, one can only demand respect of mutual obligations. In contrast, acts of love, charity and kindness are simply imperfect duties whose respect is highly recommended to maintain social order, but cannot be imposed by a sovereign. This traditional view of imperfect duties has, somehow, disqualified their legal significance. As a matter of fact, many authors of the natural law tradition seem to attach a value judgement to the dichotomy between perfect and imperfect rights. For example, according to a trajectory of authors that culminates in Emer de Vattel, imperfect rights need to be activated and turned into positive agreements to become perfect obligations, for which it is possible to demand respect.[56] There must be, in other words, a corrective to the constitutional 'deficiency' of imperfect rights.

Let us address this problem through the eyes of Taparelli. As mentioned, arguing for the primacy of love in providing a foundation for natural law raised the issue of co-causal attribution of human deeds to God.[57] This problem was exactly what caused Wolff's exile from the University of Halle, and its implications for the doctrine of grace were obvious to Suárez.[58] In book II, chapter 11 of his *De legibus*, Suárez asks whether 'the natural law imposes as an obligatory mode of action that mode which springs from the natural love of God, or from charity?'[59] Suárez claims that love is inessential to the achievement

56 See Simone Zurbuchen's reconstruction in 'Vattel's Law of Nations' and the Principle of Non-Intervention', *Grotiana* 31(1) (2010): 69–84.

57 See Ernest Fortin, 'Sacred and Inviolable: *Rerum Novarum* and Natural Rights', *Theological Studies* 53 (1992): 203–233.

58 On Taparelli, the Jesuits and scholasticism, see 'La scolastica e la politica dei gesuiti: a proposito di una polemica', *La civiltà cattolica* series 78, 3 (1927): 202; Ernesto Frattini, 'Taparelli d'Azeglio e il tradizionalismo', in *Miscellanea Taparelli*, 171–190, at 177. Taparelli explains his take on authority and Suarez's legacy in his article 'L'autorità spiegata dagli Scolastici', *La civiltà cattolica* series 2, 11 (1855): 593 ff.

59 Francisco Suárez, *De legibus ac de Deo legislatore*, II, 11 (Coimbra, 1612), in F. Suárez, *Selection from Three Works*, ed. Thomas Pink (Indianapolis, IN: Liberty Fund, 2015), 274.

of individual moral principles, 'since the latter do not all impose, as an obligation, the love of God'. Accordingly, humans must be in complete control of their actions, so as to avoid misattributions of responsibility: 'nor [...] can it be shown that God has laid down for men as ordained for a supernatural end, any special command always to discharge or to observe the precepts of the natural law, out of this sort of love or this reference of one's acts'.[60] That the purpose of perfection includes the desire to acquire the love of God does not mean that love is to be considered as a natural law precept. Love is not imposed as an obligation but, rather, is a moral guide designed by God to help us direct our behaviours.

Wolff, on the other hand, in his *Ius naturae* acknowledges a universal duty to love and formulates it as the positive version of 'the golden rule': 'universalis omnium hominum amor: uniquisque alterum quemcunque amare debet tantum seipsum'.[61] Moreover, 'we are obliged to charity by the very same law of nature'.[62] This is also true of love among nations, and not just allies.[63] However, he argues, 'it is against charity and not justice, if one nation fails in its duty toward another. Therefore although it does no wrong, nevertheless it sins'.[64]

The international implications and further articulation of the duty to love will be discussed in more detail in the next section of this chapter. As a general context for Taparelli's reflection, it is useful to recall a letter that his spiritual father Jan Roothan sent him after having read the first edition of his *Saggio*. Roothan has two major concerns: first, that the obligation to do good ('il principio: *si deve fare il bene*') seems to give rise to confusion as far as the difference between command and advice is concerned. To remedy this, Roothan recommends changing this principle into a more general 'order should be maintained' (*si deve serbar l'ordine*).[65] Second, Roothan shows some anxiety concerning the role of grace and God's intervention in human affairs. 'The expression "*participation in divine being*", when referring to creatures, and man in particular, seems dangerous, now that pantheism is so in fashion. Unless

---

60 Ibid., 283.

61 Christian Wolff, *Ius naturae methodo scientifica pertractata*, Pars Prima (Halle, 1740–1748), § 619.

62 Ibid., § 621.

63 Christian Wolff, *Ius gentium methodo scientifica pertractata* (Halle, 1749); Christian Wolff, *The Law of Nations Treated According to the Scientific Method*, ed. Thomas Ahnert (Indianapolis, IN: Liberty Fund, 2017), 122.

64 Ibid., 124; also, 'no nation ought to injure another. For every nation ought to promote the perfection of another as far as it can, consequently ought to do nothing by which the other nation or its condition is rendered less perfect', at 130.

65 'Lettera di Roothan a Taparelli', Rome, 26 December 1840, in *Carteggi*.

one explains it according to Aquinas, it seems to me, through similitude'.[66] It is useful to recall that the accusation of pantheism was also at the very core of Gioberti's critique of the Jesuits. By acknowledging that God actively concurs in the realization of good acts, Gioberti claimed, the Jesuits perverted the ontological order of beings by giving man 'the dignity of a first cause'.[67]

Roothan here suggests that Taparelli corrects these passages accordingly, and in fact they seem particularly nuanced in the later editions of his *Saggio*. Roothan is referring to a passage in Taparelli's text where the question of whether God can change divine law is addressed. Taparelli criticizes Pufendorf's claim that God could have made such law otherwise, just as he could have made man different from what he actually is. Such an argument implies, for Taparelli, that God is not a necessary being and is, therefore, himself subject to the will of some more necessary being (a clearly heretical position). Rather, he suggests that God made man in his own image, and in such a scenario mere participation in the divine being automatically makes divine law more understandable and enforceable for humans. In the 1844 edition of *Saggio*, Taparelli adds a footnote to keep Roothan's concerns at bay. The footnote clarifies that 'when we say that a limited being participates in the infinite, we do not mean this as if he was a particle of it, as dreamt by pantheists; rather, we say so because the effect must necessarily have its being in the cause from which it derives'.[68]

This, however, highlights a controversial conceptual issue with which Taparelli was clearly grappling, as shown by the many oscillations in his vocabulary.

4 Taparelli's Influential *Saggio teoretico di diritto naturale appoggiato sul fatto*: Nations and International Law

Scholars have welcomed Taparelli's contribution to international law as one of the first Italian precursors of the League of Nations, or praised the balance between tradition and historical dynamism that Taparelli puts forward in his

---

66 Ibid.

67 See note 17 of the present chapter.

68 Taparelli, *Saggio teoretico* (Napoli, 1844 edition), vol. 1, 40: 'diciamo l'essere limitato partecipazione dell'infinito, non già perché ne sia una particella, giusta il sogno de' Panteisti; ma perché l'effetto dee necessariamente avere il suo essere nella causa, da cui deriva'. In support of his thesis, Taparelli quotes Thomas Aquinas (again, to please Roothan) and Fortunato Cavazzoni Pederzini, author of *Dialoghi filosofici* (Modena: Tipi della R. D. Camera, 1842).

legal theory based on facts.[69] His originality consists precisely in bridging the gap between natural reason and the 'possibilities of historical reason', by envisaging a theory of international legal order based on moral obligation and the political necessities of interaction.[70]

In stressing the differences between the universal, natural society of mankind and the factual political unity of different nations gathering together, Taparelli also makes use of Wolff's conceptual vocabulary. Famously, Wolff conceived of the international society as a *civitas maxima*, a community governed by a fictional legislator and aimed at the promotion and achievement of communal perfection.[71]

To this effect, Taparelli uses the Italian adjective *etnarchico* to refer to Christianity as an 'ethnarchy', a society based on faith in both the Church and the Gospel. The 'ethnarchic society' is, thus, an institutional arrangement among nations, based on the idea that 'a natural principle of unity existed in Europe, according to which peoples are meant to join forces towards the achievement of a common good of order and justice'.[72] However, as both Suárez and Wolff well observed, there is a huge leap between perfection as a shared purpose and love of perfection as a legal obligation. This holds particularly true at the international level, where one nation's ideas of love and perfection do not necessarily coincide with another's convictions. Massively intervening to change that would amount to a violation of sovereign equality, which is why the duty to love is framed by Taparelli essentially as a *debt*, rather than as an obligation. By recurring to this subtle (again, Suárezian) distinction, Taparelli manages to acknowledge the obligatory force of love, although in a more nuanced and passive way (as the very term 'debt' suggests), without necessarily demeaning its legal significance.

As mentioned, it is Suárez who distinguishes *debitum* ('ought') from obligation. As a matter of fact, 'in his view, we are not obliged to do good and avoid evil before any command and prohibition. But he recognizes a moral requirement before any command and prohibition; for natural goodness and badness

69 Luciano Perena, 'La autoridad internacional en Taparelli', in *Miscellanea Taparelli*, 405–432; Robert Jacquin, *L'ordre international d'apres Taparelli d'Azeglio* (Paris: Pedone, 1939).

70 Perena, 'La autoridad internacional en Taparelli', 408–409.

71 Nicholas Onuf, '*Civitas maxima*: Wolff, Vattel and the Fate of Republicanism', *American Journal of International Law* 88(2) (1994): 280–303; Kleinlein, 'Christian Wolff: System as an Episode?', 226 ff.

72 Taparelli, *Saggio teoretico*, vol. 4, 297: 'esistea dunque in Europa un principio naturale di unità che dovea congiungere i popoli al conseguimento del comun bene di ordine e giustizia'.

tell us what we ought (*debere*) to do'.[73] For Taparelli, this 'ought' is and should be the foundation for natural law, and that is where he corrects Suárez with a touch of Wolff's Protestantism – if love is not a duty, it surely is a debt we owe to society. Suárez ascribes *debere* to the realm of morality:

> Suárez distinguishes 'ought' (*debere*) and duty (*debitum*) from obligation (*obligatio*). A class of actions that we ought to do, and that it would be right to do and wrong to avoid, is already fixed by nature; the divine command adds an obligation to do things we already ought to do. [...] The obligation imposed by a divine command is binding on our conscience if we abstract from divine command, the principles of natural law do not give rise to an obligation binding on conscience. But even without divine commands, the inherent rightness or wrongness of certain actions implies that we are required (*teneri*) in conscience to do or avoid them.[74]

Taparelli, perhaps following Roothan's suggestion to shift focus from common good to order, argues that international order has to be achieved for 'a debt of international love' ('debito di amore internazionale', but also clarifies that 'debitum' is not just a passive obligation:

> [...] respect of the negative precept is not enough: we want to also aim at the positive side of such precept and ascertain the limits of such obligation. [...] What we will say on the debt of international truth will complete the *Saggio* also as far as these duties of the will are concerned, since the will is directed by knowledge of the truth. This international veracity, that is to say, this duty to promote in neighbour nations the threefold cognition of supreme good, civic good and common relations, is, thus, the only question left for us to clarify.[75]

Taparelli acknowledges that this duty calls into question a matter of 'higher historical importance', that is, it asks to what extent a proactive promotion of Catholicism can be included in this duty to promote common good among nations. In principle, he claims that no intervention in another nation's affairs for religious reasons is allowed *per se*; it is possible to intervene only in defence of the oppressed.[76] What are, then, the 'active' international obligations deriv-

---

73 Terence Irwin, *The Development of Ethics: A Historical and Critical Study*, vol. 2, *From Suarez to Rousseau* (Oxford: Oxford University Press, 2008), 29.

74 Ibid., 30.

75 Taparelli, *Saggio teoretico*, vol. 4, 252–253.

76 Ibid., 258.

ing from the debt of international love? Taparelli seems to take a step back and concede that 'I would be a fool if I had the ambition to deduce the laws of war from the principle of love and justice'.[77] Rather, war is, according to nature, a violent defence of order, that is, a just reaction against disorder.

Order, however, can arise only from a proper society with an overarching authority. Taparelli claims that there is an international authority, otherwise there would be no proper society, strictly speaking. How do nations come together to form an international society? Taparelli argues that:

> among nations there is an overlap and, yet, at the same time a contrast of interests: therefore, there must be someone to judge on that. Now, the authority of one nation does not have the right to judge the other: there must be, then, a common authority. Since a positive law of nations exists, there must also be an authority that determines it.[78]

Such authority is essentially polyarchic, made of multiple authorities rather than just one (this resembles Suárez's idea of *ius inter gentes*).[79] The purpose of such society is different from the one pursued by domestic politics, insofar as it is given by the very same reason behind the international union, and consists in achieving happiness through the defence of oppressed nations, and in promoting cooperation towards universal good. The most perfect of these ethnarchic societies is Christianity,[80] to which Taparelli devotes a whole section, as we will see.

Thus, in Taparelli's formulation, just war amounts, if conducted to fulfil the debt of international love, to an act of international love.[81] War is an act of love because it aims at restoring order; ordered societies can declare just war against disordered societies. International disorder amounts to an offence that can be legitimately redressed by war. However, Taparelli observes:

> every society inevitably defends order whenever it comes to strict justice; but if we are dealing with perfection, since individuals are not rigorously bound to it, society must not absolutely force it onto them. It can only provide and broaden the means of knowledge, enticement, possibility, proportionally to the three elements of human action, mind, will and external force. [...] To do otherwise would be to contravene the first law

77 Ibid., 261.
78 Ibid., 289–290.
79 Ibid.
80 Taparelli, *Saggio teoretico*, vol. 5, 5.
81 Taparelli, *Corso elementare di natural diritto* (Modena: Carlo Vincenzi, 1851), 265.

> of social interaction, which consists in the exact measurement of the collision of rights; with such provision one would demand that the force of the advice to perfection overstep the right to freedom. Should such a situation occur, there would be a secret contradiction, as free advice would be confused with the exclusion from liberty. Perfection should be promoted, not commanded.[82]

So the conundrum returns. Love cannot be commanded, and neither can perfection. Is Taparelli leading his own argument to a dead end? He seems to address this point when dealing with his critique of Grotius:

> our doctrine, honest protector of the just liberty of thinking,[83] does not concede to equals any superior right on others; [...] The right to defend Christianity among foreign peoples should depend on particular facts on which the rights of Christian society build. But Grotius could not understand what such rights were, full as he was of his personal spirit and his Protestant delirium.[84]

If Grotius's natural law was a science of false deduction without a heart, Taparelli suggests that it is the emotional side of humans (values of love, charity and empathy) that makes their lives complete, precisely as much as it makes natural law more perfect and complete as a result. To promote Catholicism, Taparelli argues that using persuasion is a better strategy than force, as a nation only has a duty towards its own citizens, whereas the *debitum* of international love does not necessarily amount to a duty to command.[85] Additionally, charity bears witness to faith, according to Taparelli. His own speculations would not be of much use, he argues, if they did not invite people to a more honest realization of what their interests truly are: 'oh, how just a little unity of faith and charity could solve troubles much more than conflicts of power! And, without this unity of faith and charity, what is the point of interest, if not of dividing peoples and triggering war among them?'[86]

A very apt example of Taparelli's point comes from his essay *Della nazionalità*, where (again, against Gioberti) he discusses the relationship between barbarism and civilization.[87] When asked whether it would be right for France

82 Taparelli, *Saggio teoretico*, vol. 4, 301–302.
83 Again, a reference to the intellectual freedom Jesuits were promoting through the teaching of natural law.
84 Ibid., 303–304.
85 Taparelli, 'Epilogo ragionato del diritto naturale', in idem, *Saggio teoretico*, vol. 5, 96.
86 'Lettera di Taparelli a Roberto', in *Carteggi*, 131–133.
87 Taparelli, *Della nazionalità*, 2nd edition (Firenze: Pietro Ducci, 1849), 14.

to surrender to Algeria, Taparelli replies that this would not be right, not because it is against nature that uncivilized, barbarous and non-Christian nations conquer civilized ones. Rather, the French people should not be submitted to Algeria because the French were the ones who received the offence in the first place, with war being an attempt at mending such offence.

> These are the principles I affirmed in my international law doctrine: not the alleged superiority of Christians over barbarians. Being Christians, rather than giving us the right to conquer infidels, rather obliges us to respect their independence more religiously. That would have been something! The Dominican Vitoria pleaded under Philip II, at the times of the Inquisition, against the oppression of Indians! And today, Gioberti's civilization seeks to justify such oppression in the era of liberty![88]

Taparelli concludes with the suggestion that it is highly urgent in his time to reuse these ideas 'on the rough outline of an international society presented by Europe'.[89] 'Social love' is crucial, because it makes us want for others what we desire for ourselves. Love and altruism produce order among nations.

> Without this honest love, nations will only gather together for reasons of interests. They will come together like two fighters, just to injure each other either with hidden frauds or with open violence; but the society of intelligence and will can never be without order and love; and men, reconnected but disunited, will be a corpse of society without soul.[90]

Taparelli considers that the application of his theories to reality is far from being achieved. However, the society of Christians shows that it is actually possible to live under the rule of love, provided one turns it into a legally binding concept. The originality of Taparelli's social doctrine of natural law lies in his account of love as a debt, rather than as a duty. People who are in debt are required to give by law. It is, however, our free choice as individuals and as a society to choose God as a 'creditor' in the first place.[91]

---

88 Ibid.

89 Taparelli, *Saggio teoretico*, vol. 4, 317.

90 Ibid., 317–318.

91 On how Taparelli's notion of duty gave rise to a deeply patriarchal, family-based system of rights, see Udi Greenberg, 'Catholicism and Rights: Politics, Economics, and Sexuality', in *The Cambridge History of Rights*, vol. 4, ed. Dan Edelstein and Jennifer Pitts (Cambridge: Cambridge University Press, forthcoming).

5 Conclusion: From Love to Order

If one takes the implications of Taparelli's doctrine of international love seriously, despite its ambiguities, a number of questions arise. First, his insistence on social love as a typical feature of Christian societies echoes Ludwig Feuerbach's critical claim that Christianity's assertion of a close relationship between love and faith ends up impairing the very concept of universal love. It is impossible to be at the same time outside of the Catholic faith and within the circle of Christian love – remember Feuerbach's attack against the falseness of the precept 'love your enemy'.[92] While Taparelli's idea of social justice relied on the proactive role of Catholics in society, it theoretically implied a social consensus of religious acolytes, one that automatically excludes those who are outside it.

Proactive promotion of these values is a debt that Christians owe to society and nations to each other. Grace is, in other words, no longer a gift: it becomes disposable social currency. But there is, to this day as much as in Taparelli's times, a question of values. While respect cannot be demanded from acts of mercy, *caritas* and kindness, Taparelli aptly transforms these 'imperfect duties' into debts that members of a society have to fulfil to achieve their perfection and get closer to God. From this perspective, Taparelli's fear was that, if all sorts of individualistic values were being introduced in the political space, this would eventually favour a certain *laissez-faire* that resembled the logic of the market and commerce.

Bibliography

Abbate, Emma, 'Luigi Taparelli d'Azeglio e l'istruzione nei collegi gesuitici del XIX secolo', *Archivio Storico per le Province Napoletane* 115 (1997): 467–516.

Albrecht, Michael, *Eklektik. Eine Begriffsgechichte mit Hinweisen auf die Philosophie- und Wissenschaftsgeschichte* (Stuttgart: Frommann; Bad Cannstatt: Holzboog, 1994).

Ambrosetti, Giovani, 'Diritto come potere e diritto come ordine nel pensiero del Taparelli', in *Miscellanea Taparelli. Raccolta di studi in onore di Luigi Taparelli D'Azeglio nel primo centenario della morte*, ed. Pio Cipriotti and José M. Diez Alegria (Roma: Edizioni dell'Università Gregoriana, 1964), 1–25.

92 Ludwig Feuerbach, *The Essence of Christianity*, II, 27 ('The Contradiction of Love and Faith'), https://www.marxists.org/reference/archive/feuerbach/works/essence (accessed January 2023).

Behr, Thomas C., 'Luigi Taparelli on the Dignity of Man', in *Congresso Tomista Internazionale: L'umanesimo cristiano nel terzo millennio: prospettiva di Tommaso d'Aquino* (Roma: Pontificia Accademia di San Tommaso, 2004), 1–7.

Behr, Thomas C., *Social Justice and Subsidiarity: Luigi Taparelli and the Origins of Modern Catholic Social Thought* (Washington, DC: Catholic University of America Press, 2019).

Carteggi del p. Taparelli d'Azeglio, ed. Pietro Pirri (Torino: Fratelli Bocca, 1933).

Cataldi Madonna, Luigi, 'Il connubio della ragione con l'esperienza come fondamento e scopo del programma filosofico wolffiano', in *La filosofia pratica tra metafisica e antropologia nell'età di Wolff e Vico*, ed. Giuseppe Cacciatore et al. (Napoli: Guida, 1999), 111–129.

Catholic Social Teaching: A Volume of Scholarly Essays, ed. Gerald V. Bradley and E. Christian Brugger (Cambridge: Cambridge University Press, 2019).

Cavazzoni Pederzini, Fortunato, *Dialoghi filosofici* (Modena: Tipi della R. D. Camera, 1842).

Croce, Benedetto, *Storia d'Europa nel secolo decimonono* (Bari: Laterza, 1932).

Dante, Francesco, 'Tomismo e neotomismo a confronto nella *Rerum Novarum*', in Rerum Novarum: *Écriture, contenu, et réception d'une encyclique* (Roma: École Française, 1997), 91–105.

Dascal, Marcelo, *G. W. Leibniz: The Art of Controversies* (Dordrecht: Springer, 2008).

de Giorgi, Fulvio, *Cattolici ed Educazione tra Restaurazione e Risorgimento: Ordini religiosi* (Milano: ISU Università Cattolica, 1999).

De Rosa, Gabriele, *I gesuiti in Sicilia e la rivoluzione del '48. Con documenti sulla condotta della Compagnia di Gesù* (Roma: Edizioni di Storia e Letteratura, 1963).

De Rosa, Gabriele, 'Luigi Taparelli d'Azeglio e i moti del '48 in Sicilia', in *Miscellanea Taparelli. Raccolta di studi in onore di Luigi Taparelli D'Azeglio nel primo centenario della morte*, ed. Pio Cipriotti and José M. Diez Alegria (Roma: Edizioni dell'Università Gregoriana, 1964), 115–128.

Di Giannatale, Fabio, 'Il principio di nazionalità. Un dibattito dell'Italia Risorgimentale', *Storia e Politica* 6(2) (2014): 234–269.

Di Rosa, Luigi, *Luigi Taparelli. L'altro d'Azeglio* (Milano: Cisalpino, 1991).

Dianin, Giampaolo, *Luigi Taparelli d'Azeglio (1793–1862): il significato della sua opera, al tempo del rinnovamento neoscolastico, per l'evoluzione della teologia morale* (Milano: Ed. Glossa, 2000).

Fantappié, Carlo, *Chiesa Romana e Modernità Giuridica*, vol. 2 (Milano: Giuffré, 2008).

Feuerbach, Ludwig, *The Essence of Christianity*, II, 27 ('The Contradiction of Love and Faith'), https://www.marxists.org/reference/archive/feuerbach/works/essence / (accessed January 2023).

Fortin, Ernest, 'Sacred and Inviolable: *Rerum Novarum* and Natural Rights', *Theological Studies* 53 (1992): 203–233.

Frattini, Ernesto, 'Taparelli d'Azeglio e il tradizionalismo', in *Miscellanea Taparelli. Raccolta di studi in onore di Luigi Taparelli D'Azeglio nel primo centenario della morte*, ed. Pio Cipriotti and José M. Diez Alegria (Roma: Edizioni dell'Università Gregoriana, 1964), 171–190.

Galluppi, Pasquale, *Lezioni di Logica e Metafisica, Prima edizione livornese* (Livorno: Mazzajoli, 1854).

Gioberti, Vincenzo, *Il Gesuita Moderno* (Losanna, 1846).

Gramsci, Antonio, *Quaderni del Carcere*, vol. 3 (Torino: Einaudi, 1975).

Greenberg, Udi, 'Catholicism and Rights: Politics, Economics, and Sexuality', in *The Cambridge History of Rights*, vol. 4, ed. Dan Edelstein and Jennifer Pitts (Cambridge: Cambridge University Press, forthcoming).

Hollerbach, Alexander, 'Das christliche Naturrecht im Zusammenhang des allgemeinen Naturrechtsdenkens', in *Naturrecht in der Kritik*, ed. Franz Böckle and Ernst-Wolfgang Böckenförde (Mainz: Grünewald, 1973), 9–38.

Irwin, Terence, *The Development of Ethics: A Historical and Critical Study*, vol. 2, *From Suarez to Rousseau* (Oxford: Oxford University Press, 2008).

Iurlaro, Francesca, *The Invention of Custom: Natural Law and The Law of Nations, ca. 1550–1750* (Oxford: Oxford University Press, 2021).

Iurlaro, Francesca, 'Vattel's Doctrine of the Customary Law of Nations between Sovereign Interests and the Principles of Natural Law', in *The Law of Nations and Natural Law 1625–1850*, ed. Simone Zurbuchen (Leiden: Brill, 2019), 278–230.

Jacquin, Robert, *L'ordre international d'apres Taparelli d'Azeglio* (Paris: Pedone, 1939).

Jacquin, Robert, *Taparelli* (Paris: P. Lethielleux, 1943).

Kleinlein, Thomas, 'Christian Wolff: System as an Episode?', in *System, Order and International Law: The Early History of International Thought from Machiavelli to Hegel*, ed. Stefan Kadelbach, Thomas Kleinlein and David Roth-Isigkeit (Oxford: Oxford University Press, 2017), 216–239.

'La scolastica e la politica dei gesuiti: a proposito di una polemica', *La civiltà cattolica* series 78, 3 (1927): 202.

Leduc, Christian, 'Sources of Wolff's Philosophy: Scholastics/Leibniz', in *Handbuch Christian Wolff*, ed. Robert Theis and Alexander Aichele (Wiesbaden: Springer, 2018).

Marcolungo, Ferdinando L., 'Christian Wolff e il progetto di una psicologia filosofica', in *Christian Wolff tra psicologia empirica e razionale: atti del convegno internazionale di studi Verona, 13–14 maggio 2005*, ed. idem (Hildesheim: Olms, 2007), 15–34.

Martina, Giacomo, *Storia della Compagnia di Gesù in Italia (1814–1983)* (Brescia: Morcelliana, 2003).

Messner, Johannes, 'Die Erfahrung in der Naturrechtslehre von Taparelli', in *Miscellanea Taparelli. Raccolta di studi in onore di Luigi Taparelli D'Azeglio nel primo centenario della morte*, ed. Pio Cipriotti and José M. Diez Alegria (Roma: Edizioni dell'Università Gregoriana, 1964), 303–304.

Midgley, E., *The Natural Law Tradition and the Theory of International Relations* (London: Elek, 1975).

Miscellanea Taparelli. Raccolta di studi in onore di Luigi Taparelli D'Azeglio nel primo centenario della morte, ed. Pio Cipriotti and José M. Diez Alegria (Roma: Edizioni dell'Università Gregoriana, 1964).

Morra, Gianfranco, *La dottrina sociale della Chiesa* (Milano: Scuola di dottrina sociale, 1988).

Morte e resurrezione di un Ordine religioso. Le strategie culturali ed educative della Compagnia di Gesù durante la soppressione (1759–1814), ed. Paolo Bianchini (Milano: Vita e Pensiero, 2006).

Onuf, Nicholas, '*Civitas maxima*: Wolff, Vattel and the Fate of Republicanism', *American Journal of International Law* 88(2) (1994): 280–303.

Perena, Luciano, 'La autoridad internacional en Taparelli', in *Miscellanea Taparelli. Raccolta di studi in onore di Luigi Taparelli D'Azeglio nel primo centenario della morte*, ed. Pio Cipriotti and José M. Diez Alegria (Roma: Edizioni dell'Università Gregoriana, 1964), 405–432.

Petersen, Claes, 'What Has Logic Got To Do With It? On the Use of Logic in Christian Wolff's Theory of Natural Law', *Scandinavian Studies in Law* 48 (2005): 310–320.

Purdy, Daniel, 'Chinese Ethics within the Radical Enlightenment: Christian Wolff', in *The Radical Enlightenment in Germany: A Cultural Perspective*, ed. Carl Niekerk (Leiden: Brill, 2018), 112–130.

Riberi, Mario, 'I Taparelli d'Azeglio durante l'età napoleonica', in *'Une très-ancienne famille piémontaise'. I Taparelli negli stati Sabaudi*, Quaderni del Dipartimento di Giurisprudenza dell'Università di Torino, 13, ed. Enrico Genta, Andrea Pennini and Davide De Franco (Milano: Ledizioni, 2019), 113–138.

Salerno, Emanuele, '*Stare pactis* and Neutrality. Grotius and Pufendorf in the Political Thought of the Early Eighteenth Century Grand Duchy of Tuscany', in *War, Trade and Neutrality: Europe and the Mediterranean in the Seventeenth and Eighteenth Centuries*, ed. Antonella Alimento (Milano: Angeli, 2011), 188–202.

Scattola, Merio, *Prinzip und Prinzipienfrage in der Entwicklung des modernen Naturrechts* (Stuttgart: Fromman-Holzboog, 2017).

Scattola, Merio, 'Protestantesimo e diritto naturale cattolico nel XVIII secolo', in *Illuminismo e Protestantesimo*, ed. Giulia Cantarutti and Stefano Ferrari (Milano: Angeli, 2010).

Suárez, Francisco, *De legibus ac de Deo legislatore*, II, 11 (Coimbra, 1612), in F. Suárez, *Selection from Three Works*, ed. Thomas Pink (Indianapolis, IN: Liberty Fund, 2015).

Suárez, Francisco, *Disputationes Metaphysicae* I, I, 2 (Salamanticae, 1597).

Taparelli, Luigi, *Corso elementare di natural diritto* (Modena: Carlo Vincenzi, 1851).

Taparelli, Luigi, *Della nazionalità. Breve scrittura del p. Luigi Taparelli d'Azeglio, rivista e accresciuta notabilmente dall'autore con una risposta del medesimo alle osservazioni di Vincenzo Gioberti* (Genova: Tip. F.lli Ponthenier, 1847).

Taparelli, Luigi, 'L'autorità spiegata dagli Scolastici', *La civiltà cattolica* series 2, 11 (1855): 593.

Taparelli, Luigi, *Legge fondamentale d'organizzazione nella società*, in G. De Rosa, *I gesuiti in Sicilia e la Rivoluzione del '48: con documenti sulla condotta della Compagnia di Gesù e scritti inediti di Luigi Taparelli d'Azeglio* (Roma: Edizioni di Storia e Letteratura, 1963).

Taparelli, Luigi, *Saggio teoretico di diritto naturale appoggiato sul fatto. Opera corretta ed accresciuta dall'autore*, 5 vols (Palermo: Muratori, 1840–1843; later editions Livorno, 1845; Napoli, 1850, 2 vols; Roma, 1855, 2 vols).

The Jesuit Suppression in Global Context: Causes, Events, and Consequences, ed. Jeffrey D. Burson and Jonathan Wright (Cambridge: Cambridge University Press, 2015).

Thomann, M., 'Introduction', in Christian Wolff, *Gesammelte Werke*, II (Hildesheim: Olms, 1962), vol. 25.

Van Kley, Dale K., *Reform Catholicism and the International Suppression of the Jesuits in Enlightenment Europe* (New Haven, CT: Yale University Press, 2019).

Vian, Giovanni, 'Luigi Taparelli D'Azeglio', in *Il contributo italiano alla storia del pensiero: storia e politica*, Treccani (2013), http://www.treccani.it/enciclopedia/luigi-taparelli-d-azeglio_%28altro%29 (accessed January 2023).

von Wille, Dagmar, 'La fortuna delle opere di Christian Wolff in Italia nella prima metà del Settecento: la prima edizione veronese degli *Opera Latina*', *Rivista di Storia della Filosofia* 50(2) (1995): 369–400.

Wolff, Christian, *Gesammelte Werke*, II (Hildesheim: Olms, 1962).

Wolff, Christian, *Institutiones Juris Naturae et Gentium* (Halle, 1750).

Wolff, Christian, *Ius gentium methodo scientifica pertractata* (Halle, 1749).

Wolff, Christian, *Ius naturae methodo scientifica pertractata*, Pars Prima (Halle, 1740–1748).

Wolff, Christian, *Philosophia Practica Universalis, Pars Prior* (prostat in officina Rengeriana, 1738–1739).

Wolff, Christian, *Psychologia Empirica methodo scientifica pertractata, qua ea, quae de anima humana indubia experientiae fide constant, continentur et ad solidam universae philosophiae practicae ac theologiae naturalis tractationem via sternitur* (Frankfurt, 1732).

Wolff, Christian, *The Law of Nations Treated According to the Scientific Method*, ed. Thomas Ahnert (Indianapolis, IN: Liberty Fund, 2017).

Wolff, Christian, *Vernünfftige Gedancken von Gott, der Welt und der Seele des Menschen, auch allen Dingen überhaupt: den Liebhabern der Wahrheit mitgetheilet* (prostat in officina libraria Rengeriana, 1720).

Zurbuchen, Simone, 'Vattel's Law of Nations and the Principle of Non-Intervention', *Grotiana* 31(1) (2010): 69–84.

CHAPTER 11

The Teaching of International Law in Cagliari, the 'Italian School' and the Unification of Italy

Giuseppina De Giudici

> Ideas are the product of their times and they contribute to events with their fruitful spark; they do not stem from the human mind just out of the blue, but from all the efforts that unite in a definitive act; facts, indeed, inspire ideas, whilst ideas, in turn, govern the course of events, fortunate products of the former, propitiously triggering the latter.[1]

∵

1 The Study of International Law in Cagliari before 1850: The Missing Story

It is well known that the inception of international law as a positive science resulted from the efforts of the legal theory that, from the nineteenth century onwards, worked to get rid, on the one hand, of the alleged abstractness of natural law and, on the other hand, of the political concreteness of the old law of nations.[2] Admittedly, although the proposals deriving from Christian Wolff

1 Guido Bortolotto, 'Nazionalità', in *Il Digesto Italiano. Enciclopedia metodica e alfabetica di legislazione, dottrina e giurisprudenza* (Torino: Unione tipografica Editrice Torinese, 1905–1910), vol. 16, 11: 'Le idee sono figliuole dei tempi e agli eventi portano la loro spinta feconda; esse non sorgono ex novo dalla mente d'un uomo, ma sono il prodotto faticoso di tanti sforzi che si uniscono in un'energia definitiva; e se i fatti esse danno l'ispirazione, esse alla lor volta presiedono al corso degli avvenimenti, figlie felici dei primi, provvide genitrici degli altri'.

2 An earlier and shorter version of the present chapter has been published as 'A cavallo dell'Unità d'Italia. L'insegnamento del Diritto internazionale a Cagliari e l'adesione alla cosiddetta Scuola italiana', *Annali di Storia delle Università italiane*, 2 (2020): 213–233. On the emergence of international law as a positive science see Luigi Nuzzo, *Origini di una scienza. Diritto internazionale e colonialismo nel XIX secolo* (Frankfurt am Main: Vittorio Klostermann, 2012), in particular 4; and Luigi Nuzzo and Miloš Vec, 'The Birth of International Law as a

 | DOI:10.1163/9789004685130_013

and popularized by Emer de Vattel's widely dispersed *Droit des gens*[3] promised to overcome 'reveries' and 'misunderstandings', they did not satisfy the new international law scholars, whose aspiration, if anything, was to found a science independent of individual government policies as these were expressed in diplomatic endeavours. Indeed, the deductive method – not least in Wolff – led to the suspicion that such constructions actually disguised the attempt to 'order nature according to one's ideas, and not order one's ideas according to nature' (Gotthold Ephraim Lessing).[4]

We should also note the historical link between the labels 'international law' and 'law of nations'. Their meaning overlaps only partially, but anyone wishing to understand the situation prior to the spread of the term 'international law' in the nineteenth century should undoubtedly look into the law of nations, or natural law *and* the law of nations, or public law.[5] Accordingly, this investigation has to start with an analysis of the institution (or non-institution) of the chair of natural law and law of nations.

The reform of the University of Cagliari advocated by Giovanni Battista Lorenzo Bogino, the superintendent at the Secretariat of the Affairs of Sardinia,[6] and implemented in 1764,[7] served to restore its original task, which it had long ceased to fulfil, and made it operational again in training prospective graduates for both legal and academic practice.

Legal Discipline in the 19th Century', in *Constructing International Law: The Bird of a Discipline*, ed. Luigi Nuzzo and Miloš Vec (Frankfurt am Main: Vittorio Klostermann, 2012), ix–xvi.

3 In a vast literature see in particular Koen Stapelbroek and Antonio Trampus, 'The Legacy of Vattel's *Droit des gens*. Contexts, Concepts, Reception, Translation and Diffusion', in *The Legacy of Vattel's Droit des gens*, ed. Koen Stapelbroek, Antonio Trampus (Cham: Palgrave Macmillan, 2019), 1–25; and Elisabetta Fiocchi Malaspina, 'The Legacy of Vattel's *Droit des gens* in the Long Nineteenth Century', ibid., 267–283, and the bibliography there.

4 Quoted from Aldo Mazzacane, *Savigny e la storiografia giuridica tra storia e sistema* (Napoli: Liguori, 1976), 5.

5 See Emmanuelle Jouannet, 'Droit des gens (Du droit des gens au droit international)', in *Dictionnaire de la culture juridique*, ed. Denis Alland and Stéphane Rials (Paris: PUF, 2003), 463–467.

6 See Giuseppe Ricuperati, 'Il Settecento', in *Il Piemonte sabaudo. Stato e territori in età moderna, Storia d'Italia*, ed. Giuseppe Galasso (Torino: UTET, 1994), vol. 8, pt 1, 515–528 and 549–562.

7 Boginian reform was extended in 1765 to a second university in Sardinia, the University of Sassari, founded in 1562. On the common history of the two Sardinian universities and especially the two law faculties see Antonello Mattone, 'La storia delle Facoltà di Giurisprudenza di Cagliari e di Sassari, una storia parallela?', in *La Facoltà di Giurisprudenza di Cagliari e l'insegnamento del diritto tra Otto e Novecento. La storia e la memoria*, ed. Giuseppina De Giudici (Napoli: ESI, 2023), 17–75. Concerning the law faculty there, see Antonello Mattone, *Storia della Facoltà di Giurisprudenza dell'Università di Sassari (secoli XVI–XX)* (Bologna: Il Mulino, 2016).

Founded in 1620 as a city university and operational from 1626, the University of Cagliari did not fully function as such until the end of the seventeenth century.[8] Nevertheless, at the beginning of the eighteenth century it was essentially ghost-like: although chairs and assignments were formally decided, the secretariats did not function; student registers were not kept; although university degrees (bachelor's, licentiate and baccalaureate) were formally conferred, examinations were not held; and, above all, no actual teaching took place.[9] The aim of the Bogino's reform was to relaunch the original university, as is clear from the scope of the initiative by the House of Savoy, that is, moderate in content and, as far as legal studies were concerned, with an unwillingness to reconsider the classical curriculum of jurists *in utroque jure*.[10]

Despite this, there is no reason to rule out that the Savoy government felt the need to form new classes of intellectuals. Indeed, Bogino's reform was modelled on Turin, though adjusted due to the more limited financial resources available, and it was conceived as an essential basis for more wide-ranging reforms; in fact, a 'new flourishing of Sardinia' was expected. It is no coincidence that this phrase (in Italian: *Rifiorimento della Sardegna*) is the title of a work that was written by Francesco Gemelli at Bogino's request and which can be regarded as a manifesto of that period.[11] Effectively, the late-eighteenth-century reform of the Sardinian universities determined, as has

8 The University of Cagliari was founded by a charter granted by Filippo III of Spain. See *I documenti originali di fondazione dell'Università di Cagliari*, ed. Luisa D'Arienzo (Nuoro: Ilisso, 1997), *passim*. For a historical reconstruction on the birth of the University of Cagliari and the function of teaching during the seventeenth and eighteeenth centuries, see Gian paolo Brizzi, 'Tra Roma e Madrid: la genesi dello Studio generale di Cagliari (1543–1626)', in *La Facoltà di Giurisprudenza dell'Università di Cagliari, vol. 1, Dai progetti cinquecenteschi all'Unità d'Italia*, ed. Italo Birocchi (Pisa: ETS, 2018), 23–64, and Antonello Mattone, *Storia della Facoltà di Giurisprudenza dell'Università di Sassari*, 45–51.

9 See Italo Birocchi, 'Graduati e professori nell'età preboginiana (1709–1763)', in *La Facoltà di Giurisprudenza dell'Università di Cagliari*, vol. 1, 171–181. However, the decline of the University of Cagliari before the 1764 reform is not an isolated case in the history of Italian universities. On the topic see Emanuela Verzella, 'La crisi dell'assetto corporativo e le riforme universitarie', in *Storia delle Università in Italia*, ed. Gian Paolo Brizzi, Piero Del Negro and Andrea Romano (Messina: Sicania, 2007), vol. 1, 159–191. Regarding the review of legal studies, see Italo Birocchi, 'Contenuti e metodi dell'insegnamento: il Diritto nei secoli XVI–XVIII', in *Storia delle Università in Italia*, vol. 2, 243–261, at 253–256.

10 Law firms remained, in fact, tied to the humanistic model, as stated by Italo Birocchi, 'Università e riforme: il modello neoumanista e le facoltà giuridiche', in *Governare un Regno. Viceré, apparati burocratici e società nella Sardegna del Settecento*, ed. Pierpaolo Merlin (Roma: Carocci, 2005), 422–441.

11 On the reform conceived by the House of Savoy between the late 1750s and the late 1760s see Giuseppina De Giudici, *Interessi e usure nella Sardegna di Carlo Emanuele III* (Pisa: ETS, 2010), esp. 31–36.

been recognized,[12] an intellectual awakening and triggered a sort of revolution of ideas. This also occurred thanks to the initial recruitment of foreign lecturers, called to teach, mainly in the Faculty of Philosophy and Arts, preparatory to admission to the three higher faculties (Law, Theology and Medicine), and in that of Theology. This is what happened with the Lombard Augustinian Carlo Nicolò Fabi,[13] the Genoese Scolopian Liberato Fassoni,[14] the Carmelite Paolo Maria Oggero[15] and the Turin Dominican Gian Battista Vasco.[16]

In the Faculty of Law in Cagliari – where, as at the University of Sassari, there had been a lack of external recruitment[17] – the major themes of natural law did not find a place in the courses on *jus civile* and *jus canonicum*.[18] However, it cannot be said that law students were entirely exempt from study of

---

12 See Antonello Mattone and Piero Sanna, 'La rivoluzione delle idee: la riforma delle due università sarde e la circolazione della cultura europea (1764–1790)', in idem, *Settecento sardo e cultura europea. Lumi, società, istituzioni nella crisi dell'Antico Regime* (Milano: Franco Angeli, 2007), 13–106. See also Italo Birocchi, *La carta autonomistica della Sardegna tra antico e moderno: le leggi fondamentali nel triennio rivoluzionario (1793–96)* (Torino: Giappichelli, 1992), 53–72; Piero Sanna, 'L'assolutismo sabaudo e l'Università di Sassari. Il rinnovamento degli studi', in *Storia dell'Università di Sassari*, ed. Antonello Mattone (Nuoro: Ilisso, 2010), vol. 1, 81–97; Italo Birocchi, 'Università e riforme', esp. 57; and Walter Falgio, *Libro e università nella Sardegna del '700* (Cagliari: AM&D, 2011), 13–29.

13 In Cagliari from 1764 to 1770, Fabi taught for the first two years Ethics or Moral Philosophy and Metaphysics and Logic and for the remaining four years Moral Theology. On Fabi see Guido Fagioli Vercellone, 'Fabi, Carlo Nicola Maria', in *Dizionario Biografico degli Italiani* (Roma: Istituto dell'Enciclopedia italiana, 1993), vol. 43, 697–699, at 698.

14 Fassoni taught Moral Theology from 1764 to 1770. On Fassoni see Carlo Fantappiè, 'Fassoni, Liberato', in *Dizionario Biografico degli Italiani* (Roma: Istituto dell'Enciclopedia italiana, 1995), vol. 45, 308–311, at 310.

15 Oggero taught Sacred Scripture and Hebrew Language from 1764 to 1770. See Mattone and Sanna, 'La rivoluzione delle idee', 23.

16 Vasco was professor of Scholastic-dogmatic Theology and Ecclesiastical History from 1764 to 1766. On his teaching in Cagliari see Franco Venturi, 'Gian Battista Vasco all'Università di Cagliari', *Archivio storico sardo* 25 (1957): 12–41; idem, 'Giambattista Vasco', in *Illuministi italiani*, vol. 3, *Riformatori lombardi, piemontesi e toscani*, ed, Franco Venturi (Milano-Napoli: Riccardo Ricciardi Editore, 1958), 757–768; Gianni Marocco, *Giambattista Vasco* (Torino: Fondazione Luigi Einaudi, 1978), 24–26; and Paola Bianchi, 'Giovanni Battista Vasco', in *Dizionario Biografico degli Italiani* (Roma: Istituto dell'Enciclopedia italiana, 2020), vol. 98, 388–392. The text of his prologues to courses on Scholastic-dogmatic theology and Church history (under the name of Thomas, assumed as a Dominican) is now in Giambattista Vasco, *Opere*, ed. Maria Luisa Perna (Torino: Fondazione Luigi Einaudi, 1989), vol. 1, 15–23 and 27–28.

17 Mattone, *Storia della Facoltà di Giurisprudenza dell'Università di Sassari*, 100.

18 This statement is reflected in the guidance provided by the government on course holding (see the 'Piano per l'Instituta civile', in Archivio di Stato di Cagliari, Cagliari, Italy (hereinafter ASCa), Segreteria di Stato, series II, vol. 819; the document, undated but referable to the years of the start of the reform, is contained in the file concerning the

the topics discussed by the natural lawyers. If anything, the problem lay in the quality and quantity of the teaching.

2 Preparing for Higher Courses: The Ethics and Logic and Metaphysics Classes

As noted above, prior to specialist training, aspiring jurists – as well as aspiring theologians and aspiring physicians – were required to take courses at the Faculty of Philosophy and Arts. Here they were taught, in addition to classes in Experimental Physics, those in Ethics (or Moral Philosophy),[19] designed as an introductory discipline to the natural law sciences, and Logic and Metaphysics, useful for acquiring the principles of a 'sound criticism', away from 'superstitious credulity' or 'intemperate freedom of thought'.[20] It is interesting to consider that Ethics texts included, in addition to those of Aristotle, St Thomas and Cicero, Samuel Pufendorf's *De officio hominis et civis*, Johann Franz Budde's *Elementa philosophiae praticae* and Johann Gottlieb Heinecke's *Elementa philosophiae rationalis et moralis*, as well as works by Christian Wolff and Ludovico Antonio Muratori.[21]

For the Logic and Metaphysics lectures, on the other hand, the texts of Francis Bacon, Pierre Gassendi, René Descartes, Nicholas de Malebranche, Jean Le Clerc, Johannes Clauberg, Gerhard Johannes Voss, Willem Jacob's Gravesande, Jean-Pierre de Crousaz, Antonio Genovesi and so on were to be used.[22] It is during Ethics classes, for the purpose of highlighting the main 'errors, on which the human mind had stumbled for lack of principles and rules',[23] that Father Fabi, for example, had delivered the lecture 'De humanae

University of Sassari, but since the reform affected both universities, it also applies to that of Cagliari. It should be added that dictation from treaties left little room for in-depth studies other than those contained in the sources of Roman or canon law and perhaps also during the exercises that took place on Saturdays.

19 The Ethics course was taught by the faculty members of Logic and Metaphysics and of Experimental Physics in alternating years, as required by the *Costituzioni di Sua Maestà per l'Università degli studi di Cagliari* (Torino: Nella Stamperia Reale, 1764), tit. x, §§ 1–7, 26–27. For the course programme see the *Idea del modo in cui si avrà a dettare l'Etica*, in ASCa, Segreteria di Stato, series II, vol. 819.

20 Ibid.

21 Ibid.

22 See the *Idea del modo in cui si avrà a studiare la Logica e la Metafisica*, in ASCa, Segreteria di Stato, series II, vol. 819.

23 Ibid.

mentis, brutorumque animae discrimine adversus Petrum Baelium et Helvetium dissertatio', to criticize Pierre Bayle's rationalism and Helvétius's sensism. On that occasion he had also recalled the thought of the 'gravissimus philosophus' John Locke and referred to Antonio Genovesi and the encyclopaedists.[24]

On the other hand, Helvétius's thought was not liked by Giuseppe Gagliardi, Turin Jesuit Professor of Experimental Physics and Ethics in Cagliari from 1784 to 1789 and author of the essay *L'onest'uomo filosofo* (1772).[25] Moved by the aim of re-establishing the authority of civil laws, questioned by those who emphasized their variety and mutability, he acknowledged the existence of norms of the law of nations, as part of natural law. After critiquing the contributions of Machiavelli, Hobbes and Bayle and of many theories on the origin of sovereignty and on the rights of the citizen, he referred to Grotius, Pufendorf, Locke and Burlamaqui. He then blamed the 'extravagant and free opinions' of Rousseau and Helvétius on the equality of men and criticized the thought of Montesquieu.

Interesting spaces for the discussion of issues addressed by the great natural lawyers are found, perhaps to an even greater extent, in the Theology courses,[26] which responded to a more 'openly innovative' approach[27] but with a slant strictly functional to the aim of affirming the doctrine of the Church. The dissertations of Giambattista Vasco and Liberato Fassoni are well placed in this context.

Vasco – in addition to refuting in the dissertation *De certitudine in quaestionibus facti* (1764), inspired by the *Encyclopédie* entry on 'Certitude',[28] the opinion of those who excluded the possibility of certainty in historical subjects – quoted during lectures in the course of Theologia scholastica Thomas Campanella, Baruch Spinoza, John Locke, Gottfried Wilhelm Leibniz, Christian Wolff and Johann Christoph Gottsched as well as Voltaire, Denis

24 See Franco Venturi, 'Gian Battista Vasco all'Università di Cagliari', 25; and Mattone and Sanna, 'La rivoluzione delle idee', 25–26.

25 Gagliardi had the Cagliari position after teaching in Sassari; see Antonio Delogu, 'Gli studi filosofici nell'Università di Sassari (1765–1960)', in *Storia dell'Università di Sassari*, 344–345.

26 In-depth study of topics on natural law and the law of nations, accomplished within the bounds of thinking not unwelcome to the Church, was done within Moral Theology classes. It concerned human acts (*de actibus humanis*) and the principles that governed them, as well as topics *de justitia et jure, de legibus, de contractibus*.

27 The expression is used by Mattone and Sanna, 'La rivoluzione delle idee', 27.

28 The entry is by Jean-Martin de Prades.

Diderot, Étienne Condillac and Jean-Baptiste D'Alembert,[29] and praised John Locke for his famous work *De intellectu humano*.[30] As part of his teaching on moral theology, Fassoni,[31] on the other hand, had given a lecture later published as *De morali patrum doctrina adversum librum Jo. Barbeyraci ad disputationes de ecclesiastica historia introitus* (1767).

The criticism of Jean Barbeyrac, 'excellenti ingegno et doctrina vir',[32] was related to the positions expressed in the preface to the French translation of Pufendorf's *De jure naturae et gentium*. Here, Barbeyrac had discussed the positions and authority of the Holy Fathers in the area of the philosophy of morals, provoking the lively reaction of Rémy Ceillier, author of the *Apologie de la morale des Pères contre les injustes accusations du sieur Jean Barbeyrac* (Paris, 1718).

After the first generation of professors, however, our knowledge of the content and circulation of the thought of natural lawyers is less than episodic, due to the lack of most lecture texts.[33] The circulation in the university environment of some classic texts of natural law can, however, be verified through the increase in the number of books in the city's university library, opened to the public in 1792 with a holding of about 8,000 volumes, many of which came

29 See Venturi, 'Gian Battista Vasco all'Università di Cagliari': 17–41; Gianni Marocco, *Giambattista Vasco*, 26–27; and Gian Giacomo Ortu, 'Tra etica, diritto ed economia: intrecci di cultura e di pratica', in *La Facoltà di Giurisprudenza dell'Università di Cagliari*, 463–464.

30 The manuscript is in the Cagliari University Library (collocation: s.b., 1–4, 32–33).

31 Already author of *De leibnitziano rationis sufficientis principio dissertatio philosophica* (Senogalliae, 1754), he had also presented to the island's university the dissertation *De viro laico cun haereticis disputante* … (Liburni, n.y.), dedicated to Antonio Genovesi.

32 Liberato Fassoni, *De morali patrum doctrina adversus librum Jo. Barbeyraci et ad disputationes de ecclesiastica historia introitus* (Liburni: Ex Typographia Marci Coltellini, 1767), 2.

33 This applies to both manuscript and printed texts. On the difficulties of finding and studying lecture treatises see Silvia Conti, 'Dettati e trattati per la "studiosa gioventù": trasmissione e diffusione delle idee a Cagliari tra Seicento e Settecento', in *Circolazione d'idee, parole, uomini, libri e culture: Sardegna, Corsica, Toscana*, ed. Giancarlo Nonnoi (Cagliari: CUEC, 2009), 187–194 (in Annexes I and II, pp. 195–230, the author provides a list of the manuscripts of lectures held between the seventeenth and eighteenth centuries that have been found; since Silvia Conti wrote her work, the only change has been that the University of Cagliari's Historical Archive is now accessible). Among the printed editions, it is worth mentioning the text of the lectures of Sebastiano Deidda, *Institutiones logicae et metaphysicae* (Carali: Aloysium Lecca Paucheville, 1836, 2 vols). He asserted that Descartes, Malebranche, Leibniz, Wolff and especially Locke were responsible for a more mature metaphysics. Hume and d'Alembert had contributed to this along with Condillac, Genovesi and others.

from the libraries of the colleges following the suppression of the Society of Jesus (1773).[34]

Between 1786 and 1794 it had been expanded by the addition of volumes by Hugo Grotius, Samuel Cocceji, Johann Gottlieb Heinecke and Jean-Jacques Burlamaqui, as well as with Antonio Genovesi's *Diceosina o la filosofia del giusto e dell'onesto* and the select compilation *Les Pensées de Jean-Jacques Rousseau.*[35] We also know that the importance of Vico's *Scienza nuova* and the debates about it did not escape Giacinto Hinz, Professor of Sacred Scripture from 1770 and in charge of the Library for more than fifteen years from the end of 1785.[36] After the economic difficulties that greatly conditioned the possibilities for growth of the library holdings,[37] finally in the early 1840s, the Library, directed by Pietro Martini (from 1842 to 1866), increased the number of titles significantly for the purpose of equipping the university with useful texts for all courses.[38] The massive number of volumes purchased mostly covered science subjects. Among those acquired during that period the following stand out: Samuel Pufendorf's *De jure naturae et gentium* in the French edition by Jean Barbeyrac, the *Corso di diritto naturale* by Heinrich Ahrens, Robert-Joseph Pothier's treatises, two copies of Jean Domat's *Le loix civiles dans leur ordre naturel*, one work by Jeremy Bentham and one by Arnold Vinnen, and several works by Gian Domenico Romagnosi, Antonio Rosmini and Vincenzo Gioberti.[39]

---

34 Together with the volumes of the college libraries, the University Library also absorbed the important library of the Sardinian humanist jurist Monserrat Rosselló (which had about 4,450 titles, not only of law). On Rosselló Enzo Cadoni and Maria Teresa Laneri, *Umanisti e cultura classica nella Sardegna del '500*, vol. 3, pt 1, *L'inventario dei beni e dei libri di Monserrat Rosselló* (Sassari: Gallizzi, 1994), 11–79; and Carla Ferrante, 'Rosselló Monserrat', in *Dizionario Biografico dei Giuristi Italiani*, vol. 2, 1736–1737. On the events surrounding the establishment of the library's holdings see Giovanna Granata, 'La Biblioteca Universitaria di Cagliari e i libri di diritto', in *La Facoltà di Giurisprudenza dell'Università di Cagliari*, 383–384.

35 See the list of books purchased by Giacinto Hinz, in charge of the Library, in Archivio Storico dell'Università di Cagliari (hereinafter ASUCa), sezione I, series 5, Biblioteca, busta 157, n. 12.

36 See Granata, 'La Biblioteca Universitaria di Cagliari e i libri di diritto', 384.

37 Among the books purchased by Faustino Baille between 1827 and 1838 we find several works by Melchiorre Gioia, Adam Smith's *Wealth of Nations* in French language and some of Robert-Joseph Pothier's treatises (see the list of books in ASUCa, sezione I, series 5, Biblioteca, busta 158, n. 23).

38 See Granata, 'La Biblioteca Universitaria di Cagliari e i libri di diritto', 413–418.

39 ASUCa, sezione I, series 1.9, Deliberazioni, busta 37, n. 21 and series 5, Biblioteca, busta 158, n. 23.

Between 1852 and 1853, the Library's funding increased further and consequently the University was able to keep abreast of the evolution of faculty studies and of the teaching needs imposed by the mid-century reforms.[40] On more than one occasion the new acquisitions also included titles on – as could be expected – natural law and law of nations and international law. In the meantime, for just under a decade from 1818, the direction of the Library was entrusted to Sassari's international law scholar Domenico Alberto Azuni, who had returned to Italy after the fall of Napoleon. The purchase of volumes in the field of maritime law dates to that period.

3 Ambiguous Times: From a Discipline 'on Paper' to an Actual Course of International Law

Thanks to the 'perfect incorporation' of Sardinia into the Savoy States, which took place in 1847–1848,[41] the universities of Cagliari and Sassari were absorbed within the general university system of the Kingdom of Sardinia and started to overcome a sort of cultural paralysis which had hampered them after the eighteenth-century reform. In contrast to the lively reforms at the mainland universities, the Sardinian ones had remained substantially hidebound.[42] Thus, when the autonomy of the former Regnum Sardiniae was relinquished, this had a significant impact on the functioning of the Sardinian universities and the organization of legal studies, which had recently been heavily criticized by Carlo Cattaneo in the essay *Della Sardegna antica e moderna* (1841).[43]

The departure in 1851 from the old lecture text dictation system that had enabled the government to keep a watchful eye on the legal theories taught by the professors[44] was immediately followed by the decision to discontinue

---

40 Granata, 'La Biblioteca Universitaria di Cagliari e i libri di diritto', 416–418.

41 See Italo Birocchi, 'La questione autonomistica dalla "fusione perfetta" al primo dopoguerra', in *La Sardegna. Storia d'Italia. Le regioni dall'Unità ad oggi*, ed. Luigi Berlinguer and Antonello Mattone (Torino: Einaudi, 1998), 136–199, at 138.

42 See Mattone, *Storia della Facoltà di Giurisprudenza dell'Università di Sassari*, 157–168.

43 Carlo Cattaneo, *Della Sardegna antica e moderna con 56 lettere intercorse tra lo studioso e i suoi corrispondenti sardi*, ed. Assunta Trova (Nuoro: Ilisso, 2010), esp. 78. This work had originally appeared as 'Di varie opere sulla Sardegna', *Il politecnico repertorio mensile di studj applicati alla prosperità e coltura sociale* 2 (1841): 219–273; the essay was later published under the title given in the text.

44 In this respect, there had been a number of complaints from those who, like Borgna, opposed the system. See Italo Birocchi, 'L'impianto filosofico e il quadro normativo della riforma boginiana', in *La Facoltà di Giurisprudenza dell'Università di Cagliari*, vol. 1, 223.

the teaching of Latin (1852).[45] An even more important decision had been the opening, from mid-century, of the Faculty of Law to disciplines that were not consistent with the by now obsolete model of traditional courses shaped on the *jus civile* and on the *jus canonicum*. The introduction in legal studies of the chair of *res mercatoria* in 1846 was of little importance, since this subject was mainly aimed at meeting the needs of tradesmen. Besides, even professors publicly stigmatized the unbridgeable gap between the Faculty of Law of Cagliari and that of the main Italian universities. For instance, in Cagliari in December 1848, the young Giovanni De Gioannis went so far as to affirm, in the presence of the 'highly adorned scholars of Law', that while in Turin and Genoa 'the new chairs of civil code, public law, economics and constitutional science had been established' and while 'our young continental brothers are educating themselves for the real studies of progress', in Sardinia university students were 'doomed to feed on minutiae of old schools of thought', since they still had to study 'that law most of which reflected conditions that have remained unchanged for the past thirteen centuries'.[46]

From the first decades of the new century, there was a widespread idea that curricula needed to be renewed and adapted to educational models more in tune with the times, and in particular with the German one, which was becoming a leading example. Also in this period we have the resolute words of a renowned visiting professor, Friedrich Carl von Savigny, who in the 1820s made clear the distance between university studies in Italy and those in Humboldt's Germany.[47] It is noteworthy that Savigny's judgement, which circulated in a reduced and simplified form, further widened the gap between these cultural worlds,[48] so much so that Giovanni Carmignani in 1841 acknowledged it

---

Laura Moscati, 'La Facoltà legale e la scienza giuridica della Restaurazione', *Annali di storia delle università italiane* 4 (2000): 77–94, relates the first signs of modernization in the curricula of the Law Faculty of the Sapienza in Rome to the prohibition of dictation from textbooks.

45 See the royal decree of 7 May 1852, in ASCa, Atti governativi ed amministrativi, vol. 32, no. 1366.

46 Giovanni De Gioannis, *Parole dette agli ornatissimi studiosi di Giurisprudenza* (*23 dicembre 1848*) (Cagliari: Timon, 1849), 13. Also quoted by Mattone, *Storia della Facoltà di Giurisprudenza dell'Università di Sassari*, 167.

47 Carl von Savigny, 'Sull'insegnamento del dritto in Italia', in idem, *Ragionamenti storici di diritto del prof. C. Savigny, tradotti dall'originale tedesco e preceduti da un discorso da A. Turchiarulo* (Napoli: Tipografia all'insegna del Diogene, 1852), pt IV, 67–84. That essay follows 'Sulla qualità e sul merito delle Università tedesche', ibid., 46–66.

48 Laura Moscati, 'Un'inedita lettera di Savigny a Poerio', in *Quaderni fiorentini per la storia del pensiero giuridico* 21 (1992): 663–669; and Luigi Lacchè, 'La nazione dei giuristi. Il

as a 'serious and degrading reproach' from the learned men of Germany.[49] In the 1840s there followed the sad account by Carl (or Carlo) Mittermaier, who, after recalling that 'Italy had been the cradle of European civilization',[50] pitied it because of the 'present decay, of the impoverishment of science and art' and the 'decline of its people'.[51] Scientific speculation was, in his opinion, spoiled by the excessive pragmatism of the professor-lawyers in particular.

The issue of the modernization of studies and of the reform of the curricula was also dealt with by a jurist in the making, Francesco Forti, the maternal nephew of the great Jean-Charles-Léonard Sismondi, who, in his *Lettera sulla direzione degli studj* addressed to a friend, asserted that devoting oneself to the law of nations was 'an important part of the science of a jurisconsult'.[52]

In Cagliari, international law was first introduced as a discipline in 1850.[53] However, this is in fact a fictitious landmark date since in Sardinian universities the public law chairs were 'cumulative', that is, designed to bring different disciplines together. This was the case of the incredibly capacious chair of public, constitutional, administrative and international law, assigned to a single professor who was vested with the impossible task of covering such an extensive programme in a one-year course. Therefore, it is not surprising that the professors in question – Giuseppe Siotto Pintor (1850–1855)[54] and Giovanni De

canone eclettico, tra politica e cultura giuridica: spunti per una riflessione sull'esperienza italiana della Restaurazione', in *Diritto, cultura giuridica e riforme nell'età di Maria Luigia*, ed. Frank Micolo, Giuseppina Baggio, Edoardo Fregoso and Atti del Convegno (Parma: Monte Università Parma, 2011), 263–307, at 269–270.

49 See Enrico Spagnesi, 'Giovanni Carmignani e il problema dell'insegnamento del diritto', in *Giovanni Carmignani (1768–1847). Maestro di scienze criminali e pratico del foro sulle soglie del Diritto Penale contemporaneo*, ed. Mario Montorzi (Pisa: ETS, 2005), 463–498.

50 Carlo [Carl J. A.] Mittermaier, 'Dell'importanza d'Italia ne' progressi della civiltà in Europa, e delle speranze pel suo avvenire. Lettera dell'autore al traduttore', in idem, *Delle condizioni d'Italia con un capitolo inedito dell'autore e con note del traduttore Pietro Mugna* (Leipzig: stampato da G. B. Hirschfeld at Tendler & Schäfer, 1845), 229–251, at 236–237.

51 Ibid., 237.

52 See Francesco Forti, 'Lettera sulla direzione degli studii', in idem, *Scritti varii. Opere edite e inedite* (Firenze: Presso Eugenio and F. Cammelli Editori-Librai, 1865), 1–81, at 52.

53 See the *Regolamento provvisorio per l'esecuzione della legge del 1850 contenente alcune nuove disposizioni per le Università di Cagliari e Sassari*, approved by royal decree of 14 May 1850 (in ASCa, Atti governativi e amministrativi, vol. 27). Regarding the innovations brought about by the reform and the objectives pursued by the subalpine government by means of the same, see Mattone, *Storia della Facoltà di Giurisprudenza dell'Università di Sassari*, 183–184.

54 By his own admission Giuseppe Siotto Pintor never actually taught international law. Regarding Siotto Pintor, who graduated in Cagliari in 1832, Professor of Latin Eloquence in 1834, of Civil Law in 1839, of *Digest* in 1841 and from 1850 of Public, Constitutional,

Gioannis (1855–1859) – pointed out on several occasions the absurdity of such an arduous task, especially since it concerned subjects closely related to the achievement of 'national well-being'.[55] In 1853, Siotto Pintor suggested dividing the subjects into two different courses (one of public and constitutional law and the other of administrative and international law). The same request was subsequently made by De Gioannis on several occasions (for instance in 1856–1857).

Things eventually changed in 1859, when the Casati law, which made the study of international law compulsory in the universities of the Italian peninsula, was enacted.[56] International law was thereby incorporated into philosophy of law, and this secured the speculative foundations essential for a discipline that was considered endangered by positivism and, therefore, at risk of being represented as a *summa* of arbitrary and contingent norms, in other words, as a product of politics and power. In this way, the two subjects were mutually reinforcing,[57] all the more so since in 1852 Giuseppe Siotto Pintor had denounced the serious shortcomings of future jurists in the philosophy of law.

Certain that every provision could be traced back to natural law, 'like the streams to their source', he voiced the idea, revealed by the 'best public law scholars', that every society was not 'a product of man, but of nature'. Nonetheless, his students were not able to grasp 'the essence, the definition, and [...] the existence of a law considered as an ideal and moral entity'.[58] The will to disprove the peripatetic philosophy testified by the short-sighted closure in Ulpian's definition of natural law ('ius naturale est quod natura omnia animalia docuit') had led Siotto Pintor to endeavour for 'over two months'[59] to strengthen his students' familiarity with natural law. Indeed, international law was a science enriched by the philosophical spirit.

International and Administrative Law, see *Giuseppe Siotto Pintor*, ed. Efisio Siotto Pintor (Cagliari: Tipografia nazionale, 1855).

55 Giovanni Siotto Pintor, *Storia letteraria di Sardegna* (Cagliari, 1843–1844; Bologna, Forni, 1966), vol. 2, l. IV, 199.

56 For the legal subjects established under the Casati law, and an opinion on the latter, see Mattone, *Storia della Facoltà di Giurisprudenza dell'Università di Sassari*, 181–184 and 193–195.

57 Pasquale Stanislao Mancini, *Prelezione al corso di diritto pubblico marittimo insegnato nella R. Università di Torino nel 1852–53 pronunciata nel dì 29 novembre 1852*, in idem, *Diritto internazionale. Prelezioni con un saggio sul Machiavelli* (Napoli: Giuseppe Marghieri, 1873), 93–116. International Law was a two-year course; in the second year, public maritime law was addressed.

58 Quote from G. Siotto Pintor in his report on the teaching activity carried out in 1853 (see the document in ASUCa, sezione 2.2, series 1.2, Carteggio, busta 3, no. 59).

59 Ibid.

Those were also the years when Pietro Luigi Albini, Professor of Legal Encyclopaedism at the University of Turin, encouraged historical-philosophical studies. He was convinced that Italian jurists, 'with the exception of those who had the patience and courage to start their scientific education from scratch, remedying the imperfection of the University's narrow-minded and petty studies', ignored not only the German philosophy of law, but also that taught by 'Lampredi, Genovesi, and, above all, Giambattista Vico', not to mention that 'of the more recent [scholars]'.[60]

In addition, the establishment of a chair of philosophy and international law was in line with the proposal put forward by Giovanni De Gioannis[61] on the occasion of Pasquale Stanislao Mancini's visit to Cagliari in 1859, in the latter's capacity as ministerial inspector in charge of evaluating the functioning of the two Sardinian universities.[62] The request by De Gioannis, who later became a renowned administrative law scholar after moving first to Pavia then to Pisa,[63] must have impressed the internationalist; he had started teaching less than a decade before in the renowned course on international public law in Turin and had previously been supply professor of natural law and law of

60 Luigi Albini, 'Sull'importanza dello studio della filosofia del diritto', in Pasquale Stanislao Mancini and Terenzio Mamiani, *Filosofia del diritto e singolarmente del diritto di punire. lettere di Terenzio Mamiani e di Pasquale Stanislao Mancini accresciute di quattro discorsi di Terenzio Mamiani sulla sovranità e di una prefazione del prof. Luigi Albini* (Livorno: Coi Tipi di Franc. Vigo Editore, 1875), 5–13, at 10.

61 In the report of April 1851, the rector of the University of Cagliari considered the impossibility 'for a single professor to teach public, constitutional, administrative and international law in 140 lessons at most'. See ASUCa, sezione 2.2, series 1.1, Carteggio, busta 2, no. 45.

62 See Claudia Storti, 'Mancini, Pasquale Stanislao', in *Dizionario Biografico dei Giuristi Italiani (XII–XX secolo)*, ed. Italo Birocchi et al. (Bologna: Il Mulino, 2013), vol. 2, 1244–1248; Luigi Nuzzo, 'Da Mazzini a Mancini: il principio di nazionalità tra politica e diritto', *Giornale di Storia Costituzionale* 14(2) (2007): 161–186; idem, 'Pasquale Stanislao Mancini', in *Enciclopedia italiana di scienze, lettere e arti. Appendice* 8. *Il Contributo italiano alla storia del Pensiero – Diritto* (Roma: Treccani, 2012), 307–310; idem, *Origini di una scienza. Diritto internazionale e colonialismo nel XIX secolo* (Frankfurt am Main: Vittorio Klostermann, 2012), *ad indicem*; *Per una rilettura di Mancini. Saggi sul Risorgimento*, ed. Italo Birocchi (Pisa: ETS, 2018). See also Chapter 9 of the present volume, by Frédéric Ieva.

63 See Giulio Cianferotti, 'Lo Stato nazionale e la nuova scienza del diritto pubblico', in *Enciclopedia italiana di scienze, lettere e arti. Appendice* 8, 321. On the jurist as administrative law scholar, see idem, *Storia della letteratura amministrativistica italiana*, vol. 1, *Dall'Unità alla fine dell'Ottocento. Autonomie locali, amministrazione e costituzione* (Milano: Giuffrè, 1998), *ad indicem*.

nations (1847–1849) in Naples.[64] However, the unified teaching of philosophy and international law was short lived, since in 1872 the first chair of international law was inaugurated in Cagliari, later surviving the ministerial changes to the curricula at the Faculty of Law.[65]

4 The Principle of Nationality as the Foundation of a New Law of Nations

The establishment of an Italian legal science that took into account the specializations of the different branches almost represented the *leitmotiv* of Italy's unification. As if illuminated by a 'new light',[66] political unification did, in fact, give jurists the enthusiasm to feel part of a collective scientific movement with a synergy to construct a common theoretical heritage.

It is no coincidence that in 1869 the young international law scholar Augusto Pierantoni, Professor of International and Constitutional Law in Modena, addressed the Italians who had finally recovered their self-awareness, urging them to dedicate themselves to the 'serious task of combining political unity' with the consolidation of 'national awareness'.[67] Likewise, it is no coincidence that his *Storia degli studi del diritto internazionale in Italia* (1869) became the symbol of an idealized intellectual brotherhood of the Italian people. Dramatically divided 'between many States, with varying attitudes', Italians had to draw energy from their nation's independence in order to

64 Storti, 'Mancini, Pasquale Stanislao', 1245. The discipline of international public law was introduced in 1850 within a post graduate specialist course. On the establishment in 1808 of a chair of 'public and commercial law in relations between the State and foreign States' (diritto pubblico e commerciale nei rapporti dello Stato cogli Stati esteri), see Pasquale Fiore, *Trattato di diritto internazionale pubblico*, 2nd edition (Torino: Unione Tipografico-Editrice, 1879), vol. 1, 141, note 2; Enrico Catellani, *La dottrina italiana del diritto internazionale nel secolo XIX: lezioni alla Accademia di diritto internazionale all'Aia nel 1933* (Roma: Anonima Romana Editoriale, 1935), 10–11. In Genoa, the chair of constitutional and international law had been established in 1848 and entrusted to Ludovico Casanova, whose lectures were published after his death.

65 The main reforms following the Casati law had been introduced under the Regulations of the Universities of the Kingdom of Italy (1862), under the Regulations of 1876 and under those of 1885, concerning which see Mattone, *Storia della Facoltà di Giurisprudenza di Sassari*, 194–195.

66 Enrico Pessina, *Dei progressi del diritto penale in Italia nel secolo XIX. Discorso* (Firenze: Stabilimento Civelli, 1868), 147.

67 See Augusto Pierantoni, *Storia degli studi del diritto internazionale in Italia* (Modena: Coi tipi di Carlo Vincenzi, 1869), Prefazione, iii.

emancipate the 'native ingenuity from the overwhelming foreign power'.[68] Clearly, Pierantoni was driven by enthusiasm for the nation and perceived the effects that the same could display with regard to the law of nations. Besides, the Risorgimento events could but enhance their impact, showing that that factor was not a mere creation of the intellect. On the contrary, the concept of nation was based on naturalness and was therefore the expression of a true force, capable of actually affecting peoples,[69] the Italian events testifying to the nation that was finally constituted as a state were proof of this.

In addition to the Risorgimento restraints burdening that generation of jurists, there was yet another factor. Indeed, the legal theory of international law had long been shaken, if not by a real crisis, at least by profound restlessness. The latter called for the rejection of 'Grotius's erudition, Wolff's geometric formulas, Vattel's excessive simplicity, De Martens's practical knowledge', as effectively stated by Pellegrino Rossi in his summary in a famous review of Henry Wheaton's *Elements of International Law*.[70] In Rossi's opinion, the last century – roughly the period since the publication of Vattel's *Le Droit des gens* (1758) – had not reaped any fruit.[71] According to him, in fact, the law of nations was still too tied 'to the miseries of empiricism', since it lacked 'independent principles which could bear all the consequences of necessary deductions'.[72]

The words of Rossi, who was murdered in Rome during the riots of 1848, were bitterly true but not totally devoid of hope; in fact, the crisis could be regarded as a prelude to change.[73] Those words had not gone unnoticed.[74] Indeed, Pasquale Stanislao Mancini must have been so impressed that he quoted them in his lecture for the inauguration in 1851 of the course that had been assigned to him in Turin after he had left Naples for political reasons. It is well known that on that occasion at the University of Turin he delivered the

68 Ibid.

69 Bortolotto, 'Nazionalità', 14.

70 Pellegrino Rossi, 'Droit des gens, Intervention', in idem, *Mélanges d'économie politique, de politique, d'histoire et de philosophie publiés par ses fils. 1* (*Économie politique*) (Paris: Librairie de Guillaumin et C., 1867), 443–477, at 443. Regarding Rossi as an exponent of legal eclecticism, which combined romantic historicism, the philosophical school and liberal-moderate thought, see Luigi Lacché, 'La nazione dei giuristi. Il canone eclettico, tra politica e cultura giuridica: spunti per una riflessione sull'esperienza italiana della Restaurazione', 263–307; and idem, 'Rossi, Pellegrino Luigi Edoardo', in *Dizionario Biografico dei Giuristi Italiani*, vol. 2, 1741–1744.

71 Rossi, 'Droit des gens. Intervention', 443–444.

72 Ibid., 444.

73 Concerning the notion of crisis according to Pellegrino Rossi, see Luigi Lacché, '*La nazione dei giuristi. Il canone eclettico, tra politica e cultura giuridica*', 266–267.

74 Bortolotto, 'Nazionalità', 14.

lecture later published as *Della nazionalità come fondamento del diritto delle genti*.[75] The lecture had also been a remarkable success abroad, stimulating discussion and triggering debates.

In Italy, that lecture by Mancini quickly became the manifesto of the newly formed Italian 'school of international law',[76] which, in hindsight, sublimated the objective of reconsidering the political events, affording them a legal basis. As a result, the Risorgimento history emerged freed from the crass connotations of diplomacy-driven politics, thus becoming the history of a nation untainted by politics.

It must be noted that the concept of nationality foregrounded peoples who, having reached a certain level of development, recognized themselves as a united and highly committed natural community. According to Mancini, such a concept also testified to the triumph of natural law, as a consequence of the nation being finally acknowledged as the holder of absolute and inalienable rights, traditionally attributed to the state (equality, freedom, morality, dignity, etc.).[77] As a matter of fact, Mancini's theoretical structure adhered to the canons of natural law for the intrinsic belief that the connection between morality and the law should not be broken.[78] It also marked the success of an idea drawn from the scheme of Giambattista Vico's *Scienza nuova*, which now disruptively revealed itself with the force of a philosophical principle laying the foundations for the entire legal theory of international law.[79] This principle arose from the historicization of natural law: it was no longer the laws 'subject to the logics of change, that were universal, but the ways in which

---

75 See Pasquale Stanislao Mancini, *Della nazionalità come fondamento del diritto delle genti* (Torino: Fratelli Bocca, 1851; ed. Erk Jayme, Torino: Giappichelli, 2000). On Mancini's teaching in Turin see in particular Elisa Mongiano, 'Pasquale Stanislao Mancini. Nazionalità e diritto internazionale all'Università di Torino', *Rivista italiana per le scienze giuridiche*, new series, 4 (2013): 363–377. Notes from Mancini's lessons, taken by Giuseppe Todde, have been published by Eloisa Mura, *Mancini in cattedra. Le lezioni torinesi di diritto internazionale dal 1850–51 e 1851–52* (Pisa: ETS, 2018), 91–345. See also Chapter 9 of the present volume, by Frédéric Ieva.

76 On the emergence in Italy and abroad of the Italian school of international law see Eloisa Mura, *All'ombra di Mancini. La disciplina internazionalistica in Italia ai suoi albori* (Pisa: ETS, 2017).

77 Antonio Droetto, *Pasquale Stanislao Mancini e la scuola italiana di diritto internazionale del secolo XIX* (Milano: Giuffrè, 1954), *passim*; Nuzzo, 'Pasquale Stanislao Mancini', 307–310, at 308–309.

78 On this matter see Italo Birocchi, 'Pasquale Stanislao Mancini e la cultura giuridica del Risorgimento', in *Per una rilettura di Mancini*, 32.

79 Bortolotto, 'Nazionalità', 11.

they evolved and were affected by the succession of different phases of civil coexistence'.[80]

Having ascertained the antithesis between law and politics, the nation was valued for its inherent ability to propose itself as a natural legal subject, unlike the artificially constructed state.[81]

Professing the right to a free and harmonious development of nationality enabled Mancini and those who shared his opinions to sever their ties with the traditional law of nations. This served the purpose of moderating the craving for positivism of those who regarded international law as being rooted in 'accepted and established' historical facts, that is, in customs and treaties, believing that the same resulted from the material causes that had determined them and not from indispensable precepts of justice, which could not be disregarded.

A solution to the conflict generated by the twofold nature, rational and positive, of international law was still an open issue, as can also be inferred from a matter that is only apparently a thing of the past. The need to reconcile those two aspects – aimed at allowing international law to be studied systematically and not to become unfruitful by way of mere case studies or mere abstraction – was evident even from the title of Mancini's course. The two phrases at stake, law of nations and the more recent international law, were not used by everyone indifferently. The concern regarding the risk of turning international law into arbitrary law sometimes led to the adoption of a binary logic, in order to avoid mistaking the rational principles of the law of nations (*droit des gens*, *diritto delle genti*, etc.) for those of international law.[82]

5 Science Taught and Developed: Cagliari and Its Participation in the Italian School of International Law

A lively debate on the role to be assigned to Italian universities ensued throughout the second half of the nineteenth century.[83] Despite the different

---

80 Andrea Battistini, 'Giambattista Vico', in *Enciclopedia italiana di scienze, lettere e arti. Appendice 8. Il contributo italiano alla storia del pensiero. Filosofia* (Roma: Istituto della Enciclopedia fondata da Giovanni Treccani, 2012), 313–322, at 317–318.

81 Droetto, *Pasquale Stanislao Mancini*, 205–210.

82 See Francesco Contuzzi, 'Diritto internazionale', in *Il Digesto italiano. Enciclopedia metodica e alfabetica di legislazione, dottrina e giurisprudenza* (Torino: Unione Tipografico Editrice, 1898–1901), vol. 9, pt II, 1105–1141, at 1108–1110.

83 Cf. the interesting considerations by the Genoese professor Pietro Cogliolo, *Malinconie universitarie* (Firenze: Barbera, 1887), 4.

opinions and changes in ministerial views, it seemed clear that universities were called upon to perform at least two important tasks, both related to creating a national identity: training new professionals and contributing to the development and promotion of science. Such tasks required a modernization of the cultural habitus of the professors, for whom new forms of recruitment were put in place. In addition, the idea that, unlike the minor universities, the major ones selected professors on merit had been implemented by ranking universities in groups, which even affected remuneration.[84]

In fact, education in Italian universities seemed to change at different speeds; alongside large and important universities, there were others in which recruitment was driven purely by local factors and not based on the professor's skills or on the standard of the discipline studied and taught. This reflected the situation after the recent unification of the Kingdom, which had not yet managed to bridge the historical gaps between the territories that had been unified. As far as Cagliari was concerned, a young 'jurist by chance',[85] Giuseppe Saredo, had been entrusted with the teaching of public and constitutional law in Sassari in 1860,[86] despite the fact that he had not yet finished his own university studies. In 1861, Saredo published a provocative article addressing the need to modernize higher studies.[87] His idea was evident: the progress of legal science in France, Germany and England was a consequence of the appointment of eminent scholars to chairs, which did not happen in Italy, where 'distinguished jurists and public law scholars'[88] could be found only in major universities. With a view to corroborating this hypothesis he proposed to examine the theses in the law faculties in order to map the legal theories taught in Italian universities. The first research on this topic started precisely with the dissertations discussed in Cagliari in 1861, and concluded, in a lapidary fashion, that despite the recognized merit of some of the documents examined, in the main city of the island, 'none of the great challenging issues raised in the social sciences were discussed'.[89]

---

84 See Mattone, *Storia della Facoltà di Giurisprudenza dell'Università di Sassari*, 187–188.

85 See Lorenzo Sinisi, 'Dal giornalismo all'Accademia. Giuseppe Saredo giurista "per caso" nell'Italia postunitaria', *Materiali per una storia della cultura giuridica* 37 (2007): 225–237.

86 Concerning Saredo, see Francesco Verrastro, 'Saredo Giuseppe', in *Dizionario Biografico dei Giuristi Italiani*, vol. 2, 1801–1803.

87 Giuseppe Saredo, 'Dell'insegnamento delle scienze giuridiche nelle Università italiane. I. Cagliari', *Rivista italiana di scienze, lettere ed arti colle effemeridi della Pubblica Istruzione*, 2 (14 October 1861): 918–919.

88 Ibid.

89 Ibid.

His stance called for disproval. This is precisely what Giuseppe Orano did in 1862, in a sort of introduction to his degree dissertation *La nazionalità*.[90] The extensive work, in which he agreed with Mancini's thesis, shows the depth of his studies concerning at least the texts by Giambattista Vico (*Scienza nuova*), Vincenzo Gioberti (*Sulla nazionalità*) and Pietro Luigi Albini (*Principi di filosofia del diritto*).

Orano's assent to Mancini's theory was matched by that of other young students at the faculty in Cagliari, including Antioco Cadoni, who in 1863 had applied to become a member of the academic board, with a volume also concerning nationality,[91] and Enrico Lai. The latter, who later became a successful civil law scholar, had entitled his degree dissertation *Principii sulle convenzioni internazionali*,[92] which highlight the fact that from Grotius onwards the main concern had been to demonstrate either the inviolability of treaties or their non-existence, without, however, ever reaching a solution. Indeed, there was a divide in legal theory between those who argued that treaties should conform to the rules of natural law and those according to whom unenforceable duties between nations became enforceable only by virtue of the stipulation of conventions. In addition, he found that a large number of public law scholars, while not completely disregarding the existence of eternal principles, believed that these should be used as a supplement, that is, after flipping through the pages of 'the dusty diplomatic protocols'[93] to no avail. Thus, conventions were 'always at risk, since the peoples declared the conventions invalid as soon as they no longer felt the weight of their oppressor'.[94]

Many of the observations in his thesis on the subject at issue (and others) were biased by the significance of the person who, in all likelihood, had been his professor, namely Francesco Tronci, initially supply professor, then full Professor of Philosophy of Law and International Law, but for only five years (1862–1868), due to his untimely death.[95] He had graduated in Cagliari in 1852, then had attended the 'specialization course' in Turin, probably to carry on his specialization in international law by attending Mancini's lectures. To publicly qualify as an expert graduate, he had written an essay titled 'Delle

90 Giuseppe Orano, *La nazionalità* (Cagliari: Tipografia Timon, 1862).

91 Antioco Cadoni had published *Saggio di filosofia del diritto* (Cagliari: Tipografia della Gazzetta popolare, 1863), for the competition for the chair of Philosophy of Law and International Law. In the text there was room to explore the issue of nationality.

92 See Giuseppina De Giudici, 'Lai, Enrico', in *Dizionario Biografico dei Giuristi Italiani*, vol. 2, 1135–1136.

93 Enrico Lai, *Principii sulle convenzioni internazionali* (Cagliari: Timon, 1863), 5.

94 Ibid., 6.

95 Tronci started teaching only in 1863.

Convenzioni internazionali', aimed at demonstrating that treaties and conventions were an expression of voluntary law and that the latter, as a secondary form of law, had to comply with the law of nations (a primary form of law), that is, with rational law.[96] It is a distinction that echoes the one drawn in Christian Wolff's *Jus Gentium* and repeated by Emer de Vattel.[97]

After correcting Grotius's distinction between natural law and the law of nations, which referred the latter to consent and usage, he expanded on the theory of nationality in order to state one of its most consequential corollaries. Treaties detrimental to the nation were null and void, as were those that imposed the victor's power over the loser. He therefore proposed that international law do away with arbitrariness, which obscured 'the light shed by universal justice'.[98]

As for Orano, he had most likely been a pupil of De Gioannis, an authentic follower of Vico in Sardinia.[99]

In his 1853 *Saggio d'introduzione generale alla scienza del diritto* De Gioannis had presented his syncretism and invited the Cagliari audience to combine the three fundamental elements 'fostered by Kant [...], Savigny [...] and Thibaut' in order to obtain a balanced reconciliation of the contrasting forces.[100] At the same time, he recommended that scholars study natural law thoroughly, while he cautioned them (as well as himself) both legal positivism and exegetical studies.[101]

---

96 Francesco Tronci, *Saggio filosofico-giuridico sulle convenzioni internazionali* (Torino: Unione Tipografico Editrice, 1863), 7.

97 See Giuseppina De Giudici, Sanctitas legatorum. *Sul 'fondamento' dell'indipendenza giurisdizionale in età moderna* (Napoli: ESI, 2020), 29–32. On the nineteenth-century circulation of Vattel, see Elisabetta Fiocchi Malaspina, *L'eterno ritorno del* Droit des gens *di Emer de Vattel (secc. XVIII–XIX). L'impatto sulla prospettiva giuridica in prospettiva globale* (Frankfurt am Main: Max Planck Institute for European Legal History, 2017), *passim*, see also Chapter 7 of the present volume, by Antonio Trampus.

98 Tronci, *Saggio filosofico-giuridico sulle convenzioni internazionali*, 10–11.

99 Gioele Solari, 'Floriano del Zio a Cagliari e l'introduzione dell'hegelismo in Sardegna', *Archivio Storico Sardo* 13 (1921): 23-74, at 32, note 1.

100 See Giulio Cianferotti, 'De Gioannis, Gianquinto Giovanni', in *Dizionario Biografico dei Giuristi Italiani*, vol. 1, 678–679.

101 In *Saggio d'introduzione generale alla scienza del diritto* (Cagliari: Timon, 1853), whose content was to be partially repeated in the *Prolusione al corso di Enciclopedia giuristica nella R. Università di Pisa* (Firenze: Barbera, 1875), the lecture given in Pisa in 1875, De Gioannis underscored the undisputed success of the theories of natural public law, which he considered an 'admirable harmony of the threefold element of what is right, what is honest and what is of benefit'. On the circulation of the thought of the School of Exegesis and that of the German historical school of law in nineteenth-century Italian universities see Laura Moscati, 'Insegnamento e scienza giuridica nelle esperienze

Twelve years later, in his inaugural lecture in Pavia,[102] he explicitly stated that 'the division of mankind into Nations was not the product of violence or chance', but, rather, of a constitutive force coming from 'certain special similarities, which brought men akin together'. Such force revealed itself in all aspects of evolution,[103] including philosophy (what is true)[104] and law (what is right), as well as the native language.

Philosophy, law and the national language formed an inseparable entity in his mind, which did not merely result from Savigny's school of thought – in fact, we are led to believe that he was 'the mind' of the insurrection at the Faculty of Law of Cagliari in 1861 against the decision to stop teaching Latin and to 'embrace the heroic language of Lazio', the ancient Sardinian dialect. That request, in fact, did not derive from an 'exaggerated veneration of the past', but it seemed useful with a view to recovering 'the greatest and most glorious elements' Italy had, that is, the closely interrelated Roman language and law.

Of the three professors in charge of the chair of international law in Cagliari from 1859 to the end of the century, Gaetano Orrù appears to have been the minor figure, or at least the most elusive from a scientific point of view, since, like so many professor-lawyers of the time, he continued to practise his profession – scarcely devoted to science.

The only written contribution he left is the lecture, 'strictly observant of Mancini's theory',[105] entitled 'Dell'attività scientifica esplicata in questo secolo nel campo del diritto internazionale', inaugurating the 1885–1886 academic year. He explained that international law was an expression of a 'rational principle',[106] of the eternal norm of what is true and what is right. He publicly recalled and celebrated the fortunate shift in such a discipline. From being 'almost arcane, reserved for the privileged few, regarded by many as being useless, and excluded from university teachings by suspicious or fearful governments, as full of dangers',[107] it was now entering the milieu of jurists in the

---

italiane preunitarie', in *Studi di storia del diritto medievale e moderno*, ed. Filippo Liotta (Bologna: Monduzzi, 1999), 277–321, at 279–294.

102 Giovanni De Gioannis, *Prolusione accademica letta nella Regia Università di Pavia nel 23 novembre 1863* (Pavia: Tipografia in ditta Eredi Bizzoni, 1864), 7.

103 Ibid., 10.

104 Ibid., 13–15.

105 Quote from Laura Passero, *Dioniso Anzilotti e la dottrina internazionalistica tra Otto e Novecento* (Milano: Giuffrè, 2010), 80.

106 Gaetano Orrù, 'Dell'attività scientifica esplicata in questo secolo nel campo del diritto internazionale', in *Annuario della Regia Università di Cagliari 1885–86* (Cagliari: Timon, 1886), 22.

107 Ibid.,14.

making. That was also an opportunity to talk about Mancini's legacy, which 'was a spark almost capable of shaking the political and scientific world'.[108]

Archival Sources

ASCa: Archivio di Stato di Cagliari, Cagliari, Italy, Atti governativi ed amministrativi, Segreteria di Stato.

ASUCa: Archivio Storico dell'Università di Cagliari, Cagliari, Italy, sezione 1, series 1.9 and series 5 and sezione 2.2, series 1.1 and 1.2.

Cagliari University Library, Cagliari, Italy.

Bibliography

Albini, Luigi, 'Sull'importanza dello studio della filosofia del diritto', in Pasquale Stanislao Mancini and Terenzio Mamiani, *Filosofia del diritto e singolarmente del diritto di punire. Lettere di Terenzio Mamiani e di Pasquale Stanislao Mancini accresciute di quattro discorsi di Terenzio Mamiani sulla sovranità e di una prefazione del prof. Luigi Albini* (Livorno: Coi Tipi di Franc. Vigo Editore, 1875), 5–13.

Battistini, Andrea, 'Giambattista Vico', in *Enciclopedia italiana di scienze, lettere e arti. Appendice 8. Il contributo italiano alla storia del pensiero. Filosofia* (Roma: Istituto della Enciclopedia fondata da Giovanni Treccani, 2012), 313–322.

Bianchi, Paola, 'Giovanni Battista Vasco', in *Dizionario Biografico degli Italiani* (Roma: Istituto della Enciclopedia italiana fondata da Giovanni Treccani, 2020), vol. 98, 388–392.

Birocchi, Italo, 'Contenuti e metodi dell'insegnamento: il Diritto nei secoli XVI–XVIII', in *Storia delle Università in Italia*, ed. Gian Paolo Brizzi, Piero Del Negro and Andrea Romano (Messina: Sicania, 2007), vol. 2, 243–261.

Birocchi, Italo, 'Graduati e professori nell'età preboginiana (1709–1763)', in *La Facoltà di Giurisprudenza dell'Università di Cagliari*, vol. 1, *Dai progetti cinquecenteschi all'Unità d'Italia*, ed. Italo Birocchi (Pisa: ETS, 2018), 171–205.

Birocchi, Italo, *La carta autonomistica della Sardegna tra passato e presente: le leggi fondamentali nel triennio rivoluzionario, 1793–96* (Torino: Giappichelli, 1992).

Birocchi, Italo, 'La questione autonomistica dalla "fusione perfetta" al primo dopoguerra', in *La Sardegna. Storia d'Italia. Le regioni dall'Unità ad oggi*, ed. Luigi Berlinguer and Antonello Mattone (Torino: Einaudi, 1998), 131–199.

108 Ibid., 26.

Birocchi, Italo, 'L'impianto filosofico e il quadro normativo della riforma boginiana', in *La Facoltà di Giurisprudenza dell'Università di Cagliari*, vol. 1, *Dai progetti cinquecenteschi all'Unità d'Italia*, ed. Italo Birocchi (Pisa: ETS, 2018), 207–227.

Birocchi, Italo, 'Università e riforme: il modello neoumanista e le facoltà giuridiche', in *Governare un Regno. Viceré, apparati burocratici e società nella Sardegna del Settecento*, ed. Pierpaolo Merlin (Roma: Carocci, 2005), 422–441.

Birocchi, Italo, 'Pasquale Stanislao Mancini e la cultura giuridica del Risorgimento', in *Per una rilettura di Mancini. Saggi sul diritto del Risorgimento*, ed. Italo Birocchi (Pisa: ETS, 2018), 19–119.

Bortolotto Guido, 'Nazionalità', in *Il Digesto italiano. Enciclopedia metodica e alfabetica di legislazione, dottrina e giurisprudenza* (Torino: Unione tipografica Editrice Torinese, 1905–1910), vol. 16, 1–35.

Brizzi, Gian Paolo, 'Tra Roma e Madrid: la genesi dello Studio generale di Cagliari (1543–1626)', in *La Facoltà di Giurisprudenza dell'Università di Cagliari, vol. 1, Dai progetti cinquecenteschi all'Unità d'Italia*, ed. Italo Birocchi (Pisa: ETS, 2018), 23–64.

Cadoni, Antioco, *Saggio di filosofia del diritto* (Cagliari: Tipografia della Gazzetta popolare, 1863).

Cadoni, Enzo, and Maria Teresa Laneri, *Umanisti e cultura classica nella Sardegna del '500*, vol. 3, pt 1, *L'inventario dei beni e dei libri di Monserrat Rosselló* (Sassari: Gallizzi 1994).

Catellani Enrico, *La dottrina italiana del diritto internazionale nel secolo XIX: lezioni alla Accademia di diritto internazionale all'Aia nel 1933* (Roma: Anonima Romana Editoriale, 1935).

Cattaneo, Carlo, *Della Sardegna antica e moderna con 56 lettere intercorse tra lo studioso e i suoi corrispondenti sardi*, ed. Assunta Trova (Nuoro: Ilisso, 2010).

Cattaneo, Carlo, 'Di varie opere sulla Sardegna', *Il politecnico repertorio mensile di studj applicati alla prosperità e coltura sociale* 2 (1841): 219–273.

Cianferotti Giulio, 'De Gioannis, Gianquinto Giovanni', in *Dizionario Biografico dei Giuristi Italiani (XII–XX secolo)*, ed. Italo Birocchi, Marco Miletti, et al. (Bologna: Il Mulino, 2013), vol. 1, 678–679.

Cianferotti, Giulio, 'Lo Stato nazionale e la nuova scienza del diritto pubblico', in *Enciclopedia italiana di scienze, lettere e arti. Appendice* 8, *Il Contributo italiano alla storia del Pensiero – Diritto* (Roma: Istituto dell'Enciclopedia italiana, 2012), 315–322.

Cianferotti, Giulio, *Storia della letteratura amministrativistica italiana*, vol. 1, *Dall'Unità alla fine dell'Ottocento. Autonomie locali, amministrazione e costituzione* (Milano: Giuffrè, 1998).

Cogliolo, Pietro, *Malinconie universitarie* (Firenze: Barbera, 1887).

Conti, Silvia, 'Dettati e trattati per la "studiosa gioventù": trasmissione e diffusione delle idee a Cagliari tra Seicento e Settecento', in *Circolazione d'idee, parole, uomini, libri e culture: Sardegna, Corsica, Toscana*, ed. Giancarlo Nonnoi (Cagliari: CUEC, 2009), 177–230.

Contuzzi, Francesco, 'Diritto internazionale', in *Il Digesto italiano. Enciclopedia metodica e alfabetica di legislazione, dottrina e giurisprudenza* (Torino: Unione Tipografico Editrice, 1898–1901), vol. 9, pt II, 1105–1141.

Costituzioni di Sua Maestà per l'Università degli studi di Cagliari (Torino: Nella Stamperia Reale, 1764).

De Gioannis, Giovanni, *Parole dette agli ornatissimi studiosi di Giurisprudenza (23 dicembre 1848)* (Cagliari: Timon, 1849).

De Gioannis, Giovanni, *Prolusione accademica letta nella Regia Università di Pavia nel 23 novembre 1863* (Pavia: Tipografia in ditta Eredi Bizzoni, 1864).

De Gioannis, Giovanni, *Prolusione al corso di Enciclopedia giuristica nella R. Università di Pisa* (Firenze: Barbera, 1875).

De Gioannis, Giovanni, *Saggio d'introduzione generale alla scienza del diritto* (Cagliari: Timon, 1853).

De Giudici, Giuseppina, 'A cavallo dell'Unità d'Italia. L'insegnamento del diritto internazionale a Cagliari e l'adesione alla cosiddetta Scuola italiana', *Annali di Storia delle Università italiane*, 2 (2020): 213–233.

De Giudici, Giuseppina, *Interessi e usure nella Sardegna di Carlo Emanuele III* (Pisa: ETS, 2010).

De Giudici, Giuseppina, 'Lai, Enrico', in *Dizionario Biografico dei Giuristi Italiani (XII–XX secolo)*, ed. Italo Birocchi, Marco Nicola Miletti, et al. (Bologna: Il Mulino: 2013), vol. 2, 1135–1136.

De Giudici, Giuseppina, Sanctitas legatorum. *Sul 'fondamento' dell'indipendenza giurisdizionale in età moderna* (Napoli: ESI, 2020).

Deidda, Sebastiano, *Institutiones logicae et metaphysicae* (Carali: Aloysium Lecca Paucheville, 1836, 2 vols).

Delogu, Antonio, 'Gli studi filosofici nell'Università di Sassari (1765–1960)', in *Storia dell'Università di Sassari*, ed. Antonello Mattone (Nuoro: Ilisso, 2010), vol. 1, 344–345.

Dizionario Biografico dei Giuristi Italiani (XII–XX secolo), ed. Italo Birocchi, Marco Nicola Miletti, et al., vols 1 and 2 (Bologna: Il Mulino, 2013).

Droetto, Antonio, *Pasquale Stanislao Mancini e la scuola italiana di diritto internazionale del secolo XIX* (Milano: Giuffrè, 1954).

Fagioli Vercellone, Guido, 'Fabi, Carlo Nicola Maria', in *Dizionario Biografico degli Italiani* (Roma: Istituto della Enciclopedia italiana fondata da Giovanni Treccani, 1993), vol. 43, 695–698.

Falgio, Walter, *Libro e università nella Sardegna del '700* (Cagliari: AM&D, 2011).

Fantappiè, Carlo, 'Fassoni, Liberato', in *Dizionario Biografico degli Italiani* (Roma: Istituto della Enciclopedia italiana fondata da Giovanni Treccani, 1995), vol. 45, 308–311.

Fassoni, Liberato, *De morali patrum doctrina adversus librum Jo. Barbeyraci et ad disputationes de ecclesiastica historia introitus* (Liburni: Ex Typographia Marci Coltellini, 1767).

Ferrante, Carla, 'Rosselló Monserrat', in *Dizionario Biografico dei Giuristi Italiani* (*XII–XX secolo*), ed. Italo Birocchi, Marco Nicola Miletti, et al. (Bologna: Il Mulino, 2013), vol. 2, 1736–1737.

Fiocchi Malaspina, Elisabetta, *L'eterno ritorno del* Droit des gens *di Emer de Vattel* (*secc. XVIII–XIX*). *L'impatto sulla prospettiva giuridica in prospettiva globale* (Frankfurt am Main: Max Planck Institute for European Legal History, 2017).

Fiocchi Malaspina, Elisabetta, 'The Legacy of Vattel's *Droit des gens* in the Long Nineteenth Century', in *The Legacy of Vattel's* Droit des gens, ed. Stapelbroek Koen and Antonio Trampus (Cham: Palgrave Macmillan, 2019), 267–283.

Fiore, Pasquale, *Trattato di diritto internazionale pubblico*, 2nd edition (Torino: Unione Tipografico-Editrice, 1879).

Forti, Francesco, *Lettera sulla direzione degli studii*, in idem, *Scritti varii. Opere edite e inedite* (Firenze: Presso Eugenio and F. Cammelli Editori-Librai, 1865), 1–81.

Gagliardi, Giuseppe, *L'onest'uomo filosofo* (Cagliari: Nella Reale Stamperia, 1772).

Giuseppe Siotto Pintor, ed. Efisio Siotto Pintor (Cagliari: Tipografia nazionale, 1855).

Granata, Giovanna, 'La Biblioteca Universitaria di Cagliari e i libri di diritto', in *La Facoltà di Giurisprudenza dell'Università di Cagliari. Dai progetti cinquecenteschi all'Unità d'Italia*, ed. Italo Birocchi (Pisa: ETS, 2018), 359–430.

I documenti originali di fondazione dell'Università di Cagliari, ed. Luisa D'Arienzo (Nuoro: Ilisso 1997).

Jouannet, Emmanuelle, 'Droit des gens (Du droit des gens au droit international)', in *Dictionnaire de la culture juridique*, ed. Denis Alland and Stéphane Rials (Paris: PUF, 2003), 463–467.

La Facoltà di Giurisprudenza dell'Università di Cagliari, vol. 1, *Dai progetti cinquecenteschi all'Unità d'Italia*, ed. Italo Birocchi (Pisa: ETS, 2018).

Lacché, Luigi, 'La nazione dei giuristi. Il canone eclettico, tra politica e cultura giuridica: spunti per una riflessione sull'esperienza italiana della Restaurazione', in *Diritto cultura giuridica e riforme nell'età di Maria Luigia*, ed. Frank Micolo, Giuseppina Baggio, Edoardo Fregoso and Atti del Convegno (Parma: Monte Università Parma, 2011), 263–307.

Lacché, Luigi, 'Rossi, Pellegrino Luigi Edoardo', in *Dizionario Biografico dei Giuristi Italiani* (*XII–XX secolo*), ed. Italo Birocchi, Marco Nicola Miletti, et al. (Bologna: Il Mulino, 2013), vol. 2, 1741–1744.

Mancini, Pasquale Stanislao, *Della nazionalità come fondamento del diritto delle genti* (Torino: Fratelli Bocca, 1851; ed. Erk Jayme, Torino: Giappichelli, 2000).

Mancini, Pasquale Stanislao, *Prelezione al corso di diritto pubblico marittimo insegnato nella R. Università di Torino nel 1852–53 pronunciata nel dì 29 novembre 1852*, in idem,

Diritto internazionale. Prelezioni con un saggio sul Machiavelli (Napoli: Giuseppe Marghieri, 1873), 93–116.

Marocco, Gianni, *Giambattista Vasco* (Torino: Fondazione Luigi Einaudi, 1978).

Mattone Antonello, 'La storia delle Facoltà di Giurisprudenza di Cagliari e di Sassari, una storia parallela?', in *La Facoltà di Giurisprudenza di Cagliari e l'insegnamento del diritto tra Otto e Novecento. La storia e la memoria*, ed. Giuseppina De Giudici (Napoli: ESI, 2023), 17–75.

Mattone Antonello, *Storia della Facoltà di Giurisprudenza dell'Università di Sassari (secoli XVI–XX)* (Bologna: Il Mulino, 2016).

Mattone, Antonello, and Piero Sanna, 'La rivoluzione delle idee: la riforma delle due università sarde e la circolazione della cultura europea (1764–1790)', in idem, *Settecento sardo e cultura europea. Lumi, società, istituzioni nella crisi dell'Antico Regime* (Milano: Franco Angeli, 2007), 13–106.

Mazzacane, Aldo, *Savigny e la storiografia giuridica tra storia e sistema* (Napoli: Liguori, 1976).

Mittermaier, Carlo [Carl J. A.], 'Dell'importanza d'Italia ne' progressi della civiltà in Europa, e delle speranze pel suo avvenire. Lettera dell'autore al traduttore', in idem, *Delle condizioni d'Italia con un capitolo inedito dell'autore e con note del traduttore Pietro Mugna* (Leipzig: stampato da G. B. Hirschfeld – at Tendler & Schäfer, 1845), 229–251.

Mongiano, Elisa, 'Pasquale Stanislao Mancini. Nazionalità e diritto internazionale all'Università di Torino', *Rivista italiana per le scienze giuridiche*, new series, 4 (2013): 363–377.

Moscati, Laura, 'Insegnamento e scienza giuridica nelle esperienze preunitarie', in *Studi di storia del diritto medievale e moderno*, ed. Filippo Liotta (Bologna: Monduzzi, 1999), 277–321.

Moscati, Laura, 'La Facoltà legale e la scienza giuridica della Restaurazione' *Annali di storia delle università italiane* 4 (2000): 77–94.

Moscati, Laura, 'Un'inedita lettera di Savigny a Poerio' *Quaderni fiorentini per la storia del pensiero giuridico* 21 (1992): 663–669.

Mura, Eloisa, *All'ombra di Mancini. La disciplina internazionalistica in Italia ai suoi albori* (Pisa: ETS, 2017).

Mura, Eloisa, *Mancini in cattedra. Le lezioni torinesi di diritto internazionale del 1850–51 e 1851–52* (Pisa: ETS, 2018).

Nuzzo, Luigi, 'Da Mazzini a Mancini: il principio di nazionalità tra politica e diritto', *Giornale di Storia Costituzionale* 14(2) (2007), 161–186.

Nuzzo, Luigi, *Origini di una scienza. Diritto internazionale e colonialismo nel XIX secolo* (Frankfurt am Main: Vittorio Klostermann, 2012).

Nuzzo, Luigi, 'Pasquale Stanislao Mancini', in *Enciclopedia italiana di scienze, lettere e arti. Appendice 8. Il Contributo italiano alla storia del Pensiero – Diritto* (Roma: Istituto dell'Enciclopedia italiana, 2012), 307–310.

Nuzzo, Luigi, and Miloš Vec, 'The Birth of International Law as a Legal Discipline in the 19th Century', in *Constructing International Law: The Bird of a Discipline*, ed. Luigi Nuzzo and Miloš Vec (Frankfurt am Main: Vittorio Klostermann, 2012), ix–xvi.

Orano, Giuseppe, *La nazionalità* (Cagliari: Tipografia Timon, 1862).

Orrù, Gaetano, 'Dell'attività scientifica esplicata in questo secolo nel campo del diritto internazionale', in *Annuario della Regia Università di Cagliari* 1885–86 (Cagliari: Timon, 1886), 11–41.

Ortu, Gian Giacomo, 'Tra etica, diritto ed economia: intrecci di cultura e di pratica', in *La Facoltà di Giurisprudenza dell'Università di Cagliari*, vol. 1, *Dai progetti cinquecenteschi all'Unità d'Italia*, ed. Italo Birocchi (Pisa: ETS, 2018), 431–511.

Passero, Laura, *Dioniso Anzilotti e la dottrina internazionalistica tra Otto e Novecento* (Milano: Giuffrè, 2010).

Per una rilettura di Mancini. Saggi sul Risorgimento, ed. Italo Birocchi (Pisa: ETS, 2018).

Pessina, Enrico, *Dei progressi del diritto penale in Italia nel secolo XIX. Discorso* (Firenze: Stabilimento Civelli, 1868).

Pierantoni, Augusto, *Storia degli studi del diritto internazionale in Italia* (Modena: Coi tipi di Carlo Vincenzi, 1869).

Ricuperati, Giuseppe, 'Il Settecento', in *Il Piemonte sabaudo. Stato e territori in età moderna, Storia d'Italia*, ed. Giuseppe Galasso (Torino: UTET, 1994), vol. 8, pt 1, 441–834.

Rossi, Pellegrino, 'Droit des gens, Intervention', in idem, *Mélanges d'économie politique, de Politique, d'Histoire et de Philosophie publiés par ses fils. I (Économie politique)* (Paris: Librairie de Guillaumin et C., 1867), 443–477.

Sanna, Piero, 'L'assolutismo sabaudo e l'Università di Sassari. Il rinnovamento degli studi', in *Storia dell'Università di Sassari*, ed. Antonello Mattone (Nuoro: Ilisso, 2010), vol. 1, 81–97.

Saredo, Giuseppe, 'Dell'insegnamento delle scienze giuridiche nelle Università italiane. I. Cagliari', *Rivista italiana di scienze, lettere ed arti colle effemeridi della Pubblica Istruzione* 2 (14 October 1861): 917–919.

Savigny, Carl von, 'Sulla qualità e sul merito delle Università tedesche', in idem, *Ragionamenti storici di diritto del prof. F.C. Savigny, tradotti dall'originale tedesco e preceduti da un discorso da A. Turchiarulo* (Napoli: Tipografia all'insegna del Diogene, 1852), pt IV, 46–66.

Savigny, Carl von, 'Sull'insegnamento del dritto in Italia', in idem, *Ragionamenti storici di diritto del prof. F.C. Savigny, tradotti dall'originale tedesco e preceduti da un discorso da A. Turchiarulo* (Napoli: Tipografia all'insegna del Diogene, 1852), pt IV, 67–84.

Sinisi, Lorenzo, 'Dal giornalismo all'Accademia. Giuseppe Saredo giurista "per caso" nell'Italia postunitaria', *Materiali per una storia della cultura giuridica* 37 (2007): 225–237.

Siotto Pintor, Giovanni, *Storia letteraria di Sardegna* (Cagliari, 1843–1844: Bologna: Forni, 1966).

Solari, Gioele, 'Floriano del Zio a Cagliari e l'introduzione dell'hegelismo in Sardegna', *Archivio Storico Sardo* 13 (1921): 23–74.

Spagnesi, Enrico, 'Giovanni Carmignani e il problema dell'insegnamento del diritto', in *Giovanni Carmignani (1768–1847). Maestro di scienze criminali e pratico del foro sulle soglie del Diritto Penale contemporaneo*, ed. Mario Montorzi (Pisa: ETS, 2005), 463–498.

Stapelbroek, Koen, and Antonio Trampus, 'The Legacy of Vattel's *Droit des gens*. Contexts, Concepts, Reception, Translation and Diffusion', in *The Legacy of Vattel's Droit des gens*, ed. Koen Stapelbroek and Antonio Trampus (Cham: Palgrave Macmillan, 2019), 1–25.

Storia dell'Università di Sassari, ed. Antonello Mattone (Nuoro: Ilisso, 2010).

Storti, Claudia, 'Mancini, Pasquale Stanislao', in *Dizionario Biografico dei Giuristi Italiani (secoli XII–XX)*, ed. Italo Birocchi, Marco Nicola Miletti, et al. (Bologna: Il Mulino, 2013), vol. 2, 1244–1248.

Tronci, Francesco, *Saggio filosofico-giuridico sulle convenzioni internazionali* (Torino: Unione Tipografico Editrice, 1863).

Vasco, Giambattista, *Opere*, ed. Maria Luisa Perna (Torino: Fondazione Luigi Einaudi, 1989).

Venturi, Franco, 'Giambattista Vasco', in *Illuministi italiani*, vol. 3, *Riformatori lombardi, piemontesi e toscani*, ed. Franco Venturi (Milano: Ricciardi Editore, 1958), 755–807.

Venturi, Franco, 'Gian Battista Vasco all'Università di Cagliari', *Archivio storico sardo* 25 (1957): 17–41.

Verrastro, Francesco, 'Saredo Giuseppe', in *Dizionario Biografico dei Giuristi Italiani (XII–XX secolo)*, ed. Italo Birocchi, Marco Nicola Miletti, et al. (Bologna: Il Mulino, 2013), vol. 2, 1801–1803.

Verzella, Emanuela, 'La crisi dell'assetto corporativo e le riforme universitarie, in *Storia delle Università in Italia*, ed. Gian Paolo Brizzi, Piero Del Negro and Andrea Romano (Messina: Sicania, 2007), vol. 1, 159–191.

Index of Persons

Index of Places

Index of Subjects

www.ingramcontent.com/pod-product-compliance
Lightning Source LLC
LaVergne TN
LVHW010543300926
849162LV00002B/221